# The Law and Economics of Intellectual Property in the Digital Age

This book explores the economic analysis of intellectual property law, with a special emphasis on the law and economics of informational goods in light of the past decade's technological revolution. In recent years there has been massive growth in the law and economics literature focusing on intellectual property, on both normative and positive levels of analysis. The economic approach to intellectual property is often described as a monolithic, coherent approach that may differ only as it is applied to a particular case. Yet the growing literature of the law and economics movement in intellectual property does not speak with one voice. The economic discourse used in legal scholarship and in policy-making encompasses several strands, each reflecting a fundamentally different approach to the economics of informational works, and each is grounded in a different ideology or methodological paradigm.

This book delineates the various economic approaches taken and analyses their tenets. It maps the fundamental concepts and the theoretical foundation of current economic analysis of intellectual property law, in order fully to understand the ramifications of using economic analysis of law in policy-making. In so doing, one begins to appreciate the limitations of the current frameworks in confronting the challenges of the information revolution. The book addresses the fundamental adjustments in the methodology and underlying assumptions that must be employed in order for the economic approach to remain a useful analytical framework for addressing IPR in the information age. This book will be of particular interest to students and academics in the fields of law and economics.

**Niva Elkin-Koren** is the Dean of the University of Haifa Faculty of Law and the founding director of the Haifa Center for Law & Technology. Her research focuses on the legal institutions that facilitate private and public control over the production and dissemination of information. *Law, Economics and Cyberspace*, also co-authored with Eli M. Salzberger, was published by Edward Elgar in 2004.

**Eli M. Salzberger** was the Dean of the Faculty of Law at the University of Haifa and the President of the European Association of Law and Economics. His research and teaching areas are legal theory, economic analysis of law, legal ethics, and the Israeli Supreme Court.

## Routledge Research in Intellectual Property

Available:

**Re-thinking Intellectual Property**
The Political Economy of Copyright Protection in the Digital Era
*YiJun Tian*

**The Development of Intellectual Property Regimes in the Middle East**
*David Price*

**Intellectual Property, Community Rights and Human Rights**
The Biological and Genetic Resources of Developing Countries
*Marcelin Tonye Mahop*

**Intellectual Property in Global Governance**
The Crisis of Equity in the Knowledge Economy
*Chidi Oguamanam*

**Intellectual Property Overlaps**
Theory, Strategies, and Solutions
*Robert Tomkowicz*

**Digital Private Copying**
The Scope of User Freedom in EU Digital Copyright
*Stavroula Karapapa*

**The Law and Economics of Intellectual Property in the Digital Age**
The Limits of Analysis
*Niva Elkin-Koren & Eli M. Salzberger*

Forthcoming books:

**A Politics of Patent Law**
Crafting the Participatory Patent Bargain
*Kali Murray*

# The Law and Economics of Intellectual Property in the Digital Age

## The limits of analysis

Niva Elkin-Koren and
Eli M. Salzberger

Routledge
Taylor & Francis Group
LONDON AND NEW YORK

First published 2013
by Routledge
2 Park Square, Milton Park, Abingdon, Oxon OX14 4RN

Simultaneously published in the USA and Canada
by Routledge
711 Third Avenue, New York, NY 10017

*Routledge is an imprint of the Taylor & Francis Group, an informa business*



*British Library Cataloguing in Publication Data*
A catalogue record for this book is available from the British Library

*Library of Congress Cataloguing in Publication Data*
Elkin-Koren, Niva.
The law and economics of intellectual property in the digital age : the limits of analysis / Niva Elkin-Koren, Eli Salzberger.
p. cm. — (Routledge research in intellectual property ; 5)
ISBN 978-0-415-49908-8 (hardback) — ISBN 978-0-203-10438-5 (e-book) 1. Intellectual property—Economic aspects. 2. Intellectual property—Information technology. 3. Intellectual property—Computer network resources. I. Salzberger, Eli M., 1960- II. Title.
K1401.E45 2012
346.04′8—dc23

2012004444

ISBN 978-0-415-49908-8 (hbk)
ISBN 978-0-203-10438-5 (ebk)

Typeset in Garamond
by RefineCatch Limited, Bungay, Suffolk

MIX
Paper from responsible sources
FSC www.fsc.org FSC® C004839

Printed and bound by CPI Group (UK) Ltd, Croydon, CR0 4YY

# Contents

# Table of cases

# Table of legislation

# Acknowledgments

This book is the outcome of a study funded by the IT and Law (ITeR) Program of the Netherlands Organization for Scientific Research (NWO). We wish to thank the Institute for Information Law (IViR) at the University of Amsterdam for acquiring the funding. We are particularly grateful to IViR director, Professor Bernt Hugenholz, for inspiring us to undertake this research project. We thank our research assistants, Karni Chagal, Amir Kolton, Nir Servatka and Ran Carmi, whose dedication and excellent skills were instrumental to the completion of the book.

# Part I

# Intellectual property, law and economics

# Introduction

Until the last decade of the 20th century, intellectual property law was a small branch of legal research and practice, focusing mainly on *copyright*, with a relatively small group of practitioners and a tiny segment of scholarly writings. The wider public was hardly aware of intellectual property (IP) altogether. The technological revolution of the Internet and accompanied technologies resulted in a huge increase in informational goods and intellectual creations that became potential candidates for the protection of Intellectual Property Rights (IPR). Parallel changes characterize *patents*, the value of which was increasingly acknowledged with the significantly accelerated pace of technological advancement and the growing number of patent disputes.

Intellectual property law became one of the fastest growing fields of law. The increasing overall interest in intellectual property, and in particular the growing economic interest, is a byproduct of the information age. In the age of *information economy*,[1] creative works and inventions are claimed to be the single most important factor driving growth and affecting the wealth of nations. As intangible goods such as software, drugs, film and music constitute an increasing percentage of the gross national product (GNP) of industrial countries, there is a growing interest in the economic implications of intellectual property. IPR grant exclusive entitlements over informational works and since the volume and pace of information production is rapidly growing, the stakes involved in intellectual property are rising. The world discovered that intellectual property is the new most significant source for wealth and economic growth.

The increasing significance of intellectual property laws generated a growing interest in the economic analysis of intellectual property. Intellectual property has not been a serious focus of the science of economics until the current technological revolution. Yet in the last two decades we are witnessing

1 Information economy is defined as the 'new economy' – an economy based on information as its primary resource. The main characteristic of the information economy is rapid innovation, in which networks and network economics are playing very substantial roles (Shapiro 1999).

an emerging economic literature on intellectual property, innovation and technological advancement, both empirical and theoretical. The rise of *Law and Economics* as a dominant movement for the analysis and evaluation of the law has been accompanied by an increased economic discourse related to intellectual property policy debates. The economic discourse seemingly offers an objective ground, which enjoys a scientific basis, and provides a methodology for promoting societies' shared goals. However, while traditional economic studies defer the determination of these social goals to policy-makers, the law and economics approach attempts to provide a grand theory of which normative analysis (setting the social goals) is an integral part (for more on the differences between the science of economics and the law and economics movement see Chapter 1). Thus, the increasing economic discourse, and especially the law and economics analysis of intellectual property, weakened other discourses, such as rights discourse, or justice discourse, which are perceived as relativist, often sectarian, and not providing objective criteria for resolving conflicting claims.

Currently, the economic discourse of intellectual property (originating from both law and economics and pure economics studies) dominates law-making processes and policy debates related to the regulation of the information environment. It has affected intellectual property laws in various junctures related to legislative processes and court litigation in the United States, Europe and elsewhere. This is especially surprising in Europe, where the foundations of IP law are deontological. Copyright, for example, has been viewed in Europe as protecting a set of natural entitlements of authors. In contrast, the US Constitution, which authorized Congress to legislate in the area of intellectual property, has taken a teleological-consequential approach. Congress was authorized to grant authors and inventors exclusive rights for a limited time, in order *to promote the progress of science and useful art* (Article 1, Section 8 of the US Constitution). Yet, the economic discourse has been explicitly applied by US courts to intellectual property law only from the mid 1980s. Despite its deontological origins, economic arguments are playing an increasing role in the European intellectual property regimes and affecting law-making processes related to intellectual property both on the European Union level and on the national state level. It seems that the economic discourse of IP became dominant globally, mitigating the moral foundations' differences.

The economic approach to intellectual property is often described as a monolithic and coherent approach. Yet, the growing literature of law and economics on intellectual property, and indeed pure economics writings in this field, do not speak in one voice. The economic discourse used in legal scholarship and in policy-making encompasses several strands, each reflecting a fundamentally different approach to the economics of informational works, and each grounded in a different ideology or methodological paradigm. Identifying the different economic approaches to intellectual property is critical for understanding the ramifications of using economic analysis of law in policy-making. Careful analysis of the underlying assumptions of these approaches is also necessary in order to appreciate the frameworks' limitations in confronting the challenges of the information revolution.

A deep understanding of the economic analytical framework and its application to intellectual property is therefore a key for comprehending recent developments in intellectual property law. But a critical inquiry of the economic approach to intellectual property and its limits is also a key for participating in policy-making and providing a sound basis for defining the desirable scope of legal intervention. Identifying the limits of the economic framework is particularly essential for designing policies that would fit the needs of the information environment in the 21st century.

This is the purpose of the current book. This book is situated at a junction of three major transformations: a changing legal regime – the expansion of intellectual property protection on the national and international levels; a changing technological environment, which increases the value of informational goods but also transforms the way works and inventions are generated and disseminated; and, finally, a paradigmatic shift in the theoretical framework pertaining to IPR. These changes are not simply simultaneous; they are also interconnected and affect one another.

## Law

The basic doctrines and positive laws relating to the different segments of intellectual property law (i.e. copyright, patent, trademark, designs, trade secrets) had been crafted long before the technological and information revolutions. These independent doctrines were not conceived as part of property law until they were grouped under a unified legal title of 'intellectual property law' in the late 1960s. This alignment under a new title changed the substantive content of these rights in an expanding course. Over the recent decades intellectual property has been facing serious challenges. It has attracted endless reform initiatives, on the national and international levels, aiming to adapt IPR to the evolving information environment.

The growing economic value of informational goods increased the pressures towards expanding the scope of intellectual property protection to cover more subject matters, to last for a longer period of time and to include a wider range of rights. This pressure originates from powerful players, especially the content and pharmaceutical industries that may benefit the most from such expansion, but also from scholars and policy-makers who perceive IPR as a key to economic growth in the information society.

The adoption of the Agreement on Trade-Related Aspects of Intellectual Property Rights (TRIPs) in the mid 1990s reflects a similar phenomenon among nations. Pressure to enhance a new IP world order comes from those nations that can benefit economically from a broader IP regime, supplemented by arguments of scholars and policy-makers that IPR are central for world economic growth and development. TRIPs addresses intellectual property issues that were governed by special international treaties administered by the World Intellectual Property Organization (WIPO), an organization that was established only in 1967. The purpose of TRIPs was to achieve some minimal level of harmonization. TRIPs turned the field of intellectual property rights, an essentially private law issue, into an area of public law, and public and private international law, enforced through trade sanctions and administered by the World Trade Organization (WTO). Consequently, many trade and economic disputes were turned into international disputes related to intellectual property and those were turned back into economic disputes, promoting the use of economic insights in intellectual property rule-making and dispute resolution processes.

Over the past two decades the field of intellectual property law and its economic significance, aggregate and distributive, national and global, has also turned out to be an important battleground for interest groups, politicians and different voices in civil society. The borderless nature of informational goods highlights national interests, which are reflected in internationalization of legal arrangements and institutions in this field and in growing controversies among nations and governments.

IPR are not pertaining only to growth, wealth and the economy. They are also affecting personal freedoms and political liberty. The use of IP protected works has become inevitable, and access to information is vital to our daily life in the *information society*.[2] Every use of works in a digital format requires copying and, consequently, copyright law becomes an obstacle on access and use of all types of content, from reading scientific articles to browsing the daily news. The use of copyrighted materials might be essential for generating new creative works and technological innovation, as well as for the ability of citizens to integrate in their communities and actively participate in political and cultural life. Likewise, market structure and monopolies created by patents might affect individual rights, such as the rights to health care and education, freedom of speech and freedom of occupation.

Currently there is no good fit between the existing IPR and the needs of our information economy, our politics and culture in the information society. The intellectual property framework is failing to address the 21st century needs of creative and innovative economies. IPR play a major role in structuring the creative environment, and may stifle growth by imposing high transaction cost, creating impediments on access to innovation and knowledge, which is essential for further innovation and growth.

2 'Information Society' is defined as society in which the creation and distribution of information is its main activity, affecting cultural, political and social aspects. The main characteristic of the information society is the high level of transmission of information by individuals, in both workplaces and homes, using a compatible technology such as computers and phones (Webster 2002).

Take copyright for example. Copyright law, the legal regime mostly tied to the emergence of the printing press, has come into question in the digital environment. As millions of users are using the Internet to access works in digital format, uploading and downloading is difficult to control. The cost of copyright enforcement against illegal downloading is becoming prohibitively high. Ordinary individual conducts, such as listening to music or watching films may turn out to be infringements under current copyright law. Applying old rules to the digital environment has become so cumbersome that the average user is getting confused. In many cases, such as mass digitization initiatives, the costs of licencing create a serious barrier to the development of new kinds of businesses and uses. As the copyright framework is showing signs of collision it becomes increasingly difficult to enforce IPR (Depoorter and van Hiel 2010; Hargreaves 2011) and there is a growing disregard for the law, which potentially endanger the authority of law in general.

## Technology

New technologies are challenging the basic tenets of intellectual property laws on various levels. Digital technology shifted various individual conducts that had been perfectly legal before the new information revolution into formal infringements of IP laws. Copying, for example, is much more common in the course of the operation of computer related activities than in equivalent activities in the pre-digital age. Thus mere technological change had an immense effect on the core of copyright – the exclusive right to copy. Likewise, the pace of technological progress and the growing number of patent applications completely changed the role of patents and their effects vis-à-vis their original function of incentivizing innovation. These changing realities require new conceptual thinking and implementation. The traditional doctrines, concepts and positive laws establishing copyright, patent, trademark, designs and trade secrets, which were crafted independently from each other in the past millennium, are ill-equipped to treat the changing modes of informational goods.

The information environment further gives rise to new ways of governing information by technology and via private ordering. Digital networks provide new technical means for excluding informational goods (digital rights management (DRM) systems); digital networks offers new opportunities to govern information through licences and contracts. These new ways of governing information challenge norms made by democratic institutions and transform their real world outcomes. They ought, therefore, to be a core factor in the prescription of desirable government intervention. These new institutions for governing information further blur the boundaries between public and private ordering, and are challenging some of the fundamental tenets of the economic analysis of intellectual property.

Finally, digital networks are fundamentally transforming the way we generate and disseminate informational goods. Intellectual property was essential for the growing wealth of Western economies at the end of the 20th century, but now it is facing new challenges as new modes of production are emerging, transforming the content and innovative industries. The mass production of content and inventions, which characterized the second half of the 20th century, is losing its dominance to user-generated content (UGC) and social production facilitated by mega-platforms (Benkler 2006; Elkin-Koren 2011). One of the main justifications for intellectual property rights is that without their protection innovations and creations will not be produced. New modes of production and distribution are creating new business models and new institutions that may challenge some of these underpinning rationales.

As we are entering the second decade of the 21st century it becomes clear that our regulatory framework must change and adapt to the new creative and innovative environment. So far, many of the reform initiatives have overlooked these fundamental changes and opt instead to create some patches and fixes to the current IPR system. But designing policy that would promote innovation, creativity and growth in our times requires a comprehensive overview of the IPR system and a critical review of its underpinning theoretical framework. One of the prime objectives of this book is to examine the normative and positive analyses of intellectual property in the light of the technological revolution. A first step in reforming the IP regime is to identify the underlying economic rationale of legal intervention and examine whether this theoretical framework still holds water. Technological change and its ramifications should be incorporated into the economic analysis of intellectual property to provide a sound theoretical framework for policy-making.

The book addresses the fundamental adjustments in the methodology and underlying assumptions that must be employed in order for the economic approach to remain a useful analytic framework for addressing IPR in the information age.

## Shifts in the economic theoretical framework

As mentioned above, until recently intellectual property law as such did not attract significant attention by economists. In fact, economic theory has neglected altogether the economics of innovation and technological progress, with the bold exception of Joseph Schumpeter's writings (1912, 1928, 1942). Early writings on the economics of intellectual property questioned the necessity of legal rights for stimulating innovation. Arnold Plant, for instance, claimed that most inventions are spontaneous and, moreover, that first mover advantages and imperfections in markets provided inventors and publishers with sufficient rewards to create and distribute their works, even with no intellectual property rights. Thus, he argued, granting patent protection will eventually lead to a waste of resources (Plant 1934a: 30–51, 1934b: 167–95). Others stated that innovators could extract substantial revenues from the private utilization of proprietary information, without the need for property rights, by speculating in the market on the basis of their discoveries prior to such discoveries becoming public knowledge (Hirshleifer 1971). The skepticism of economists regarding IP (for a more recent example see Stiglitz 2008) has not crossed over to the mainstream law and economics writings.

The *Economic Analysis of Law*, or the *Law and Economics* movement, which can be defined as an application of economic methodology to explain and evaluate the formation, structure, process and impact of law and legal institutions (Salzberger 2008), has been emerging in recent decades as a dominant theoretical paradigm for legal academia and it is gradually capturing various segments of legal practice as well. Law and economics is a methodology for both the explanation of legal rules, judicial decisions and their consequences (positive analysis) and the evaluation of legal rules and judicial decisions and the prescription of the desirable ones (normative analysis). As the result of the growing importance of IP law, on the one hand, and the intensifying discourse of law and economics, on the other hand, it is not surprising that there has been a massive growth in the law and economics of intellectual property literature in the past decade in both normative and positive realms (Scotchmer and Menell 2007 is a good survey).

Economists have been rather skeptical, or at least unconvinced, as to the significance of intellectual property rights in generating innovation and growth, and they have spread their attention vis-à-vis promoting innovation and technological progress to other legal fields such as competition and corporation law. This cannot be said about the mainstream law and economics literature. While one can hardly find law and economic literature on other legal fields in connection with innovation and technological progress (for a survey see Salzberger 2012), the more recent studies that have explored the economic analysis of intellectual property law as a whole (e.g. Granstrand 1999; Landes and Posner 2003; Towse and Hozhauer 2002; Braga, Fink and Sepulveda 2000) perceive a strong intellectual property regime as efficient and inductive to growth and thus desirable. These studies are already captured in the property rhetoric and focus on the ways to extract the highest value or profits, presuming informational products as property.

A review of the law and economics literature reveals a shift in the paradigmatic framework that dominates the economic analysis of intellectual property, from the incentives – public goods framework to the proprietary paradigm. This book delineates these two economic approaches and analyses their presupposition, tenets and consequences. It maps the fundamental concepts and critically reviews the theoretical foundations of current economic analysis of intellectual property law.

This is not a monolithic book. We attempt to discuss theories at a high level of abstraction, alongside accounts and analyses of the legal and extra-legal realities. The discussion is conducted on both levels of positive and normative analyses; in both we review the theories and describe and evaluate their applications. We also contribute some new theoretical conjectures. We do not focus on a specific legal system, but most of our examples are taken from the US, on the one hand, and from Europe, on the other. Comparison between the two regimes can shed interesting light on the theories on both levels of analysis. We focus on the two most important segments of IPR – copyright and patent, which are founded on the basis of the same economic rationales.

The book is written and organized in such a way that both experts and novices in intellectual property law and/or law and economics can find an interest. Scholars and students of economic analysis of IP will hopefully benefit from the broad economic approach we introduce and from the critical approach we take. Practitioners and students of intellectual property law could benefit from the general theoretical frameworks offered in the book that can serve as a basis for new arguments in courts and policy-making debates. For those who are familiar with neither IP law nor law and economics the book can serve as a good introduction. Consequently, each chapter stands on its own, and readers might wish to read only a selection of the chapters or opt to read all the chapters but in a different order than they are organized here. The book is divided into four parts – foundations, normative analysis, the new information environment and positive analysis. We conclude this introduction with a short overview of the chapters that can assist the reader to make informed reading choices.

Chapters 1 and 2 introduce the two pillars of the law and economics of intellectual property, which set the framework for the rest of the book: the paradigm of law and economics and the concept of intellectual property. Chapter 1 introduces the economic approach to law – its historical origins, evolution in the framework of several generations or sub-paradigms, its main normative and positive premises and, indeed, some critique on the approach as a whole. Those who are already familiar with the growing literature of law and economics or the economic analysis of IP might want to skip this chapter. However, we believe that it is useful to know our perception of the economic approach towards law. We define law and economics in a broad way, which focuses on its unique methodologies, rather than on its subject areas or ideologies. This chapter is meant to negate the common view that law and economics as a discipline to analyse and evaluate the law has a principled right wing socio-economic ideology, that it is pro-markets, anti central intervention and thus on the pro-propertization side of the current debate regarding IP laws. Our definition of the economic approach highlights the possible gaps in the existing literature of law and economics, in general, and law and economics of IP, in particular.

Chapter 2 provides a general introduction to the history, definition and scope of intellectual property. It maps the primary theoretical justifications to intellectual property – deontological and teleological, which provide a context to the law and economic approach to IP. We further describe the rise of the economic studies, as well as law and economics writings, to intellectual property as a dominant framework in IP scholarship and policy-making. Since most of our substantial discussion in the rest of the book focuses on two sub-branches of IP law – patent and copyright – this chapter provides an overview of this legal field as a whole, and especially the sub-branches that we do not venture into.

Chapters 3 and 4 address the law and economics normative approaches to IP and portray the implicit paradigmatic shift within law and economics from the incentives paradigm to the propriety paradigm. The evolution of the economic approach towards IP law can be viewed as comprising three generations or mini-paradigms. The first generation of literature is what we dub an economic version of the utilitarian approach to IP (as derived from the wording of the US Constitution). The second generation focuses on market-failure analysis and perceives informational goods as suffering from a public good market failure, for which intellectual property provides a remedy. This is the most common association of economic analysis of IP law, as it includes the much discussed incentives framework. The third generation is the propriety paradigm. The rise of this third paradigm brings the American and the European theoretical approaches to IP closer to each other.

Chapter 3 introduces the incentives paradigm, within which the vast majority of economics and law and economics writings about IP have been carried out. The incentives paradigm views information as public goods that bring about a market failure, and thus requires central intervention by granting IP rights. The goal, according to this approach, is to design laws, which will maximize society's welfare or wellbeing. The justification for IPR under this framework is of a second order type as opposed to first order justification of IPR as protecting natural rights of creators. After laying down in detail the different premises of the incentives paradigm, the chapter critically examines these premises' convincing force, and whether the actual role IPRs play today corresponds to correcting the identified market failure. In this chapter we question whether a real need for monetary incentives for creation and innovation exists, what are the different forms of generating incentives and whether intellectual property rights offer the best legal regime. Special emphasis is put on IPR in the information age, and on digital information products, arguing that these technological developments present new challenges to the traditional analysis.

Chapter 4 introduces the propriety paradigm. This emerging paradigm in the law and economics approach to IP originates from the veteran 'tragedy of the commons' rationale for property in general. We critically account for the application of the 'tragedy of the commons' framework to intellectual property. We show how this new approach abandons the public good analysis and presumes intellectual creations to be property, i.e. implicitly shifting to a first order justification of IPR. We argue that this shift was brought about for two main reasons: first, the frustration from the failure of the incentives paradigm to strike the right balance of IPR in terms of scope and duration; and, secondly, actual legal developments, such as the legislation in the US of the Copyright

Extension Act in 1998, which added 20 years to copyright including to existing works. These developments could have not been endorsed on the bases of the incentives paradigm. Chapter 4 discusses some of the criticism raised against the proprietary approach, which applies property theory to informational works. It further addresses the functional role of property rights in organizing the use of informational work, and examines whether property rights generate an adequate organizational framework for the new challenges posed by the information environment.

Chapters 5 and 6 describe the rise of private ordering as a dominant strategy for governing informational goods, and explores the changing nature of information governance in the digital environment. It critically examines the law and economics approach to IP in light of the fundamental changes in information governance from central regulation to regulation by technology and private ordering. It further addresses the implications of the digital revolution for the fundamental assumptions and core economic analysis of IPR.

Chapter 5 describes the rise of contracts and end user license agreements (EULA), which are becoming a dominant mechanism for governing intellectual creations in the shadow of the propriety regime of IP. Private ordering is used to expand but also to limit rights. We describe the economic analysis of private ordering and its critique, offer explanations for these phenomena and analyse the effects of private ordering on the actual operation of IPR, as well as on the desirable intellectual property laws. We further examine whether the changing nature of knowledge production and the rise of user generated content and social production give rise to different considerations related to private ordering for governing access to creative works.

Chapter 6 explores the implications of digital locks vis-à-vis the justifications for central intervention in the market for informational goods. It focuses on the economic analysis of technological protection measures (TPM) or digital rights management (DRM) and on the major tool of central intervention that has been employed in this context so far – anti-circumvention legislation. We offer some insights related to the economic analysis of information in the age of regulation by the code and question the premises of the traditional economic justifications for IPR. We further analyse the economic implications of TPMs for competition, and for consumer protection. One of the important unique features of DRMs – their ability to control uses long after purchase was made – has some important implications for the economic analysis of information and consumers' rights. We discuss the economic analysis of anti-circumvention legislation and its effects on the general economic model of informational markets and offer tentative alternative courses for central intervention in the shadow of regulation by technology.

Finally, Chapter 7 focuses on the positive analysis of IP laws, offering an explanation as to the actual IPR rather than the desirable one. It suggests three basic models of positive analysis of legislation – the Pluralist model, the Republican model and the Public Choice model (the last of which can be associated with the law and economics approach). Various developments in IP legislation in Europe and the US are presented as supporting or negating these models. Special attention is given to the reasons and effects of the growing international rule-making in this field.

The book does not adopt a single analytical framework to the analysis of IP. It does not reach a conclusive verdict on the success of the whole project of economic analysis of IP laws. It does not point to the best framework of analysis within the economic approach. It leaves many questions open or unanswered, which might frustrate the reader. But if the book contributes several original insights and arguments, if it highlights some missing links in the various frameworks of analysis, if it contributes to the setting of the research agenda – both theoretical and empirical – in the field, then our goals are satisfied.

# 1 Introduction to law and economics

The economic analysis of law, or the law and economics movement, will soon celebrate its first half century. In recent decades it is emerging as the dominant theoretical paradigm and scientific methodology for legal scholarship, and it is gradually capturing various segments of policy-making and legal discourse of legislatures, courts and legal practitioners.[3] Although initially law and economics prospered mainly in North America, in the last decades it is rapidly increasing also in Europe and elsewhere. Yale Law Professor, Bruce Ackerman (1984), referred to it as 'the most important development in legal scholarship in the Twentieth century'. Law and economics is an offspring of American legal realism, which flourished in the mid 20th century. Legal realism emerged as a response to the positivist-formalist paradigm to law that replaced the natural law paradigm.

Legal research and the methodology employed to analyse and evaluate the law are conducted within paradigmatic thinking. The term 'paradigm shift' was coined by Thomas Kuhn (1962) to describe the development of the natural sciences. Kuhn disputed the modernistic description of Francis Bacon who presented scientific inquiry as one of constant and accumulative progress, like a building, which is constructed stone after stone. Kuhn argued that science develops in leaps. Regular scientific research is conducted within a set of boundaries that are based on presuppositions left unquestioned by the contemporary scientific community. These boundaries were dubbed by Kuhn 'a paradigm'. Scientists in their research (and in their research agenda) are trying to complete a jigsaw puzzle, whereas the framework of the puzzle is predetermined by the paradigm. However, in the course of scientific research it turns out that not all pieces fit their spots, and some pieces tend to cross the preset boundaries. Scientists try to force the pieces into the slots they think are meant for them but at one focal point the framework collapses. Doubts

3 For a good introduction the two most important textbooks are Richard A. Posner, *Economic Analysis of Law* (7th edn 2007) and Robert D. Cooter and Thomas Ulen, *Law and Economics* (6th edn 2011). For a comprehensive bibliography see *Encyclopedia of Law and Economics* (http://inprem.rug.ac.be/gremer/encyc/index.html).

bring about rethinking of the preset presuppositions. The paradigm shifts; a new paradigm is constructed, which sets new presuppositions and a new research agenda. Regular scientific research continues within the new paradigm, until it too is ripe for replacement.

Kuhn's analysis can be applied to our thinking about the law and the methodology of legal research. One qualification might be in place – that in legal research, and in the social sciences more generally, different paradigms can coexist in parallel. However, one could argue that this is the case also with regard to the natural sciences, and therefore no real difference vis-à-vis the development of knowledge exists between the different spheres of human inquiry. Be that as it may, law and economics is a current dominant paradigm for legal research. This statement does not only reflect the increasing share of law and economics papers in law journals and other scientific journals, but also the fact that law and economics jargon and thinking is present in many other law articles and books, which are not strictly speaking law and economics works. The economic analysis of law affects also those legal researchers who do not belong to the law and economics crowd and it infiltrates also to judicial decision-making and to modes of thinking and reasoning of policy-makers. The field of intellectual property is an obvious example of this trend, as will be unveiled in the course of this book. One of the significant factors that make law and economics a paradigm in legal research is the unquestioned premises, both positive and normative, that most contemporary writings in this field take as pre-given. One of the key examples is the normative goal of efficiency determined in terms of wealth maximization, which is the baseline of most contemporary writings. We will return extensively to this point in Chapter 3.

In this introductory chapter we will place law and economics within the more general picture of the development of legal theory (section 1.1), offer a definition of the economic approach to law (section 1.2) and point to some weaknesses of this approach (section 1.3), which are specifically relevant in the field of intellectual property.

## 1.1 The historical roots of law and economics

Natural law dominated legal thinking until the paradigm shift of the 18th century Enlightenment. It did not distinguish between the questions what is law and what law ought to be, and treated positive analysis of law and normative analysis of law as one. The natural law portrayed law as deriving from morality – either in a religious form – the source of law is God – *à la* Thomas Aquinas, or in a secular one – the source of law is human nature – *à la* Immanuel Kant, emphasizing either natural duties, obligations and prohibitions and in modern times – natural rights. Natural law was an apparent framework to justify the right of property and indeed intellectual property (see the following chapter), and it left significant footprints on contemporary concepts of moral rights in intellectual property. It can be further argued that the Continental European thinking about IP is still to some extent dominated by the natural law paradigm, according to which it is the natural right of every creator and innovator to own his or her ideas.

Legal positivism that emerged in the 18th century became the dominant paradigm in the context of broader changes – meta-paradigmatic shift of the Enlightenment – and coincided with the emergence of an alternative moral theory, Utilitarianism, and with the emergence of the social sciences, among them the science of economics. Legal positivism attempted to separate the two levels of analysis, the positive and the normative, acknowledging that law is not necessarily what we desire the law to be. It claimed that the law is a pure concept, separated from morality or political philosophy, and attempted to create a science of law by developing an independent methodology and doctrine to analyse law and legal institutions. Thus, for example, explanation and evaluation of the common law under the hegemony of natural law (judges do not create laws, they merely declare the ancient laws of the English nation) were distinctly different from the description and analysis of common law in the framework of legal positivism (judge-made laws), which is yet distinct from the way common law is portrayed and evaluated by law and economics (individual decisions which follow each other with fine tuning corrections along time, resulting in efficient solutions to common disputes).

During the 19th century the formalist approach towards law, which was based on legal positivism, prospered. It saw the law as a set of coherent rules, which are clear-cut, predictable or foreseeable and readily available. Facts were perceived as something that can be verified objectively. The legal process, therefore, was portrayed as a routine application of the law to a set of facts and, thus, save in cases of bad judges, every reasonable judge could derive from this process the 'correct' decision. The approach to law and legal research became doctrinal; dogmatic and normative analysis of law was pushed out from law schools.

The American legal realism of the mid 20th century (alongside the Scandinavian legal realism) claimed that this ideal picture of law is not true, that courts' decisions are not a mechanistic application of legislation, and that the law and legal rulings are influenced by the identity, ideology and politics of those who administer them – legislatures, politicians, enforcement agencies and judges. Legal realism coincided with a crisis of legal positivism on the other side of the Atlantic brought about in the aftermath of the Second World War, where the positivist approach enabled German judges to approve racist and cruel legislation. The realists advocated a much more pragmatic approach towards the law, pointing at the gap between the ideal formalist description of law and the complicated and specific circumstances realities. But with this grand insight the realists stopped, without offering any systematic explanation to this gap and its sources. One of the important footprints of legal realism was a call to the social sciences to come to the assistance of legal scholars in order to study the law and legal institutions. The critical legal studies (CLS) movement and the law and society movements emerged in the last quarter of the 20th century to fill the realists' chasm and explain the sources of the gaps between the ideal description of the law and legal realities. One of the main insights of CLS portrays the law as a tool of control for dominant groups over other groups in society and as a tool of Western liberalism to maintain its ideological, economic and political hegemony.

The law and economics movement is another offspring of legal realism. Indeed, it can be seen as a direct response to the realist call for help of the social sciences in analysing the law and legal institutions. It emerged as a parallel response to the realist challenge and is perceived, at least in the American academic context, also as a rival response to the CLS. While the CLS literature challenges the liberal foundations of law, the law and economics movement operates within these foundations. The CLS is often associated with the left, while law and economics is associated with right-wing ideology, capitalist or libertarian thinking, which favors free markets and is against central intervention (Gazal-Ayal 2007; Kennedy 2002; Hunt 1986). In many American law schools these two movements became a source for academic and political rivalry. As we will elaborate later, we do not share this view and classification. Law and economics is not necessarily a right-wing movement and we believe that there are many common insights of the two movements, certainly when compared with traditional 'black letter' doctrine and formalist legal thinking. Be that as it may, the nature of the relationship between these two off-springs of legal realism is less relevant today, because in recent years we witness a significant decline of CLS, side by side with further expansion of law and economics, both in the subject areas it addresses and in the methodological tools it employs (Gabel 2009).

While the association of law and economics with right-wing ideology might have been convincing in the past, today the law and economics world is much more diverse. European input to this movement, institutional law and economics, behavioral law and economics and other theoretical streams expanded this paradigm and made room for much more diversity in terms of ideologies and public policies. The field of intellectual property is a good example in hand, to which we will return in the final words of this chapter. One can talk today about law and economics as the dominant paradigm in the study and analysis of law, but one can no longer associate this paradigm with a specific political or ideological agenda. In a sense, the law and economics movement has even had a significant impact on the science of economics in general. Whether the directions of the contemporary developments of law and economics can still be regarded within the same paradigm, whether we are witnessing the emergence of different paradigm or sub-paradigm, a paradigmatic shift within law and economics, will remain as open questions here, but an answer to these questions begs a definition of law and economics, which leads us to the next section.

## 1.2 What is economic analysis of law?

Most students of law are familiar with various law and economics theorems, arguments and insights, such as the Coase theorem, efficient breach, or rent-seeking, but will encounter a difficulty in defining law and economics and drawing its boundaries. The same, in fact, applies to definition of the science of economics. In order to understand what law and economics is all about it is important first to define 'economics'. This definition itself has been influenced by the law and economics movement.

### *1.2.1 What is economics?*

When 'economics' is mentioned our intuitive thoughts are about markets, prices, demand, supply, inflation, unemployment etc. In fact, the 18th century founder of the modern science of economics, Adam Smith, dealt with much broader issues. His analysis of the economic world intertwined with insights into political theory and moral philosophy, politics and culture. Only subsequently did economists – first the classical theorists and then the neo-classicists – narrow down their interests and focused only on pure economic markets. This was partly the result of the development of more rigorous methodology and graphic models, especially by the neo-classicists in the 19th century, with the addition of advanced mathematics in the 20th century.

However, in recent decades we have witnessed the rebroadening of economics to encompass analyses of areas outside the traditional economic markets: Politics, international relations and other types of collective decision-making, are some of these new frontiers. This imperialism of economics has also reached the law – with the law and economics movement. In this sense, the economic analysis of law has an interesting common feature with CLS. This rival movement can also be seen as part of a broader movement of the deconstruction and post-modern paradigms, originating in the humanities. Law and economics and CLS are fresh attempts to return to a 'grand theory', abolishing the 19th century emergence of the social sciences, their division into sub-fields, each with its distinct object of analysis and scientific methodology and the general division between the social sciences, the humanities and even the exact sciences (Skinner 1985). Law is one of the fields in which these two grand theories collide.

The expansive course of economics can be demonstrated by the changes of its definitions offered by key economics scholars. The famous neo-classic economist, Alfred Marshall, who developed the demand and supply curves, defined 'economics' as 'A study of man's action in the ordinary business of life; it inquires how he gets his income and how he uses it' (Marshall [1890] 1961: 2). George Stigler, a contemporary economist, defined economics in 1952 as the: 'Study of the operation of economic organizations, and economic organizations are social (and rarely individual) arrangements to deal with the production and distribution of economic goods and services' (Stigler 1952: 1). These two definitions are narrow and focus on the traditional economic market. But already in 1932 economics was defined more broadly by Lionel Robbins as 'the science which studies human behavior as the relationship between ends and scarce means which have alternative uses' (Robbins 1932: 15). This definition broadens the domain of economics to cover every human or social choice in conditions of scarcity and, indeed, in recent years we include within economics fields such as game theory and public and social choice, which focus on all types of human decision-making. According to Robbins, every human activity has an economic aspect (Robbins 1962: 16). But maybe even Robbins's definition is not wide enough to include all the types of studies that are conducted today under the umbrella of economics. Some of the questions that are dealt with by social choice and game theory are not connected to scarcity, or its traditional definition. In a sense, law and economics believes not only that every human activity has an economic aspect, but that the economic aspect (broadly defined – see below) can be presented as the sole or exclusive aspect which explains human behavior.

A possibly broader and more accurate definition of the science of economics focuses not on the subject matter of economics but on its methodology. According to this definition economics studies human behavior in a set situation by (1) transforming the complex reality to a simplified reality, using simplifying assumptions, (2) operating a rigorous (mathematical or graphical) model on this simplified reality, (3) deriving conclusions as to the variables of the model and the causal connections between them, and (4) transforming these conclusions into statements and policies concerning the real world.

The soft points of this methodology are the first and last stages – the assumptions stage and the real world policy conclusions. One of the major points of criticism against the economic approach, in general, and against the economic approach towards law, in particular, is that the economic models never faithfully represent reality. This criticism is not justified because the economic models do not pretend to represent the real world as it is. One has to remember that even the most basic and simple micro-economics model of first year economics courses – studying the connections between price, supply and demand of a simple product – is based on simplifying assumptions such as set tastes, set prices of other products etc. Having said that, a question remains whether the canon models of the economic analysis of law focus on the important aspects of human behavior vis-à-vis the law, or whether the choice of the simplifying assumptions by law and economics mainstream literature are neutral or biased. As we shall see later these are crucial questions in the economic analysis of intellectual property.

The advantage of economic models applied to traditional economic markets is that their underlying assumptions are less controversial or are more faithful to reality as it is being transformed to the model. One of the key assumptions, which characterize most economic models, is rational behavior. The *homo economicus* behaves rationally when his decisions are geared to maximize his welfare (or utility or wellbeing). He has a set order of preferences and makes his choices on the basis of information. The rationality and self-maximization assumptions are less controversial when we analyse activity within the traditional economic market, for example, the individual decision-making with regard to investing one's money, or whether to purchase a certain product or service. When we operate in the stock market we usually aim to make more money. Rationality is thus transgressed to maximization of wealth. But when we move away from pure markets into other spheres of human behavior, this assumption becomes more controversial. How can we apply rational behavior in the context of a decision whether to get married, to enlarge one's family or to commit a crime? Unlike the stock market example, here we will not necessarily assume that rational actors are maximizing wealth and that wellbeing or utility maximization equals wealth maximization, although we can still assume that the decision-maker is operating in order to maximize his or her happiness or to satisfy his or her order of preferences.

It ought to be noted that according to the broad definition of the economic approach the rationality assumption is not an integral part of economic analysis. It is still dominating the work being done within this field, but the new sub-branch of economics – behavioral economics – focuses on relaxing the narrow rationality assumption. In theory economic models can offer analyses based on the assumption that individuals are not rational or are only partly rational, or that their operation is motivated by deontological moral perceptions.

What are the broader advantages of the economic methodology? One main advantage is that economic study is scientifically evolutionary: one can construct a simple model based on far-reaching simplifying assumptions and develop this model gradually by relaxing or complicating some of these assumptions. Following the construction of a simple model of supply and demand and market equilibrium, we can further enrich our insights by examining what happens if there is no full information, if there is uncertainty, what happens if the decision-making itself is costly etc.

Another significant advantage of economics thinking is that this methodology provides a common language for discussion. It helps focus some debates by distinguishing between the model and its mathematical validity, the policy conclusions from the model regarding the real world and, indeed, the set of simplifying assumptions. This makes it easier to identify flows, qualify the underlying assumptions, improve the mathematical modeling or refine the policy conclusions regarding the real world. Economics, therefore, offers us not only a better tool for deliberation (we can agree on what are the exact points we disagree about) but it is also an evolutionary study – the models can be constantly improved and become more sophisticated. Other scientific approaches used in legal discourse and research also have distinctive common language. However, the terms of the economic science are much more precise and agreed upon. Thus, terms such as wealth, transitivity, rent, or monopolistic and competitive price have a broader common understanding, even among non-economists, than reasonableness or good faith (vis-à-vis black letter or doctrinal analysis), or hegemony or socialization (vis-à-vis sociological discourse).

Yet a further advantage of the economic methodology when applied to legal questions is that it easily crosses geographical borders and different legal systems and cultures. When using doctrinal analysis a legal scholar is usually bound to his or her legal system or culture or legal family, while an economic analysis is more detached from the local specifics and thus enables an easier import and export of ideas and a real global discussion of various common legal issues. This advantage itself is an explanatory factor for the success of law and economics, as it makes it easier for scholars to publish internationally and engage in global and comparative discussions, but it also highlights the importance of law and economics in the fields of IP, as the global characteristics of this field are rapidly increasing.

### *1.2.2 The economic analysis of law*

The intersection between law and economics is not a new phenomenon. There are legal fields that are aimed to regulate the activities in the traditional economic markets. The laws and legal concepts in those fields are derived from traditional economic analysis of markets, their special characteristics and failures. The 'old' law and economics focuses on these fields. Corporation law, tax law, antitrust and competition law are a few examples of such legal branches, where the economic considerations are only natural and the market analysis is an integral part of the legal framework. The 'new' law and economics is an approach that does not focus on legal analysis of the economic world but on the economic analysis of the legal world. It is not limited to the branches of the law dealing with economic issues but views the whole legal system – private law as public law, substantive law as procedural law, as well as legal institutions – as targets for economic analysis.

The roots of the new law and economics can be found in the 18th century with the writings of Smith ([1776] 1961), Beccaria ([1764] 1986), Condorcet ([1785] 1976) and Bentham ([1789] 1948), but in our times it emerged as a significant branch in legal theory only in the 1960s, with a famous article by Ronald Coase – Nobel Prize Laureate in Economics – entitled 'The problem of social cost' (Coase 1960). Worth mentioning as pioneering works are also the writings of Calabresi on the law of torts (Calabresi 1961, 1970, 1975) and Alchian and Demsetz on property law (1972). These works coincided with the publication of two important journals – the *Journal of Law and Economics* and the *Journal of Legal Studies*. But the important impetus of the movement came in the 1970s with the popular book by Richard Posner entitled *Economic Analysis of Law* (1972).

The (modern) economic approach towards law extends the traditional economic models designed to analyse traditional markets and applies them to non-economic markets, such as the market of crimes, the market of conflict resolution or the market of innovation. It also emphasizes the role of law and legal institutions within economic and non-economic markets. In performing these tasks the economic analysis of law also shifted traditional economic analysis to put more weight on normative analysis, pointing to the desirable legal rules and institutions to achieve certain goals (such as efficiency).

Similarly to the definition of the science of economics, the definition of the economic approach towards law or the law and economics movement is not agreed upon. The diversity of definitions reflects, among other factors, also an ideological stance, as we will demonstrate below. As regards the definition of economics, we prefer the broad methodological definition according to which law and economics is a specific way of dealing with legal questions, a way that emphasizes particular methodology.

The law and economics movement is engaged in two different projects – normative analysis and positive analysis, and some scholars add a third mode of descriptive work. Descriptive law and economics is an attempt to describe legal rules, judicial decisions or legal institutions, using the language of economics. The emphasis here is on description rather than prediction or prescription. One of the examples of a body of literature on this level of analysis is the attempt to describe the common law as an efficient set of rules or as competitive market equilibrium (see for example Rubin 1977).

Positive economics is the major branch of economics, which is seeking with the assistance of mathematical models and empirical tools to offer an explanation to the causal connections between various variables, as well as predictions as to the effect of changes in one variable on others. The classical example for this kind of work is micro-economics' core supply and demand model. It shows the connections between price and supply, on the one hand, and price and demand, on the other. The model predicts that with the rise of price demand will decrease while supply will increase. These relations are examined when other variables are set to be fixed. These theoretical causal connections can be tested empirically with the usage of another branch of economics – econometrics, and its major tool – multiple-regression. In the realm of law, what law and economics scholars are mainly interested in are the effects of different legal rules on various phenomena which the law is set to deal with, as well as the effect of different institutional factors on legal decision-making. For example, positive economic analysis of law can deal with the influence of different methods of punishment and enforcement and, indeed, substantive criminal law norms on the level of crime. Positive economic analysis of law may also explore the influence of alternative liability rules on the rate of car accidents, or the influence of the methods of judicial appointments on the degree of judicial independence and on the outcome of judicial decision-making, or the influence of various IP laws on the level of innovation.

Normative economic analysis is geared to rank alternative solutions or to identify the desirable legal or institutional arrangements. In other words, normative analysis tells us not what the legal rule is nor why it exists, but whether it is a good rule and what is the desirable legal arrangement or judicial outcome. This branch of analysis is significant because it can help us to evaluate various legal rules and judicial decisions. In the example of criminal law mentioned above, based on positive analysis, which offers insights about the correlations between various variables, normative analysis will point to the best rule. If criminal law aims only to minimize the level of crime (or the costs of crime, which include costs accruing from criminal activities and the costs of crime prevention and enforcement), then on the bases of the positive analysis we can detect the best punishment guidelines and substantive principals of criminal law. If the only purpose of regulating liability for car accidents is to minimize social costs, the analysis can tell us that the desirable rule is strict liability. Similarly, if the goal of IP laws is to maximize social welfare, on the basis of positive analysis we can prescribe the optimal legal rules – creating property rights limited in time and scope, or perhaps offering grants and prizes.

To perform a normative analysis one has to define a normative objective, the source of which is outside the scope of the science of economics. In this sense and in the framework of our broad definition of 'economics', the normative goal can be considered as one of the simplifying assumptions within the economic methodology. The leading normative goal of most law and economics literature is efficiency. There are several competing definitions of efficiency, such as maximization of utility, maximization of wealth and Pareto optimality. There are also competing views as to the status of efficiency, either as the primary normative goal as advocated by Posner (1979) or as a second best to utility maximization, unattainable owing to measurement problems, as advocated by welfare economics. In addition, efficiency is not necessarily an exclusive normative goal. Any teleological principle, including distributional principles (for example Rawls's theory of justice), can be set as the normative goal of economic analysis. A major share of constitutional law and economics relates to a different normative goal, which coincides with one specific notion of efficiency – consensus or Pareto optimality. This normative goal evolves from different historical roots, primarily from the social contract theories of the state (Coleman 1988: ch 6). In principle, non-teleological principles can also serve as goals for normative economic analysis.

One can describe the law and economics movement as comprising several generations, which can be perceived as separate sub-paradigms of sorts: the traditional Chicago school, alongside the Yale school of economic analysis of law; transaction cost and neo-institutional law and economics; behavioral law and economics; and the most recent emerging generation of development law and economics, which will have a particular relevance for intellectual property law. We use the term 'generation' because it reflects the chronological history of the movement and, indeed, its evolutionary nature. However, by this we by no means imply that the early generations are gone. The first generation – the Chicago School – is very much alive. In fact, a significant amount of work in law and economics is being carried out in this framework. These generations or sub-paradigms reflect a specific attitude towards the nature of the simplifying assumptions of each model, but also different normative goals, a fact sometimes overlooked.

The Chicago school views the neo-classical micro-economic model as the suitable and preferred theoretical framework for the analysis of all legal questions, including those that are not traditional market issues. The tools of micro-economic theory – the curves of supply and demand – are applied to analyse the market of crimes or the market of innovation, just as they are applied to the market of apples. The Chicago framework does not distinguish between rational individuals and other, more complex, market players such as firms, governments or agencies. The state, its structure and institutions are reduced through one of the simplifying assumptions to be regarded as an individual decision-maker geared to maximize self-welfare. Furthermore, within the micro-economic model this 'dogmatic' approach assumes that the players on both the demand side and the supply side are fully rational and motivated only by the quest to maximize personal wealth. It also assumes that everything can be transformed and measured by money units. Full information is assumed, as well as full knowledge of the legal rules that guide the players' choices. Preferences are assumed to be exogenous to the analysed market. The normative goal is assumed to be efficiency, in terms of wealth maximization, and any considerations of distributional justice are excluded. The result is a strong preference for markets and contracts and the rejection of regulation and government intervention. Only a few market failures are recognized – monopolies, public goods, externalities and information asymmetry – and those alone justify central intervention. This type of analysis associated the law and economic movement with the political right.

The Yale school of law and economics (led by Guido Calabresi), which had been developed in parallel with the Chicago school, uses more complex and less rigid assumptions. Thus individuals are assumed to be self-maximizers, yet their self-interest can include not only personal wealth but other factors such as others' wellbeing. More complex assumptions as to information and knowledge of legal rules are introduced. Likewise, on the supply side the firm or the government is perceived as a body of assets and individuals organized with certain structure and operated by agents. Thus the supply curve is not assumed to represent only maximization of the firm's (or the supplier's) profits. On the normative level additional goals to efficiency are recognized, such as distributional justice, and the meaning of efficiency is more complex. These differences result with a recognition of a much broader range of market failures and desirable interventions by the government. The law is perceived as strengthening the market and not as substituting it. The Chicago approach has the advantage of being simpler to model, operate and apply, and is often presented as an earlier evolutionary stage. However, such a presentation is misleading mainly because of the differences in the normative goals between the approaches.

A transitional generation in the development of the law and economics thinking is transaction cost analysis. Its starting point is, in fact, an extension of the Chicago school's focus on the basic micro-economic model of markets; and it is a transitional generation because this extension eventually gave rise to the neo-institutional law and economics. The core of transaction costs analysis is the 1960 Coase theorem, which undermines the categorization of the traditional market failures and especially the analysis of the remedies to correct them. The Coase theorem predicts that in a world with no transaction cost legal rules do not matter because market transactions will by-pass any inefficient legal arrangement. But since the real world is a world with transaction costs, Coase's analysis points at transaction costs as the focal factor to take on board when legal rules are considered (Coase 1960). The concept of transaction costs, which was originally used to analyse the interaction between individuals in the market, was soon broadened to include the analysis of the emergence of institutions, their internal decision-making processes and their external interactions, incorporating Coase's earlier work (1937) on the nature of the firm as a substitute to contracts in the market. In doing so the methodological tools used for the analysis were expended and hence the shift towards the second sub-paradigm.

This second generation of economic analysis of law – the neo-institutional sub-paradigm – is a much broader framework of economic analysis compared with that of the Chicago school insofar as it incorporates institutional structures as endogenous variables within the analysis of law. Thus, neo-institutional analysis views the political structure, the bureaucratic structure, legal institutions and other commercial and non-commercial entities as affecting each other. Political rules intertwine with economic rules, which intertwine with contracts (Williamson 1993). The tools used by the neo-institutional law and economics are the traditional micro-economics or welfare economics models, alongside public choice, game theory, agency theory, institutional economics and Virginia school of economics.[4]

In recent years law and economics has been looking into new directions. The traditional theories have been put to empirical tests, and one of the results is the incorporation of studies and insights from the fields of psychology and sociology regarding, among other factors, the rationality assumption (Simon 1957), behavior under risk (Kahneman and Tversky 1979), path dependence in decision-making and the endowment effect (Kahneman, Knettsch and Thaler 1991). Fresh emphasis is placed on the role and function of social norms (Ellickson 1991; Eric Posner 2000). The recent emergence of this behavioral law and economics, which focuses on the relaxation of the pure rationality assumption (Sen 1982) and blends empirical findings from the field of psychology, is bound to complicate economic analysis and shift its policy recommendation further apart from those of the Chicago school. A third generation of law and economics is thus emerging.

4 For a broad definition of neo-institutional law and economics, which consists of the works of Coase, Williamson, Stigler, and Buchanan and Tullock, among others, see Mercuro and Medema (1997) ch 5.

Alongside the emerging behavioral approach there are signs of another transformation of economic analysis, which might be most relevant to the analysis of intellectual property. We refer to the emergence of development law and economics. Neo-classical economics and, by derivation, the Chicago school focuses on static efficiency, examining how effective any set of legal norms (or other social and economic arrangements) is in generating maximum goods and services for any current level of inputs using existing technology. However, in recent years the attention of policy-making worldwide is geared to achieve maximum economic growth, which can be translated to the economic goal of dynamic efficiency. In contrast to static efficiency, which attempts to recommend rules generating the maximum welfare from existing resources, dynamic efficiency aims at recommending the rules, which are likely to increase collective (national or global) resources. In other words, static efficiency assumes a set level of resources to be allocated in the most efficient way, while dynamic efficiency is geared to maximize the future growth in resources. The level of technology (achieved by innovation) is the new focal point for development law and economics, as it is mainly technological change (rather than changes in the traditional production means of natural resources, labor and capital) that enables economic growth. Intellectual property law is perceived by law and economics as the most important field of law vis-à-vis innovation, technological change and thus for development and growth.

Economists have always recognized the central importance of technological innovation to economic growth and collective welfare. Adam Smith's *Wealth of Nations* emphasizes 'improvements in machinery', and Karl Marx's model of the capitalist economy ascribes a central role to technological innovation in capital goods. Likewise, Alfred Marshall described knowledge as the chief engine of progress in the economy. However, until the second half of the 20th century economists devoted very little attention to technological change or innovation as part of their theoretical models or empirical analyses. For example, Paul Samuelson, in his principal textbooks, has always acknowledged the importance of technological change but then proceeded, like all the other leading texts, largely to ignore it. Others, including Solow (1957), incorporated technology into their models, but assumed technology to be an exogenous variable in market equilibrium analysis. This had brought Joseph Stiglitz (1987: 885) to lament that: 'while it is the dynamic properties of capitalism . . . that constitute the basis of our confidence in its superiority to other forms of economic organization, the theory – at least the version we teach our students – is based on a model that assumes an unchanging technology'. Assuming technology as an exogenous factor is also true, as will be elaborated below, for the foundations of the law and economics movement.

A bold exception was the work of Schumpeter (1912, 1928, 1942) who placed innovation at the core of his economic theory, at the expense of abandoning the traditional neo-classical micro-economics equilibrium paradigm in exchange for a less rigid and less stylized evolutionary model with a strong emphasis on path dependency (Nelson and Winter 1982). One of Schumpeter's important early insights, which highlighted one of the differences between his analysis and the conventional neo-classical model, is that monopoly and oligopoly provide a more favorable environment to nurture innovation (Schumpeter 1928). Later, Schumpeter himself changed his view, pointing to individual innovative entrepreneurs as the main vehicle to promote innovation (Schumpeter 1942). This point is still under heated debate in theory and empirical studies.

Things changed in the second half of the 20th century, when more and more economists made technological change and innovation a central focus of their writings, although there is still neither a general theory of innovation nor incorporation of technological change as a full endogenous variable to the traditional micro-economics and macro-economics models. In addition, the role and functions of innovation highlights a 'sharp inconsistency between the macro-growth literature and the micro literature on technological change *per se* – that calls into question the basic tenets of neoclassical theory' (Nelson and Winter 1974: 886). The law and economics movement is still captured by the neo-classical model, which is a more rigorous theoretical framework but fails to capture various critical aspects of innovation, such as the role of education, infrastructure, firm inter-relations and other factors.

Almost no attention has been given so far within the law and economics movement to the emerging neo-Schumpeterian literature, which is less rigorous, but captures these background and less formal variables that are significant sources for innovation. The later sub-paradigm challenges the neo-classical view that have a full trust in free competition and market equilibrium. The ramifications of the neo-Schumpeterian literature to law and economics are very significant, as it has bearing on various legal fields that have been so far outside the radar of scholars writing on innovation, such as labor law, contract law, commercial law in general and public law. Many neo-Schumpeterian economists believe that the prime attention given to intellectual property law as the main vehicle to promote innovation is exaggerated. We thus envisage that in the coming years we will witness a major transformation in the law and economics writings related to technological change and thus significantly relevant to the analysis of intellectual property.

## 1.3 Shortcomings and challenges of the economic analysis of law

Many points of criticism were raised against the law and economics movement in general and, in particular, against the Chicago school, which is still its main sub-paradigm. In this framework we will not be able to cover the wide range of critical literature and instead we will focus on several points that are relevant to the economic analysis of IP and relate mainly to the methodology of the whole project of law and economics, especially to the challenges it faces in light of the changing world of the 21st century.

### *1.3.1 The overemphasis on normative analysis and the internal fallacy of law and economics*

The methodology of the science of economics is positivist in nature. As explained above, the normative goal of economic analysis is exogenous to the economic analysis. Indeed, most of the work within economics itself is on a positive level of analysis, aiming to provide improved bases for policy-makers to make their choices according to their normative considerations. This was also the nature of the writings of Ronald Coase – one of the law and economics movement's pioneers. Coase enlightened, in a revolutionary way, what should be the considerations of law-makers and judges in the field of private law, but did not point to one specific normative goal or one specific desirable legal arrangement. In this sense his 1960 article on the problem of social cost resembles his earlier 1937 article on the nature of the firm. But lawyers attribute greater importance to normative analysis, which is the direct consequence of the nature of their occupation and discipline. When economics was imported to legal research by law professors, therefore, the emphasis was shifted to normative analysis and the normative goal was presented as endogenous to economic analysis. This was the way in which Richard Posner, for example, interpreted and applied the Coase theorem.[5]

Wealth maximization emerged as the dominant normative criterion in law and economics, among the wide-ranging normative criteria employed by the economics methodology. There are at least two main reasons for this – internal and external. The internal explanation is that wealth maximization is the simplest normative criterion to model. In this sense, although in theory economics (as broadly defined above) is neutral vis-à-vis the normative goal of law, in practice it is biased towards a particular ideology as the result of its easier application, or as a result of its scientific methodology. Adopting wealth maximization as the prime normative goal results in preference of markets to public or legal ordering, privatization to government intervention and total wealth or growth rates to distributional justice.

The external explanation is rooted in the political-ideological dominance of the right, which coincided with the great rise of the law and economics movement in the 1980s. Wealth maximization was embraced by the Reagan and Thatcher regimes in the US and in the UK, and the influence of their socio-economic ideology left its significant marks on the post Reagan-Thatcher era. Thus, the Labour party in the UK, Democrats in the US and social democracy platforms worldwide have shifted to the right in the course of the last decades and have become very different, in comparison to the ideologies of pre Reagan/Thatcher political left and center. Wealth maximization or GDP growth has remained an important segment of politics and socio-economic policy. It was

5 See the interesting debate between Posner, Coase and Williamson on this issue in the 1993 volume of the *Journal of Institutional and Theoretical Economics* (vol 149).

thus an easy path for law and economics scholars to adopt and entrench it (Mattei 2005). It is difficult to establish the exact nature of the causal relations between the ideological hegemony in the political world and the success of law and economics and particularly that of the Chicago school, but we believe that this causal connection is not one sided (that is, the influence of law and economics on politics) and at least it operates in both directions, as can be seen from the appointments of two of the leading scholars of law and economics – Frank Easterbrook and Richard Posner – to senior judicial posts in the USA.

The founders of the law and economics movement had debated the normative goals and were aware of the critiques against wealth maximization, as well as of the fact that the normative goal is exogenous to the economic methodology.[6] It seems that the young generation of law and economics scholars who grew into the paradigm is much less aware of these normative debates and thus wealth maximization has become one of their presuppositions. The vast majority of law and economics writing today, using a high degree of modeling and mathematical techniques, is grounded on the unquestioned assumption that the normative goal of their analyses is wealth maximization. If it is not the mathematics that makes this literature less accessible to the wider legal community, it is this presupposition that makes much of these writings of reduced relevance for the legal world and also for the efficacy and contribution to legal research. It is noteworthy that the technological revolution of the last decades and the rapid development of behavioral law and economics may bring about improved abilities in the future to measure and compare utilities – the prime original normative goal of the science of economics, and thus the need to resort to wealth maximization for those who perceive it as a second best, would be weakened.

The emphasis on normative analysis is related to another soft point of the economic analysis of law project – the inner equilibrium between normative and positive analyses. Many law and economics scholars are engaged in both projects of normative and positive analyses. Normative analysis tries to tell us what is the desirable legal or constitutional arrangement. Positive analysis tries to explain why things are as they are or to describe legal phenomena in economic language. The distinction between normative and positive analyses is not exclusive to the economic approach. Thus the core questions of jurisprudence or the philosophy of law are what law is and what law ought to be and what are the inter-relations between these two questions. However, this distinction is crucial in law and economics, because both positive and normative analyses are founded upon specific common assumptions as to human behavior, and what is the use of constructing a normative theory if the same

6 See for example the arguments of Posner and the criticism of Ronald Dworkin and Jules Coleman in 'Symposium: Efficiency as a Legal Concern' in the 1980 volume of *Hofstra Law Review*.

assumptions which are in its bases direct us to predict that the recommended solutions do not stand a chance to be selected?

In other words, an inbuilt incoherence of the law and economics project as a whole is that, based on the rigid pre-suppositions of the paradigm, its positive analysis cannot predict the adoption of its normative recommendations. This generates a lack of inner equilibrium between normative and positive analyses. In this sense a major difference exists between free and fully competitive economic market and the political market. Within the former, the conduct of individuals, each of whom is lead by self-interested goal of maximizing his or her preferences, is expected to lead to efficient equilibrium, ie to utility maximization (as well as wealth maximization and Pareto optimality), creating equilibrium between positive and normative analyses. In the latter, self-interested conduct by politicians, bureaucrats and judges, which is the consequence of the very same pre-suppositions that are the bedrock of the normative goals of mainstream law and economics, does not necessarily lead to such efficient or utility maximizing collective choices. Once central intervention is required as a result of a market failure, the economic analysis cannot predict that this intervention will lead to the desirable solutions. As we shall elaborate later (Chapter 7) this is an acute problem in the economic analysis of IP.

This problem of lack of equilibrium between normative and positive analyses is less acute in the realm of traditional private law and, in Calabresi and Melamed (1972) terminology, in the realm of second order rules designated to protect allocation of entitlements. Thus if normative analysis points to the desirable rule regarding the leading remedy for breach of contract, or to the desirable rule regarding contingency fees, or indeed to the desirable remedy to protect an intellectual property entitlement, there is a fair chance that legislators, who do not have direct stakes in the selected solution or who are not under specific pressure to enact a certain arrangement by powerful interest groups, will vote for such an arrangement. Partly, this is the result of the high degree of generality of legislation, which cannot be perceived as acting for the benefit of certain and constant individuals or groups. Likewise, a whole body of literature showed why the common law – norms derived from individual precedents of courts – is geared towards efficiency. Given that efficiency is the leading normative goal, this literature points to equilibrium between normative and positive analyses.

Lack of equilibrium between normative and positive analyses is a much more acute problem in the realm of public law and in first order rules of whom to allocate entitlements. When politicians are voting on rules that bind their future discretion, either through the establishment of other institutions to check and balance their output (structural rules of government – either constitutional or post-constitutional) or through constitutional or administrative substantive limitations on political power, or when they are asked to vote on allocation of entitlements – such as the creation of intellectual property rights, it will be difficult to present their choices as falling in line with normative arguments regarding separation of powers, bill of rights or efficiency, growth and justice. If one assumes self-interested politicians, then it is not straightforward to present the positive analysis of intellectual property laws, for example, as falling in the same line as the normative argument that is usually used by legal theorists to describe the concept, as a major share of legislation in the area of IP is of first order decisions, that is, allocation of entitlements. The vast majority of law and economics writing ignores this internal fallacy.

### *1.3.2 The assumptions of rationality and exogenous preferences*

The shift of emphasis from positive to normative analysis with wealth maximization as the dominant collective normative goal and the lack of equilibrium between normative and positive analyses are connected to another implicit assumption that characterizes most of law and economics writings – the rationality assumption. Most law and economics literature assumes that preferences are exogenous and that individuals act rationally in the rigid sense of rationality; namely, they aspire only to maximize their personal wealth and that everything is measurable in monetary units.

The economic approach assumes that individuals' preferences are given, and seek to explain their behavior in response to changes in price, cost and information. Preferences are, thus, exogenous and fixed: they are unaffected by processes, market exchanges and social institutions. Just as wealth maximization has become an unquestionable component of the law and economics paradigm, the rigid assumptions of exogenous preferences and rational behavior are implicit in the majority of writings of law and economic scholars, so much so that they became part of the paradigmatic thinking. The latter usually boils down to assuming that human behavior is directed to maximize self-wealth. Here too, the major reason for presuming individual self-wealth maximizing behavior is the simplicity of modeling and applying advanced techniques of analysis, combined with the ideological belief in wealth maximization as the desirable prime collective goal. When wealth maximization is assumed to motivate individual conduct, the path to the collective goal of wealth maximization is straightforward (although not lacking logical and philosophical difficulties). Mainstream law and economics ignores the deficiencies of the shift from assuming self-maximization of utility to assuming self-maximization of wealth, disregarding the decreasing marginal utility of wealth, or the endowment effect.[7] The insistence of most scholars to continue the Chicago path in this realm too, therefore, makes their work of little contribution to the real world of law.

7 The decreasing marginal utility of wealth means that the utility generated from any additional unit of wealth is lower than the one from the previous unit and thus there is no strict correlation between wealth and happiness. For the endowment effect see Kahneman and Tversky (1979).

Likewise, the assumption of exogenous preferences, used by most law and economics writings, is reductionist and unrealistic, given that a number of our more important social institutions, including the law itself, are designed largely to alter preferences, not merely to structure their aggregation (Dau-Schmidt 1990). Many social institutions, such as families, schools, religion, advertising and ideologies, and indeed the law, operate largely independent of price signals and instill strong psychological aversions to stigmatized activities. Although in recent years there has been some literature on endogenous preferences (for example Stern, Dethier and Rogers 2005; Lichtenstein and Slovic 2006), it is still in the margins. Ignoring this role of key social institutions decreases the attractiveness of the canon law and economics literature.

The assumption of exogenous preferences is used by most law and economics writings not only because it is more straightforward to handle and model but also because it is an essential component in advocating wealth maximization as the desirable normative goal. Once one expands economic models to include the possibility of preference changes resulting, among other things, from legal rules, and takes those preference changes into account in any overall normative assessment, justification for the use of wealth maximization criterion weakens considerably. To apply the criterion, and once central intervention by the law is justified, one must first choose whether to measure the willingness-to-pay consequences of a policy on the basis of the affected persons' pre-policy or post-policy preferences (Crespi 1997). Recognizing that post-policy preferences might be different from pre-policy preferences undermines the coherence of wealth maximization as deriving strict recommendation as to the desirable rule or legal decision, and makes wealth maximization dependent on the order of decisions. This may be one of the reasons why to date the attempts to relax the exogenous preferences assumption, as well as the rigid rationality assumption, for example by the behavioral scholars, still remain peripheral to the core and the number of contributions by law and economics scholars and their public voice.

The weakness of assuming exogenous preferences is blatant in the area of information and the markets of informational products and services, which are the object of IP laws. This is due to both the inherent nature of information as one of the most important foundations of preferences and to the very rapid changes in these markets, in which technology advancements frequently precede the crystallization of preferences. The consumption of information, as well as constraints on information, may shape preferences. Moreover, while a blunt assumption regarding preferences might be applicable in the case of corporations that are specifically designed to maximize profits, it may not apply to individual actors. The introduction of the Internet and information technologies in recent decades brought the individual to the forefront of processes of production and consumption of information (see the discussion in Chapter 5). Information technologies and the rise of a global network further transform altogether the notion of the individual, who is the basic unit for economic analysis. We elaborated on this in relation to the effects of cyberspace on the economic analysis of law (Elkin-Koren and Salzberger 2005: ch 9).

One reason for keeping preferences exogenous is the fact that preferences are affected by a variety of social and cultural variables, which make it difficult for economists to control them. Conventional economic analysis assumes that our basic identity, which can be framed in terms of various sets of preferences, is the result of distinct historical, cultural, linguistic and even climatic different backgrounds. Those background factors are givens and predate any formation of markets and collective action organizations, such as states or other political units. The definitions of state boundaries, however, are very much influenced by these ancient groupings of preferences. Even if preferences change as the result of market interactions, such as successful marketing and advertising, they are initially founded upon and developed from these ancient differences, some of which are presumably almost permanent. The global information network is challenging this perception, because it blurs historical, cultural, national and even climatic boundaries. The online information environment constitutes the human condition of our time. The comprehensive character of the online environment makes individuals more vulnerable to external effects that shape their preferences. The emergence of media, communications and multinational software conglomerates and the rise of new monopolies affect not only economic competition in the market for ordinary goods, but also the very bases of individual autonomy.

While conventional economic thinking, neo-institutional and behavioral law and economics included, perceives individual preferences as exogenous to the political process and to the economic markets, the emerging information environment requires us to internalize not only the analysis of individual preferences but also the concept of the individual.

### *1.3.3 Law and economics in a changing global environment*

The law and economics movement was born and had established itself before the technological revolution of the last three decades and the accelerated globalization process. It has not adapted yet to the new realities or, put differently, the vast majority of contemporary law and economic literature ignores the deep global changes of the last couple of decades. Several points can be emphasized in this context. The first relates to the role of technology within the economic models and legal theory.

Traditional economic models presume the state of technology to be fixed or exogenous to their analysis. Take, for example, the path-breaking Coase theorem, which predicts that in a world with no transaction costs the choice of legal rule would not matter, since the market will by-pass any inefficient legal rule and would stabilize on efficient equilibrium. The technologies relevant to the actual examples – trains and sparks – given by Coase in his 1960 article were not likely to change significantly as a result of the choice of legal rules (although one could have assumed that the technology of operating trains will be affected by the decision whether to hold the train companies liable for damages caused by them to the cultivated fields through which they run, or not). In today's information environment, where technologies are constantly evolving at an accelerated pace, the outcome of Coasian analysis may be different with every diverse technological advancement. The pace of technological change today is disputable and there are many ways to measure it. Some believe that the speed of the chip, which doubles every two years, is a good measure of technological change. A common assumption in the high-tech environment is that technology reinvents itself every six to twelve months. This very brief timeframe and the elasticity of technology, call for different treatment of technology within economic analysis. The crucial shortcoming of the transaction cost analysis when applied, for example, to the Internet is that it regards technological development as static. It overlooks the interdependency and reciprocity between technological developments and legal rules. This multi-layered relationship between law and technology is a key factor for understanding technological innovation in the information environment, which is also characterized by decreasing traditional transaction costs. Thus, an analysis that takes the state of technology as an exogenous component suffers from a serious shortcoming when applied to an environment with rapid technological advances and innovations. Such an analysis fails to consider the effects of legal rules on innovation (Elkin-Koren and Salzberger 2004: ch. 8), which have a significant relevance for the field of intellectual property law.

Technology is not the result of nature or the necessary sole outcome of predetermined scientific progress. Scientific progress depends on investment in R&D, which in turn is likely to hinge on the legal regime and specific legal rules regarding allocation of entitlements and liability. Therefore, technological states of the art, cannot be regarded as independent factors and should not be exogenous to the analysis of the cheapest avoider or the greatest maximizer. Indeed, the availability of certain technologies is contingent upon various socio-economic factors, of which law is a prime player. If we require that the steam engines of railway companies release fewer sparks, we create a demand for more effective devices. Such a demand is likely to attract more investment in research and development of better devices, and to stimulate competition among developers and producers. Large investments and high levels of competition are likely to increase innovation in spark-reducing measures and push down the prices of such devices. Likewise, anti-circumvention laws are likely to have an effect on the system security and deciphering technologies, which in turn will have an effect on society's progress and wellbeing and ultimately on future laws. The ramifications of the choice of a legal rule on the likelihood that preventive technologies will emerge are not taken into consideration by the standard law and economic analysis.

Technology also affects other important pillars of the standard law and economics analysis. Thus, agency theory, applied, for example, to analyse representative government (Musgrave and Musgrave 1989) should be revisited. The easier and relatively cheap access to information and the lower costs of collective deliberation and action, rendered by information technologies are likely to increase the effective monitoring level and thus reduce agency costs, thereby extracting significant influence on economic analysis of politics and on the theory of the firm. The technological revolution affects the structure and role of firms in the organization of production and the use of resources. According to Coasian (1937) analysis, firms are likely to emerge when it is more efficient to organize economic activity through hierarchies than through contracts or markets. The potential reduction in the organizational cost of firms would arguably turn them into a more efficient option for conducting economic activities. However, the reduction in transaction costs of collective action is also evident in markets, thus changing the balance between firms and markets. If firms were conceived as the outcome of high transaction cost in markets, advanced technologies are bound to shift activities back from firms to markets, as we are witnessing in the informational products environment (Benkler 2002).

Likewise, the theory of collective action and economic analysis of the state, constitutional and public law and institutions have to be revisited. Mainstream public choice literature assumes that small interest groups will be able to seek rents and acquire gains through pressure on representatives at the expense of the general public. Interest groups are able to succeed in their actions because of the costs of collective action. These costs allow only small groups to organize, groups whose potential gain from collective action is higher than the costs of organization (Olson 1965). This theory is decisive for the normative and positive analysis of constitutional law and state institutions but, as we elaborate in Chapter 7, it is also crucial in the analysis of IP laws. The Internet lowers the costs of collective action, which in turn enables broader interest groups to organize, bringing more equality to the political markets and diffusing the impact of narrow interest groups; this will affect the traditional analysis of separation of powers, constitutional law and regulation (Elkin-Koren and Salzberger 2004: ch. 10).

Moreover, technology is also an emerging hidden source of law, as well as an enforcement system. Law can no longer be perceived as generated exclusively by premeditated rule-making processes of legislatures and courts, and even those laws that are deliberately created by political institutions are no longer the sole monopoly of the institutions of state governments. The code has become an important source of law and an enforcement mechanism (Reidenberg 1998; Lessig 1999). These phenomena have, until now, been overlooked by the mainstream law and economics literature. A possible explanation is that recognizing technology as an endogenous factor, in a similar way to the attitude towards individual preferences, shakes up the leading law and economics normative goal of wealth maximization. Endogenizing technology affects the coherency of the argument in favor of wealth maximization, primarily because of the vague geographical and time units of maximization and the order in which decisions are taken, which will have much more bearing on the possible efficiency frontiers.

A second feature characterizing the new world is globalization. It is itself related to the current technological revolution and the fact that markets today – both economic and political – cross traditional geographical borders and undermine the traditional structure and powers of a world divided to independent and sovereign states. Like the treatment of technology, the traditional law and economics models view as exogenous crucial factors, including the existence of states, the borders between them, their central governments, their enforcement powers and the correspondence of markets and states. Public choice theory attempted to remedy part of this deficiency of traditional micro-economic theory by analysing the emergence of the public sphere, the state, public law and collective decision-making processes. Neo-institutional theory is the broadest framework of economic analysis insofar as it attempts to incorporate public choice analysis with the traditional micro-economics or welfare economics. Accepting Coase's (1937) insights with regard to the emergence of firms and their internal structure, neo-institutional law and economics regards institutional structures as endogenous variables within the analysis of law. Thus, neo-institutional analysis views the political structure, the bureaucratic structure, legal institutions and the other commercial and non-commercial entities as affecting each other. Political rules intertwine with economic rules, which in turn intertwine with contracts.

## 1.4 Conclusion

Law and economics has emerged as a dominant contemporary paradigm for the analysis of law. One cannot hide the fact that one of its driving forces is publication. Legal scholars find it easier to publish law and economics papers because they are more abstract, less contingent upon local law or specific legal systems and thus they appeal to broader readership and easily cross geographical and language borders, and also because the criteria for their evaluation are more objective. At first sight this might not seem to be a justified reason for the success of the law and economics movement or for its methodological dominance in the research and study of the law, but, looked upon more deeply, this phenomenon ought to be welcomed. It allows better communication between legal scholars worldwide and a real advancement of the science of law and the methodology for legal research. This is specifically important in the area of IP law in which national legal arrangements have real ramifications on other jurisdictions, much more than in other areas of the law, and as a result internationalization, harmonization and globalization of the law is more apparent than in other fields.

The explanation for the paradigmatic contemporary dominance of law and economics is not very different from the explanation for the dominance of previous paradigms in legal studies; they too were rooted in developments outside the immediate realm of the law. The current dominance of law and economics is also manifested by its influence on non-law and economics discourse, thinking and theorizing of law (Landes and Posner 1993). Indeed, formalist, comparative, law-and-society and critical scholars have a fruitful dialogue with law and economics. They incorporate law and economics insights, way of thinking, reasoning and discourse into their writings, some of which are the background of new angles of criticism, which are the source for innovative non-law and economics insights about law. This phenomenon contributes to legal scholarship and to better understanding and evaluation of the law.

Having said that, the mainstream scholarship of law and economics, which originated from counter-dogmatic and pragmatist approaches towards the law – transformed over the years into dogmatic thinking. The law and economics movement originated from a pragmatic view of law and legal research which characterized legal realism and which was a response to the dogmatic approach of positivism-formalism. But it transformed to become another form of dogmatism, reflected by the rigid assumptions inbuilt into its mainstream literature (Katz 1990; Hovenkamp 1990). It is interesting to note that, ironically, one of the big prophets of the law and economics movement and the scholar who is primarily responsible for its dogmatic character – Richard Posner – reveals a much more pragmatic face in some of his writings in recent years. Taking into account factors such as intuition, subjectivity, ignorance, learning and political motivations, Posner's recent analysis of legal decision-making does not seem to assign to economics the same role that was assigned by the traditional theory, in which law-making was supposed to reflect a mechanical balancing of social costs and benefits (Krecke 2004). It is time for mainstream scholarship of law and economics to turn around back to pragmatism. We hope that this book is a contribution in this direction.

# 2 The rise of intellectual property

Intellectual property is playing a growing role in society, culture, the economy and politics. This chapter provides a short overview of intellectual property and the major debates surrounding the field. We begin by elaborating on the growing significance of IP (section 2.1) and proceed with the definition and sub-branches of intellectual property (section 2.2) and whether it is really property (section 2.3). Finally, we inquire into the four different major philosophical justifications of IP (section 2.4) and in their context vis-à-vis the law and economics scholarship (section 2.5).

## 2.1 The rising significance of intellectual property

Intellectual property has become a very serious matter. Some estimates conclude that the current value of intellectual property significantly outweighs the value of physical property – land, tangibles and intangibles together. According to Idris (2004), for example, while in 1982 only 38 percent of corporate assets in the United States were non-physical assets, by 2000 this figure rocketed to 70 percent. Greene (2001) asserts that the value of IP in corporations of all the industrialized countries amounts to more than two-thirds of their total value. A growing percentage of the GDP in industrial countries is now comprised of informational goods such as software, movies, music, drugs and databases. Shapiro and Hassett (2005) estimate the value of IP in the United States in 2005 at US$5 trillion, which equates to roughly 50 percent of its GDP.[8] The scope of IP protection has of course had a significant effect on this economic value and the laws regulating intellectual property in the information age are perceived as key for economic growth. Intellectual property law, therefore, has become of immense importance. It has seen in the last two decades the most significant changes since its birth following the invention of printing.

8 According to the US Chamber of Commerce, in 2008, the gross output of US intellectual property companies in the manufacturing and non-manufacturing sectors generated nearly US$7.7 trillion in gross output, accounting for 33.1% of total US GDP.

The importance of intellectual property is reflected not only by its economic value. Intellectual property law has significant effects on the pace of technological advancement, with some important implications for the course of scientific research, for food security, health and human welfare. It also has a far-reaching impact on our social and cultural life – on the kind of entertainment and culture we consume, on the nature of gadgets we use and the timescale within which we are compelled to replace them. Intellectual property is also affecting the distribution of wealth and social structures of societies that have been transformed as the result of IP with the emergence of new classes of young professionals, trained in high-tech related professions, whose earnings are skyrocketing and significantly influence the redistribution of income. The growing importance of IPR amplifies the power of individual authors and inventors and shakes the structure of labor markets, marking the decline of unionized labor. Intellectual property has also affected politics, institutions, the structure and size of corporations, organizations and the role played by interest groups in both the national and international domains.

A good way to understand the impact of intellectual property on our contemporary lives is to imagine how the world would have looked like without intellectual property rights – no Hollywood mega productions, different types of entertainment products and cultural artifacts, fewer gadgets with much longer shelf lives and perhaps a slower pace of technological change, different modes of communication and collective actions, different structure of societies, of the labor markets and indeed of the financial markets.[9] Whether in this hypothetical world individuals would have been happier or better-off is one of the key questions which cannot be precisely answered.

The crucial impact of intellectual property on all avenues of the human condition nowadays is the result of the technological revolution of the information age. Intangible goods, software, pharmaceutical drugs, music, books and movies are driving the economic growth in the 21st century. Intellectual property law has significant effects on the pace of this technological advancement and the technological revolution has no less significant effects on the scope and importance of intellectual property law. The growing economic value of informational goods brought about a process of commodification and propertization. Informational goods and services are increasingly protected as property, either by legal rules that grant the owner a set of exclusive legal rights, or by other means such as technology, which itself is protected by law against circumvention. The law became a major tool for economic gains and the immense economic potential of intellectual goods and their borderless nature has led to globalization of legal arrangements in this field. Intellectual

9 The abolishing of IPR would have considerably diluted the financial markets (Fisher 2001; International Chamber of Commerce 2005). In addition, world trade would have been significantly affected in volume and indeed in structure (Helfer 2007; Sykes 2002).

property issues have also turned into trade issues, administered by the World Trade Organization.

The globalized nature of information markets and the subsequent harmonization of intellectual property regimes have also become a source for tension and growing controversy among nations and governments. IP law has become an important battleground for interest groups, politicians and different voices in civil society. The expansion of intellectual property and its significance for economic growth, national and personal wealth and for human rights raised a variety of calls amounting to a social movement advocating a counter-process that will halt and indeed reduce proprietary regimes.

The public domain is a key feature of this movement. The public domain consists of those aspects of intangible goods that are not subject to intellectual property. Over the past two decades scholars have emphasized the role of the public domain as a vehicle for promoting the goals of innovation and technological progress (for example Boyle 2003). Indeed, the public domain is not a graveyard of intellectual property laws, but rather its ultimate purpose (Patterson and Lindberg 1991). Intellectual property seeks to stimulate creative output and inventions that would ultimately be accessible to all, for the benefit of humanity as a whole (Wagner 2003). The public domain is also fueling innovation by providing the raw materials for further inventions and new creative works. As Jessica Litman aptly explained, as early as 1990, the public domain should be viewed as a source of creativity: 'The public domain should be understood not as the realm of material that is undeserving of protection, but as a device that permits the rest of the system to work by leaving the raw material of authorship available for authors to use' (Litman 1990: 968).

Advocates of the public domain argue that legislatures and courts surrender to the big media, to mega corporations and to powerful interest groups and enhance the scope of intellectual property, thus shrinking the public domain, increasing corporate control over creative activities and posing a serious threat to free culture and also to technological progress itself (Boyle 2003a; Samuelson 2003; Lessig 2004). This claim highlights the significance of the right regime of intellectual property rights not only vis-à-vis the economy but also vis-à-vis civil society and the future of democracy (Birnhack 2006).

## 2.2 What is intellectual property?

The term 'intellectual property' is relatively new (Sterk 2004). It was coined in 1967 when the UN decided to establish the World Intellectual Property Organization (WIPO). It brought under one roof very different issues ranging from rights of authors to protect the integrity of their works, through the right of pharmaceutical companies to prevent the competing manufacturing of their drugs, to the rights of celebrities to prevent the presentation of their photos. The TRIPs Agreement covers seven categories of intellectual property rights: copyright and related rights, trademarks, geographical indications, industrial designs, patents, layout-designs (topographies) of integrated circuits and the protection of undisclosed information.[10] The three major categories of intellectual property are copyright, patents and trademarks. Copyright law protects creative works, patent law protects inventions and trademark law protects symbols. Specific regulations also address issues such as databases, trade secrets, design patents; plant patents, plant variety protection, semiconductor mask work protection, digital audio recording devices, broadcast and cable retransmission, protection of rights management systems against circumvention, and sometimes even publicity rights.

All these categories were treated separately in the past and only recently were named by a single tag. Each category has its own unique characteristics and constitutes a different market for a particular informational good (that is, designs, symbols, creative expressions, data). Thus, the market for brand names, for instance, is established on the basis of trademark law. In the absence of trademarks and complementary claims, no transactions in brand names could have been possible since everyone would have been free to copy brand names as they pleased.

Yet, it is often the case that several types of intellectual property govern the same tangible good, creating distinct markets for various aspects of the same material object. Consider computer programs for instance. The expression embodied in the program could be protected by copyright as a literary work, while its interface could be protected as both literary and artistic work. Sometimes software will also qualify for patent protection if it includes novel and non-obvious invention (that is under the US legal regime but not always in Europe). The name of the application and symbols used to mark the program could win trademark protection. Those different aspects are governed by different rules, each of which offers a distinct type of protection. Intellectual property law is thus a set of legal doctrines that govern the use of informational works. The feature shared by all objects of intellectual property is that they are all intangibles. These objects of intellectual property protection may often be embodied in a tangible medium, but the economic value of them would be the knowledge they incorporate.

Intellectual property is not a coherent notion and the classification of a bundle of rules under the single notion of intellectual property could lead to some confusion regarding its underpinning theoretical framework. The economic rationale for copyrights, patents and related rights, as further explored in the following chapters, is very different from the economic

10 See Agreement on Trade-Related Aspects of Intellectual Property Rights (TRIPs) art 1(2) available at http://www.wto.org/english/docs_e/legal_e/27-trips.pdf.

rationale of trademarks and related rights. While the economic rationale of the former is founded upon market failures of public goods and externalities, the latter involves market failures connected to a-symmetric information. Trademark law protects intangibles, and is often referred to as a type of intellectual property. Yet, this body of law is not directly linked to innovation policy. This distinction was explained by the US Supreme Court in determining whether US Congress is authorized to enact federal trademark legislation under the intellectual property clause of the Constitution (see *In re Trade Mark Cases*, 100 US 82: 94):

> The ordinary trade-mark has no necessary relation to invention or discovery. The trademark recognized by the common law is generally the growth of a considerable period of use, rather than a sudden invention. It is often the result of accident rather than design, and when under the act of Congress it is sought to establish it by registration, neither originality, invention, discovery, science, nor art is in any way essential to the right conferred by that act. If we should endeavor to classify it under the head of writings of authors, the objections are equally strong. The writings which are to be protected are the fruits of intellectual labor, embodied in the form of books, prints, engravings, and the like. The trademark may be, and generally is, the adoption of something already in existence as the distinctive symbol of the party using it.

The prime focus of this book is on copyright and patents, which affect the production of knowledge. It will allow us to explore those aspects of intellectual property that are relevant to innovation and creativity and which raise the greatest challenges for the economic approach.

## 2.3 Is intellectual property a property right?

The term *intellectual property* is, to some extent, a metaphor. First, it is not really *intellectual*, as it does not apply merely to intellectual creations. Creative works such as *The Sound of Silence* by Paul Simon, *Hamlet* by Shakespeare or the invention of the electric bulb by Thomas Edison could certainly be considered the fruits of the author's inventive imagination and intellectual skills. The protection of such an output of the human mind and spirit would often reflect a perception of the *romantic author* – a creator that is conceived as the sole originator of the work (Jaszi 1991; Boyle 1992). Yet, in many cases intellectual property rights also cover intangibles that do not reflect any intellectual effort, such as a compilation of horse racing information or a telephone directory, or a brand name that acquired secondary meaning due to massive investments in marketing. In those circumstances, when protection is granted it would practically reward the efforts and the investment of labor and resources, which do not necessarily involve any exceptional intellectual effort.

Second, *intellectual property* is not strictly property. Indeed, intellectual property shares some significant features with conventional property rights: It defines a set of exclusive rights, created by law, which constitute rights against the whole world (rights in rem). The right to exclude is considered a core element of any property right and a defining feature, which arguably makes intellectual property a type of property right (Merrill 1998; Merrill and Smith 2007). The exclusive rights might be limited in scope, but within that scope it imposes a duty upon strangers to avoid using the intellectual property without the permission of the owner. The interests of rightholders are usually protected by a *property rule*, within the Calabresi and Melamed typology (Calabresi and Melamed 1972), which entitle them to an injunction prohibiting the injurer from bypassing their rights. Potential injurers must therefore negotiate with the owner and reach an agreement regarding the exploitation of the informational works that are covered by the intellectual property right. Supplementary protection is often provided by torts and common law claims such as false advertising, passing off, misappropriation and restitution.[11]

However, there are significant differences between intellectual property and property rights in tangible assets. First, the legal protection provided by IPR is limited in time and scope. While real property will generally last forever, intellectual property is only granted for limited periods. Patents would generally last for 20 years from the date the application for the patent was filled, while copyrights would last for 70 years after the death of the author. When duration, however long, expires, the copyrighted work or patented invention will fall back into the public domain. The *public domain* is therefore a fundamental tenet of the intellectual property regime, defining the legal status which applies to those intangible works for which intellectual property rights had expired, or those aspects thereof that are not protected by intellectual property rights. While intellectual property laws define a set of exclusive rights granted to rightholders with respect to their work, the public domain is a regime in which everyone is privileged to use any given resource and no one is legally entitled to exclude others.

Another feature differentiating intellectual property from property in tangibles is its non-rivalry nature. While intellectual property regulates the use of informational resources, which do not suffer from scarcity, real property

11 The exclusion-centrism in property theory was recently criticized by Dagan (2009), arguing that limits of the right of the owner to exclude are quite common in property law, and that manifestations of inclusion (the right of non-owners to buy, rent or physically enter a property) are intrinsic to property as those of exclusion. Dagan demonstrates this by using the fair use doctrine in US copyright law, as an example of such principle. However, his starting point is that IPR are property rights, the mere categorization disputed here.

regulates the management of scarce resources. Land, for instance, cannot be used by more than a limited number of users. One cannot use the same parcel of land for both a coalmine and a holiday resort. Therefore, property rights must presumably allocate the use privileges among potential users of the land. Economic theory would suggest that rights will be allocated to the most efficient user. Physical resources, such as chattels or minerals are also scarce. The use of such resources by one often denies others from using it, especially in cases of minerals and food, where the use of the resource consumes it. Intellectual property law applies to resources that do not suffer from scarcity; consuming an informational good does not prevent others from consuming it subsequently or simultaneously. Quite the contrary, the nature of informational goods (e.g. software) is such that their usage by an additional user may often increase the value of that good to the original user and to the public at large. The lack of rivalry in using intellectual property subject matters means that intellectual property law is not facing the allocation challenges faced by law of physical property.

Moreover, in some cases, informational assets protected by intellectual property would not have come into being in the first place without intellectual property protection. Whereas property rules are designed to allocate rights in existing subject matters (ie land, tangible assets), intellectual property seek to encourage human action and interaction that would generate the creation of informational works. Intellectual property is inherently ex ante, and seeks to establish the social institutions that would generate new subject matters. Therefore, the main challenge for intellectual property laws, in contrast to traditional property law, is to design a legal regime that would stimulate creation of new resources and not merely manage the use of pre-existing assets, while enabling the widest usage possible to the benefits of society at large.

The most obvious feature that characterizes intellectual property and distinguishes it from real property is its intangible nature. The notion of property is rather intuitive. Property rules define rights and duties related to an asset, and depend on compliance by strangers who are not bound by any contractual relationship with the owner. It imposes a duty, defined by law, to refrain from any of the actions exclusively granted to owners. We often assume that if we are not the owners of something – a piece of land, a car, a golden necklace; it must be *owned* by somebody else and we need to ask for permission to use it. We do not normally think the same way about virtual assets such as stories, images, music or new inventions. Sometimes we might not even be aware that we were using them in creating our own works. When we use such virtual assets we do not usually have to cross any physical barriers. This makes the identification of intellectual property more cumbersome, requiring a high level of awareness and understanding of the legal regime.

A novel could be embodied in a tangible copy of a printed book, but the intellectual property rights related to it extend beyond the protection of a particular physical copy and apply to the original narrative, the characters, the choice of language and other aspects of the expression that make up the novel. The boundaries of legal protection do not coincide with the physical boundaries of the copy that embodies the work. The physical boundaries of the book cover do not signal the scope of rights and duties imposed on potential users of such property. With the introduction of eBooks, and digital content in general, such boundaries are further blurred. The definition of the subject matter of rights is entirely dependent on legal definitions. For instance, a novel may include aspects, some of which are protected by copyright (expression) and others that are in the public domain (ideas). The distinction between idea and expression would often require legal analysis.

The virtual nature of intellectual property also makes it relatively difficult to exclude and therefore vulnerable to free riding. While the object of physical property has visible boundaries that can be clearly marked and noticed, enabling exclusion even with a lack of legal rule or enforcement agents, intellectual creations are lacking any obvious or natural boundaries that enable exclusion without a clear and efficiently enforceable legal rule. This aspect of intellectual property is further discussed in Chapter 6.

These differences between intellectual property and real property suggest that intellectual property is not strictly property. The unique features of intellectual property require caution in applying the conceptual framework, the theoretical foundations and the policy analyses pertaining to real property. As aptly put by Benjamin Kaplan, referring to copyright:

> To say that copyright is 'property', although a fundamentally unhistorical statement, would not be boldly misdescriptive if one were prepared to acknowledge that there is property and property, with few if any legal consequences extending uniformly to all species and that in practice the lively questions are likely to be whether certain consequences ought to attach to a given piece of so-called property in given circumstances.
>
> (Kaplan 1967: 72)

Even though intellectual property might only be a metaphor, legal metaphors may prove to be very powerful in framing policy issues and legal analysis. The rhetoric of property has indeed affected legal theory and legal analysis (Rose 1994). When we group these different legal rights together under a single roof, call them 'property' and establish an independent regime of intellectual property, we are likely to affect the actual scope and general attitude towards these rights. In recent years alternative metaphors for the information environment were suggested, such as the environmental metaphor, viewing culture as 'a system of interconnected and interdependent resources that includes both natural and built resource systems' (Madison, Frischmann and Strandburg 2010), or the dialogic metaphor, viewing cultural and knowledge resources as information flows and ingredients of social discourse and human interaction (Elkin-Koren 2005).

In Chapter 4 we show further how the notion of property has affected a theoretical shift in the economic analysis of intellectual property, where the general concept of intellectual property moved away from the notion of *trade regulation* and *business tort* towards a unified notion of proprietary rights, perhaps partly due to the title 'property'. The rhetoric of property is thus very powerful; the property discourse is very influential and strikes fundamental intuitions regarding entitlements. Consequently, it advances stronger and broader property protection (in its traditional meaning).

## 2.4 The normative sources of intellectual property law

What are the philosophical justifications for intellectual property rights? There are two grand conflicting foundations for normative analysis of intellectual property rights: deontological foundation and teleological (consequential) foundation. The former can characterize the dominant historical source of IP legal discourse in the civil law world (Continental Europe), while consequential thinking is perceived to be the dominant foundation of IP law in the Anglo-American legal tradition. Within each of these domains we can identify two major normative theories of IP (Fisher 2001).

One group of deontological-based theories for justification of IP rights includes natural law and natural rights theories. The deontological paradigm is mostly outside the scope of law and economics, as it judges whether a law, decision or action is right or wrong on the basis of its intrinsic moral value regardless of its consequences in terms of individual subjective values or preferences. In other words, traditional natural law thinking perceives morality or the basic distinction between good and bad as pre-human, originating either from God or from the essence of human nature, and it also believes that positive laws ought to reflect and enforce morals. Although natural law tradition can be traced back to ancient times, it was 13th century Thomas Aquinas who framed it in the context of a theory of law, and John Locke (1690) who based on it justifications for the right of property, intellectual property included (Shiffrin 2001).

A natural law Lockean type justification to property rights asserts that every person has a natural right to own his or her self-creations or fruits of labor – whether they are physical or intellectual. These include creations of which the raw materials were not owned or held in common (Nozick 1974). Whether the six different reasons given by Locke form a coherent justification for a natural intellectual property right is an open question (Fisher 2001: 22). However, there is no doubt that Locke's writings were instrumental in shaping the European approach to intellectual property, which borrows from the natural law tradition (Gordon 1993). If such a natural right is recognized it cannot be compromised, even if allocating it decreases the total social welfare or utility, hinders a just distribution and alike. In this sense the natural law discourse is outside the realm of law and economics and it also cannot justify current positive intellectual property law. Thus, from a natural law/natural rights perspective, intellectual property rights cannot be limited in time; they ought to be allocated to the inventor or creator and not to the investor or the corporation in which the creator is employed.

A second group of deontological theories for the justification of intellectual property rights focus not on the natural right to one's fruits of labor, but on intellectual property as an inherent ingredient of the self or of personality. These theories are associated with Kant and Hegel's self-fulfilling or self-flourishing arguments. They might be perceived as an important source for moral rights in intellectual property law, but certainly cannot conform with the contemporary positive scope of intellectual property law (Fisher 2001). Accepting this normative foundation will mean that IPR are unlimited in time, but those will be granted only for real creative expressions or real intellectual creations, which express the self, and not for discoveries, which are the result of sheer luck, on the one hand and creations, which are only information compilation, such as databases, on the other hand. Like the natural rights foundation, since the self-fulfilling, personal autonomy rationales are also deontological in their nature they fall outside the realm of law and economics and therefore will not be further discussed in the framework of this book.

The two main groups of theories within the teleological realm are the utilitarian theory and its derivatives, as well as classical republican theories. The utilitarian moral theory is one of the historical sources for modern economics, especially normative economics, and hence it is only natural that it is the main focus of the law and economics discourse, including the economic analysis of IP. But, as we argue below, the republican moral and political philosophy can also be discussed in the framework of law and economics and it might be the most interesting challenge of the discipline vis-à-vis intellectual property.

Utilitarianism as a modern moral theory originates in the writings of Jeremy Bentham (1789) and was further developed by John Stuart Mill (1863). It rejects deontological moral theory, natural law and rights in particular, arguing that good and bad are subjective and individual values. Every person defines what is good for her and legitimately strives to promote it. This starting point leads to the sole collective moral criterion – the maximization of aggregate utility or the greatest good for the greatest number. Utilitarianism is an attractive moral theory in the sense that in principle it can judge the desirability of any decision, action or law by examining whether this decision, action or law increases society's aggregate utility. In cases of alternative actions, decisions or laws, the moral choice is the one that maximizes aggregate utility. However, utility is difficult to measure and compare and thus when economists adopted utilitarianism they resorted to a second best. Welfare economics substituted utility with wealth (Kaldor 1939), acknowledging that wealth maximization is a second best, primarily because it overlooks the decreasing marginal utility of wealth – an additional dollar to a wealthy person generates less utility when compared with an additional dollar to a poor person. Thus welfare economists attempted to correct this shift by social welfare functions, which attribute different weights to the willingness to pay.

The shift from utility to wealth might solve the measurement problem, but it retains two other key questions, which are very crucial in the IP context – the geographical unit for maximization and the time framework for maximization. The former question relates directly to the internalization of IPR and the heated controversy whether the balance struck by the IPR regime in the developed world also maximizes utility (or wealth) for the rest of the world. The time frame for maximization is related to the goal of static versus dynamic efficiency. The latter seeks to maximize wealth over time, but what should be the horizons of development and growth? Should we aim at maximizing growth for the next year, the next five years, the next decade or the century? We will address some of these questions in the next chapter.

Another direction in economic theory attempting to solve the measurement problem of utilitarianism was constructed on the premise that since utility cannot be measured and compared we have to assume individuals' order of preferences rather than utility functions. This direction was further developed by social choice theory and by the Pareto principle, according to which a decision, action or law are justified as long as at least one person is made better off while no one is left worse off. In principle, any utility enhancing law is Pareto optimal, because those who object to it can be compensated by those who are in favor and the latter still remain better off. The Pareto criterion coincides with consensual decision-making as the only justifiable collective decision-making rule, which is the foundation of the social contract tradition in political philosophy from Hobbes (1651) to Rawls (1971).

In 1979 Richard Posner came forward with an original argument according to which wealth maximization is not a second best to utility maximization but is in fact to be preferred normatively, and that it ought to be the leading normative principle for law (Posner 1979). Posner's argument set the main normative framework of the Chicago school of law and economics which we elaborated and indeed criticized in the previous chapter.

The utilitarian foundation of intellectual property and its offspring justify intellectual property rights as far as granting such rights maximizes social utility or social welfare or individual preferences, or social wealth or economic efficiency. There are significant differences between each of these consequential goals, which will be partly addressed in subsequent chapters, but all of them can be analysed under the methodology of economics. The incentives theory is maybe the most common framework to analyse IP law within this paradigm. It justifies a limited form of intellectual property rights which will generate the incentives to creation and innovation, taking into account the public good nature of the products, implying that once they are produced, maximizing their usage enhances collective utility and wealth. Property rights for intellectual creations, therefore, have conflicting consequences vis-à-vis the goal of utility or wealth maximization and thus the right balance to generate an optimal solution has to be struck, leading to property rights limited in time, terms and scope.

In other words, the incentives paradigm asks: what are the desirable laws to maximize society's utility or welfare or wealth? It recognizes the fact that while property rights will give incentives to create and thus ought to be established by law, propertization also hinders the creation process, as new creations in most cases rely on previous ones and, if the latter are kept private property and are too costly, then the likelihood of new creations decreases. In this sense, one cannot describe the law and economics model based on utilitarian foundations as pro-propertization and anti-public domain. The challenge is to design the appropriate scope of IP rights, and by derivation the public domain, so that IPR will maximize society's wellbeing. We will return to these themes in detail in Chapter 3.

A republican theory of IP might be considered as the most complex one. The republican tradition in political philosophy overlaps with the social contract tradition, as can be exemplified by the writings of Jean-Jacques Rousseau (1762). It can, therefore, be viewed as connected to the teleological moral framework. Yet, the republican tradition adds an important twist. The general will of Rousseau or the common good of the American founding fathers is not a mere aggregation of individual preferences. The republican emphasis on participation, deliberation and responsibility vis-à-vis the state can be interpreted in various ways in the context of economic thinking and modeling. The republican goal in the context of the philosophical justification of intellectual property is to achieve an attractive and just society and culture (Fisher 2001), to enable the flourishing of civil society (Elkin-Koren 1996) and to promote 'discursive foundations for democratic culture and civic association' (Netanel 1996).

We argued elsewhere (Elkin-Koren and Salzberger 2005) that republican thinking is not outside the scope of law and economics but is perhaps its most interesting challenge. From a law and economics perspective, the primary difference between the classical utilitarian (and derivative) moral and political philosophy and the republican one lies with the assumptions regarding individual preferences. The utilitarian approaches view individual preferences as given, or exogenous to the collective decision-making process, or to market processes, and therefore outside the scope of economic analysis. The republican approach, by contrast, views individual preferences as endogenous to the analysis. In other words, from a republican perspective the legal arrangements themselves, as well as institutions and procedures, can affect the basic individual preferences in a way that will make them more other regarding or cooperative, allowing the extension of the collective utility frontiers.

These very general and philosophical observations are important for understanding many contemporary debates regarding intellectual property, such as the controversy between the pro-propertization advocates and the defenders of the public domain. The concept of the public domain exists beyond the specific IP context and is part of a republican discourse. The public domain, like the public sphere, is a metaphorical space in which individuals are encouraged to interact, exchange views and information and attempt to influence each other's opinions and preferences. Thus, under an analytical framework, which assumes endogenous preferences, the development and preservation of such a space is beneficial from a welfare or utility maximization point of view. If individuals change their preferences towards more other-regarding ones the collective is able to reach utility or wealth frontiers or other consequential goals, which were not available given the initial preferences. In the context of intellectual property the public domain does not only enable a free flow of information and opinions, it is also a means of production and, unlike other traditional resources of production, such as land, labor and to a lesser degree – capital, the public domain is not rivalrous or exclusionary. This point regarding individual preferences is one of the most important points of criticism against the dominant law and economics literature in general (Salzberger 2008), and it has far-reaching ramifications for an IP theory. In the course of this book we will examine how this multipurpose public domain affects the traditional analysis regarding efficiency in both production and allocation.

As we indicated above, the common wisdom is that while natural law thinking dominated the Continental legal approach to IP, utilitarian or consequential thinking dominates the Anglo-American approach. One important argument of this book is that in the last decade both traditions have moved closer to each other. In Europe, more and more economic arguments are made in debates related to IP legal reforms, and indeed new policies, legal norms and judicial decisions reflect those arguments. In addition, positive analysis of the legal arrangements in this field reflects economic interests and can be explained against the basic framework of positive analysis of legislation. In the US, law and economics discourse has been shifting from the utilitarian or consequential framework towards a new version of natural law – libertarian, according to which every potential economic value ought to be propertized. In other words, a growing segment of literature presumes intellectual creations to be property and economic analysis is employed on the basis of this presupposition, thus bringing the discourse closer to the traditional European school of thought.

## 2.5 The law and economics of intellectual property

Intellectual property has not been a serious focus of the science of economics until the current technological revolution. In fact, economic theory has neglected altogether the economics of innovation and technological progress, with the bold exception of Joseph Schumpeter's writings (1912, 1928, 1942). In the last two decades we have witnessed an emerging economic literature on intellectual property, innovation and technological advancement, both empirical and theoretical. Historically, in contrast to legal scholarship, there had been more economic studies in the area of patent law than in the area of copyright law and trademarks (Landes and Posner 2003a: 403–19; Menell 2000).

Patents were considered industrial property, and therefore have always been linked to industrial and business environments, in which efficiency and economic indicators were routinely studied. Studies in this area addressed issues such as the effects of the patent system on competition, on social and private benefits, on the production process and on market structure. The significance of patents for industry and business during the 19th and 20th centuries also secured sufficient funding for empirical studies in the economics of the patent system (Samuelson 2003).

There has been a massive growth in the law and economics of intellectual property literature in the past decade in both normative and positive realms (Scotchmer and Menell 2007 is a good survey). An increasing volume of economic research explores specific rules and examines their economic effects vis-à-vis the purpose they mean to serve. Studies in the area of copyright law explore, for example, the economics of the 'fair use' exemption (Gordon 1982), the economic outcome of increasing the duration of copyright protection (Gordon 2002; Kilbey 2003), the economic effect of performers' rights on the music industry (Towse 1999) and the economics of cultural products (Towse 2003).

Early writings on the economics of intellectual property questioned the necessity of legal rights for stimulating innovation. Arnold Plant, for instance, claimed that most inventions are spontaneous and, moreover, that first mover advantages and imperfections in markets provided inventors and publishers with sufficient rewards to create and distribute their works, even with no intellectual property rights. Thus, he argued, granting patent protection will eventually lead to a waste of resources (Plant 1934a: 30–51; 1934b: 167–95). Others stated that innovators could extract substantial revenues from the private utilization of proprietary information, without the need for property rights, by speculating in the market on the basis of their discoveries prior to such discoveries becoming public knowledge (Hirshleifer 1971).

In general, it can be stated that economists were rather skeptical, or at least unconvinced, as to the significance of intellectual property rights in generating innovation and growth. Their attention vis-à-vis promoting innovation and technological progress was spread to other legal fields such as competition and corporate law. This cannot be said about the mainstream law and economics literature. The skepticism of economists regarding IP (for a more recent example see Stiglitz 2008) has not crossed over to the mainstream law and economics writings.

While one can hardly find law and economic literature on other legal fields in connection with innovation and technological progress (for a survey see Salzberger 2012), the more recent studies exploring the economic analysis of intellectual property law as a whole perceive strong intellectual property regimes as efficient and inductive to growth and thus desirable (Granstrand 1999; Landes and Posner 2003; Towse and Hozhauer 2002; Braga, Fink and Sepulveda 2000). These studies are already captured in the property rhetoric and focus on the ways to extract the highest value or profits, presuming informational products as property.

The rise of law and economics as a dominant methodology in intellectual property scholarship and the proliferation of economic studies related to intellectual property, however, tells us little about the impact that this growing body of scholarship has on policy-making.

Law and economics discourse has become dominant in intellectual property policy-making, causing policy-makers to focus exclusively on the economic ramifications of intellectual property. This narrow economic perspective leaves out many aspects of creativity and innovation, such as the sociology of arts and science or the complexity of human motivation that could be crucial to policy-making in this area. Thus, there is a need for the reconstruction of existing scholarship and methodologies to address fundamental issues that were left outside the scope of inquiry (Cohen 2000; Boyle 2003).

One would expect that economic arguments would be found in the US intellectual property regime and less so in Europe. While the foundations of European IP law are deontological, the US Constitution, which authorized Congress to legislate in the area of intellectual property, has taken a consequential approach. Congress is authorized to legislate for the purpose of securing incentives to authors and inventors. The constitutional authority of the US Congress is defined in Article 8 of the US Constitution, stating that:

> Congress shall have Power . . . To promote the Progress of Science and useful Arts, by securing for limited Times to Authors and Inventors, the exclusive Right to their respective Writings and Discoveries.

The economic rationale is therefore considered the principal justification for intellectual property rights in the United States.

In sharp contrast to the instrumentalist approach of the American law, copyright is viewed in Europe as protecting a set of natural entitlements of authors. It could, therefore, be expected that economic arguments will play a less significant role in the European intellectual property regimes than in the US (Samuelson 2001). Yet, the law and economics discourse in the area of copyright has also been increasing in Europe in the recent years (Koelman 2004).

This is rather puzzling given the traditional difference between the EU and the US legal systems. Several scholars have suggested that the fundamental differences in copyright rationales between US and European copyright regimes are fading (Samuelson 2001; Koelman 2004). This process could be attributed to several reasons, one being the rise of the global information economy that is governed by international agreements and the growing trend of harmonizing intellectual property laws. Koelman explains that European and US rationales are coming closer together as a result of the rise of economic arguments in European copyright doctrine (Koelman 2004). The European Commission has focused on facilitating an internal market and advancing the Community's economic goals. Therefore, the legal activism of the Commission in the area of intellectual property has increased the use of economic arguments in policy debates related to intellectual property.

The analysis of economic discourse in European legislative processes shows that economic arguments were generally used to justify strengthening property rights. They focused on the need to reward authors for their efforts but failed to explore the need for incentives and the scope of incentives necessary for stimulating creation. The somewhat superficial focus on incentives and reward further overlooked the non-rivalrous nature of information and the economic consequences that follow. Providing incentives in the form of exclusive rights could sometimes go against the economic goals of the IP regime. The introduction of economic discourse in Europe did not change much at the theoretical foundation of intellectual property, and therefore did not require re-examining the legal regime altogether. Economic arguments basically serve to justify further a regime that was already in existence.

Finally, the observation that theoretical rationales of intellectual property in the US and EU increasingly merge, could also be attributed to changes in the American approach to intellectual property and the rise of the proprietary approach as further described in Chapter 4.

# Part II

# Normative analysis

# 3 The incentives paradigm

The incentives theory has been for decades the dominant law and economics paradigm for the analysis of intellectual property, copyright and patent law in particular.[12] It was only in recent years that some of the law and economics literature has shifted to the proprietary paradigm, on which we elaborate in the next chapter. The incentives paradigm assumes that economic incentives are necessary to generate sufficient innovative activity. Informational goods (inventions and creations) are non-excludable and therefore inventors and creators lack sufficient incentives to invest in their development. Central intervention is therefore necessary to remedy this failure, by creating property rights that would enable producers legally to exclude non-payers. The normative goal of the incentives paradigm is efficiency, and since it involves central intervention – the creation of property rights for a limited period – only one specific kind of efficiency can be aimed at (see our discussion in Chapter 1). The incentives paradigm aims at efficiency measured in terms of wealth and is geared towards wealth maximization.[13] The incentives paradigm can, therefore, be associated with the Chicago school of law and economics.

The incentives paradigm rests upon two assertions. The first is that information is a public good and thus without central intervention the investment in creative expressions and the resulting cultural and technological progress will be insufficient. The second is that property rights are the cheapest and most effective way for society to hold out these incentives (Andersen 2004, 2006). Yet, intellectual property rights come at a cost; they create monopolies and barriers on access to works and inventions and therefore may also stifle innovation. The public goods analysis leads to the limited nature, in time and in scope, of intellectual property rights: the need for the societal optimization

12 It is noteworthy that not all forms of IP are analysed solely within this framework. The economic rationales for trademarks, trade secrets and the right of publicity derive also from other types of market failures, such as the lack of information and asymmetric information, which will not be discussed here.

13 For an explanation why central intervention tilts efficiency measurement towards wealth maximization see our discussion in Chapter 1.

function to balance the two contravening forces – the benefits from the increase of new intellectual creations which is the result of granting property rights to creators, and the output-limiting effect that excessive protection of IPR would impose on the rest of society (Valkonen and White 2006).

The technologic and information revolutions of the past decades have paused serious challenges to the incentives paradigm. Mass production of knowledge and information bypassing intellectual property rights or making a subversive use of them, such as 'Open Content', 'Access 2 Knowledge', 'Open Source' and 'Free Culture' have become a significant part of the informational landscape, and point to the inefficiency of current intellectual property laws. Moreover, as the means of producing informational goods become more distributed, engaging new players in generating informational goods, the incentives analysis becomes more complex and requires adjustments. The balance struck by IPR in the past may no longer be optimal today. The information age enhances our dependency on informational goods, which become essential for basic business and political functioning. As our dependency on informational goods grows, the costs implied by the IPR system become more severe.

This chapter will discuss and evaluate the economic rationales of the incentives paradigm and its manifestations in legal arrangements and judicial policies. We will put a special emphasis on IPR in the information age, and on digital information products, arguing that these technological developments present new challenges to the traditional analysis. Following a discussion in section 3.1 of the economic foundations of the incentives paradigm and an analysis of public goods failure of the market, we will question in section 3.2 whether a real need for monetary incentives for creation and innovation exists. Under the assumption that incentives are necessary for promoting innovation, we will discuss in section 3.3 the different forms of generating incentives and whether intellectual property rights offer the best legal regime, including discussion of the specific design and tailoring of intellectual property rights. Section 3.4 will conclude the chapter.

## 3.1 Market failure of public goods as the foundation of intellectual property law

Modern economic theory has always been skeptical of government intervention in the market. Free and open markets, it has been thought, will function efficiently if not interrupted by government actions. Equilibrium of a free and competitive market will be utility maximizing, wealth maximizing and Pareto optimal. Therefore, a prima facie case for central intervention requires a demonstration of a failure of the free market (Cooter 1997). The Chicago school of law and economics, with which the incentives paradigm can be associated, adopts the traditional neo-classical theory and welfare economics' identification and classification of market failures. According to this approach a market failure exists when there are no multiple players on both sides of the market (the problem of monopolies, cartels and monopsonies), when the market players do not have full or symmetric information relevant to their market activities, when any of the players bypasses the market through involuntary actions (the problem of externalities), or when the traded commodity is a public good. Later in the development of the market approach, and following Ronald Coase's groundbreaking article 'The problem of social cost' (1960), the framework of these market failures shifted to a more general setting of transaction costs. It is important to note that these four categories of market failures (sometimes prescribed as five categories, positive transaction cost being the fifth) are not mutually exclusive. Particular issues could be analysed in more than one framework. For instance, the production of informational products can be analysed either as an externality or as a public good.

The incentives paradigm views the legal regime of intellectual property as a justifiable central intervention to tackle a public good failure of the market. Once it is established that intervention in the market is required, the materialization of utility maximization, wealth maximization and Pareto optimality cannot all be guaranteed and a primer normative goal has to be set. This goal, as explained in Chapter 1, is in theory external to the law and economics analysis. In practice, however, law and economics literature has always been biased towards efficiency defined in terms of wealth maximization, as best exemplified by Richard Posner's leading book in the field first published in 1972, and later endorsed by Landes and Posner in the IP context (Landes and Posner 2003a: 11–36).

### *3.1.1 **Public goods analysis***

A pure public good is a commodity with two distinctive characteristics: non-excludability and non-rivalry. In some cases, central intervention might be justifiable for goods or services, which are partly public goods, ie goods that are partly non-rivalrous and/or partly non-excludable (e.g. roads and other physical infrastructure).

Non-excludability occurs whenever it is either impossible to exclude non-payers (free-riders) from using the good or service, or the costs for such exclusion are so high that it would be inefficient to exclude. Informational goods are thought to be non-excludable, as it is often rather cheap to copy them (Landes and Posner 1989; Menell 1987, 1989). The costs of creating multiple copies of a music file or a piece of software, or the cost of manufacturing a life-saving drug, knowing its formula, are often negligible. The non-excludable characteristic of informational goods derives from their virtual nature. Information has no physical boundaries, and its duplication and distribution involve relatively low costs. The marginal costs of exclusion are often greater than the marginal costs of provision, so it is inefficient to spend resources to exclude non-payers. Therefore, in the absence of impediments on copying, the prices of works in a competitive market could fall to near zero (Geroski 2005). The potential producer of non-excludable products, knowing that the competitive market price of the product will equal the (very low) marginal cost of production and thus would not cover the fixed cost, will not produce the product at all. Free-riding of non-payers reduces incentives for investment in generating new information, and without government intervention information tends to be under-supplied.

Book publishing is a classic example. Historically, the development of the first copyright law, the English Statute of Anne 1709 (8 Anne c. 19) was tied to the emergence of the printing press (ie significant decrease in the cost of copying) and was designed to promote a book industry (Birrell 1899). Publishers invest the necessary resources to cover the author's expenses in preparing the manuscript, paying his fee, designing a cover and covering the graphic and editorial expenses. The publisher also bears the marginal cost of producing a large number of copies of the printed book, and distributing it via various distribution channels. In the absence of copyright, once the book is released in the market a second comer could easily copy it, bearing only the marginal (relatively low) costs of creating additional copies, and avoiding the substantial cost of producing the manuscript. Thus, the second comer who made no investment in creating the work could easily distribute the copies for a lower price, driving the original publisher out of the market. Publishers would therefore lack incentives to invest in the production of informational goods, such as books. The same analysis applies to the production of drugs or sophisticated high tech gadgets for which the research and development investment significantly outweighs the actual marginal cost of per unit production.

A second feature of a public good is that it is non-rivalrous. Non-rivalry characterizes goods or services for which consumption by one person does not detract from the ability of others to consume. Tangibles, as well as real estate are usually rival goods, meaning that their usage by one person precludes others from using them. Informational goods are usually non-rivalrous. They cannot be exhausted. If I use a parcel of land for growing wheat, it cannot be used at the same time by entrepreneurs who want to build a resort. In contrast, if you hear a symphony by Mozart you do not prevent others from enjoying it too. If you read a book, you do not deprive others from reading it, even though a number of users may not be able to use the same tangible copy of the book simultaneously. The tangible media, in which works are embodied, such as printed books and plastic CDs, are not public goods. They would be subject to the rivalry suffered by other scarce resources. But this scarcity does not apply to the information contained in them. In contrast to tangible goods, the use of informational resources is not consumptive. We do not 'consume' a book in the same way we 'consume' chocolate or water. Consumption of informational works does not exhaust the resource. Quite the contrary; the use of an idea, the reading of a text, or the implementation of a mathematical theory by one person does not prevent others from using it and often the actual benefits of individual usage increases as more individuals use the same product simultaneously or subsequently.

The non-rivalrous nature of informational goods means that there is no social loss associated with their usage, since no one else is deprived of that use. Therefore there is no need to allocate informational resources to the most efficient user. Quite the contrary; since everyone can use informational goods simultaneously it is in the general interest that once produced they will be used by as many people as possible. This peculiar character of informational goods was beautifully described by Thomas Jefferson's poetic passage:

> Its peculiar character, too, is that no one possesses the less, because every other possesses the whole of it. He who receives an idea from me, receives instruction himself without lessening mine; as he who lights his taper at mine, receives light without darkening me.
>
> (Jefferson, letter to Isaac McPherson 13 August 1813)

Moreover, the use of informational goods is beneficial on top of the immediate value for the user, in that it engages readers, viewers and other users in a mutual productive experience. The readers of books learn of their content, the users of software acquire some skills. The use of information in this sense is nurturing the human capital that could subsequently contribute to the production of more informational goods. In economic terminology, the consumption of information – be it a cultural product, software or a scientific invention – creates positive externalities. Consequently, once informational goods are created there is a benefit in their widest possible usage in order to maximize welfare in society and as a basis for further innovation.

While the non-excludability character of informational goods justifies central intervention in order to secure incentives for further investment in producing new works, the non-rivalrous nature of these goods justifies setting limits on the bundle of rights in scope and duration, in order to maximize their usage to the extent possible, for the greatest collective welfare. Hence the incentives paradigm treats IPR as an inevitable evil that must be limited to the scope necessary for serving its goal, as reflected in the famous quote by Lord Macaulay (1914), that copyright is 'a tax on readers for the purpose of giving a bounty to writers'.

Moreover, even limited property rights on information come at a cost. Granting exclusive rights, even for a limited period of time, gives owners monopolistic powers. Instead of competitive price – the marginal or average cost of production (taking into account the fixed cost or the R&D costs), which maximizes social welfare, owners can set the price as they please. They are likely to set the price that maximizes their profits, bringing to a reduction in total social welfare. This collective loss in economic language is called deadweight loss, which comprises all potential users who value the informational product between its competitive price and the monopolistic price, who would therefore not purchase it.

These losses are particularly significant in the informational goods market, as these goods are the primary resource for further creation. Technological innovations are built one upon another. Artistic works refer to one another, use symbols, metaphors and characters, and often cite from other works. The skills of human capital – the author, inventor and other innovators of informational goods – depend on access to previous works. Exposures to the books of the past, to modern art, or to available computer programs, may all become crucial for writing a new novel or developing a new word processor. Human capital requires training and knowledge of the current state of the art. A too strong incentivizing regime will thus increase the price of future works, and may prevent their creation altogether. IP law attempts to mitigate the later phenomenon through limiting not only the duration of rights but also their scope. It protects only certain aspects of works (ie *expressions* are protected by copyright but not *ideas*), and recognizes several privileged uses or exceptions (ie *fair use* under copyright law).

### *3.1.2 Are incentives necessary?*

The core of the economic justification for IPR, as elaborated above, is the need to create incentives for the production of information, which results from its non-excludable nature. Skepticism regarding the necessity of such economic incentives provided by central intervention in the context of copyright, was expressed as early as 1970 by Harvard Professor and now US Supreme Court Justice Steven Breyer.[14] In his seminal article 'The uneasy case for copyright: a study of copyright in books, photocopies, and computer programs', Breyer explored what would have happened had copyright protection been abolished altogether.

In challenging the need for copyright protection, Breyer argued that creators have several advantages over competitors that offset the lower production costs of free-riders. One such advantage is lead time. If copies produced by the creator reach the market first, creators could sell original copies before they are confronted with competition by copiers. The need for incentives is of course a function of the easiness of copying; copyright did not exist prior to the invention of the printing press by Gutenberg, and likewise it was expanded following the invention of photocopying. One can argue, therefore, that digital technology made copying much cheaper, quicker and commonplace and, thus, even if Breyer's argument was sensible in 1970 it is not so anymore. Yet, the prime example discussed by Breyer in 1970 was a new and sophisticated technological product at the time – software.

Breyer used the software industry to demonstrate the significance of lead time as a factor that can provide economic incentives to potential investors.

14 Similar arguments in the context of patents were made as early as 1934 by Plant. See the Introduction to this book.

Thus, he argued, application programs are sold, not directly 'off the shelf', but in 'packages'. Those packages contain 'copyrighted documentation manuals and a promise that the seller will install the program, iron out its "bugs", update it as advances are made, and make adjustments from time to time to keep it compatible with others in the machine'. A computer user is often buying services and expertise as much as he is buying a particular computer program. Thus, the copier's need to develop this support independently would often provide the initial programmer with sufficient lead time to recover his development costs. Indeed, the shift of content providers from the sale of copies to the supply of services is evident in the growing markets for free software and open source, where copies are made available free of charge and revenues are often extracted by charging for additional goods and services, selling support, consulting services and training (Arno 2005).

Nevertheless, the technological advancements of the last two decades and the introduction of digital technology certainly shortened the lead time in comparison to the 1970s. Pirated copies of new films are often leaked and distributed on the Internet within hours of the movie's release and sometimes even before the film opens. The ease of digital copying and mass distribution actually often eliminates altogether the lead time of publishers, as digital copying is made possible within seconds of the release of the original content, be it a music file, a movie or an eBook. This was one of the reasons for the demand of the chip industry in the late 1970s and the early 1980s, to extend IPR to chips: 'The advances in chip manufacturing technologies dramatically reduced the cost and time required to make exact or near-exact competing chips, thereby shortening considerably the lead time innovators could expect and reducing the costs of copying' (Samuelson 2002: 1598).

Digitization further affects other types of revenues of the initial publisher that could keep profits sufficiently high and maintain incentives to create even without copyright. One variable discussed by Breyer is the threat of retaliation – namely, the fear on the part of the copying publisher that she will not be able to recoup the (lower) cost of copying and distributing the original, as the initial publisher will sell copies below the copier cost (Breyer 1970: 300–301). In a digital environment, copiers face minimal risk, as the cost of digital copying and distribution are negligible.

Other countervailing forces may turn out to be more feasible in the digital age. Breyer argued that copyright would be unnecessary if other means of sustaining publishers' revenue were undertaken, such as prior funding by the government or by buyers. He envisioned groups of buyers that may contract to buy books in advance. During the 1970s these types of solutions to the incentives problem were not quite practical and raised many difficulties, such as the high administrative cost of organizing the group of buyers and the need to delegate buying decisions to a group of people. In the digital environment, however, the cost of communicating, coordinating and raising funds from large groups of unorganized individuals is relatively low. The first author to experiment with direct sales of eBooks for upfront payment was Stephen

King, who announced in 2000 that he would publish a new book, *The Plant*, in up to 10 instalments, subject to an honor system. King asked readers to pay US$1 for each instalment downloaded. He promised to release the next instalment only if at least 75 percent of the readers complied. Following the success of the first instalment, the experiment was eventually suspended after only 46 percent of the downloads were paid for.

Overall, the low cost of digital copying increases the non-excludability of informational works and therefore suggests that copyright protection should be strengthened to secure the publishers' return on their investment. At the same time, however, technological advancement of the recent decades made easier and cheaper not only copying, but also exclusion. The new exclusion practices of informational goods have some important implications for innovation policy as well as for consumer rights and civil rights such as privacy and free speech. We further address these issues in Chapter 6.

Another way in which emerging technologies have changed the economics of information, is by introducing new production and distribution methods and new players to the scene. Digital networks give rise to user-generated content (UGC) and new forms of social production. Individual creators and inventors are playing a greater role in the production of content than they did in the past, owing to greater accessibility and lower cost of digital distribution. Low communication costs further facilitate new forms of coordination and collaboration outside of the organizational structures of corporations and states (Benkler 2006). These fundamental changes in the production and distribution of informational works are challenging the incentives paradigm and require careful consideration of some of its tenets. We further elaborate on the implications of these changes in the following sections.

It is noteworthy that Breyer's article endorses the basic teleological normative foundations of intellectual property rights, ie the presumption that they are justified and desirable only if they enhance total social welfare. He offered a thorough economic analysis of copyright protection based on the data available at the time, examining the necessity of copyright given the changing economies of publishing and the introduction of software. Aware of the limitations and practical problems in conducting cost-benefit analyses, which cannot be precise as there are not enough facts available to make exact quantitative estimates, Breyer insisted that 'one can identify the sources of benefit and loss, estimate whether the amounts involved are significant, and draw approximate conclusions about whether copyright protection seems sufficiently valuable to justify not only retaining it, but also extending its scope' (Breyer 1970: 292). Unfortunately, up to date economists have not completed a decisive calculation of the cost-benefits of copyright.

In the following sections we examine more carefully additional arguments and empirical findings regarding the need to generate monetary incentives for creators and inventors by central intervention. We will distinguish between the role of incentives on the individual creator's level and the role of incentives on the organizational level.

### *3.1.3 Incentives to create – the individual level*

Creations or innovations can be made by individuals working alone or by individuals working within firms and other organizations. The incentives patterns of individuals might be different from those of organizations and the picture is even more complicated as the legal regime, on the one hand, and technology, on the other hand, may affect not only on whether creation will occur but also by whom – individuals or firms. One can argue that IP laws in fact contributed to a shift from creation by individuals to creation by firms, by tailoring incentives to corporations and large organizations. The technology nowadays has a reverse effect. The focus on incentives to create and innovate on the individual level has become ever more important in recent years, as digital technology and distributed networks brought individuals to the forefront of creative and innovative processes. This process is further described in section 3.1.5 below. The growing power of individual users to produce high quality content and to distribute it to a wide audience (using the Internet) increases the share of individuals in the overall production of information. This requires paying special attention to the incentives of individual creators and innovators.

The incentives paradigm presumes that monetary incentives are a necessary condition for inducing creativity and innovation. This assumption involves an empirical claim that is based on shaky grounds: that monetary incentives (derived from IPR) would actually induce more creative and innovative activity and even further, that potential authors and inventors will not engage in creative activity unless they are promised some monetary profits (Moore 2003: 610–613). There is very limited empirical support for these propositions.

Various scholars in recent years have been paying more attention to the non-monetary incentives that motivate creators, thus challenging the dominant view that monetary rewards are necessary and sufficient for inducing human creativity (e.g. Zimmerman 2011; Tushnet 2009; Cohen 2007). Creative activities are performed by human beings, be it a musician working alone or a scientist working in a lab of the pharmaceutical industry. Human creativity involves a complex matrix of motivations and incentives, often working simultaneously to induce or halt a particular behavior. While the economic literature pertaining to intellectual property focused almost exclusively on monetary awards, there is a wide body of research which explores the different types of motivations which derive creative and innovative activities (Tushnet 2009).

There are many non-monetary benefits that people gain from creative activity; there is a natural drive to create, creative passion, the need to express oneself and to communicate one's ideas and talents, to be acknowledged and to enjoy and be satisfied (Moglen 2002). Most scientists, creators and inventors are motivated by the intrinsic satisfaction of investigation and discovery, and also by the wish to gain recognition among their peers and the general public (Martin 1998: 46–50). In order to provide a sound basis for policy-making in this area it is necessary to reach a better understanding of the matrix of the motivations to create and innovate. This is particularly important as a growing segment of our information environment is generated by individuals, working alone or collaborating with others.

There are different ways of classifying non-monetary motivations. One useful distinction is between intrinsic motivations (self-oriented) and social motivations (other-oriented) (Peddibhotla and Subramani 2007). 'Self-oriented motives' refers to intrinsic motivations such as fun, self-expression or personal development, and also to utilitarian motives. 'Other-oriented motives' refers to social affiliation, altruism, and reciprocity.

Self-oriented motives focus on the benefits that people derive from creative activity. First and foremost there is a natural drive to create. People are creative beings. Creation often reflects a human desire, a passion to act upon the world, a desire to constitute something from nothing (Buber 1955). Poets, sculpturers and musicians created monumental works of art long before there was any intellectual property system offering them a legal right over their creations; they created simply for the sake of making art and science. As Hurt and Schuchman noted back in the 1960s: 'The massive literary and dramatic production during the centuries before copyright protection was enacted demonstrate that there are other motives for the creation of intellectual property than the expectation of monopoly profits' (Hurt and Schuchman 1966: 425). Browsing the rich reservoir of user-generated content on the web nowadays is probably the best contemporary example of the human longing for creative self-expression. From blogs, through homemade video clips posted on YouTube, to pictures shared on Flickr and music distributed in MySpace, the web demonstrates that creative activity is not all about money. This rich display of UGC reflects the human longing to engage with the world, to create meaning.

Creativity provides socio-psychological rewards, which are a function of the cultural meaning associated with the act of creation. These include the benefits from acknowledgement and reputation, but also social relations such as a notion of belonging and friendship (Benkler 2006: 92–99). Other types of passions – ego, a hunger for power, competition, and confrontation – may also drive creation.

Moreover, empirical research suggests that monetary rewards can sometimes actually stifle creativity. Studies which explored creative motivations distinguish between external rewards such as money and inherent rewards such as pleasure, curiosity and positive experiences of autonomy and competence. These studies show that intrinsic motivations are often undermined by extrinsic rewards and that people may become less creative when they are offered monetary rewards (Deci, Koestner and Ryan 1999; Lawrence 2004). Likewise, cognitive evaluation theory (CET) focuses on the negative effects of monetary rewards and predicts that rewards given for achievement could sometimes reduce the sense of autonomy of the creators (Cameron, Pierce, Banko and Gear 2005). Such rewards might actually reduce the quality of work (Kohn 1999: 136–38) or shift its direction.

Social motivation must be viewed within a rich matrix of different motivations to create, including monetary rewards. Individual creators or scientists might not be engaged in creative processes just for the money – but this does not mean that they never expect to profit from their creativity. Content generated by users can be distributed in a commercial setting and might, in fact, generate revenues. For instance, artists and amateurs often profit from advertising, by incorporating advertisements into their content or monetize the traffic attracted by their content through online services, such as Google AdSense, which automatically delivers targeted ads to blogs and personal homepages for a share in revenues. Therefore, even though content created by artists or amateurs is often not generated for profit, it is increasingly being shaped by market forces. The mixture of social motivation and commercial interests may destabilize social motivation. On the individual level, the mixture of for-profit and non-profit activities motivated by monetary and social interests may sometimes undermine intrinsic motivation. Monetary rewards may further interfere with the sense of social solidarity, which provides the basis for engagement in social production, thereby reducing the motivation to collaborate. In other words, incentives to create on the individual level might be required, but not primarily in the form of direct monetary incentives (such as IPR), but rather in infrastructure, education and promotion of innovative culture – features which are generally ignored by the incentives model and neo-classical approach altogether, as has been argued by the neo-Schumpeterian approach (see Chapter 1).

To sum up, the growing share of individual creators and inventors in the overall production of new content and the rise of UGC may increase the significance of incentives on the individual level. Viewed from the perspective of individual creators, and in sharp contrast to industrialized content, creative works and inventions are not generated for the sole purpose of maximizing profits, even though they could be distributed in a commercial setting and may, in fact, generate revenues. Moreover, there is some empirical evidence that monetary incentives may undermine social motivation to engage in creative enterprises. A legal policy for promoting creative and innovative activities should be designed to minimize these negative effects. As social motivation is playing a central role in inducing creative activity on the individual level, legal policies that aim at promoting creative and innovative activities must facilitate social motivation. For instance, in some cases the authors' right to get proper credit for works they have created (moral rights) might be sufficient and more effective in generating incentives than the economic rights to exploit the work.

### *3.1.4 The need for incentives – the organization level*

So far we have focused on the incentives of the individual creator operating alone to invent or create. But at least until recently, most of the creative and innovative activities, including technological research and development, the source of patents, have been conducted within organizations – commercial or public institutions. The early Schumpeter writings (1928) even claimed that innovation originated primarily from big and monopolistic firms. Likewise, during the second half of the 20th century, the production and mass distribution of content, the subject matter of copyright, were dominated by the content industry: mass media, book publishers, record companies and the movie studios. In contrast to the early Schumpeter writings it can be argued that copyright regime itself incentivized this mode of content production. A different regime of copyright would have not resulted with less creation but with a higher share of creation by individuals as opposed to creation by firms and other organizations.

There is a significant difference between the motivation of individual creators, and those of publishers, producers of content and inventions, as well as universities and research institutions. While a passionate poet is likely to write her poems even if she lacks financial incentives, the book and music publishing industry would not necessarily publish her work and, in general, undersupply works, without the monetary incentives to do that. There are also important differences between the incentives of organizations and those of the individuals working for them and between individual creators who do not work within organizations and those who are employees of the information industries. While, as we have seen in the previous section, individuals working alone are not incentivized only by monetary considerations, corporations maximize profits, and this will have an effect also on the motivation of the individuals working within firms compared to individuals working alone.

A better way to understand the economic function of IPR on the institutional level is to view it within the framework offered by Stiglitz (2008), who distinguishes between the motivation to create and financing. Stiglitz argues that IPR should serve innovation by financing the production of knowledge that is not costless. While non-monetary incentives are playing a major role in motivating individual creators and inventors, the production of some works involves high cost at the time of production, such as a movie production or the development of environmentally friendly industrial production machinery. In the absence of sufficient returns on investment, it is argued, it would be difficult to attract sufficient funds to be invested in rather expensive and risky enterprises such as the production of content or R&D in commercial enterprises. Innovation is risky since inherently there is a high level of uncertainty regarding its success. Underinvestment, so the argument goes, will consequently lead to undersupply of resources and thus to less creative works and discoveries, which are beneficial to society. Without these industries, passionate creators would be unable to disseminate their artefacts to the public. This is particularly evident in the pharmaceutical industry. A report by the Tufts Center for the Study of Drug Development Outlook (CSDD) estimates the cost of developing a new drug at about $1.3 billion (CSDD 2011). Other studies are citing lower, but still substantial, numbers: $59 million (Light and Warburton 2011) and $22 million (Love 2003). On average these costs are high, including the direct cost of R&D, the cost of the delay involved in satisfying the standards of regulatory agencies (such as the Food and Drug Administration or health authorities) and the high risk involved in this type of development activity. Covering these costs may require high investments and some assurances that investors will get a return on their investment. In the absence of IPR the costs of creation or R&D are not incurred by the copier and, therefore, copiers can drive the initial investor out of the market.

However, studies conducted recently (e.g. Johnson 2011) indicate that, as a general matter, the incentive theory for corporations has been empirically refuted. Those studies show that corporations simply do not pin their hopes on the rewards offered by IPR when they face decision-making regarding innovations and investment in R&D. The basic incentive theory in fact does not apply in the real world – creation and innovation are profitable in most of the cases even without the externally provided rewards. In this context, it should be mentioned that many business managers overlook their IP entitlement prospects, and sometimes are not even aware of them. From their point of view, marketing strategies – such as 'lead time', first-mover advantage, sales-and-service expertise, superior manufacturing capacity – are much more significant as considerations toward success. The conclusion of these studies is that while there is evidence of a need for external incentives in certain fields, such as pharmaceuticals, those fields are clearly the exception and not the rule. Indeed, in most of the fields and areas, the markets already price much of the R&D costs, without government interference, in an efficient way (Johnson 2011). This description coincides with empirical findings according to which no correlation was found between number of patent applications and the level of innovation (Zoltan and Audretsch 1988).

Distinguishing between the motivations of individual creators and the incentives' structures which drive organizations becomes critical in the digital era. Until recently, the production and the dissemination of content to the public have been orchestrated by profit-maximizing firms who worked within a market framework. Communication to the masses used to be costly; the distribution of physical copies or the broadcast of TV shows required an expensive infrastructure, one which was owned and operated by broadcasters and publishers. The content industry invested in producing a master copy of the work (a novel, a news report, a television series or a movie) and recouped the investment by selling copies at a monopoly price or by licencing exclusive broadcast rights. Although copyright discourse has always emphasized authors' rights, copyright law, in fact, served the needs of the content industry. It provided a mechanism for securing monetary incentives for those who invest in the creative process, rather than for those who engage in the creative process itself. In fact, those incentives were biased towards large organizations. Consequently, while the traditional economic analysis of IPR assumed market structure as an exogenous variable, it can be argued that the expanding intellectual property rights regime had in fact significantly influenced market structure by incentivizing mega-corporations at the expense of individual creators and inventors.

Recent technological advancements are changing this picture. In particular, lower transaction and communication costs are pushing production from hierarchical firms back to individuals contracting in markets. For instance, encyclopedias and dictionaries, which were often given as a classic example of works that are produced for profit and require large upfront investment for their production (Hurt and Schuchman 1966) are now being generated by peers, the classic example being Wikipedia. Similarly, significant production of software and other high-tech products is conducted by individuals contracting with each other rather than in the framework of a firm, or by small firms rather than big corporations. For this new mode of production the current incentives structure of IPR might be an obstacle rather than an incentive mechanism for innovation.

The institutional perspective complicates the simple and naïve picture portrayed so far. It further invokes a distinction between different organizations. Firms differ from each other in their organizational structures and profit distribution. Research performed at a university or a public research institute might be driven by a different set of incentives compared with research in a commercial firm. Moreover, public research institutions and universities as opposed to private firms are funded by the government or the public and this funding itself might be sufficient to overcome the public good nature of its products. This may challenge the justification for allowing such publicly funded institutions also to benefit from IPR.

The insights of institutional and neo-institutional economics could further our understanding of the role of incentives. This body of literature teaches us that we cannot portray producers as we portray consumers – individuals geared to maximize utility or profits from market interactions. The actual shape of a supply curve of a firm is dependent upon the firm's structure and the procedures in which the interaction between owners, directors, managers and employees (each group with its unique preferences or utility function), yield decisions and actions. Those insights should be incorporated into the incentives analysis and organizational structures ought to be endogenized into the existing models.

Furthermore, the institutional level requires a distinction between incentives to invest at the corporate level, required for financing the creation or R&D, and incentives to create on the individual level of freelancers and employees. For example, the financial agreements with employees differ from firm to firm and might be crucial for the incentives to innovate on both the organizational and the individual levels. Within organizations, monetary rewards could be a dangerous motivator if improperly or inequitably managed (Fromer 2012; Sauermann 2007). Studies have shown that employees often lack the proper motivations if they are 'bought out' for limited rewards (Lawrence 2004). Moreover, these rewards could damage the employees' intrinsic motivation, as phrased by Eric Raymond, a famous hacker and open source advocate: 'You cannot motivate the best people with money. Money is just a way to keep score. The best people in any field are motivated by passion' (Fast Company Magazine 1999). To further understand the motivation of employees one must look at socio-psychological studies which show that the desire for self-expression is a main reason why inventors invent (Fromer 2012). Other studies indicate that while extrinsic incentives for the employees – such as pay raises, career promotion and recognition by their peers – usually increase the quantity of their production, it is the intrinsic incentives – such as challenge and interest in the task – that usually increase their quality. In addition, it was found that intrinsic incentives may stimulate creativity and innovation by encouraging riskier and more exploratory activity, while extrinsic incentives might undermine and enfeeble creativity, causing the employees to choose safe, risk-free and inanimate approaches in solving problems (Sauermann and Cohen 2008).

To sum up, even on the organizational level the connection between monetary incentives in the form of IPR and the level of innovation is not straightforward. Monetary incentives to create and innovate are not identical to monetary incentives to establish mega-corporations, which seek to maximize profits. Moreover, the old IP balance might not be appropriate for the current technological age, as will be elaborated below.

### *3.1.5 The rise of alternative modes of production and monetary incentives*

Digital networks introduced new modes of production and distribution of information and new modes of consumption, all of which further challenge the need for monetary incentives in the form of IPR, or at least the current IP balance in terms of duration of rights and their scope.

As numerous scholars have noted, digital networks facilitate the rise of UGC and the emergence of social production as a major type of content production (Benkler 2002, 2006; Litman 2004; Tapscott and Williams 2006; Howe 2008; Elkin-Koren 2010). In this environment, individuals are playing a more significant role in the production of content and innovation compared with that in the past. When *Time* magazine selected 'You' as the 2006 'Person of the Year', it expressed a sentiment shared by many that individual users had acquired a central role in the online environment. The Web 2.0 brought individuals to the forefront of creative processes, where Internet users generate their own content and share it with communities of their choosing. The availability of Internet access at low cost enables the distribution of creative materials to a large audience, thus increasing their potential impact on users. UGC flourishes: bloggers post news and analysis, independent musicians distribute their recordings on MySpace and amateur photographers post their photos on Flickr and distribute their homemade videos on YouTube. The volume of blogs, tweets and video sharing demonstrate how millions of people around the world are uploading their self-generated content to the web in the form of video files, audio files or online diaries. Individuals are expressing themselves and share content without worrying about intellectual property issues, and often without even being aware of them.

Moreover, individuals today can work together on big joint projects outside the framework of firms or other formal institutions. Low communication costs enable new forms of coordination and collaboration outside of the organizational structures of firms and states (Benkler 2006; Shirky 2008). Coordination is often facilitated by social media platforms, both commercial and non-profit. Online coordinating tools enable collaboration without a legal organizational structure, orchestrating the tasks undertaken by different contributors. Contributors are not working under any legal duty to perform particular tasks and are usually acting voluntarily. Over the past decade, we have witnessed the flourishing of social production of content. In the area of software development, for instance, communities of users have produced significant informational products. Open source projects, such as Linux, are comprised of the contributions of thousands of unorganized developers, located in different places around the globe, who voluntarily contribute to a common project without direct monetary compensation.[15] The development of free software stands in sharp contrast to Microsoft Windows, which was written by employees of Microsoft and is protected by copyright, patent and trademark laws, prohibiting unauthorized copying, redistribution and modification of the software. One can ask what drives open source developers to dedicate their time and resources to the creation of such products. Studies have shown a high sense of personal creativity in these projects. Contributors are being motivated mostly by the enjoyment-based intrinsic motivations and community-related social motivations (Lakhani and Wolf 2005). It seems that writing codes for projects is a form of intellectual stimulation for such developers.

But software is by no means the only example of the new mode of production. Other online phenomena have similar attributes. Compare, for instance, the production of news by corporate employees of CNN with news generated by subscribers of newsgroups, in which individuals contribute news items that are rated by their peers over time for credibility and reliability; or the well established encyclopedias versus Wikipedia, which is constructed on the basis of individual efforts of many who do not operate for any monetary incentives. Another example is the creation of categories for classifying online web pages. While Yahoo is a commercial directory in which categories are created by paid employees, the Open Directory is run by volunteers, each editing a

15 The GNU/Linux operating system and Apache server software, which were developed in a common non-proprietary regime, are increasingly gaining popularity and are considered more stable than comparable commercial programs (Gillen, Kusnetzky and McLarnon 2003). There is no way of knowing exactly how many people use GNU/Linux – that's the whole point of open-source rationale. Users do not have to register or ask for permission to use free OS and nobody is tracking them. However, the number of users can be estimated and one such recent estimate is that there are 91 million machines running GNU/Linux these days (http://mrpogson.com/2011/03/27/how-many-people-use-gnulinux-lots/).

sub-category. The contributions of all individual editors is merged into an Open Source directory that everyone is free to use, and is indeed used by some of the major search engines, including Google. Another example is the online communities of movies or TV shows translations. Teams compete against each other (surprisingly not for money) but also share knowledge and technological skills. Translations into English, Spanish, Italian, Russian and Hebrew are very common on file-sharing software such as eMule and Torrent clients.

As contended by Benkler (2002), new technologies enable a new radically decentralized type of production mode, which is the commons-based peer-production of information. These social and economic phenomena reflect a non-proprietary regime where content is developed through collaborative efforts without any claim for exclusive rights in it. Production of information, knowledge and culture, Benkler maintains, no longer requires management by the hierarchy of firms, or the price signals of the market. When projects are modular in the sense that they can be divided into small independently produced components, they can rely on non-monetary motivation of individuals. Large-scale collaborations will be possible as long as diverse motivations can be pooled and merged into a single effort. The low cost of communicating and processing information makes such coordination and integration cost-effective in a way that was unavailable before. The development of such powerful informational products, which are non-rivalrous and non-excludable, without any apparent monetary compensation and any guaranteed return for financial investment is challenging the incentives paradigm and its basic premise – the need for monetary incentives for informational, technological and intellectual creation. Indeed, Smith and Kollock (1999: 230) called Linux 'the impossible public good'.

Digital technology also transforms the nature of consumption. The experience of content consumption becomes exceedingly social: we watch videos rated by our peers, listen to music recommended by our contacts and seek to share content with our different communities. Social plug-ins such as Facebook's 'like' button or 'recommendations' and 'activity feed' allow users to see what their friends have liked, commented on or shared with sites across the web. With the introduction of eBooks, reading a book, that used to be a solitary experience, may now turn into a social experience. For instance, the 'popular highlights' feature of Amazon.com eBooks highlights the passages that were appreciated by the greatest number of readers without revealing their identity. The 'public notes' feature further allows readers to share their highlights and notes with others. In 2010, participating in social networking sites was the most popular online activity. We increasingly seek to engage with content rather than simply acquire access to a copy of it. A common example is the reading of news reports together with the stream of responses. Another example is the remixing and mash-ups of videos and music. The flow of information created by such interactions often becomes part of the content itself. Consumption and production of content are increasingly converged. Web users are not interested in UGC simply because it provides a fresh perspective or is viewed as more reliable and unbiased; users are also seeking participation in a community. A recent study shows that users are even willing to pay a premium for the opportunity to participate and contribute to a community (Oestreicher-Singer and Zalmanson 2010).

From an economic perspective the new modes of production and consumption can be analysed within three frameworks, all of which point towards a decreasing need for central intervention in order to provide monetary incentives to create. The first framework is the Coasian theory of the firm (1937), which views the creation of the firm as a substitute to the nexus of contracts in the market, where the transaction costs involved in the hierarchical nature of a firm are lower than the costs of transacting within markets. The new technological frontiers decrease contractual transaction cost significantly and thus shift back productive activity from firms to markets, from industrial production of intangible goods to production by individuals, groups and unorganized crowds (Benkler 2002), for which there are significant non-monetary incentives schemes.

The second framework is the Coasian 1960 theorem, according to which in a world with no transaction costs legal rules (the allocation of entitlements as well as the choice of remedies for their infringement) do not matter because individuals will bypass inefficient rules. In contrast, in a world of positive transaction costs such bypassing of inefficient rules may not materialize and thus the choice of legal rules does matter; the prime consideration in their crafting ought to be minimization of transaction costs. The transformation of content production modes described above is at least partly the result of a significant decrease in transaction costs and can confirm Coase's prediction that inefficient rules will be bypassed by individuals. The emergence of content production which does not rely on IPR can signal the inefficiency of the current IP laws.

The third economic framework for the analysis of this new mode of production is the traditional division between work and leisure. The atomization of efforts can shift activities that were regarded in the 'old' world as work, to activities that are regarded by individuals in the digital world as leisure (Elkin-Koren and Salzberger 2005: 62–63). Work is what people do for a salary and leisure is what they do for fun. Yet, online activities we usually associate with leisure now generate a value that we usually associate with the output of 'work'. Reviews of books and movies, for instance, are routinely shared by users as a matter of social practice, but when such reviews are posted online, they become economically valuable for such platforms as Amazon.com, which use them to improve the service they provide to their customers. The fact that Amazon extracts an economic value from user-generated reviews, however, does not necessarily turn this practice into work, and does not create an employment relationship among the parties. At the same time, however, our definition of labor may also be changing, and may expand to cover forms of labor that were not treated as work, such as participating in chats, posting comments in online forums and playing online games.

Content is increasingly created outside professional routines or employment agreements and simply emerges out of social interaction, play and fun. Indeed, these processes are challenging the boundaries of some professions. Take bloggers for instance. As more individuals report the news on their blogs, it becomes harder to distinguish between traditional journalism and blogging, between news reporting by licenced and paid reporters and news reported by participants in online news forums. Journalism, as a profession, may also be transformed. Bloggers may not be professionals, but one may no longer need to be a professional journalist in order to report the news (Shirky 2008: 70–80).

UGC is blurring the distinction between amateurs and professionals. Amateur content is not produced within an industrial structure and it is not linked to any particular business model. It is often created for fun and exchanged for free within a social framework. Although much online content is generated by amateurs, some UGC is also produced by professionals, outside the scope of their employment agreement. A typical example is the thousands of software developers who hold regular jobs in high-tech companies and contribute, after hours, to a whole variety of open source projects. Some companies encourage their employees actively to engage in UGC communities and to contribute to collaborative projects. The output of these employees is simply mixed with contributions of other users, and it is neither claimed nor branded by the company.

The blurring distinction between work and leisure and the increased significance of non-monetary incentives in the overall production of content may challenge professional authorship. The need to support professional authors, who are fully devoting themselves to authorship, is one of the economic arguments in support of copyright. It is assumed that even though artists are motivated by non-monetary incentives, they will not become professional authors unless they can profit from their copyrighted works. The professional author who emerged during the 19th century may decline.

Finally, creative and innovative production is driven by social motivation. Promoting creation and innovation in this environment should therefore take into account the *social nature* of these activities and the social design that could facilitate it. Social motivation represents a special type of non-monetary motivation that arises from a social context – a context that transcends the individual creator. Although it shares some qualities with self-oriented motives, social motivation is fundamentally other-oriented. While self-oriented motives focus on the individual creator, in other-oriented motives the social context plays a key role. Users who generate and distribute content in social media platforms often engage in a social activity such as sharing opinions (as in blogs), sharing skills and knowledge (as in forums), rating films and articles, or tagging photos and sharing videos (as in social networks). Sharing something you have created yourself or simply something you have watched or otherwise experienced is a type of social interaction that adds a layer of meaning to the experience of reading and writing.

Individuals not only have an instinctive motivation to act upon the world, but as social beings may simply want to interact, communicate, connect with other people, be heard by their fellow users, feel they belong and affiliate themselves with groups (Wellman et al. 2003). Rather than focusing on self-expression for intrinsic satisfaction, individuals may often seek to perform communicative acts, aiming to engage others in a conversation, gain their attention and get feedback.

Another aspect of social motivation is a sense of belonging to a community. A classic example is Wikipedia. Several studies exploring why people write and edit entries on Wikipedia have focused on Wikipedia's communal nature (Rafaeli and Ariel 2008). A sense of community reflects a commitment of community members towards other members of the community and also to the group as a whole. It is often based on reciprocity, which is the tendency to contribute for the benefit of those from whom you have benefited in the past (Peddibhotla and Subramani 2007). Accordingly, individuals sometimes produce content (write reviews, edit entries on Wikipedia) to reciprocate for the benefits they have received from their fellow users. This type of reciprocity is a strong social motivation, as it encourages further contribution by individuals in a particular social context where it becomes the norm. Several studies have focused on social interaction, defined as the desire for affiliation and belonging (e.g. Rafaeli, Havat and Ariel 2009). One study of early experimentation with the crowd-sourcing site Google Answers showed that even when significant monetary rewards were involved, the economic incentive was strongly moderated by social variables (Rafaeli, Raban and Ravid 2007). This suggests that the process of social production is focused not on individuals but on groups and communities.

While self-oriented motives can sometimes serve as a substitute for monetary rewards, social motivation cannot. This is because it reflects a continuum, an ongoing process, rather than a single, one-time exchange with an indistinct party. Social motivation involves a relationship with a concrete or partially imagined community. The act itself – sharing a photo, discussing the news – derives its meaning from the actual engagement and interaction with others. These aspects of social motivation are not reducible to a market exchange and therefore call for a reconsideration of the way we capture and design these markets for content.

The transformation of the industrial production of content and the rise of social production destabilize some of the fundamental premises of intellectual property law and pose new challenges for the governance of intangible goods. The economic analysis of intellectual property assumes that creators and inventors are simply selfish, rational actors who maximize profits. Corporations, which dominated the production of informational goods during the second half of the 20th century, were profit maximizers and therefore required economic incentives to invest in the production of new content and inventions. The rise of social production and the growing significance of social motivation are challenging this view of the creative environment and therefore the prevailing economic rationale of IPR. Social production is driven by communities. In sharp contrast to the industrial model, individuals who generate content in social contexts are driven by a wide range of social motivations. Social production is therefore less dependent on a firm's business model that secures a financial return for each creative investment; it depends instead on voluntary contributions by individuals, often large crowds of individuals, and on their continued engagement and enthusiasm, which in turn, is related to various micro indicators such as education, communication, infrastructure and culture.

The rise of social production and the greater share of UGC in the overall content that is available to the public imply a shift in the balance mandated by the public good equation. The 'public good' nature of creative works entails that intellectual property law must balance two contradicting forces: the need to provide exclusive rights for incentivizing the creation of new works and the need to minimize restrictions on access as a result of excessive protection. Such limits on access to pre-existing materials will hinder further creation and deny society the benefits of the IPR system. While monetary incentives were necessary in the past to induce mass production by the content industries, the rise of social production suggests that other considerations should now be given more weight, namely, maximizing the use of (non-rivalrous) informational works. Legal policies related to the social web should aim at promoting social production by nurturing social motivation, facilitating collaboration and enhancing the social capital of creative communities.

### *3.1.6 Technological change and the need for incentives*

The digital environment also has a significant bearing on the non-excludability character of informational goods, which is a prime source for the law and economic incentives paradigm. New technologies enable not only easier and cheaper copying but also enable much easier and cheaper exclusion. The Internet enhances the ability to exclude and control the distribution of information to the extent that makes significant fractions of it no longer a public good. The nature of information in the Internet and also on other digital platforms such as DVDs, computer games, electronic books and the like allows the application of cost-effective self-help technical measures to control its consumption and use.

Consider, for instance a book. Books in a digital format (eBooks), unlike printed books, are tied to a reading device (eReader), a tablet computer, a smart phone or a dedicated reader such as Kindle, which converts the binary code into a readable text. Printed books are usually widely distributed as commercial products and typically consumers are not required to undergo any approval process or to undertake any additional commitments before they can use the book. The online purchasing of eBooks, however, often requires identification, and the eBook is subject to a license agreement, setting limits on the freedom to use the book in a certain way, such as lending it, listening to it aloud, or selling the copy to others. DRMs often set additional limits, preventing the preparation of copies, the ability to cut and paste text, print the eBook, or transfer the eBook to another location. A striking example of the effective publishers' control in the use of the book after it was purchased by the user is the Orwellian 1984 saga, in which Amazon.com remotely removed purchased copies of George Orwell's book, *1984*, from Kindle due to certain copyright concerns. Following a public outcry, Amazon.com apologized and later settled a class action brought against it for violating its terms of service by remotely deleting purchased copies of the book. The incident demonstrates the power of online retailers remotely to control the collection of eBooks stored on an electronic device.

Digital technology may turn information which was previously non-excludable, to an excludable asset. Indeed, the creation of digital copies involves very low cost, yet distribution of copies protected by IPR is no longer the sole way of generating profits. Technical ways to prevent copying and to charge a fee are more widely available. In addition, the digital environment facilitates a shift from selling copies to charging for access. Distribution methods such as streaming enable online providers to facilitate access without granting the end users control over copies. This arrangement releases providers from the need to worry about piracy. The music and film industries are moving away from the sale of records, CDs and DVDs, into streaming services such as Spotify, which offers DRM protected music streaming services. Users can register for a free account, supported by advertising, or pay for subscription to receive streaming without ads and with additional features. Digital networks enable collecting a fee for access to a website and charging one-time fees for use of the information provided. It allows temporary entrance permits and restrictions on usage of information to online individual use, blocking the possibilities of copying information or forwarding it, and more (Bell 1998; Dam 1998).

The result of this new state of technology seems to be ideal. On the one hand, it brings about a significant increase in the production and distribution of information, and, on the other hand, that information can no longer be regarded as suffering from the public good deficiencies. Thus, government intervention might not be required or desirable. This, however, is not the full picture. The development of self-help exclusion measures is likely to encourage users to develop counter code-breaking and hacking tools. This, in turn, is likely to lead to sophistication of the exclusion tools and a continuous technological race between the two sorts of devices. Such a race may divert funds that might otherwise be invested in more productive directions. This infertile race might cause resources waste and may require central intervention, which is very different from government intervention within the traditional public goods framework. Here the government will not be called upon to provide the public good or the legal means to enable its production by private firms. Central intervention may be required to halt or control the technological race between exclusion tools and their counter technologies. The American 1998 Digital Millennium Copyright Act (DMCA) provides an example of such regulation. This legislation includes a prohibition on anti-circumvention activities. However, when interpreted by the courts this clause was extended to prohibiting anti-circumvention of non-protected IPR activity (*Lexmark International Inc.*, 387 F.3d 522; *Chamberlain Group Inc.*, 381 F.3d 1178), further restricting the availability of information. We will return to this legislation in Chapter 6.

### 3.1.7 *Summary*

To sum up, the extent to which information today is a public good meriting incentives in the form of central intervention is debatable. It depends, among other factors, on the technological state of the art, which is changing at a rapid pace and this pace is not only the cause but also the result of the IPR regime. Consequently, the public good analysis may not be very conclusive in determining when government intervention is necessary and to what extent, and it is possible that incentives in the form of contemporary IP laws even achieve the opposite goal – suppressing innovation and creation. The fact that the principles of IP laws have not been revisited in light of these technological developments (and, in fact, in some fields, notably copyright, protection was actually amplified in recent years) and that law and economics analysis has not recommended a shift of balance, (in terms of duration for example) ought to raise some question marks. These observations and the indeterminacy of economic analysis as to the right amount of incentives needed for tackling the traditional public goods problem, might be a possible explanation for the shift of the law and economics literature to the proprietary paradigm of IP, on which we elaborate in the next chapter.

## 3.2 Incentives for what?

A different angle of looking into the incentives paradigm is to examine who should be granted monetary incentives – the investor, the creator or the producer? And for which activity: the initial creation, its management and distribution, or maybe its improvement? One can find very different stances on these questions, which imply different sizes of monetary incentives and a variety of forms. At one extreme there are those who suggest that it is necessary to grant a monopoly on the creation, enabling creators to collect every cent generated by an innovation because only such a method would repay the risk of failure. For example, as Frederic M. Scherer argues, recoupment is not an adequate measure of return necessary to stimulate the optimum level of creativity since in creative industries the likelihood of failure is very high and hard to predict. Thus, the law must insure that successful products generate high and sufficient returns to compensate the creators for their efforts in unsuccessful endeavors (Scherer 2001: 3–23). In economic terms, the monopolistic pricing facilitated by intellectual property rights is justified to compensate for the risk involved in creative and innovative activities.

On the other hand, there are those who believe that it is sufficient to allow creators to collect a little more than a return on their investment. The reason is that any extra value awarded to creators represents a loss to consumers. Mark Lemley (2005: 1060–62), for instance, warns that the meaning of giving inventors control over all the positive externalities associated with their inventions is giving them control over improvements and new uses that might be made of their works. As a result, there will be fewer incentives for future improvers to invest in developing the first generation technology, ie the original invention. Competition on improving the first generation technology will be stifled.

In considering the types of incentives vital for stimulating optimal creative activity it is necessary to define exactly the type of activity that the incentives scheme aims to induce. In this context it is useful to draw several distinctions as discussed in the following subsections.

### *3.2.1 Incentives to create or incentives to produce?*

To understand the incentives paradigm in greater depth we need to take a closer look at the particular market behavior that this type of government intervention seeks to promote. For this purpose it is necessary to distinguish between incentives to create and incentives to produce and distribute. The exclusive right to reproduce and distribute in copyright law, for instance, provides little incentive to authors but greater incentives to distributors and publishers (Shih Ray Ku 2002). Indeed, the emergence of copyright was led by publishers who argued that not only the author but also the publisher's considerable investment in bringing a book to the market must be protected (Zimmerman 2003). The same can be said about patents vis-à-vis Schumpeter's (1928) characterization of the innovation process, which includes the invention stage, the innovation stage, the diffusion stage and the imitation stage. Patents do not necessarily promote investment to invent; they promote more incentives to diffuse and of course are a hurdle to imitation.

The law and economics literature on intellectual property generally treated the interests of authors and inventors, and the interests of publishers, producers and investors as identical (Landes and Posner 1989; Breyer 1970; Sunder 2006; Fisher 2001). An exception is Hurt and Schuchman who argued that the incentives of authors and publishers should be distinguished as their degree of dependence upon the copyright system is different (Hurt and Schuchman 1966: 425).

The distinction between incentives to distribute and incentives to create has become even more important in recent years. The market for content has undergone a fundamental transition in the past two decades where the role of publishers and producers of content is rapidly diminishing. Book and music publishers were essential for the production and distribution of content in the pre-digital era. In the digital era, authors are increasingly making their works available directly to their potential readers and audience. The reason is that digital technology enables direct distribution at very little cost, thereby minimizing the reliance on publishers (Elkin-Koren 1996: 254–58). Online dissemination of informational works of all sorts can easily be made directly by individuals, using their personal computers to convey their ideas or share informational works with other individuals using the same protocols. Users of file-sharing systems, for example, are capable of making files available for downloading by other users, by simply placing files at a designated directory on their personal computers. Electronic delivery of information involves low costs and does not require any large investment in the production of copies and the establishment of distribution channels. Digital networks provide cheap, global and easy ways of sharing or selling digital information without any investment by the creators or users (Peukert 2005).

The elimination of intermediaries in the information supply chain is called *disintermediation*, a term which first appeared during the revolution in financial services precipitated by the high interest rates of the 1970s. At that time, consumers discovered that they could get better returns on their money by disintermediating, ie cutting out banks and directly investing in the same money markets used by the banks. The Internet cuts out the middlemen by placing consumers in direct contact with businesses or indeed individuals. Musicians, for instance, can make their works available online. For example, Ann and Nancy Wilson, the sisters who founded *Heart*, one of the most successful rock and roll bands of all times, released their popular song *Jupiter's Darling* on the Internet and it has been shared on P2P networks. Janis Ian, a recording artist who received two Grammy awards, benefits from the use of P2P file sharing networks. The traffic to her website (www.janisian.com) has increased dramatically since the rise of P2P technology, going from approximately 60,000 unique visitors annually to five times as many (Brief of Amici Curiae Sovereign Artists, *Grokster*, 125 S. Ct. 2764). Another example is the Chicago-based band *Wilco*. The band was dropped from Reprise Records in 2001 over creative conflicts surrounding their album *Yankee Hotel Foxtrot* and subsequently released it free of charge on the Internet. The album was a great success and later on the band released it officially through Nonesuch Records (Jardin 2004). The incentives to create were thus maintained, without granting exclusive rights to copy and distribute, and in fact without relying on any exclusive IPR.

Similarly, authors of scientific papers relied in the past exclusively on publications distributed by publishers of scientific journals for publishing their scholarly work. These journals in a paper format were expensive to produce and distribute and since they were targeted at relatively small audiences journals became disproportionately expensive (Boczkowski 2005). While scientists usually do not receive any monetary rewards for their scientific journal contributions, some of the publishers made fortunes. Scientists are increasingly using open access mechanisms for making scientific knowledge available online. See for example the Public Library of Science (PLOS) journals. This is a non-profit scientific and medical publishing venture that provides scientists and physicians with high quality, high profile journals in which they can publish their most important work, while making the full contents freely available for anyone to read, distribute or use for their own research). Another open access initiative is the Johns Hopkins University Scholarly Communications Group, whose aim is to allow open access to quality information, as a way of encouraging learning, scholarship, research and patient care.

The role of intermediaries in attracting incentives and managing risk is also declining as digital technology also lowers the cost of production. To take eBooks as an example, some of the cost of producing an eBook remains the same as producing a physical copy, such as editing, cover design, ISBN, interior layout and design, marketing and promotion. Nonetheless, the production of eBooks saves on the cost of print runs, storage and shipping copies to bookstores. Consequently, digital publishing is no longer tied up in the substantial investment required for printing a large number of paper copies in advance and managing an inventory that may not be sold (Elkin-Koren 2011).

Digital networks diminish the role of some traditional intermediaries, such as the recording or publishing industries, while at the same time introduce new players to the scene. New intermediaries in the online environment may come into play: online retailers, search engines and online aggregators, social media platforms, communication carriers, ISPs and device manufacturers might all play a role in bringing together authors and their readers. Online intermediaries facilitate access to digital content in a variety of ways. Major distributors of music, applications and eBooks are online retailers, such as iTunes and Amazon.com. Access to digital content is also provided by communication carriers, such as mobile phone companies, which are integrating content offerings into their communication packages. Another model is access by peers to social media such as Facebook, where informational goods, such as music, movies, pictures and news items become available in a social setting. Finally, there is access by search – where digital content posted by users is identified and located with the assistance of a search engine. Consequently, the distribution and marketing of creative content in this environment are taking a different form.

What makes the new online intermediaries interesting in the context of the incentives analysis is the fact that their business models do not necessarily rely on the sale of copies, and therefore these models are less dependent on copyright. For instance, distribution by online intermediaries, such as search engines and social networks, depends on traffic. Content enables intermediaries to attract more users and to benefit from selling users to advertisers. Intermediaries can share advertising revenue with authors. Advertising services, such as Google AdSense, automatically deliver targeted ads to blogs and personal homepages, sharing the collected revenues from advertising with the hosting website. As we further discuss below, such business models, based on advertising, are less dependent on the legal right to control copies, and do not necessarily require the restriction of unauthorized copying.

The above discussion and examples demonstrate how digital networks may affect the creation of information and its dissemination in a way that could render current incentive schemes unnecessary or out of date. The lower cost of online dissemination weakens the need for securing incentives to distributors. The emerging business models of new online intermediaries suggest that financial incentives for distributing works could also be achieved without placing unnecessary restrictions on the preparation of copies and their distribution to the public.

### *3.2.2 Incentives to create or incentives to improve?*

A second distinction that is essential for defining the purpose of incentives is the distinction between incentives to create and innovate and incentives to improve. The first scholar to raise this distinction was Edmund Kitch in his paper from 1977. According to his analysis, patent rights are necessary as a means of encouraging efficient usage of existing inventions. Kitch argued that we should grant patents in advance of an invention, making a patent a right to 'prospect' technological improvements in a particular field. Kitch's theory is one of the foundations of the proprietary paradigm, which we discuss in the next chapter. It lies on two basic assumptions. The first assumption is that inventors will not invest in putting their invention to efficient use unless they obtain exclusive rights to the invention. Without exclusive rights the inventors will fear that their investment will result in unpatentable information appropriable by competitors. The second assumption is that enabling the holder to control any improvement of the invention will lead to efficient investment in further innovation. It is based on the presumption of perfect information, perfect rationality and zero transaction costs. Accordingly, the exclusive patent right should lead to an efficient licencing to both users and potential improvers.

Kitch's argument reappeared in a somewhat different form as a supporting argument for the US Copyright Term Extension Act (CTEA), which added an additional 20 years to the already long copyright term. Advocates of the CTEA argued that extending intellectual property rights was necessary to give existing copyright owners an incentive both to preserve films they had already made, and to distribute books they had already published. The rationale behind the law was to prevent works from entering the public domain. Saving works from such destiny is allegedly necessary because once a work entered the public domain it is, arguebly, 'orphan' and no one has any incentive to take care of it and invest in its improvement. The argument that incentives are necessary to encourage further improvement of works was also put forward by Landes and Posner (2003a). Incentives, they argue, are needed for promoting not only marketing efforts, but also persistent improvement of the good in order to preserve its value. They emphasized that their support of the copyright extension is based on the traditional incentive-based argument for property right, but with a 'new twist'. Incentives are not exhausted in the initial creation of the intellectual property goods. The incentives are further necessary to 'maintain the value of the property and also to resurrect abandoned or otherwise unexploited intellectual property' (Landes and Posner 2003a: 231–33).

This theory has strong counter arguments. Mark Lemley (2005), for example, argues that this theory contradicts the entire competitive market paradigm. Competition and the invisible hand is what drive the market to efficiency. The meaning of Kitch's argument and its successors is that only one skilled firm in the market can reach the efficient outcome, and for doing so society must provide it with the adequate incentives. The fact that goods in a particular market had been protected by exclusive rights in the past, either by patent rights or copyrights, does not change his belief in the idea of competitive market. Lemley invites us to compare the market of IP to the market of paper clips. Companies will make and distribute paper clips if they can sell them for more than it cost to produce and supply them. Granting one company the exclusive right to make paper clips would likely result in an increase in the price and a decrease in the supply of paper clips. Books, in Lemley's opinion, are not different from paper clips. As books, paper clips were once patented. Similar to the books market, the competition in the paper clips market is not a perfect one, since in both markets there are no perfect substitutes to the goods. And, finally, in the paper clips market as well as in the books market, once an intellectual property right expires many companies can compete to make the good, and they will do so only as long as they can manufacture and distribute it for less money than people will pay to buy it.

According to Lemley, empirical evidence strongly supports the intuition of the market. A comparison of copyrighted works from the 1930s with public domain works from the 1910s and 1920s reveals that far more public domain works than copyrighted works are actually distributed to the public, and generally at a somewhat lower price. Twice as many books published in the 1920s (and therefore in the public domain) are in print today compared with books published in the 1930s.

A powerful example that supports Lemley's findings is the Google Book Search (GBS) initiative in which Google has scanned millions of books from major research libraries in order to make them searchable online. As of March 2012, Google has scanned more than 20 million books. The scanned copies were delivered to the partnering libraries and the electronic database of books was made available for online search. Google was willing to invest the cost of scanning books that were not born digital, and make them searchable and digitally available for online search. It created an added value to consumers from which it was planning to draw profits. The lack of copyright was not an impediment to Google's investment. In fact, copyright presented an obstacle on the development of this added value service. In 2005, the Authors Guild and five publishers brought a class action against Google in the Southern District of New York, alleging copyright infringement for scanning copyrighted books. The parties announced a settlement in 2008, but the approval of the Amended Settlement Agreement (ASA) was recently denied by the US District Court (*Authors Guild, Inc. v. Google, Inc.*, 05 Civ. 8136 (DC), 2011 WL 986049 (S.D.N.Y. March 22, 2011)). We will return to this debate in the next chapter.

### *3.2.3 Incentives to create or incentives to disclose?*

A third important distinction is between incentives for creation and disclosure. Patent law is said to promote further innovation by encouraging disclosure. Without patents people might continue to create but will keep the invention secret and will try to conceal its nature in the final commercial product that is based on the invention. Coca Cola opted to keep its recipe for its famous drink secret rather than registering it and receiving an exclusive IP right for a limited time. It thus has been enjoying the exclusivity of its recipe for a much longer period than would have been its legal right under IPR. Disclosing a particular invention in a manner sufficient to permit one skilled in the art to which the invention pertains, to make and use the invention effectively, means that the invention is given to the public. The disclosure is made in exchange for the exclusive right granted to the inventor. These exchanges between the inventor and the public constitute the quid pro quo of a patentee's deal with the public. Some even argue that insufficient patent protection will lead inventors to keep their inventions as trade secrets, as a way to obtain a competitive advantage, harming social welfare (Sommer 2005: 153–55).

There are cases that support the argument in favor of the need to generate incentives for disclosure and thus for IPR as a mechanism for generating advancement. For example, Flavio Alterthum, a Brazilian professor, and two American academics invented, while working at the University of Florida at Gainesville, a genetically altered microbe, which digests the bio-waste of the sugar harvest to produce ethanol efficiently. The US Patent Office awarded the invention a United States patent. Similar patents were eventually obtained in five other large sugar-producing countries, but not in Brazil, where such inventions were not patentable at that time. Commercial development of the invention is progressing in the United States and elsewhere, but not in Brazil, where this new technology could bring substantial benefits. The Brazilian co-inventor returned to Brazil and attempted to get local sugar companies to invest in the development of the process, but in the absence of local patent protection at the time he was not successful (Sherwood 2000: 352–53).

However, the sugar story is anecdotal and in fact it does not prove the main argument that incentives to disclose are vital to advancement, because the option to register a patent was available but it was simply not exercised.

It can actually support a counter argument according to which without mandatory disclosure content providers and inventors will apply the most beneficial strategy for them (as in the Coca Cola case) or more than one strategy for legal exclusion. With software, for instance, patenting provides protection for the functional elements of the software. However, the downside of patenting software is the disclosure requirement. Disclosing the technology exposes it to the competitors and makes it more vulnerable to improvement. Thus, some programmers prefer to keep their software code as a trade secret and avoid disclosing it in a patent application (Campbell-Kelly and Valduriez 2005: 277–78). Similarly, in the case of copyright law, the economic purpose of the law is to ensure that more works become accessible – the equivalent of disclosure. The introduction of DRMs allows copyright owners to distribute the copyrighted works, but at the same time further to limit the technological access to works. We will discuss this issue further in Chapter 6.

In any case, even if incentives are needed for disclosure, intellectual property rights are not the only mechanism to generate these kind of incentives, and in fact they might be inferior to other forms of incentives, such as grants or subsidies that can require disclosure as a precondition. We elaborate on the different regimes for generating incentives in the next section.

### *3.2.4 Summary*

The three distinctions made here boil down in legal terms to the object and scope of the right; in the case of IP rights – to their duration and exceptions. Incentives needed for creators, distributors, promoters, improvers and for disclosure would mean a totally different scope and scheme of IP rights than incentives needed for innovation and creation only. Although we cannot prescribe here the optimal scheme, we believe that the discussion above refutes many of the arguments made in recent years on behalf of the incentives paradigm for expansion of IPR, and in fact advocates quite the opposite.

It is not clear whether incentives are really necessary to encourage all types of innovation and creation on both the individual and organizational levels. The technological revolution of the last decades has transformed the process of creation and innovation without any corresponding changes in the law and economics analysis of these issues. This poses a big question mark on the viability of this analysis. While in the past incentives might have been necessary for carrying on an invention or creation to wide distribution, the technological tools of today significantly decrease this rationale, and it is possible that incentives in the form of contemporary IP laws achieve the opposite goal – they in fact suppress innovation and creation. We will return to some of these themes in the next sections, but there is no doubt that more empirical work has to be carried out and the question regarding the need for incentives should be an important challenge also for behavioral law and economics and development law and economics.

## 3.3 Central intervention in the form of intellectual property rights

The incentives paradigm encompasses two major premises: (1) monetary incentives are necessary in order to generate efficient level of creation and innovation; and (2) intellectual property rights are the best way for providing such incentives. So far we have critically examined the first premise of the incentives paradigm. In this section we will assume that incentives are necessary and we will examine whether IPR is the best mechanism for generating such incentives. Unlike the deontological rationales for IP, which justify *ownership* in self-created works and inventions based on a natural right, and thus provide a first order justification in favor of intellectual property rights, the incentives paradigm is not hooked to a particular proprietary solution. The starting point of the incentives paradigm is the market failure of public goods. The incentives paradigm justifies IPR only to the extent they remedy this market failure. The law and economic justification for IP rights is, therefore, of a second order nature. In other words, one thing is to examine whether a failure does exist in information markets; a separate issue is to identify the desirable remedy for this failure.

What is the best way to secure incentives to invest in creation and innovation? Are property rights – the legal right to exclude others – the most effective way for society to hold out these incentives? In the following sections we critically discuss some of the arguments raised against this legal mechanism. We begin (section 3.3.1) by describing the inherent tension between exclusive rights, as the means for generating incentives, and access to knowledge that is the ultimate goal which IPR seek to promote, and highlight the intrinsic paradox involved. We analyse some drawbacks associated with the monopoly powers that might be acquired by IPR, and other drawbacks of IPR related to administrative and transaction cost. Subsequently, in section 3.3.2, we turn to examine alternative mechanisms for generating incentives, such as liability rules, unjust enrichment, subsidies and prizes, and argue that they have significant advantages over intellectual property rights. Finally, in section 3.3.3 we examine the viability of the traditional distinction between the various types of IPR (copyright, patent, design etc) vis-à-vis the incentives paradigm and whether a different categorization of IPR according to the type of industry involved (tailored IPR) might be more appropriate.

### *3.3.1 Generating incentives by intellectual property rights*

Intellectual property laws seek to secure incentives by granting creators and inventors with a set of legal rights, which allows them to trade their works and inventions in the market. In a sense, IPR provide legal excludability to remedy the non-excludability of intangible informational goods. This regulatory scheme creates several difficulties from a law and economics perspective.

#### *3.3.1.1 Monopolistic deadweight loss and the intellectual property paradox*

The main drawback of IPR as a tool to generate incentives is that IPR provide their holder with a monopoly power, thus replacing one market failure with another. The exclusivity and excludability created by IPR is meant to enable rightholders to sell the information they created at a price above the competitive price of marginal cost of the end product, and thereby capture their sunk costs in R&D. But this power can be used to set prices that maximize the producer's profits, well above the price that covers their investment, bringing to societal loss dubbed deadweight loss. All those who value the informational product above competitive market price and below the monopolistic price will not purchase the product. The sum of these potential buyers' values is the deadweight loss.

One can argue that this description is inaccurate because some creations and inventions have substitutes and thus would not enable the IPR holder to set a monopolistic price. The exclusivity applies to a particular copyrighted work or a particular patented invention. When these works or inventions have appropriate substitutes their owners will be forced to sell them at a competitive market price. Here we get to the IP paradox (Lunney 1996: 556–70). Those creations that have substitutes will be priced at near competitive market price, thus IP protection would not make much of a difference. In contrast, the most useful inventions, which do not have substitutions, would be sold at a monopolistic price. But these particular creations have the pinnacle justification for a broad access. The more utility is driven from any particular invention, the stronger the need to make it accessible to as many users as possible in order to maximize social welfare. This is a direct consequence of the non-rivalry nature of intellectual creations. Granting intellectual property rights in extremely useful inventions such as critical drugs in order to stimulate their production generates a monopoly power of the right holders that most likely will limit access to those critical inventions for which we sought to maximize access. Granting IPR to those creations that are really path-breaking, unique and essential means that they will not reach the wider population, which is the ultimate goal of providing incentives in the first place. Hence we have a paradox.

Consider, for instance, incentives in the pharmaceutical industry. When a company invests in developing a new drug for headaches it will face competition with the many drugs available on the market. Thus, despite any property rights that might be granted to the pharmaceutical company it will not be able to set its price much above the competitive market price. The new drug will therefore be broadly available for use by many. In contrast, a drug curing AIDS, if found, would be one of a kind. Once such medication becomes available social welfare maximization would mandate making it accessible to as many infected patients as possible. If, however, the drug does not have substitutes, and it is subject to a patent, it would be sold at a monopoly price, and only a few would be able to purchase it. This is the reason for the strong objection raised by global health activists to patent legislation that prevents the production of life-saving drugs at marginal cost. Yet, the pharmaceutical industry argues that without patents the life saving drugs would have not been invented at all. If drugs for fatal diseases do not receive full patent protection, the industry argues, it would lack sufficient incentives to invest in those drugs, and R&D efforts would be diverted into more promising markets, such as anti-aging drugs. This is a two-edged sword argument: incentives by IPR will direct R&D into directions of profit maximization. A disease of the rich will attract much more investment and efforts than a disease of the poor (see also Fisher and Syed 2007). In addition, there is no full match between the amount needed to develop a drug or another invention and its level of uniqueness or lack of substitution. Thus drugs that were discovered by mistake, such as Viagra, will enjoy monopolistic power, while immense investments to develop a new drug, which eventually failed, will not be compensated by potential IPR.

The most notable example for this conflict over AIDS drugs occurred in South Africa, which has one of the highest percentage of HIV patients in the world. There are 22.5 million South Africans who are HIV positive, a figure that is approximately two-thirds of all HIV infected people in the world. In 2009 alone 1.8 million South Africans became infected with HIV, and 1.3 million AIDS-related deaths were reported (UN AIDS Report on the Global AIDS Epidemic 2010). South Africa has one of the poorest populations in the world where the average annual income is US$2600 and the GNI per capita in 2009 was US$5770 (Unicef). While the patented AIDS drugs produced in South Africa cost almost US$3 per patient per day, a generic version of the drug, produced in Brazil, costs only 1.55 percent of this price (Lewis 2002). In 1997, the South African Government of Nelson Mandela passed the Medicines and Related Substance Control Amendment Act. The purpose of the Act was to enable the government to make the HIV drugs treatment more affordable by allowing parallel importation of patented drugs from countries where the drug company sells the drugs more cheaply, and by permitting the use of generic version of the HIV drugs treatment as a substitute for the patented drugs. South Africa defended this legislation by relying on its government's obligations under its own constitution to ensure a right of access to health care, and its obligations under international human rights law to respect, promote and fulfill the fundamental human right to the highest attainable standard of health for its people.

In response to this legislation in February 1998 the Pharmaceutical Manufacturers' Association of South Africa (PMA) and numerous pharmaceutical companies commenced legal proceedings against the government to block the law, alleging that its provisions were in violation of the South African Constitution and of the World Trade Organization's Agreement on Trade-Related Aspects of Intellectual Property Rights (TRIPs). The case was scheduled for hearing on 5 March 2001, and the South African Government agreed not to implement the legislation until the court case was decided. In

February 1999 United States Vice President, Al Gore, commented in a memo that the protection of pharmaceutical patents should be 'a central focus' in upcoming talks with South Africa's Government officials. Gore explained that the South African Government has to assure it would 'not undermine legal protections' for patent holders (Scherer 1999). In April 1999 the US administration went even further and placed South Africa on a trade 'watch list'. Moreover, Mr Gore, as chairman of the US/South African Bi-national Commission, threatened sanctions against South Africa if it went ahead with the law. However, after a furious demonstration against the Pharmaceutical Manufacturers Association (PMA), it announced on 19 April 2001 that it was unconditionally withdrawing its legal action against the government (AIDS Legal Network).

From an economic analysis perspective, the AIDS example raises further conceptual and theoretical problems. When legislation is geared to maximize wealth (or welfare or utility) by the right balance between creating incentives to overcome non-excludability and restricting them due to non-rivalry, what should be the territorial unit for such maximization? If maximization of wealth is conducted on the level of South Africa, the legislation proposed by the South African Government might have been well justified. If maximization of wealth is conducted on a global level, the outcome might be different. Any wealth maximizing legislation for a certain jurisdiction creates externalities to other jurisdictions if the intellectual creation crosses the jurisdiction's borders, and it is the nature of intellectual creations easily to cross geographical borders. We will return to this point when we discuss positive economic analysis of IP in Chapter 7.

#### *3.3.1.2 Intellectual property and market power*

Another shortcoming of IPR as an optimal method for generating incentives arises from the proprietary nature of the rights, which may lead to market power beyond monopolistic price. Rendering exclusivity in informational goods gives right holders strategic advantage in informational markets and enable them to exercise control over informational goods far beyond the carefully defined list of rights and the economic purposes they were designed to serve. Intellectual property laws have turned out to be a major means of expanding market power, reducing competition and concentrating control over production and distribution of informational and derivative goods and services.

Consider, for instance, copyright law. The fundamental copyright is the exclusive right to copy or the right to exclude unlicenced copiers. Yet, copyright law in recent years has become a vehicle of control, and copyrights are being claimed for accomplishing strategic ends (Elkin-Koren 2002; Litman 2006: 77–88). Copyrights had been used strategically in order to increase barriers on entry (which are otherwise low) and to reduce the risks of competition. Thus, even when royalties were offered, copyrights were the bases for gaining control over distribution channels, such as cable retransmission of broadcast or Internet streaming. One example is the 2000 lawsuit launched in the USA by major copyright holders, including the National Football League, National Basketball Association, Twentieth Century Fox Film Corporation and a number of other Hollywood producers against iCraveTV and TVRadioNow Corp., both private Canadian companies (*iCraveTV*, 53 U.S.P.Q.2d 1831). iCraveTV had streamed copyrighted programs, such as professional football and basketball games as well as programs such as '60 Minutes', 'Ally McBeal', and 'Star Trek Voyager', framed with advertisements obtained by iCraveTV, to Internet users in the United States. The streaming technology allowed iCraveTV to capture United States programming from television stations in the US, convert these television signals into computerized data and stream them over the Internet from their website. Any Internet user could have accessed iCraveTV.com simply by entering three digits of any Canadian area code.

The US district court held that iCraveTV violated the plaintiffs' rights to perform their works publicly and to control the authorization for others to do so. In addition, iCraveTV also engaged in contributory infringement by making the plaintiffs' copyrighted programming available on the Internet with the knowledge that third parties could and would further infringe the plaintiffs' copyrights by further transmitting and publicly performing the programming. The irreparable harm that the plaintiffs were likely to face, according to the court, constituted a loss of control, which Congress vested with the copyright holders of the copyrighted materials.

This lawsuit demonstrates how IPR could be used for strategic gains. Internet streaming, which simultaneously retransmits television programs to Internet users, apparently does not compromise revenues in existing markets. Broadcasters derive revenues from selling show time to advertisers, where the selling price will depend on the size of the forecasted audience. When the expected audience of a television program is larger, the price would arguably be higher. Therefore, when retransmission expands the rating for television programs, copyright holders suffer no direct monetary harm and have no reason to object to retransmission other than for strategic purposes. The lawsuit against iCraveTV was not about remuneration or even about capturing a share in the benefits created by new technologies. In fact iCraveTV.com offered to pay the copyright fees and did not deny that rightholders should be paid for their works. At stake was control over Internet streaming of TV signals, and whether those could be picked up without authorization and retransmitted over the net. Even though the movie studios didn't suffer an immediate loss, they sought to maintain their decision-making power over the distribution of their works: at what timing, in what format, and in which context their works may be made available to the public. Internet streaming offers a whole new range of business opportunities that challenge existing licencing schemes and allow international coverage, interactivity and customization. Rightholders sought to govern this new distribution method (Elkin-Koren 2002).

Interestingly, retransmission by cable operators was also controversial during the 1970s and 1980s. US copyright holders similarly claimed that such retransmission is pirated and interferes with the owners' rights to authorize use of their works. However, that controversy was resolved differently. Although simultaneous retransmission of broadcasts was not subject to royalties until January 1978, under the 1976 Copyright Act it was eventually subject to a compulsory licencing system, which successfully separated remuneration and control (Botein 1998). Strategic use of copyright, such as in iCraveTV law suit, is becoming more common in the information environment, where entry barriers are lower. In the absence of a central bottleneck in the infrastructure, market players increasingly rely on the right to exclude for protecting market domination and expanding market power.

Another example of a strategic use of copyright, beyond the interest in gaining remuneration, is of Google Books. Google commenced an immense project of digitization of books, by scanning books pursuant to collaboration agreements with several major research libraries. Since 2004 Google has scanned millions of books stored in partnering libraries in order to make them available for online search. Google offered publishers the opportunity to join the Partner Program, in which copyright holders could authorize Google to scan the full text of the book into its database, and make it available to the public. In return, Google offered to share advertising revenues. The agreement allowed publishers to remove their books from the Partner Program at any time. Books that were not authorized by the rightholders under the Partner Program were not made available in full text. The scanned books were used only for indexing and search, and a few sentences of the text around the search term ('snippets' of text) were displayed in response to search queries. Google argued that it was entitled to scan copyright-protected books and display such 'snippets' of them in response to search queries, under fair use doctrine (Band 2009). The publishers disagreed and together with the Authors Guild brought a class action against Google in 2005, alleging copyright infringement for scanning copyrighted books. The parties announced a settlement in 2008, but the approval of the Amended Settlement Agreement ('ASA') was denied by the US court (*Authors Guild, Inc. v. Google, Inc.*, No 05 Civ. 8136 (DC), (S.D.N.Y. 22 March 2011).

Filing of the lawsuit by the publishers and the settlement negotiated between the publishers and Google demonstrate how IPR could be used strategically. Book publishers could have viewed the Google Books initiative as free marketing, enabling consumers to search inside books and efficiently identify the books they need to purchase. The service offered by Google did not pertain to full text and therefore did not substitute a purchase of a copy of the book. Access to full text, licenced by the publisher, could have further made book purchasing friendly to consumers around the world, offering books in a digital format that could have been more useful to consumers. Overall, this could have been viewed as an opportunity to expand the market for books and had the potential of actually raising the revenues publishers extract from their titles. Yet, the publishers insisted that any use of books required prior permission and objected to the opt-out system offered by Google, which enabled publishers to give a notice that their books should be removed. Most likely the publishers were concerned that they would be cut out of the publishing business, as Google and other online intermediaries were gaining growing dominance in online publishing. The lawsuit demonstrates how IPR could be used to prevent new players from offering added value to existing works without the permission of the rightholder.

The settlement reached by the parties in the class action (which was subsequently rejected by the court) further demonstrates how Google was trying to rely on the publishers' copyright to gain dominance and prevent competition in their search market. The settlement granted Google a license to make scanned books available in digital format, thereby making it very difficult for any company to compete in the foreseeable future. The court recognized the concern over this attempt. In denying approval of settlement, the court held, inter alia, that Google would have the right to make complete copies of orphan works and use them for both display and non-display purposes under the ASA, but that competitors who attempted to do the same might be liable for statutory damages. The court concluded that: 'Google's ability to deny competitors the ability to search orphan books would further entrench Google's market power in the online search market' (*Authors Guild v. Google*: 37).

The legal strategy employed successfully in these cases allows rightholders to expand their market power and accumulate control over additional markets. As Lawrence Lessig described it, strengthening copyright law will stifle technological advancement, and the opposite – strengthening technology – will weaken the rightholder's control (Lessig 1999: 125–26). According to Lessig, in real property the legal protection is necessary in order to create incentives to produce and protect the right of possession. In intellectual property law, in contrast, there is a need only to generate sufficient incentives to create. Thus, with regards to intellectual property there is a need only for less than perfect control, while in real property the law must provide perfect control to the owner. Intellectual property law, therefore, should include built-in limits on the power of the rightholders to control the use of their works (Lessig 1999: 133–34).

The excessive market power created by IPR is not confined to copyright law. A similar problem characterizes patent law. As many commentators observed, the economic value of patents is not confined to the expected value that could be extracted from each patent. Patents reward innovators by granting a patentee the right to exclude others from practicing the patented invention. However, unlike copyright, in order to be granted IPR, a patent application is required. The property right is granted in exchange for disclosure – and not all applications for registration are approved. Moreover, as

Lemley and Shapiro (2005) assert, a patent does not provide absolute exclusion, but rather presents a legal right to try to exclude. The patent right is therefore a probabilistic property right. According to empirical data the vast majority of patents that are issued are never litigated, and roughly half of those patents that are fully litigated are found to be invalid, therefore, most patents represent highly uncertain or probabilistic property rights.

The patent system creates strong incentives to file a patent application very early in the invention process, since inventors have a limited time from the commercialization of the product and disclosure of an idea until the deadline for patent application. In the US this time period is only one year. In Europe there is no such grace period, and hence the incentives to file a patent application as soon as possible are even stronger. As a result, many inventors file patent applications without any clear idea of whether the invention will be commercialized, and in some instances whether the category of invention is even patentable at all (Lemley and Shapiro 2005: 77). The outcome of the vast volume of patent applications every year and the early phase of their filing is that the examination process in the patent authorities is not broad and deep. The overwhelming majority of patent applications in the United States, at least 85 percent, ultimately result in an issued patent (Lemley and Shapiro 2005: 79). Only a small percentage of the patents turn out to be of economic value and even smaller proportion are enforced or reach litigation. On average only 1.5 percent of all patents are ever litigated and only 0.1 percent are litigated to trial (although the litigation rate is 6 percent in biotechnology). Out of the patents litigated to a final determination (appeal, trial or summary judgment), 46 percent are held invalid (Lemley and Shapiro 2005: 80). In this sense, patents are a mixture of a property right and a lottery. Inventors who are uncertain of the value of their ideas ex ante file to patent many of them, knowing that most of the resulting patents will turn out to be worthless but hoping that a few of the resulting patents will generate large profits. In fact, research shows that the expected value of many individual patents is small. Industry participants do not consider patents an effective appropriation mechanism. Patents are even considered inferior to other methods, such as lead time, learning curve advantages and even secrecy (Cohen, Nelson and Walsh 2000; Levin, Klevorick, Nelson and Winter 1987: 793–802).

In addition, the costs involved in registration are huge in proportion to the actual usage of the vast majority of registered patents; these costs might actually outweigh the value of patents. Wagner and Parchomovsky (2005) estimated that the cost of filing a patent application with the PTO in the US, including attorney, filing, issue and renewal fees, is between \$10,000 and \$30,000. The average cost of patent litigation is \$799,000 for each party through the end of discovery, and \$1,503,000 through the end of trial and appeal. The estimates reported by WIPO in 2010 are even higher, quoting an average of about \$3 million per litigation (WIPO Magazine 2010). However, on the value side, empirical data shows that the value of a patent is low. A study from 1986 found that 90 percent of the patents in France, Germany and the UK have a value of less than $25,000 (Pakes 1986: 774). A more recent study from 1998 reinforced that conclusion. In this study it was estimated that the average pharmaceutical patent value is $4,313. It is $4,969 for chemical patents, $15,120 for mechanical patents and $19,837 for electronics patents (Schankerman 1998). Despite the high private cost of patent protection and the relatively low expected value of individual patents an empirical study of patenting records in the US has shown that the number of records has steadily increased since the 1890s in all the technological sectors, with an exception over the period of the Second World War (Andersen 2004).[16] A report made by WIPO in 2007 shows statistics on worldwide patent activity. According to the report, about 1,660,000 patent applications were filed worldwide in 2005, which is an increase of 7 percent over 2004. The largest recipients of patent filing are the patent offices of Japan and the United States (WIPO Patent Report 2007). What can be the explanation for this growth? Arguably, patents are serving an important function of attracting investments. Clarissa Long (2002: 627–37) asserted that the prime value of patent rights is in their function as credible signals. The patents are used to convey credible information about the invention and the inventors to those she calls observers, ie the non-owners. The signals are necessary since otherwise the observers will probably not invest in gathering that information themselves. In this sense the value of the patents is the reduction of the informational asymmetries between patentees and third parties.

It seems, therefore, that filing for patents is serving functions other than securing incentives to create or invest. Indeed, patents are being used strategically, often in aggregation, in order to defend against hostile acquisitions and patent wars, to prevent competitors from entering a market, and to maintain a strategic market lead. A striking example relates to the smartphone market. Patents here are not invoked to fight against pirated copies of smartphone but instead are employed as a strategic asset to enable manufacturers to push competitors out of the market. The use of lawsuits and threatening letters in the race for dominating the smartphone market demonstrates the strategic power of patents. A notable statement that exemplifies these patent wars is the allegation of the late Steve Jobs: ‘I will spend my last dying breath if I need to, and I will spend every penny of Apple’s $40 billion in the bank, to right this wrong. I’m going to destroy Android, because it’s a stolen product. I’m willing to go thermonuclear war on this’ (*The Guardian* 21 October 2011). The

16 Once issued, a patent can remain in force, in most legal systems, for 20 years after the patent application was originally filed. To keep a patent in force for the full duration, the patent holder must pay certain maintenance fees after a certain period. Between 55% and 67% of issued US patents lapse before the 20 year period for failure to pay the maintenance fees. Nearly half of US patents do not even reach the 10 year mark, and two-thirds lapse before the full 20 year statutory protection term, since most inventors opt not to pay the required renewal fee (Cornelli and Schankerman 1999). This indicates that many patents are of little value to their owners.

purchase of Motorola Mobile by Google, in August 2011, for the record price of US$12.5 billion, demonstrated the extent to which patent wars have grown to dominate the technological scene. Motorola Mobile owned about 17,000 patents in smartphone technology. Experts believe that any smartphone involves about 250,000 patent claims, some of which are likely to be overlapping (*The New York Times* 16 August 2011). The patents of Motorola Mobile did not include any particular invention which was a must for building a mobile phone or any of its components. In fact, Google actually managed to develop its operating system for its smartphone – the Android – without a need for any of these patents. Yet, the purchase of Motorola Mobile and its patent portfolio, was intended to assist Google in facing the strategic threat posed by an alliance of its competitors, including Apple and Microsoft, who had teamed up a few months earlier to purchase 6,000 wireless patents owned by Nortel.

Out of the 1,900 patent lawsuits filed in the US by the middle of 2011, 270 pertained to mobile phones (Stanford News Center 2011). Among the key players in the smartphone market, everyone is suing everyone else. Google Android is attracting many lawsuits. When Motorola Mobile was purchased by Google there were over 40 lawsuits for patent infringement related to Google's Android. Google is a deep pocket, but the lawsuits brought by key mobile manufacturers, such as Apple, are intended to prevent Google from entering the mobile phone and tablet markets. Competition with Google is particularly difficult in this market, as Google is an online service provider, selling search and advertising services. It does not sell its operating system and the Android, which is an open source software, is often distributed for free (Android Open Source Project). Using a patent to stop Google from distributing the Android could prove to be very effective.

A patent is often described as merely a 'license to sue', and purchasing patent portfolios provides the ammunition for a patent war. It could serve as an offensive measure to chill a competitor from entering the market. It could also be used for a defensive strategy, when patent holders can lower their risk of litigation by threatening potential claimants with a counter patent lawsuit. The risk of litigation provides incentives to expand the patent portfolio and can sometimes lead to a patent thicket. Providing incentives via the *exclusive right to exclude* creates the risk of anti-competitive behavior. The power of the right-holder to get an injunction could prove very effective in stopping competitors from entering a market. Yet, the patent wars described above do not necessarily generate incentives for innovation. In fact such use of patents shifts large resources from R&D to handling litigation and reducing the risk of litigation, thus imposing a tax on innovation (Lloyd, Spielthenner and Mokdsi 2011).[17]

17 It should be noted that the costs of managing patents litigation is enormous – the average patent litigation costs about $3 million, and lasts about two years. An appeal can add another $2 million and one year to that estimate (Managing Intellectual Property 2009; *WIPO Magazine* 2010).

The most extreme example of strategic use of IPR is connected to the rise of 'patent trolls', or what is often referred to as non-practicing entities (NPEs), which buy up patents not for manufacturing the invention but simply for bringing up lawsuits (*Tex. Data Co., L.L.C. v. Target Brands, Inc.*, 2011). The NPEs never practice their patents – leaving them immune to a counterclaim for patent infringement. Those entities usually do not suffer any direct harm, in spite of the infringement of the patent, and they bring litigation purely for personal gain (*Forest Group, Inc. v. Bon Tool Co.*, 2009). Nevertheless, these entities own a legitimate property right – the patent – that they are seeking to enforce. The courts have not found a way to distinguish these entities and to apply different rules regarding their conduct (*Tex. Data Co., L.L.C. v. Target Brands, Inc.*, 2011). There are many types of NPEs – failed companies, universities and even individuals. Many NPEs are in business simply to accumulate patents (Risch 2012).

In a 2004 case involving Intel, a patent licencing company purchased a patent for $50,000 and then sought $7 billion from Intel for alleged infringement by the company's Pentium II semiconductor. Although the court dismissed the case, Intel was forced to pay $3 million in legal fees (Landers 2006). NTP, another non-practicing entity, filed a lawsuit against RIM, the Canadian manufacturer of Blackberry, for a patent infringement of cellular email. The parties settled for US$612.5 million, even though the US Patent Office invalidated most of NTP's patents in a later procedure (CNN Money 3 March 2006).

Patent trolls are very controversial. Some argue that they actually generate incentives for R&D by purchasing patents of small inventors, who cannot undertake an expensive patent litigation, and enabling them to profit from their inventions. Furthermore, it is argued that patent trolls help to create an efficient market for patents, by making them more available and by 'clearing' the market. Instead of manufacturing a product based on the invention or licencing the patent, the patentee can sell his patent rights to a patent troll for cash. Through this practice patent trolls increase the availability of patents and make them more marketable. Patent trolls, it is argued, help making the market more efficient, by becoming intermediaries, who match multiple buyers and sellers. So, in a search of a manufacturer for a certain technology, there is no need to contact many inventors or patentees, but only the patent trolls that specialize in that certain technology. Patent trolls may thus prevent, or at least minimize, the potential information gaps between the parties (Shrestha 2010).

Others argue that patent trolls increase the risk of litigation and increase the cost of innovation by imposing high legal costs on the developers. In addition, patent trolls extract high licencing fees from patentees and manufacturers (such as in the NTP case). These high licencing fees are increasing the costs of the products as they are rolled over to the consumers. The critics also argue that patent trolls increase 'patent thickets problems', i.e. they increase the likelihood of negotiation failure in cross-licencing agreements leading to higher prices of the products (Shrestha 2010).

Another common strategy adopted by patent owners is patent pools. A patent pool is a cooperative agreement between several patent owners to bundle the sale of their respective licenses (Dequiedt and Versaevel 2007). Despite the pool's anti-competitive characteristics, competition authorities have recognized the virtues of such an agreement – reducing transaction costs, avoiding costly infringement litigation and so on, and therefore tend to approve them. Examples of such patent pools are the DVD-Video, DVD-ROM and the MPEG-2 Digital Video. Dequiedt and Versaevel explain that there are two perspectives for patent pools: ex ante and ex post. It is unrealistic, they argue, to consider that firms first invest in risky R&D and in case of a success consider forming a pool with other patent holders. Therefore, they examine the ex ante perspective. By looking at the different considerations of incentives, Dequiedt and Versaevel propose a dynamic model for innovation and the formation of a patent pool, balancing, inter alia, the size of the pool and value of participating.

A possible economic theory explanation for filing for patents despite the negative cost-benefit calculus is behavior under risk. Patents are essentially lottery tickets. Unlike gambling, though, filing for patents manifests a risk-averse attitude in a similar way to buying insurance. However, unlike insurance, big companies who file for many patents and win from time to time, can set the price of the winning patent in such a way that it covers all the expenses of the vast majority of unsuccessful patents. In other words, the costs are shifted to the consumers. Pooling is a mechanism to decrease the risk even further. According to this defensive theory the acquisition of patents is a kind of an arms race. In addition, competing firms use patents as bargaining chips to negotiate with competitors and to secure certain niches in the marketplace. The assumption in the base of this theory is that courts enforce the patent rights harshly, and hence the possibility of patent litigation threats towards competing firms (Hall and Ziedonis 2001: 105–107).

The differences between copyright and patent are the consequence of the significant costs involved in obtaining patent protection, while copyright is granted automatically with no cost at all. However, the effects of granting IP rights in both realms are similar. The inter-relations between patents and copyright, on the one hand, and incentives to create, on the other hand, remain very vague, and it seems that the effects of granting patents and gaining copyright go beyond the immediate protected creation or innovation. The ultimate contemporary example of how IPR (of all kinds) are used as a means to control the market and generate monopoly power that can be used to leverage further monopoly power is Microsoft, which has leveraged its monopoly power in operating systems to obtain a dominant position in applications such as word processing and Internet browsers (Stiglitz 2008: 1702).

To sum up, intellectual property laws have turned out to be a major tool for expanding market power, reducing competition and concentrating control over production and distribution of information, far beyond the deadweight loss involved in the monopoly they create for the particular information protected by IPR.

### *3.3.1.3 Transaction cost and administrative cost*

A third point of criticism against IPR as the optimal mechanism to secure incentives relates to transaction costs. We have already discussed in the previous section the administrative cost of maintaining a patent system – registration and litigation – which are estimated to outweigh the total value of patents. But the high transaction costs invoked by IPR are not limited to rights, which require registration, such as patents. High transaction costs are inherent to any IPR as it generates incentives by requiring prior consent in a form of a license for every use. An unlicenced use would be subject to injunction. The increasing transaction costs of both obtaining IPR and licencing them have raised the cost of content and inventions, which are essential for any further creation, thus creating impediments on generating new works and innovations. The cost associated with licensing inventions and copyrighted materials has increased exponentially in recent years as the intellectual proprietary regime is covering more and more informational works and affords protection to types of works, or new aspects of works, that used to be in the public domain.

For instance, copyright and neighboring rights today cover facts and mere data (e.g. Directive 95/46/EC in the EU). The bundle of rights defined by copyright was expanded in recent years to cover a wider range of uses, for example, the right to prevent unauthorized access to works in digital format, a right to control digital distribution and all of this for an extended duration. Some characteristics of the digital environment also mean that informational works are less available. For instance, overlapping rights held by different rightholders make it more costly to secure a license to use a copyrighted work (Lemley 1997). Overall, expansive copyrights, supplemented by extra protection under other bodies of law, such as anti-circumvention legislation,[18] create new barriers to accessing pre-existing materials.

Licencing is becoming more expensive not only for users but also for the rightholders. It may require legal counseling regarding the scope of IP protection, a profound understanding of the scope of legal rights and the authorized uses (e.g. the meaning of *fair use* under US copyright law, or *non-commercial use* under creative commons licenses) and familiarity with the legal language used to describe them. Rightholders often need a lawyer

18 Anti-circumvention legislation (e.g. 17 U.S.C. §1201) protects digital rights management (DRM) systems which govern the use of copyrighted works and physically limit access and usage even for information not entitled directly to copyright protection or for which such protection has expired. We will elaborate on this legislation in Chapter 6.

to manage their IP rights. They are more likely to incur the cost of licencing when they expect to benefit, ie when they intend to licence the work or the invention for commercial use. They may be reluctant, however, to incur the high cost of licencing for non-commercial uses. Consequently, licencing costs may prevent the use of works that would otherwise become available, thus impeding access and subsequent creation and innovation. The high transaction costs associated with the IP system, therefore, not only reduce the level of desirable uses, but also have an increasingly unequal distributive effect. Licenses are more affordable and accessible to businesses, which can roll over the cost to consumers. It creates a more notable chilling effect on creation by individuals and small businesses. This inequality is likely to have far-reaching ramifications on the nature of innovation and the future of culture.

The chilling effect of transaction costs involved in licencing is particularly evident in the online environment with the increasing power of individuals to generate and mass distribute content and the subsequent rise of user-generated content. Since IPR require prior permission, any person who wishes to make use of a pre-existing work must first acquire an appropriate – and often costly – license. The user must determine which license is necessary, identify the different copyright owners, negotiate a license to use the work and pay the license fee. The high cost involved in licencing could create barriers that make it difficult for users to participate in generating content. This is especially so when the costs are higher than the anticipated benefits from the use of the work. In such cases, the transaction costs of licencing could prevent a use that might otherwise be beneficial.

Indeed, the legal mechanism of prior consent was tailored to serve the interests of industries and business. Industries producing mass content are relatively new and were significantly strengthened during the 20th century (Benjamin 1968: 217–52). The mass production of content involved generating a single prototype, orchestrated by the content industry, and the production and distribution of copies to the masses. Copyright law, which was designed to serve the needs of the culture industry, may carry different consequences when exercised by users or authors. While the content industry could handle the costs of licencing, these costs present a problem for amateur creators both as potential licensors and as potential licensees. As licensors, they often lack the legal knowledge required for designing a licensing strategy. As licensees, amateur users also face difficulties: on the one hand, they have a greater capability for actively transforming pre-existing works, which may require more licenses. On the other hand, they often lack the legal training, organizational support, or financial funds necessary for acquiring such licenses. The lack of a fee structure makes it especially difficult to cover the cost involved in acquiring a license. Simply avoiding copyright infringement, therefore, becomes a major challenge for amateur creators, and the risk of liability erects new barriers to creative and collaborative activities in the UGC environment.

The increasing propertization and IP-involved transaction costs were the main forces motivating several movements that try to bypass the rigid IPR system. Notable examples are the free software movement and creative commons. Free software is an innovative legal framework based on contracts, which is intended to address the impediments on access created by intellectual property. Free software is protected by copyright, but is subject to a license called the general public license (GPL). The GPL basically authorizes the unlimited copying, redistribution and modification of the software. The license is a 'viral contract', meaning it applies to future users in an attempt to make whole commitments run with this digital code (Radin 2000). It includes a viral provision requiring that any derivative work that contains free software or derivatives from it will be subject to the same license. GPL annuls the need for license fees and the burden of negotiating a license. This subversive use of copyright law does not utilize the proprietary regime for generating 'incentives' (or rather profits), but for creating an alternative non-proprietary regime, often referred to as 'copyleft'. Creative commons applies the same principles to a much broader range of informational creations. This initiative offers an infrastructure, legal and technological, that arguably could overcome the impediments to accessing creative works, for the purpose of reducing the chilling effect on creativity caused by the high cost of licencing. The automated licencing platform allows authors to retain copyright in their respective works, and authorize as many uses of the work as they choose. The hope is that such a mechanism would make it easier for rightholders to share their works under more generous terms. Yet, in contrast to the GPL, creative commons' licencing schemes include a wide variety of licenses. Every license that goes beyond absolute exclusion qualitfies for promoting, sharing and reuse of copyrighted material.

From a law and economics perspective, the emergence of these private ordering regimes to bypass the impediments created by IPR can be analysed in the framework of the 1960 Coase theorem. This path-breaking theorem demonstrated how inefficient legal rules would be bypassed by individuals achieving efficient allocation of entitlements, but this will happen only when there are no transaction costs. The Internet and related technologies are dramatically reducing transaction costs (Elkin-Koren and Salzberger 2004: ch 7) and therefore enabling parties to bargain in the shadow of inefficient IP laws. Those recent developments can therefore be explained not only in terms of altruistic behavior and political agenda but also in terms of traditional economic theory. Nevertheless, they point to the inefficiency of the current IPR regime.

#### *3.3.1.4 The optimal pace of progress – conceptual and practical problems*

A final point of criticism against IPR as an incentives-generating mechanism is more philosophical and is linked to a broader critique of the economic methodology. It has to do with the inability to determine what is the desirable or optimal level of creation or innovation incentives ought to aim at and, consequently, the inability to determine the exact scope of IPR necessary to achieve this optimum. There is no doubt that as a result of extending IPR we are witnessing a vast expansion of the entertainment industry, as well as high tech related industries. Without this expansion we might not have had some of the mega production Hollywood movies: Avatar, for instance. But do these movies really represent efficient levels of informational and artistic production? Are they comparable to great artistic masterpieces that were created under the much more limited copyright regime or prior to copyright protection? Equivalents can be drawn to patents motivated industries and the enormous number of new gadgets, which last in our lives for an ever shorter period because the legal regime and IPR incentivize us to replace them with new ones. The same questions can even be asked with regard to the pharmaceutical industry, which, generally speaking, is geared to a worthy and important cause – improving our health. But it can be argued that it produces many insignificant products, motivated by generating profits from intellectual property. The incentives paradigm assumes that more creation is better for the world. It stands for *more* works and it seems that the economic analysis is indifferent to the quality of the innovations. Extension of the IPR might increase the quantity of creations and innovations, but might not affect its overall quality (Birnhack 2006).

The current regime of intellectual property generates wealth. As we indicated in Chapter 1, the value of intellectual property today outweighs the value of physical property. But one can draw parallels between intellectual property and the artificial and imaginary financial instruments that were the prime causes for the global economic crises of 2008–2009. The wealth generated by intellectual property can be portrayed as a bubble, which might be the source for future global economic crises.

As a growing number of patents are filed over trivial inventions, for no economic reason, except for defensive purposes, the IP system represents a waste. It is detracting resources from R&D and increases the spending on litigation and licensing. The wealth created by the current IP regime also highlights in full force the indirect connection between wealth and wellbeing or utility. A society which is forced to go through too rapid technological and indeed also cultural changes might not be a happier society than a society with a slower pace of change – progress. The fact that the average income today in the OECD countries is 10 times greater than the average income 100 years ago does not mean that people today are 10 times better-off than they were more than a century ago.

When central intervention is called upon to create incentives to create, a normative goal of how much creation and innovation are desirable has to be set and positive laws that are tailored to achieve these goals has to be legislated. Economic analysis has not yet produced a rigorous model of both the desirable pace of innovation and creation and the exact rights to achieve these goals.

The significant disadvantages of IPR as a mechanism to generate incentives for creation begs an inquiry as to other potential legal tools that can better function within the general framework of the incentives paradigm. This will be the theme of the next section.

### *3.3.2 Alternative forms of incentives*

Central intervention to correct a public good failure in the market of informational goods can take many forms other than intellectual property rights. The canonic law and economic literature has not yet taken these alternatives seriously, assuming that IPR is the best mechanism to generate efficient incentives. Furthermore, it has not recognized the fact that when other forms of central intervention do exist side by side with IPR there might be overlapping incentives and the justification for granting intellectual property rights may diminish.

The alternative mechanisms for generating incentives can be divided into two categories: one is substituting incentives by public funding and the other is generating incentives by private law. Public funding itself may take several forms. Governments may opt to produce informational goods themselves, or sponsor research and development activities by funding research institutions, universities and cultural institutions. Public funding can be also arranged by offering governmental research grants for specific projects initiated and performed by the public or the private sector or indeed called for by the government. While IPR is an ex post reward system, generating incentives by promising a financial reward to a commercially successful invention, the public funding is usually ex ante, offering funding to research and development projects upfront.

But public funding could also be designed as an ex post prize system. In recent years there have been some elaborate proposals for an alternative mechanism to generate incentives. One example is the prize system advocated by Abramowicz (2004). His proposal considers a variety of design issues, such as delayed versus immediate payouts, funds versus open-ended programs, and tradable versus non-tradable rewards. The essence of Abramowicz's proposal is that the prize system will be based on delay: instead of distributing the money to the claimants shortly after they file a request, the money should remain in an investment account and, only after a few years or perhaps a decade later, the government will release it to the claimants. The delay provides a more meaningful measure on the inventions' significance, exposes potential flaws and errors and subjects them to the test of time. In addition, the delay in distributing the rewards will continue to incentivize patent holders and innovators. In this way, the right owners will continue to invest in commercializing and promoting their products to receive the reward. Such a mechanism will further encourage researchers to release research results. This will invigorate research activities that might produce social benefit, and will reduce the deadweight loss problem. In this context, the delay prevents a natural monopolist from obtaining a patent reward while still charging monopoly prices.

A similar suggestion tailored specifically to the pharmaceutical industry was put forward by Hollis (2005a), who characterizes the pharmaceutical market as dysfunctional and advocates for an ex post central payment based on the incremental therapeutic benefits of the product.[19]

Private law may also facilitate incentives, by a variety of legal rules other than proprietary. Liability rules may offer a possible remedy to the public goods market failure in information and ideas. Calabresi and Melamed (1972) highlighted the distinction between the question of whether to allocate an entitlement and to whom, and the separate question as to the desirable method of its protection. In the information goods context the need to grant incentives is equivalent to the question of whether to allocate an entitlement, while the form of creating incentives is equivalent to the method of protection. With regard to the latter, Calabresi and Melamed set up the framework for choosing between property and liability rules. The choice, according to their model, should depend on the structure of transaction costs. The entitlement to your own ideas (either as a first order justification or a second order one) can be protected by property rules that prohibit others from making use of these ideas, or by liability rules that do not ban such usage, but entitle the creator to compensation.

Which of the two remedies is more desirable? According to Calabresi and Melamed, property rules should be preferred when negotiation costs are lower than the administrative costs of an enforcement agency or a court determining the value of the entitlement. In such a case, central intervention ought to be minimal as, following the construction of the legal rule, the parties are likely to negotiate for the efficient end-result, adhering to or bypassing the initial allocation of the entitlement. By choosing a property rule, entitlements will change hands through a voluntary exchange in the market, where the government's sole function will be to prevent bypassing of the market through injunctions and criminal law. Liability rules ought to be preferred when the cost of establishing the value of an initial entitlement by negotiation is higher than that of determining this value by an enforcement mechanism. In addition, liability rules might be preferred in order to avoid bargaining costs. Lack of information or uncertainty as to the most effective avoider of costs is likely to point us, according to Calabresi and Melamed, in the direction of the liability rule as well. Liability rules involve additional central intervention by a state organ deciding on the objective value of the entitlement. In this

19 Recently, David Leonhardt, a journalist at *The New York Times*, published an article calling for the return of prizes as a reward system for innovation (Leonhardt 2007). He reminds us that in the 18th century prizes were a common way to reward innovation but nowadays they are replaced by grants that reward money upfront. The worthless merit of grants is that they are easier to be monitored by government bureaucrats. Leonhardt argues that grants are a failure and his bold example is that governments all around the world have handed out grants and subsidies for finding various alternative energy sources but that nobody has ever found such a source. Leonhardt therefore suggests a return to the prize system.

case, if the creator has the entitlement, she has the right to be compensated, but she cannot prohibit others from using it.

One of the features of information and ideas is the uncertainty as to their value and their possible changing value over time. Granting property rights in informational goods means that speculators can make a fortune by purchasing them for modest prices and then enjoying huge profits on their future market value. If this is the case, the property rule does not achieve at all its purpose of providing sufficient (but not more than that) incentives for creation. In addition, unlike tangibles, the apparatus of registering IP rights (patents, trade marks, designs etc) involves significant transaction costs and when registration is not required, as is the case of copyright, it is sometimes very difficult to locate the owners of IP. The costs of trading copyright might be very high as, for example, is illustrated by Lessig (2004: 100–107), when he discusses the process of clearing rights before engaging in an artistic creation based on various previous creations. Informational goods, as we have mentioned, are non-rivalrous, and this means that granting monopolistic property rights over them is less efficient than enabling everyone to use them, subject to appropriate compensation paid ex post. Liability rules can, therefore, offer an interesting alternative to traditional intellectual property rights. Applying liability rules is likely to enhance the public domain, because those who want to use the liability protected entitlements cannot be prohibited; they just have to pay for the usage.

Caroline Nguyen (2004) goes even further in her suggestion of a *compensated IP proposal*. In her opinion the current IP system is over-incentivizing. The circumstances of artificially high prices and low supply create significant monopolistic deadweight loss and generate unintended consequences that undermine social progress. Nguyen's suggestion of the *compensated IP proposal*, in contrast: '. . . retains financial incentives for producers but lowers them to a merely sufficient level, transferring much producer surplus to consumers. The Compensated IP Proposal contains two components: creators of intellectual products receive cost-based compensation from the government for their products and in exchange their products immediately are granted to society for unrestricted use. Inventors retain all public credit and recognition for their work. This system would alleviate desert-based objections to current IP practices while satisfying utilitarian calls for financial incentives to encourage research and development' (Nguyen 2004: 115).

When discussing liability rules, Calabresi and Melamed referred to compensation calculated in terms of the losses for the entitlement holder (damages), but their framework of analysis can also include compensation on the bases of the gains made by the party who used the entitlement. The legal framework for this possible approach is unjust enrichment or restitution law, which may suit better the application of their model to the analysis of entitlements in information (Elkin-Koren and Salzberger 2000). Such a regime, in which the entitlement holder would not be entitled to prevent usage by others but rather will be entitled to the gains made by others using the entitlement, eliminates the monopolistic effects of IPR, enables much wider usage of the information and thus might be more efficient than the traditional regime of IP. Since in any case the enforcement of IPR through legal proceedings is much more costly than the enforcement of property rights in tangibles and real estate, the additional costs in administrating such an alternative regime, if any, might be negligible in relation to the gains from such a system.

Each of these alternative remedies has advantages and disadvantages. For example, on the one hand, direct government production or funding of creation, and to a lesser degree a prize system, has the dangers of a hidden or explicit political agenda or, more broadly, a danger from the vantage point of democratic and liberal values. On the other hand, direct subsidies of government for creation activities, instead of granting IP rights, will diminish monopolistic powers of IPR holders and will result in a greater public domain, which enhances the sources for future creations. In addition, IP rights have the danger of limiting production means and can create a backfiring effect, constraining the frontiers of intellectual production. One can also argue that IPR have no less dangers from a liberal and democratic theory perspective, by enhancing the powers of mega corporations that replace democratically elected officials in dictating to us what information is available and, in fact, dictating to us the way we conduct our lives. Stiglitz (2008) compared IPR with grants and prizes and argues that the latter have the advantages of lower transaction costs, lower risks, a less distorted incentives structure, a less distorted finance structure and much better dissemination incentives (the result of the fact that grants and prizes do not generate monopolistic powers), while the only advantage of an IPR system (although a significant one) is the less distorted selection process.

It seems that law and economics scholars prefer IP rights to government's own creation activities or subsidies, grants and prizes, because the former is thought to facilitate trade in markets and therefore the value of informational goods is determined by market forces. If no free market activity in ideas and creations occurs, how will we be able to determine how much creation to finance? How many subsidies to grant and to whom? However, this is not such a trivial issue. First, in order for IP to be traded in competitive markets there is a need for an initial central intervention to define those rights in the first place – scope, duration etc. This definition itself is not a result of free market activity, and of course it will have a decisive impact on the future market outcome regarding the actual objects of the rights. Second, the IP regime creates monopolistic powers and thus the real market value of protected creations cannot be detected by the sheer operation of the market. Third, IPR constitute a problematic finance structure in the sense that they create a benefit tax system, meaning that, for example, sick people have to finance the information which is the basis for their medication (Stiglitz 2008). Fourth, giving inventors control over all the positive externalities associated with their inventions encompasses control over improvements and new uses that might be made of their works. As a result, there will be fewer incentives for future improvers to invest in developing the first generation technology, ie the original invention. Competition on improving the first generation technology will be stifled (Lemley 2005: 1060–62).

Moreover, granting subsidies, grants or prizes for creation can be conducted on the bases of competitive variables and the actual products and services resulting from these subsidies will be traded according to their marginal prices in markets and therefore will generate much more competition than the trading of IP protected products and services, which are monopolized by their holders. Indeed, most basic research is funded with no direct connection to its predicted market value and patents usually do not cover it. Nevertheless, we have witnessed in recent decades increasing attempts by research institutions to commodify their research products, which of course lead to the shrinkage of the public domain, as well as to redirecting research efforts from basic research to more applied research. As will be explained below, this sort of patent extension cannot be easily justified by candid economic analysis.

It is important to emphasize that from a law and economics perspective not only that an ex ante grant system and an ex post prize system are substitutes for each other but that they are both substitutes for an IP regime and central production. In other words, incentives to invent and create can be formed by either an IP regime or by a grant or prize system and to have both regimes might be inefficient, or at least the scope of IP rights to those who can enjoy prizes and grants should be different from the scope of IP rights for those who are not entitled to compete for them. It should be emphasized that this point is different from the question of whether it is justified at all to provide incentives for government funded research institutions who might not suffer from the public good failure of the market in the first place. The fact that universities in recent years rank very high in the statistics of patent applications and patent revenues is inconsistent with economic analysis. Government funded research and information production should not enjoy the same IP protection as private enterprises – individuals or firms, because they already enjoy monetary incentives through direct government funding for the creative activity.

### *3.3.3 Tailoring intellectual property rights*

Our discussion has so far relied on a homogenized concept of intellectual property – a mechanism of exclusive rights meant to generate incentives to create, limited in time and scope in order to enable the widest distribution of these non-rivalrous commodities. The last crucial stage of the analysis is the most acute one vis-à-vis the actual legal regime and it is also the least developed within the law and economics literature – what is the optimal duration of intellectual property rights? What is the optimal set of exceptions? Does the traditional distinction between the various types of intellectual property make sense? This section briefly discusses these issues within the law and economics framework. We first address the traditional categorization of different IPR, and then examine whether a uniform duration and list of exceptions within each category of IP is optimal.

### *3.3.3.1 Incentives and different forms of intellectual property*

As we noted in Chapter 2, the term *intellectual property* is relatively new and it has brought under one roof very different issues ranging from rights of authors to protect the integrity of their works, through the right of pharmaceutical companies to prevent competing manufacturing of their drugs, to the rights of celebrities to prevent the presentation of their photos. We discussed some theoretical differences between the two most important forms of IP – copyright and patent, which are mainly related to the distinct different organizational forms of creation processes. These result in differences in the legal regime, primarily the requirement of registration and its effects. Let us try to approach the issue from the other end, examining whether the traditional distinction between different forms of IP makes sense vis-à-vis law and economics.[20] We believe that the historical distinction between copyright, patents, designs, trademarks, trade secrets and other particular types of IP rights, is not so clear-cut when being applied to the rapidly changing real world, although this categorization has significant implications on the incentives generated, the wealth created and its distribution. It is not clear whether this traditional division and categorization is sufficient and suits our times, especially vis-à-vis the major insights of the incentives paradigm.

Let us consider software, for instance. As eloquently demonstrated by Samuelson et al. (1994), although a computer program is a text, which in itself can be valuable, the most valuable aspect of software lies in two other elements: behavior and industrial design. In other words, the value of a computer program is in the set of results which materialize when program instructions are executed in the framework of industrial design responsible for producing behavior and conceptual metaphors that gives this behavior coherence. These elements are often expensive to develop and inexpensive to copy, because the know-how necessary to construct the functionality of the software is reflected at the end product sold in the marketplace. Thus, competition from copiers has the potential of destroying the incentives to develop the program in the first place. Furthermore, complex software products are constructed from the combination of elementary modules into a global architecture. This evolution makes the distinction between private and public property much more vague.

20 It is noteworthy, however, that in the 18th century when copyright and patents were considered royal privileges rather than property rights there was no real distinction between creative expression and innovation (Carroll 2004).

None of the existing legal regimes offer adequate protection (Samuelson et al. 1994). While software can be treated in principle as an object for copyright, it can also be regarded as an object for a trade secret and for patent, incurring a totally different legal regime (ie requirement of registration, scope of protection time span of the property right and possible exceptions). Trade secret law does not protect behavior or other know-how borne on the face of a mass-marketed software product because such know-how cannot be kept a secret. Even if the necessary know-how is not evident on the surface, trade secret law has long regarded reverse engineering of products available in the marketplace as a fair means of acquiring the secrets.

Patent law also fails to provide adequate protection for the valuable aspects of a computer program. Patents are typically granted for particular methods of achieving results, rather than for the results themselves and therefore could not prevent the use of another method for achieving these same results. Furthermore, the innovations of functional program behaviors, user interfaces and the industrial design of programs that produce behaviors, are typically of an incremental type. Protecting such incremental innovations program behavior through patent law would thwart the economic goals of the patent system: to grant exclusive rights only when an innovator has made a substantial contribution to the state of the art and advanced competition to a new level, as noted by Samuelson et al. (1994).

Copyright law does not provide adequate protection either. Copyright law clearly protects computer programs as text. Copyright does not protect the behavior of physical machines brought about by the execution of program instructions (see also Samuelson et al. 1994: 2316–57).

In a recent report about patents and competition (FTC Report 2003), the American FTC acknowledged the differences between patents in the pharmaceuticals and biotechnology industries, on the one hand, and in the software and hardware industries, on the other. In the pharmaceutical and biotechnology industries it was found that one firm's questionable patent might lead its competitor to forgo R&D in the areas that the patent improperly covers. Such effects deter market entry and follow-on innovation by competitors and increase the potential powers of the holder of a questionable patent to suppress competition. According to industry representatives, innovation in the pharmaceutical and biotechnology industries is costly and unpredictable. Patents allow the firm to prevent its rival firms from free-riding on discoveries, and hence to recoup the substantial capital investments made to discover, test and obtain regulatory approval of new potential drug products.

By contrast, in the software and hardware industries, as acknowledged by its representatives, competition to develop more advanced technologies is what drives innovation in this rapidly changing industry. The innovation process in the software and hardware industries is significantly less costly than in the pharmaceutical and biotech industries, and the product life cycle is generally much shorter. In addition, computer hardware manufacturers would rather keep the invention secret than publicly disclose it in a patent application and risk third party misappropriation of patent rights that they will be unable to discover. Thus, in the software industry firms obtain patents for rather defensive purposes. Firms may sometimes require access to a large number of patents to produce a single commercial product. Many of these patents overlap, with each patent blocking several others. This tends to create a 'patent thicket' that is a dense web of overlapping intellectual property rights. Much of this thicket of overlapping patent rights result from the nature of the technology. Computer hardware and software contain an incredibly large number of incremental innovations. The firms seek more and more patents in order to increase their bargaining power while attempting to access others' overlapping patents and commercialize their desired technology (FTC Report 2003: 110–65). None of the existing legal regimes, therefore, is well suited to tackle the increasing role and the growing markets of software.

The software example demonstrates that different intellectual property rights work differently with regard to incentives to create and also that the same type of IP right works differently in a variety of creation contexts. Thus, the application of the general incentives rationale to different sectors is certainly not straightforward, and the variety may even frustrate the general rationale itself and is a potential for manipulation of the system, as well as for much higher transaction costs. A question arises, therefore, even under the assumption that IP rights are the optimal method to generate incentives to create and innovate, whether the traditional categorization of IP rights into patents, copyright etc is viable in the general framework of the incentives paradigm or that a better system is one with a single exclusive and uniform right (Dinwoodie 2008). The law and economics literature is yet to answer this question.

#### *3.3.2.2 Tailoring duration and scope of each intellectual property right*

A different approach to unification of all intellectual property rights into a single homogeneous one is tailoring different rights for different types of creative activities, either within the traditional categories of IPR (patents, copyright etc), or after discrediting the traditional categories of rights. Some de facto legal developments in this direction are the special regulation of plant patents, semiconductor chip masks and several other sui generis arrangements. In fact, the two strategies can even be integrated, by creating one single intellectual property right instead of patents, copyright etc, which will overcome the need to classify certain creative activity, such as developing computer software, into the traditional IP categories, but granting this right for different durations according to the area of creative activity.

Currently all patents are granted for a uniform period of 20 years after the application has been filed (with some differences between legal systems regarding the need to apply for extensions within this maximum period), while most copyright laws provide an exclusive right for 70 years after the death of the author. The most critical shortcoming of the incentives paradigm is the lack of any theoretical or empirical proof that 20 years for patents and life plus 70 years for copyright is exactly the optimal scope that balances the need to generate incentives, on the one hand, and the need to maximize usage of information, on the other hand. The recent extension of copyright in the USA from 50 to 70 years might serve as a good source for examining whether 50 or 70 years are the optimal duration, but so far the law and economics literature have not produced such studies.

Even if 20 years and life plus 70 years are the optimal duration on average for patents and copyright respectively, there are obviously social losses for those creative activities that require shorter exclusive rights and those which require longer terms to generate the optimal incentives. Some scholars have argued that the policy of one-size-fits-all is inefficient (Carroll 2006), especially in the patent realm (Burk and Lemley 2009; Bessen and Meurer 2008) where the cost for research and development vary significantly from one industry to another. It is asserted, for example, that the necessary investment in R&D in the pharmaceutical industry is much higher than that in the high-tech industry (Burk and Lemley 2003), implying very different optimal patent duration for the two industries. The fact that patent duration has not been changed as opposed to copyright might be the result of the conflicting interests within the patent protected industries and we will return to this insight in Chapter 7 dealing with positive economic analysis of intellectual property. But from a purely normative analysis point of view one has to acknowledge the cost of uniform rights and to ask whether tailoring IPR according to the field of creation might be a viable solution.

Michael Carroll (2010) suggested a framework to analyse this question, which comprises a cost benefit analysis of: (i) relaxing uniform rights; (ii) the administrability costs of such an exercise; and (iii) political economy costs, which are essentially the costs resulting from the gap between the optimal tailoring and the actual one. While tailoring IP rights decreases uniformity cost, it increases the costs likely to result from interest group activities aiming to get a better (extended) right for their particular activity (termed by Carroll 'political economy' cost). Although on a first look tailoring activity is also predicted to increase the administrative cost of tailoring (through legislation or regulation) and categorizing specific creations (by administrative and/or judicial bodies and accompanying lawyers' costs), Carroll asserts that a more specific and exact definition of rights might also decrease cost by substituting vague and thus costly terms as 'fair use' with more particular and precise rules.

While Carroll's framework seems to make sense, it is limited to the normative goal of efficiency in terms of wealth maximization and thus overlooks the distributional questions as well as the connections between wealth and wellbeing or utility, which are crucial in the context of intellectual property. This framework also overlooks many of the other points of criticism we discussed in this chapter, such as the optimal degree of progress, the implicit assumption of technology as an exogenous variable and the geographical and time units for the maximization (or cost-benefit) exercise. With the accelerating pace of technological change as opposed to the much slower pace of legal adaptation, tailoring IPR by law might prove to be a very problematic strategy. In addition, if tailoring is exercised on the basis of the current regime it is likely to result in more extensions of IPR than with curtailment of rights. But most important, this is a general framework the specifics of which rely on empirical data and information, which is very difficult to obtain in the domain of intellectual creation. In a similar way to the incentives paradigm as a whole, even if the principles are correct, their application to specific legal rules and rights is extremely shaky and, some will argue, arbitrary.

## 3.4 Conclusion

The incentives paradigm has been the main law and economics framework for the analysis of intellectual property. Its starting point is the identification of information as a public good, which implies a market failure. Free and competitive markets will not produce or will under-produce information because of its non-excludable nature. Thus, central intervention is required, and the optimal way for intervention, according to the incentives paradigm, is by the creation of intellectual property rights. However, informational goods as public goods are also non-rival, and this means that once these goods are produced, economic efficiency would seek for their maximized usage. This is the reason that intellectual property rights are limited in scope and time and contain various exemptions and exceptions, attempting to balance the conflicting forces of propertization.

In this chapter we have critically examined several premises of the incentives paradigm. We argued (and provided some evidence) that monetary incentives, intellectual property rights or others, are not always necessary to generate creation on the individual level and might even stifle creation. There are other in-built incentives to create, such as individual satisfaction and society's acknowledgement and respect. Lead times of creators and inventors, reputation, service and packaging, and network effects might also supply sufficient incentives to create, negating the need for IP rights. The incentives analysis is more complicated on the organizational level, but in such an analysis the structure of institutions cannot be taken as an exogenous variable because this structure itself is affected by the IP regime.

Subsequently, we examined the premise that IP rights provide the optimal incentives mechanism. One of its major shortcomings is that an IPR regime brings about a paradox: those creations that have substitutes will be priced at near free economic market price, so perhaps the IP protection is not needed for their creation in the first place. Granting IP rights to inventions that are really path-breaking, unique and essential will create monopolistic power of the creator and thus such inventions will not reach the wide population that has a real need for them. We showed, further, that rendering exclusivity in informational goods gives rightholders strategic advantages in informational markets and allows them to exercise control over informational goods far beyond the carefully defined list of rights and the economic purposes they were design to serve. Increasing transaction costs is an additional disadvantage of the IP regime. We discussed several alternative mechanisms to generate incentives and emphasized that IP rights are only one among various substitute mechanisms, which are not perceived as such by most policy-makers and the law and economics literature.

We also examined in this chapter several possible objects of incentives or different types of activities that require incentives and different groups that they serve: incentives to create versus incentives to disseminate and distribute, incentives to create versus incentives to disclose, and incentives to create and innovate versus incentives to improve. Each of these targets, activities and groups justifies a different form and scope of IP rights, in order to secure the desirable monetary incentives. In the next chapter we will show how the shift of the target of incentives has brought about a shift in the paradigmatic thinking about intellectual property.

We paid a special attention to new technologies, which generate new modes of production and distribution, questioning the suitability of the traditional IP regime to this changing environment. Since IP rights are meant to balance the two opposing characteristics of the public good nature of creations and innovations, it is striking that this balance, reflected by the term of IP rights, their scope and list of exceptions has not changed despite the technological revolution of the last decade. This applies also to the traditional division between different forms of IP rights – patent, copyright, designs etc.

The incentives paradigm has several common features with the 'tragedy of the commons' paradigm, which we discuss in the next chapter, but also several important differences. One of the differences is related to the normative-positive distinction within the law and economics movement. The incentives framework is a pure normative analysis, while the 'tragedy of the commons' emerged originally from a positive analysis. In this sense, the 'tragedy of the commons' framework for property rights can be presented as creating an inner equilibrium between positive and normative analyses. The incentives paradigm, because of its pure normative nature, has to be implemented by law-makers in order to be materialized. It is, therefore, exposed to manipulation by interests groups, social choice problems and other public choice obstacles, which we further discuss in Chapter 7. It is lacking an equilibrium between normative and positive analyses or, in other words, it cannot be forecasted that the desirable (optimal) solutions will indeed be implemented on the bases of the same fundamental assumptions of the law and economics framework, especially the assumption of rational, self-maximizing, behavior.

This point is especially important in the context of the debate about the current expansion of IP laws, or the commodification of things that in the past were not objects of intellectual property protection, and about the implications of such commodification on the public domain. While the supporters of IP extension and enlargement comprise a relatively small group of people, who are likely to be well organized because the costs of organization will be lower than the expected benefits from such organization, the supporters of a greater public domain encompass many individuals whose gains from organization is likely to be smaller than the immense organization costs, and thus their ability to influence the decision-makers will be much lower than that of the IP lobbies. The legislative results, therefore, are likely to reflect a bias (in terms of the optimal point according to the incentive analysis) towards the pro-IP camp, and thus distort boundaries between IP and the public domain. We will return to the positive analysis of IP laws in the last chapter of this book.

# 4 The proprietary model of intellectual property

In recent years we have witnessed within the law and economics literature the emergence of a new framework for the analysis of intellectual property, alternative to the incentives/public good paradigm on which we elaborated in Chapter 3. This new framework can be entitled the 'proprietary paradigm' of IPR. Rather than asking how to allocate resources for optimizing investments in creative and innovative activities, this approach focuses on the organizational function of IPR and the management of intangible assets once created. Consequently, this approach implicitly overlooks basic foundations of the incentives paradigm, the most important of which is the initial justification of allocating IPR. In other words, the new law and economics paradigm departs from the teleological normative justification for granting intellectual property rights in the first place – maximizing society's welfare, assuming the 'natural' right of a creator of information to own the creation. This version of the proprietary approach to IPR is constructed upon the economic justifications of real property, primarily the 'tragedy of the commons', which justifies property rights in land and tangibles.

This chapter begins by briefly describing the rise of the proprietary approach in the law and economics literature of intellectual property and introducing its main tenets (section 4.1). It then moves to discuss the 'tragedy of the commons', which is the oldest and major law and economic framework for the *positive* analysis of property in general, and land law in particular (section 4.2). We subsequently describe how this analytical framework was extended to explain intellectual property, and to offer a *normative* analysis and how it entrenched the view of law and economics scholars that any intellectual creation is to be considered as an object of property (section 4.3). We discuss some of the criticism raised against the proprietary approach, which applies property theory to informational works, and address the functional role of property rights in organizing the use of informational work, and whether property rights generate an adequate organizational framework for the new challenges posed by the information environment (section 4.4). Finally, we discuss briefly the application of the 'tragedy of the commons' theory to the positive analysis of intellectual property (section 4.5).

## 4.1 The rise of the proprietary approach in the law and economics literature of IPR

As elaborated in Chapter 2, the basic doctrines and positive laws relating to intangibles, such as copyright, patents, trademarks, designs, trade secrets have been crafted separately over the last millennium. These independent doctrines were not conceived as part of property law until they were grouped under a unified legal title of 'intellectual property' in the late 1960s. The new grouping under the title 'property' had an effect on the analysis of these legal rights and their justification. In 1998 the American Congress enacted the Copyright Term Extension Act, which extended copyright for an additional 20 years. This extension was granted not only to future creations but also to existing ones. The law could have not been justified by the incentives – public goods framework of analysis, as no incentives were needed for creation of already existing works. Many law and economics scholars supported this legislation and thus had to come up with a new justification or framework of analysis; hence the birth of the propriety paradigm of the economic analysis of IPR.

An early bird within this new paradigm was Edmund Kitch, who argued as early as 1977 in support of viewing a patent as a full property right. Kitch held that propertization of patents is essential to facilitate the efficient use of existing innovations rather than the creation of new works. His argument focused on managing investments in informational creations for further exploitation and improvement, implicitly assuming that the original creation was already made and merited property rights. We elaborate on this line of argument in section 4.3.

It took some 20 years for Kitch's argument to reappear in the context of the debate about the Sonny Bono Copyright Term Extension Act and its retroactive extension of copyright. Support for this legislation among several law and economics scholars and the shift from the incentives paradigm to the proprietary paradigm is best exemplified when we compare the 1989 work of two law and economics icons – William Landes and Richard Posner – who were among the pioneers to articulate the framework of the incentives paradigm, with their recent work (Landes and Posner 2003, 2003a). In their early work Landes and Posner portrayed copyrights (and by extension other types of IP) as a mechanism to enhance incentives to create, which should be balanced against the benefits of wide access to information – the main source for new ideas and creations. This was the prime reason for their advocacy for limiting the duration of intellectual property as opposed to real property, which is exclusive and rivalrous in its usage. In the later papers, however, Landes and Posner changed their analysis and advocate an indefinitely renewable copyright. In the new analysis they ignore the prime reason for limiting the duration of IP – the obstacles IPR pose to future creations. They also disavow the non-rivalrous character of informational goods, which is one of the prime foundations of the public goods analysis, arguing (in a similar way to the 'tragedy of the commons' theory) that overuse of ideas, images, literary characters and the like, will decrease their value and hence their usage is, in fact, rivalrous, meriting proprietary protection.

A classic example of the proprietary paradigm of IPR is Richard Epstein's (2003) analysis of trade secrets protection. Traditionally, trade secrets have been analysed as contractual rights. Epstein conceptualizes them as *property* rather than a web of confidential arrangements. Treating trade secrets solely as a web of confidential arrangements, he argues, will result in a narrow definition, which will not encompass protection against third parties who acquire the trade secret outside such confidential arrangements. In addition, it will not prevent strangers from stealing information or acquiring it from a person whom they knew had acquired the information by unlawful means. However, Epstein argues, the current law does not reach any individual who misappropriates the information, and does not limit itself only to the case of contractual breach. Moreover, there is no obvious reason why a single person cannot develop and keep a trade secret for himself, thus not in the framework of contractual agreement. The fact that the information was not shared with anyone else does not preclude legal protection of trade secrets. On the contrary, the right of an individual to keep that secret to himself is what allows him, later on, to disclose it to other individuals under a condition of confidentiality. The ownership of land is what allows the landlord to lease it. The ability to lease is not what gives the individual the ownership. In Epstein's words: 'After all, we do not say that someone becomes the owner of property because he has leased it; rather the reverse is true: because he is the owner, he is normally in a position to lease the property' (Epstein 2003: 5). Similarly with a trade secret, Epstein argues, that property right is what allows an individual later to contract with others about disclosing it (Epstein 2003: 3–6).

As is well demonstrated by Epstein's analysis of trade secrets, the proprietary approach to intellectual property is not simply a rhetoric move. When trade secrets are grouped together with copyright and patents under the title of intellectual property, they become property. When intellectual property is understood as *ownership*, then any benefit obtained from another person's investment is considered *free-riding* and *inefficient* (Lemley 2005). The unlawful use of someone else's property is considered a *theft* (Sterk 2004). The proprietary approach would generally support policy choices that strengthen owners' rights and would therefore often be invoked by proponents of stronger intellectual property rights. When scholars analyse various questions relating to copyright or patents under the proprietary paradigm they tend to ignore the fundamental questions raised by the incentives paradigm, simply assuming information to be the property of its creator.

As many scholars have observed (Sterk 2004; Lemley 2005; Menell 2007; Fagundes 2010), an increasing number of jurists, subscribing to the economic approach to intellectual property, are treating copyright and patents as mere property. The new paradigm is well demonstrated by an *amicus* brief filed in the US Supreme Court in a patent infringement case in 2005 by a group called 'various law and economics scholars', contending that the plaintiff merits the award of injunction in much the same way as protection against trespassing of real estate is granted (*eBay v. MercExchange*, 547 U.S. 388 (2006)).

The shift from the market failure approach (the incentives paradigm) to the proprietary model is the most significant theoretical development in the economic analysis of intellectual property in the past decade. The proprietary approach to IPR may take the form of a *positive analysis*, explaining the emergence of intellectual property rights and the reasons they have developed as a property regime. More significantly, as a *normative framework*, the proprietary approach to IPR claims that property rights are necessary in order to achieve efficient management of informational works. In essence it argues that granting property rights, in what otherwise would be considered a commons, will prevent both over-use and under-utilization of these resources. A key theorem utilized by the proprietary paradigm is the veteran 'tragedy of the commons'. In the following section we elaborate on this theory and critically examine its application to intellectual property.

## 4.2 The economic foundations of the proprietary approach: the 'tragedy of the commons'

### *4.2.1 The theory of Harold Demsetz*

Parallels were drawn between the English enclosure movement, which lasted from the 15th to the 19th centuries, and the expansion of IPR – the commodification of information – over the past two decades. The enclosure movement involved the process of fencing off communal land and turning it into private property. The past two decades have been characterized by a similar process in IPR, where informational works are increasingly commodified and various uses of such works, which were previously in the public domain, became largely restricted and legally controlled by rightholders (Boyle 2003a). From a law and economics perspective the rise of private property and the first enclosure movement were explained and indeed justified by reference to the 'tragedy of the commons', which can fall into the category of the market failure of externalities.[21]

Although the term 'tragedy of the commons' is attributed to Garrett Hardin (1968), it was in fact Harold Demsetz (1967) who first offered this theoretical framework to analyse the emergence of private property rights. Demsetz argued that property rights come to light in response to the demands of interacting individuals for adjustment of existing relationships to new cost-benefit possibilities. Thus, he held that 'the emergence of new private or state-owned property rights will be in response to changes in technology and

21 For a categorization of market failures by the basic micro-economic model see Chapter 1.

relative prices' (Demsetz 1967: 349). His analysis begins with an implicit *state of nature* – a world lacking property rights, thus rejecting the natural law concept of property rights and by derivation the natural rights concept of intellectual property. In the *state of nature* land and everything on it, is owned by no one, or rather by everyone. This can be an optimal and static equilibrium if every individual can use and produce from the land everything he or she is seeking. Population growth and density may change this equilibrium. So does an increase in demand, which is beyond the consumption needs of the local population. Once such circumstances occur, a clash between individuals over the land and what it generates will take place. This may lead to overconsumption, which will result in a decrease in the total value of property and thus all those who consume it will very quickly become poorer and thus worse off. This is the 'tragedy of the commons'. Individuals acting rationally, therefore, will attempt to prevent this 'tragedy of the commons' and will agree on the establishment of private property rights.

Demsetz compared the creation of property rights among Native Americans in the northeast with the absence of such a development in the southwest. In the northeast, hunting was initially for purposes of food and obtaining the relatively few furs that were necessary for the hunter's family. Under such circumstance, Demsetz wrote: 'Hunting could be practiced freely and was carried on without assessing its impact on other hunters . . . There did not exist anything resembling private ownership in land' (Demsetz 1967: 351). But the fur trade that originated from the increase in demand from Europe changed that equilibrium. First, the value of furs, as far as the Native Americans were concerned, increased considerably. Second, and as a result, the scale of hunting activity rose sharply. Without collectively agreed upon rules, this change meant exhausting resources in the present and creating shortage for the future. So the tribes developed territorial hunting and trapping rights to make sure that the resources were cared for prudently and to enhance long-term availability of animals to hunt. Why have the indigenous peoples of the American southwest not developed similar institutions? Demsetz cites two reasons. First, in their areas there were no animals of commercial importance comparable to the fur-bearing animals of the north. Second, those animals that did populate the southwest were primarily grazing species that tended to wander over large tracts of land, making it difficult to associate them with specific land boundaries and to allocate limited rights of hunting them to specific individuals or groups. According to Demsetz: 'Hence both the value and cost of establishing private hunting lands in the Southwest are such that we would expect little development along these lines. The externality was just not worth taking into account' (1967: 352).

It is important to emphasize that Demsetz provides us with a positive analysis of the development of property rights, which is also a dynamic analysis portraying the process of propertization (and, as we shall see later, depropertization). In contrast to the public goods analysis of the incentives paradigm, this description precedes property rights granted by a legal system in the framework of a modern state or central government, which is called upon to intervene in market activities. Individuals will act in accordance with their own interests to create agreed upon rules, in a similar way to Hobbes's (1651) general description of the shift from the state of nature to the emergence of the state and central government. Implicitly the description of Demsetz (similarly to Hobbes's) is also a normative analysis (Frischmann 2007). In other words, Demsetz endorses the market creation of property rights because it fulfills the efficiency criterion, defined probably in terms of welfare and utility maximization as well as Pareto optimality (see Chapter 1). His theory is based on an equilibrium between normative and positive analyses (Demsetz 2008), which is not the case for the analysis of the incentives model.

Subsequent literature transformed the positive analysis of the shift from commons to property to an externality type market failure analysis that also provides a predominant justification for central intervention by the government. Garrett Hardin (1968), who coined the term 'tragedy of the commons' advocated privatization of the commons, arguing that '[f]reedom in the commons will bring ruin to all' (Hardin 1968: 1244). When too many individuals are privileged to use a resource, such as a lake, they will tend to overuse it. This is because each individual will bear only the benefits of consuming the resource, such as maximizing fishing, but will not bear the full cost of such a use, namely exhausting the fishery. In other words, individuals do not internalize the negative consequences that their consumption may have on the resource and therefore the separate action of each individual may bring to collective over-consumption of the resource. In addition, when the commons is free for all to use, no one has the incentive to make the necessary investments in cultivating the resource and assuring its long-term sustainability. In micro-economic theory this phenomenon is regarded as an externality, a market failure that requires central intervention. Although externalities and public goods failures of the market can overlap, the overgrazing example is not of a pure public good problem because it does not involve the failure to produce the good in the first place.

### *4.2.2 From the 'tragedy of the commons' in land to intellectual property*

The proprietary approach in the law and economics of IPR is based on replacing the public good analysis with the externalities/tragedy of the commons analysis, as the core theoretical foundation for justifying property rights in information and creations. Its proponents argue that intellectual property fits into the general framework of physical property rights and, therefore, that informational works should be treated similarly to physical property (e.g. Easterbrook 1990; Hardy 2011; Epstein 2010).

At first glance, the application of the 'tragedy of the commons' to intellectual property seems compelling. Overuse of land and its resources and lack of incentives for private investment to optimize the production capabilities from the resource and its potential value, in the absence of property rights in land are equivalent to overuse of commonly owned innovations and intellectual creations: a lack of investment in their improvements and a crucial decrease in their production, in the absence of intellectual property rights. Demsetz himself linked the two phenomena when he wrote in the last part of his path-breaking article: 'Consider the problems of copyright and patents. If a new idea is freely appropriable by all, if there exist communal rights to new ideas, incentives for developing such ideas will be lacking. The benefits derivable from these ideas will not be concentrated on their originators. If we extend some degree of private rights to the originators, these ideas will come forth at a more rapid pace' (Demsetz 1967: 3). Note, however, that Demsetz advocates 'some degree of private rights'.

Moreover, current developments in intellectual property laws are in line with Demsetz's theory, according to which the emergence of new property rights will take place in response to a technological change. Over the past decades we have witnessed a colossal expansion of intellectual property rights covering more subject matters, extending the duration of rights, expanding the bundle of rightholders and overall reducing the volume of informational works that are freely available in the public domain. These developments are only partly the result of legislation. As further explained in the following chapters (Chapters 5 and 6), it is also the outcome of powerful self-help means facilitated by emerging technologies. These developments, described by the literature as increasing 'commodification of information' (Elkin-Koren and Netanel 2002) and the 'second enclosure movement' (Boyle 2003a), correspond to Demsetz's analysis and predictions. His observations are particularly powerful for explaining the emergence of private ordering regimes for supplementing copyright law. The use of digital rights management systems (DRMs), other self-help technological means and contractual arrangements for expanding control over the use of increasingly valuable informational goods reflect a response to the instability introduced by information technologies and new legislation.

However, a meticulous look at the application of Demsetz's theory to the contemporary analysis of the expansion of intellectual property and as a general framework for the positive and normative analysis of IPR reveals several major differences, which must be analysed more carefully in order to examine whether this framework really works for informational goods.

First, Demsetz focuses on the allocative function of property and its role in facilitating the management of existing resources. In contrast to land and other physical resources, informational goods do not exist in nature; they are created by man. Intellectual property rights, therefore, would not be established primarily to prevent over-consumption but to enable production and, perhaps, profit-making. This difference raises questions, which do not exist with regard to land and natural resources, such as what is the optimal level of information and innovation for society. Indeed, as we further explain below, the embracement of the 'tragedy of the commons' by the proprietary paradigm overlooks this difference, by implicitly assuming the existence of the intellectual creations and focusing on their over-consumption and/or lack of incentives to improve them.

Second, the same rationale, which points towards the propertization of ideas – the incentive to create – also points to the fact that such propertization will leave fewer ideas to be the source for new creations. In other words, propertization of ideas works in both directions when the goal is to maximize creation and innovation, knowledge and progress. It is arguable that this phenomenon has an equivalent in the 'tragedy of the commons' in the physical world, as the tragedy is not only reflected by over-consumption, but also by lack of investment to enhance the value of the property. But in the context of IP this consideration works in an opposite direction: while propertization in physical objects works mainly as a positive incentive to invest and enhance the value of the property, propertization of ideas will also decrease the sources for new creations and thus future volume. Propertized information will give an exclusive right to its holder to develop it further, while if the information is in the commons or the public domain everyone is entitled to do so and competition will be likely to increase its value. For these two reasons IP rights, unlike property rights in land and tangibles, are thought to be a good mechanism to maximize society's welfare only if they are given for a limited time and with various exceptions, such as fair use. The 'tragedy of the commons' theorem does not assist in prescribing the optimal scope of IPR, which is the core of the policy debates about IPR.

It is interesting to note that Demsetz himself ignored these two differences and pointed to another difference between IP and physical resources. He wrote (1967: 359):

> But the existence of the private rights does not mean that their effects on the property of others will be directly taken into account. A new idea makes an old one obsolete and another old one more valuable. These effects will not be directly taken into account, but they can be called to the attention of the originator of the new idea through market negotiations. All problems of externalities are closely analogous to those, which arise in the land ownership example. The relevant variables are identical.

Demsetz's point is a little vague because it is unclear whether this is an argument from a distributive justice perspective or whether it is an inner efficiency one (and if so, what is his precise concept of efficiency). It is true, however, that when IPR are discussed within the 'tragedy of the commons' framework, the consideration of negative externalities on markets of substitute products and services, is generally overlooked. Demsetz ignored the two differences mentioned here probably because his argument is constructed within the category of externalities as a market failure, which requires central intervention and correction, while the traditional analysis of IP has been conducted in context of the public goods category of market failures.

Third, applying Demsetz's theory to intangibles assumes that they can be overused or over-consumed. However, unlike land and tangibles, which are limited resources, informational goods do not have capacity limits. Their usage or consumption does not exhaust the resource. The prime functions of property rights in the case of information would thus not be to prevent over-consumption, but to incentivize creation and perhaps to optimize value (or profits). These functions are very different from the traditional role of property rights under the 'tragedy of the commons' analysis. As we discussed extensively in the previous chapter, information is non-rivalrous; its use or consumption does not prevent others from parallel consumption. This implies, again, that the purpose of IP rights is different from property rights in land or tangibles. One can argue that instead of over-consumption of physical objects, in intellectual property we will witness a decrease in value for users with the increase of the number of other users. But the opposite can also be argued: that increasing parallel use creates a positive network effect, as the wide use of informational goods often increases the utility that each user can derive from it. Indeed, the non-discretionary adoption of the 'tragedy of the commons' framework to intellectual creations has an inherited bias to overlook the fundamental issues of creation and progress in favor of questions of management and value or, rather, profit maximization.

A fourth difference between Demsetz's theory and intellectual property relates to the role of technology in the analysis. Although Demsetz attributes an important significance to technological changes and their impact on the creation and modifications of property rights, his analysis assumes technology to be an exogenous variable in the process of the emergence and transformation of property rights. Since technological changes today are much more rapid and dynamic it is problematic to ignore them as an essential endogenous variable in the analysis of intellectual property. As we argued elsewhere, technological development cannot be considered exogenous to the legal analysis (Elkin-Koren and Salzberger 2004). That is because the availability and cost of exclusion measures and the ability to exploit resources efficiently may depend, among other things, on legal rules defining the scope of intellectual property rights. The ease with which information technologies can be shaped and modified and the rapid pace of technological change suggest that in the information environment it is necessary to consider the long-term impact of legal rules on the availability and nature of technological progress and the directions in which it is developed, and vice versa, an analysis which is likely to take a different form and direction to the traditional 'tragedy of the commons'.

Fifth, Demsetz portrayed the emergence of property rights as the result of market activities without the intervention of the state or central government. In his description property rights are the result of social norms. Therefore, he overlooks the public choice aspects regarding the emergence of the new property regimes. Collective action problems, interest groups and rent seeking are absent from the analysis. Nonetheless, these factors were highly influential in shaping the 'second enclosure movement' (Boyle 2003; Litman 2006) and in the emergence and scope of IPR in general. We must take those differences on board when applying Demsetz's observations to the current debates regarding changes in intellectual property laws. Put differently: unlike Demsetz's original theory of property in which positive analysis is in equilibrium with normative analysis, the same cannot be concluded with regard to intellectual property. This is partly due to the fact that while land and what is on it are essential for everyone and thus their over-consumption will have a tragic effect across the board, the commercial production of informational goods is limited to relatively few people (and even fewer who make their primary living out of them) and consumed by many. Hence there is a small likelihood that efficient rules will be established by spontaneous collective action like the small likelihood that efficient rules will be generated by a central government or by spontaneous individual self-help means. This difference has significant consequences not only on normative analysis, but also on the positive analysis of the emergence of IPR. This last point will be further discussed in Chapter 7.

These differences point to a conclusion that the theory of Demsetz certainly cannot help us in the justification of IPR and their ideal prescription, as it is used by the proprietary paradigm. It remains, however, a powerful tool in the realm of positive analysis in explaining changes in this realm. In the following sections, by further elaborating on some of these differences, we will see how the moderate law and economics view of IP developed into an extreme proprietary paradigm.

## 4.3 The proprietary paradigm of intellectual property – sources and main arguments

Over the past two decades a large share of the contemporary law and economics literature on intellectual property departed from the incentives paradigm, as well as from the traditional 'tragedy of the commons' framework, and generated a new paradigm which assumes information to be an object of property. In this section we aim to describe the shift from incentives to property and to put forward several arguments regarding the fundamental nature of property and, by derivation, of intellectual property.

### *4.3.1 The shift from incentives to proprietary regime as an escape from the methodological and empirical problems of the incentives paradigm*

As a pure normative analysis, the departure point of the incentives paradigm was the normative goal of efficiency defined in terms of wealth maximization (Landes and Posner 2003a: 11–36). The incentives paradigm asks what are the desirable laws to maximize society's wealth. It assumes that without property rights there will be low incentives to create, thus endorsing monetary incentives in the form of property rights in information, while at the same time recognizing that propertization may also hinder the creation process. New creations rely on previous ones, and if the latter are kept private or are too costly, then the likelihood of new creations decreases. Granting property rights, therefore, has two opposing consequences that have to be mitigated and optimized. In this sense, one cannot describe the incentives paradigm as a-priori pro-propertization and anti-commons or anti-public domain. The question is the right scope of IPR, and by derivation of the public domain, or the right mixture of the two, which will maximize society's wealth.

However, economists have not succeeded in the main task – empirically testing whether the current balance (for example of the duration of life plus 70 years for copyright and 20 years for patents) is the efficient one. In addition, this phrasing of the question in the context of the contemporary policy debates leaves two important factors that were not addressed by the core model – the definition of society for which we are seeking to maximize wealth and the definition of a time frame for such maximization. These two factors are less crucial (but not absent) in the analysis of old property – tangibles and land – as physical property is connected to specific territory, save exceptional externalities; and it usually already exists and has a relatively long-term and steady value. Informational products have no geographical barriers (or minor geographical barriers of language) and their term of value can change significantly from news items with momentary value to scientific breakthroughs or major ideas with a long-term, even eternal, effect. In addition, the new property is mostly hypothetical or pre-creation and thus the impact of current IP laws is crucial for future creation of potential property. For the new property, therefore, the two questions – whose wealth are we seeking to maximize and what is the time frame for such maximization – become highly important. The lack of a solid analytical framework to discuss these two variables – time and space – together with the inability to obtain clear empirical findings to strike the right balance (for fixing the exact optimal duration of IPR) can be viewed as one of the reasons for the paradigmatic shift from incentives to assumed property.

Indeed, the debate between the developing world countries and the industrialized world regarding patents on medications (discussed in the previous chapter) exemplifies the two crucial factors of territory and time span. If the departure point of this debate is incentives to promote efficiency (even when phrased solely in terms of wealth maximization) identifying the unit for which we seek to maximize wealth is a preliminary task. Should we maximize wealth for the traditional national state or for the whole world? This question is crucial when international treaties, such as TRIPs, are deliberated. It is clear why American IP laws do not take into account their impact on the health of people in Africa, save for some minor potential effects on Americans' wealth, such as the decreasing level of exports to Africa. Similarly, it is clear why a country that is mainly an importer of intellectual creations, rather than a producer, will find it more efficient for its members to set a low degree of IPR protection. But it is unclear why the American IP rules are justifiable as a basis for the global environment. The shift from incentives to the a priori assumption that information is property serves an easy escape route from this question. This shift brought some supporters of the proprietary model to publish in May 2007 an op-ed page advertisement in *The New York Times*, under the title 'Stolen Property, Stolen Future', which reads: 'What if strangers showed up in your backyard and held a block party? America's fiercely defended tradition of private property rights wouldn't tolerate this. But that is in essence what's happening to the intellectual property . . . of American businesses overseas' (Menell 2007).

Similarly, different time units for wealth maximization will have a significant impact on the cost-benefit analysis of propertization and depropertization. If, for example, maximization calculations are conducted on a momentary or short time span, then most intellectual property ought to be in the public domain: similarly, the price of medications should be their marginal production cost, because the potential effect on future creation is not taken on board, as well as past incentives to create. If the time unit for such maximization is long, shifting from static to dynamic efficiency, then the incentives to create should be taken on board. But how long should this time unit be, and how can we possibly predict the impact of today's regulation on future creation, especially in an environment in which technological progress (which itself depends on the current IP regulation) is so rapid? The growing pace of technological change decreases even the relevancy of the few empirical studies on the impact of IP laws on cultural and scientific progress. In short, setting the time frame for wealth maximization is problematic from both the conceptual or theoretical point of view and from an empirical one. Hence, the easy solution is to abandon the incentives framework altogether and resort to the a priori assumption that information is property.

### *4.3.2 From incentives ex ante to incentives ex post and managing improvements*

The new law and economics paradigm has not abandoned the rhetoric of incentives, but rather shifted its meaning from an ex ante incentives justification for intellectual property towards an ex post incentives justification for IP laws (Lemley 2004). The traditional ex ante framework focuses on behavior, which occurs before the creation comes into being. In this framework, the consideration of too strong IP rights as an impediment to creation is crucial, and hence the policy recommendations for various limitations on these rights. The ex post justification looks at intellectual property as a means of managing informational works after they have been developed. The major consideration for limiting the extent and scope of IP rights is, therefore, missing in this framework.

One of the pioneers of the ex post incentive framework or the new proprietary paradigm was Edmund Kitch (1977), who argued in the patent law context that propertization is essential to facilitate the efficient use of works by allowing their commercialization. In other words, Kitch argued that patents are necessary as a means of encouraging efficient usage of existing innovation rather than the creation of new works. We should grant patents in advance of an invention, he argued, making patent a right to 'prospect' a particular field for an invention. This argument focuses on managing investments in informational creations for further exploitation and improvement, implicitly assuming that the original creation has already been made and merits property right.

Kitch's theory lies on two fundamental assumptions, neither of which is supported by empirical findings or theoretical explanation. First, it is assumed that creators will not invest in putting their invention to efficient use unless they obtain exclusive rights to the invention. Without exclusive rights the inventors will fear their investment will result in unpatentable information being appropriated by competitors. It is necessary, therefore, to exercise central management over the production and improvement of creations. This argument is often raised with respect to the industrial implementations of scientific inventions of academic institutions and was made in the context of the US Bayh-Dole Act (35 U.S.C.A (1980)). The Act aimed at promoting the industrial utilization of inventions arising from federally supported research, which prior to the Act were in the public domain. The concern was that no entrepreneur will have any incentive to invest in scientific inventions in the public domain, knowing that they will not enjoy any exclusive rights (Miller 2005). That might be true for inventions that require a major investment to bridge the gap between the scientific breakthrough and the industrial application, such as pharmaceutical drugs that require investment in costly clinical trials. Yet, as shown by Rai and Eiseberg (2003), not every type of invention requires such a large investment in developing a commercial application, and in fact the majority of scientific inventions generated by the academic institutions they studied, did not require such investments. In the majority of cases non-exclusive licenses were sufficient to incentivize private entrepreneurs to invest in the commercializing of scientific inventions.

The second assumption is that the creator is in the best position for managing these rights, or that there is perfect information and zero transaction costs, which would lead to an efficient licensing to both users and potential improvers. This assumption is unsound, as the initial inventor (such as a scientist) is often not best positioned to manage the commercialization of her invention. While there might be good reason to remunerate the initial inventor (ie incentives, rewards), there is no reasons to assume that she will have any advantage in centrally managing her inventions. Commercializing creative works and inventions requires different expertise and skills than those required for a successful creative or innovative process.

In addition, concentrating the decision-making power regarding the exploitation of an invention with the initial owner is inconsistent with the emerging decentralized modes of production. The emergence of new modes of production suggests that such central management may not be necessary and may, in fact, impede the development of further improvements and new developments. As argued by Benkler (2002), the digital networked environment opens up opportunities for new modes of production and distribution of information. The information economy, he argues, introduces a new radically decentralized type of production mode, which is the *commons-based peer-production* of information. The proprietary regime, which was designed to secure incentives, can, in fact, impede production of content by individuals and communities as well as management and improvement. That is because informational works are necessary resources for producing new works. The use of existing works protected by intellectual property is costly: works are priced above marginal cost, and transaction costs of licencing are often high. The high cost of licencing may reduce, and sometimes even prevent new creation by peers collaborating in non-commercial settings. Furthermore, unilateral appropriation of the common project by any individual contributor could reduce intrinsic benefits of participation and reduce motivation of other contributors. Attempts to dominate the common project to reflect one's values or advance one's private gains could alienate others. Defection in the form of excluding others from the fruits of their joint effort, or abuse of the common project to benefit a single participant could weaken the will of others to contribute (Benkler 2002).

Moreover, it is uncertain that property rights and exchanges governed by contracts will lead to optimal allocation of rights. The allocation of property rights and transfer by contracts rely on market forces and price signaling. But price may not be the optimal mechanism for rights allocation in informational resources. One reason is that it is often impossible accurately to determine the value of information prior to its use. Some information becomes valuable at a later stage, when combined, for instance, with other sorts of information or with new technologies. Another reason is that the availability of financial resources at the hand of potential exploiters does not indicate their ability to develop further the resource and therefore would not guarantee optimal allocation. The further development of works and inventions often depend on issues such as intellectual capacity, circumstances, collaboration with others and sometimes even luck. These are not necessarily tied to any market power. The chances of coming up with an innovative breakthrough in computer technology, or creating an exceptional artistic expression, are not higher for powerful economic players. They rather depend on wide exposure to existing works or recent technologies. This suggests that widespread information will increase the chances of further innovation and improvement.

### *4.3.3 The shift to proprietary model by the founding fathers of law and economics*

It took some 20 years for Kitch's argument to reappear in the context of the debate about the Sonny Bono Copyright Term Extension Act and its retroactive extension of copyright, which could have been justified only on the bases of ex post incentives justification. Support for this legislation among several law and economics key scholars can be seen as the turning point in the paradigmatic thinking of law and economics. We mentioned the transition in the analysis of Landes and Posner between 1989 and 2003. Let us elaborate on their arguments. While the analysis of Demsetz focused on externalities as the main rationale for property rights, the early writing of Landes and Posner (1989) focused on the market failure of public goods as the main justification for IP rights. The focal point of the public goods analysis was that since the marginal costs of copying works are minimal (almost zero) the market price of non-propertied works will be so low that it will not cover the initial investment of their creators and thus new works would not be developed. Only propertization of such works, they argued, will grant sufficient incentives for their creation in the first place.

However, they also acknowledged that the benefits should be outweighed with the administrative costs of registration and enforcement and, more importantly, with the benefits of wide access to information, which is the main source for new ideas and creations. They wrote (1989: 332):

> . . . beyond some level copyright protection may actually be counterproductive by raising the cost of expression . . . Creating a new work typically involves borrowing or building on material from a prior body of works . . . The less extensive copyright protection is, the more an author, composer, or other creator can borrow from previous works without infringing copyright and the lower, therefore, the costs of creating a new work.

In their later work Landes and Posner (2003) changed their analysis and advocated an indefinitely renewable copyright, instead of IP rights limited in duration. It is puzzling how in this article the authors ignored the major reason, mentioned in their earlier piece, for limiting the duration of IP – that propertization, while, on the one hand, provides incentives for creation, on the other hand, limits the sources for new creations and thus is likely to reduce such creations. Instead they specify six other reasons, connected mainly with transaction costs, for limiting the duration of IP and argue that these reasons are not convincing anymore.

The main thrust of their later argument overlooks the difference between land and informational goods – the public good nature of the latter, which would prevent a 'tragedy of the commons' even if there is no propertization. Posner and Landes argue that overuse of ideas, images and literary characters will decrease their value and hence their usage is, in fact, rivalrous. Their main example is Disney's Mickey Mouse, about whom they write (Landes and Posner 2003: 487–88):

> If because copyright had expired anyone were free to incorporate the Mickey Mouse character in a book, movie, song, etc, the value of the character might plummet. Not only the public would rapidly tire of Mickey Mouse,

> but his image would be blurred, as some authors portray him as Casanova, others as cat meat, others as an animal-rights advocate, still others as the henpecked husband of Minnie.

Posner and Landes's point is similar to Demsetz's qualifications regarding the potential effects of new ideas and creations of old ones, and in this sense the differences between land and informational goods might not be so great. Posner and Landes overlook, however, two distinct attributes of informational works. One is the network effect of informational goods, which is likely to balance the decreasing value caused by a wide usage of the creation. Wider usage of informational goods improves connectivity. If more people use the same software or communication technique then everyone can benefit more from this software or communication platform. Similarly, it can be more generally argued that widely shared fictional characters, symbols, stories and the like enhance the total value of these cultural icons for each user and for society as a whole, in contrast to Landes and Posner's description. A second element missing from Landes and Posner's analysis is the contribution of ideas in the public domain to incentives and the likelihood of developing new ideas and creations, which is the main characteristics of informational goods, distinguishing them from tangibles and real estate. In other words, they do not distinguish between the economic value of an informational good and its commercial value. In this sense the major difference between the informational public domain and the physical public sphere or commons is that the former is not only a common pool for non-rivalrous consumption but also a common means of production, which can foster Pareto improvement not only in consumption but also in production.

Supporting the retroactive extension of copyright, Landes and Posner also endorse Kitch's argument that incentives are needed in order to encourage the investment in the distribution and promotion of creations. They write (Landes and Posner 2003a: 230):

> Recording companies differentiate their product by promoting the performer or artist who has signed an exclusive contract with the company. Because a recording company can, for example, copyright the Chicago Symphony Orchestra's recording of Mahler's *First Symphony*, it has an incentive to promote that version; it has little incentive to promote the public domain work of an unknown composer, since it could not appropriate the benefits of its promotional efforts, as distinct from benefits that might accrue from a recorded performance of the unknown composer's work by a popular performer.

They go further to contend that incentives are also needed for promoting not only marketing efforts, but also persistent improvement of the creation in order to preserve its value. They emphasize that their support of the copyright extension is based on the traditional incentive-based argument for property right, but with a 'new twist'. Incentives are not exhausted in the initial creation of the intellectual property goods. The incentives are further necessary 'to maintain the value of the property and also to resurrect abandoned or otherwise unexploited intellectual property'. The example they use again is the most popular mouse ever, Mickey Mouse. Disney Corporation has spent over the years enormous amounts of money refurbishing the Mickey Mouse character, both by subtle alterations in the character and by situating it in carefully selected entertainment contexts in an effort to increase the appeal of Mickey Mouse to the current generation of young children. Landes and Posner argue that it seems unlikely that only the most recent version of the character retains commercial appeal (Landes and Posner 2003a: 231–33).

The later work of Posner and Landes emphasizes the goal of maximizing the value of IP to its producers, thus revealing the paradigmatic shift and the presumption that intellectual creations are to be considered as a priori natural objects of property of their creators. Ironically, the new proprietary paradigm not only ignores the initial normative justifications for intellectual property rights but it also undermines some fundamentals of competitive market theory. As Mark Lemley (2004) justifiably writes, competition and the invisible hand is what drive the market to efficiency. The meaning of Kitch's argument and its successors is that only one skilled firm in the market can reach the efficient outcome, and for doing so society must provide it with adequate incentives. The fact that goods in a particular market were protected as the result of exclusive rights in the past, either patent rights or copyrights, does not mean that their initial inventors are the most efficient producers forever. On the contrary, granting one company the exclusive right to make these goods would be likely to result in an increase in the price and a decrease in the supply. Even if a manager is necessary for efficient distribution of intellectual property goods, it does not mean that the creator is the best and adequate manager. Creators are often terrible managers. They frequently misunderstand the significance of their own inventions and the uses to which they can be put. Moreover, even if creators have the perfect management skills, their successors, who will hold the exclusive right later on, may not be as good. In any case, the more recent analysis of Landes and Posner shifts the normative goal from maximizing society's welfare to maximizing the profits of the IP owner. This shift cannot be rationalized without presupposing the natural right of the creator to enjoy all economic benefits related to the creation.

### *4.3.4 The normative analysis of the proprietary paradigm*

So far we have focused on the 'tragedy of the commons' as the prime source of argument on behalf of the proprietary approach towards intellectual property. But there are other arguments or extensions of the traditional arguments regarding land and natural resources, made within the normative analysis of the proprietary paradigm, advocating for a strong intellectual property regime. Let us summarize the major arguments. One set of arguments is based on the *signaling value* of a property system: Property rights aid in establishing efficient markets by internalizing costs and benefits into packages that can be traded (Demsetz 1967). Markets and price will provide efficient signals on questions of allocation: how much to produce and how much to consume. Absent transaction costs a clear property right will internalize the costs and benefits of the owner's activity and permit the sale of that right to others who may value it more. In a world with transaction costs property rights are justified when the social gains from internalizing an externality exceed the costs of doing so (Demsetz 1967: 349–50).

A second set of arguments relates to *transaction costs*: Property rights are efficient because they can reduce transaction costs. Property law addresses the problem of verification by assuming that a single owner owns all property rights in any given asset unless there is an adequate notice to persons who might be affected. Thus, by awarding clear property rights a more efficient trade can be facilitated (Hansmann and Kraakman 2002; Merrill and Smith 2001). A related argument concerns the minimization of conflicts over resources. Property is understood as a mechanism for reducing social disorder. Since Aristotelian times, legal thinkers have justified property as a mechanism for avoiding disputes and settling conflicts. The property rules regarding land aim to decrease the likelihood of conflicts among potential users of land. However, there is no need for privatization of the land. Common ownership would be also sufficient for preserving social order, as long as the boundaries are set clearly by the law. A rule that allocates each scarce usage right to a particular person or group, or a rule that provides a mechanism for resolving disputes over use rights, is sufficient (Smith 2002: 454–55). Yet, when the resource is not scarce, or when the resource is characterized as a public good, property rules are not necessary in order to avoid conflicts. In the case of public goods, such as road or lighthouse, property rules might be needed for assurance that appropriating the resources is devoted to creating these public goods (Rose 1986: 752). As Stewart Sterk puts it: 'two men cannot plow the same furrow, but two boats can be guided by the same beacon, and two travelers can take the same road' (Sterk 2004: 15). With regards to intellectual property goods, not only that they are characterized as public goods, but also as a result of the network effect, sometimes they might be more valuable if they are used widely (Sterk 2004: 13–15).

Another justification to the proprietary paradigm relates to *incentives*. In contrast to the incentives paradigm, and to the market failure approach, the proprietary approach focuses on incentives to invest in existing resources. A property system is thought of as providing adequate incentives to invest in improving what you already 'own'. Note that this type of argument is different from the *incentives paradigm* discussed earlier, in that it focuses on incentives to improve what is already there, rather than creating new resources. That is because property rights in real estate could induce owners to invest in improving their land, but they cannot provide incentives for creating more land (Sterk 2004: 17–18).

Finally, property is arguably a social institution that could potentially protect *individuals' autonomy* against the coercive power of the state. Markets allow people to pursue their own ends, and lead to sufficient instability to promote freedom (Hayek 1960: 141, 1978: 109). One version of this argument in the context of intellectual property is Netanel's approach to copyright and democracy discussed in Chapter 2 (Netanel 1996). Intellectual property rights establish a market, thereby enabling different parties, such as authors, journalists and newspapers to accumulate property and gain their independence vis-à-vis the state.

The property approach raises serious questions regarding the applicability of tangible property analysis to informational works. To what extent are the justifications for real property applicable to information, which is non-rival? These aspects are further discussed in the next section.

## 4.4 A critical view of the proprietary approach

Our critique of the emerging proprietary model was laid down in the previous sections, alongside the description of the main tenets of this approach. In this section we elaborate on the main points of criticism, adding some fresh insights into the debate.

### *4.4.1 Can information be over-consumed?*

The law and economics literature, as we specified above, perceives the 'tragedy of the commons' not only as the explanation but also as the predominant justification for privatizing commons (Hardin 1968). When too many individuals are privileged to use a resource, such as a lake, they will tend to overuse it. While the 'tragedy of the commons' may occur in the case of fisheries or overgrazed fields it need not occur in the case of information. The use of informational resources will not lead to any 'tragedy' since information cannot be over-consumed. That is simply because the use of information does not consume it at all, and therefore it can never be exhausted. While scarce resources, such as oil or water, should be put to their highest valued use, information does not raise the same allocation dilemmas since it is non-rival in the sense that its use by one person does not deprive others from using it. For physical resources, in the absence of transaction costs, bargains in the free market will guarantee efficient allocation because the user with the highest valued usage will also be able to offer the highest bid. Since the use of information is non-rival, it does not raise similar allocation problems. Consequently, it is unlikely that the absence of property rights in informational works will lead to the 'tragedy of the commons' in the sense of over-consumption.

Some scholars have questioned the non-rivalry nature of informational goods, arguing that more use may decrease the commercial value that could be extracted from any single work (Posner and Landes 2003: 485–87) or that even informational works may invoke conflicts among users, when some uses are interfering with others' conduct, or where there is a certain limit to the number of people who can use the resource (Duffy 2005).

As we suggested in section 4.3.3 above, the value of informational works to each individual user is actually likely to increase as its use becomes more pervasive, especially when we are talking about communicative products – software, cultural creations etc. Network externalities would emerge when the value of some informational works is enhanced as more people use them. A classic example is the benefit of using a single operating system. Digital networks rely on common standards and shared programming languages. Whenever the value of informational works depends on exchange and coordination with others, additional users may inflict positive externalities on all users. The same argument can be made not only with regard to infrastructures but also regarding content. When content, such as literary or entertainment creation, is more widely known its value for consumers through communicative and derivative activities is enhanced. In addition, some level of free access to information is essential for further innovation and creation, which is not the case with tangibles or land. Information is developed incrementally. Existing information stimulates the creation of more information and, therefore, extensive use of information may increase the likelihood of further development, ie enhanced value.

Be that as it may, our main point here is that the 'tragedy of the commons' framework is misused in the context of the debate about commodification of information. The primary 'tragic' nature of intellectual creations common is the likelihood that without the protection of property rights they will not be produced in the first place rather than their management, consumption and producers' profits. Unlike land, information has to be produced in order to be consumed, and free usage by everyone can affect the likelihood of producing it in the first place. Put differently, the potential tragic element of commons in informational goods takes a different shape from the 'tragedy of the commons' in land, and thus employing it in the IP context requires a more serious study of the differences between the propertization of land and propertization of information, which is substantially different from Demsetz's description. While land and other natural resources will always remain scarce, information is not.

### *4.4.2 Propertization of the commons and the anti-commons*

While informational works cannot be overused, they can be underused. The notion of 'anti-commons' as developed by Michael Heller (1998) may clarify this point. Heller distinguishes between three types of property regimes: private property, commons and anti-commons. The dichotomy between the first two types of property regimes, private property and common property, is fundamental to the neo-classical economic approach to property (Rose 1994). A resource may be either privately owned, so that rights of exclusion are vested in private parties, or may be such that control over its use may not be efficiently divided among private owners (Gordon 1954). It is in the latter case that a common property regime will emerge in which the use of the resource is open to the public and is not subject to exclusive rights of any particular party. Thus, the private/commons distinction focuses on the level of control exercised over a resource: from the strongest right of exclusion in a private property regime to the total absence of exclusion rights in a commons.

Heller's theory of anti-commons property adds another dimension to the analysis of propertization by considering the organizational function of property rights. An anti-commons regime is defined as 'a property regime in which multiple owners hold effective rights of exclusion in a scarce resource' (Heller 1998: 668). An anti-commons regime emerges whenever several owners have rights of exclusion in a resource that each of them wants to use. Such a regime creates 'horizontal' relations among competing owners of overlapping rights. An anti-commons regime may lead to what is described by Heller as the 'tragedy of the anti-commons': when too many individuals have rights of exclusion in a scarce resource, rational individuals, acting separately, may collectively waste the resource by under-consuming it compared with a social optimum (Heller 1998: 677).

The anti-commons analysis is of great importance to the intellectual property discourse. Heller and Eisenberg (1998) demonstrated how patents granted on upstream technology might impede downstream product development. They warned against the proliferation of patent rights in biomedical research, which could lead to anti-commons by fragmenting intellectual property rights in potential future products or by allowing too many upstream patent owners to stack licenses on top of the future discoveries of downstream users. For decades, the literature on intellectual property has focused on the appropriate level of control that should be accorded to intellectual property owners. It sought to define the appropriate scope of rights that would stimulate creation and at the same time would not stifle future innovation. The anti-commons analysis expands the current debate over the appropriate scope of intellectual property rights to consider not merely the level of protection, but also the organization of rights, namely the way rights are designed and held. This analysis, thus, focuses on the effects of the organization of rights on the efficient use of information.

The anti-commons analysis is particularly relevant to the emergence of new rights by private ordering using contracts or DRMs, which result in the same outcome as property rights. The reason why private ordering may lead to anti-commons is that it enables the proliferation of rights of exclusion. Using self-help means to acquire a property-like control over the use of works, such as by enforcing contracts/licenses against third parties or developing exclusionary technology, not only affects the strength of rights, but may also transform the division and allocation of rights. There are several features of propertization by contracts or technology that deserve special attention. A property regime constituted by copyright law is very different from a web of exclusion rights (quasi-property regime) constituted by contracts. Copyright law defines the sort of informational works that are entitled to protection. It further defines the limited scope of rights that are accorded to copyright owners with respect to such works. By contrast, propertization by private ordering is not subject to any such limits. Exclusive rights are established by contracts that as a practical matter become enforceable against all users of any particular work to which the contract applies. We further elaborate on this point in Chapter 5.

### *4.4.3 Managing informational commons*

The proprietary approach suggests that full property rights are required to ensure that users internalize externalities associated with the use of common resources, preventing the over-consumption or under-production of the resource. The tragedy of the anti-commons points to the same sort of tragedy when common resources are fully privatized. Is there a third option for treating common resources? Nobel Prize winner Elinor Ostrom demonstrated how some communities developed intuitions, falling short of privatization, to manage common pools of physical resources. Ostrom's work provides a third reaction to the 'tragedy of the commons'. If the solutions offered to the overuse of resources were privatization, where each member of the community becomes an owner and internalizes the cost of use, or regulation of the scope of use, Ostrom showed that different communities develop a variety of different strategies that avoid the 'tragedy of the commons' and facilitate a sustainable use of natural resources. In this section we demonstrate the shortcomings of the proprietary model in handling a cultural commons and explore a different form of intervention to prevent the 'tragedy': social norms and institutions aiming centrally to coordinate the use.

Ostrom, who studied the use of the common pool of physical resources, identified formal and informal institutions, which substitute private property, enabling sharing and making a productive and a sustainable use of natural resources (Ostrom 1990). Such diverse institutional arrangements for managing natural resources helped communities avoid the exhaustion of the common resource. These institutions and rules, she argued, are contextual and tailored to particular environments, although they share a similar design. Ostrom offered an institutional analysis and development framework for addressing a variety of questions related to natural resources commons. She identified eight 'design principles' of stable local common pool resource management, including clearly defined boundaries of the community, collective-choice arrangements that allow most resource appropriators to participate in the decision-making process, effective monitoring by accountable monitors, a scale of graduated sanctions for violation of norms and accessible mechanisms of conflict resolution.

This approach is raising a few challenges in the context of governing knowledge. One issue is whether the institutional framework identified by Ostrom for the governance of natural resources may equally apply to the governance of knowledge and informational resources. Here again, the distinct characteristics of the informational resources we discussed above come into play: non-rivalry, and the dynamic nature by which each informational resource are both the input and output of creative and innovative processes. Rather than building a theory on the basis of managing physical assets, Madison, Frischmann and Strandburg (2010) argue that the same type of inductive studies, which revealed the governing structures of commons natural sources, are necessary for the study of commons informational resources. Thus, they argue, further research is necessary for systematic studying the organizational structures of arrangements such as patent pools, open-source software development and academic scientific research, within a unified conceptual framework of 'cultural commons', to enable the development of a comprehensive approach to the governance of informational resources.

Another issue relates to the role of informal institutions. While social norms can play a significant role in managing the behavior of users of natural resources, it is still unclear whether they can serve a similar function in communities of users and producers of informational works. Recent studies identified the role of social norms in managing the use of intangibles. For instance, Fauchart and von Hippel (2008) identified norm-based semi intellectual property systems among French chefs, showing that social norms provide group members with rights, which are similar to intellectual property rights in their nature and protection. Similarly, Oliar and Springman (2008) demonstrated how stand-up comedians protect their jokes using a system of social norms and Loshin (2008) showed how magicians protect their tricks. While such informal institutional structure may serve the needs of distinct, relatively homogenous communities, it is unclear whether it could fit large scale collaboration, where it is harder to establish trust and reciprocity.

### 4.4.4 *The proprietary model and large scale collaborations*

The basic tenets of the proprietary model fail to address the organizational challenges posed by social production in large-scale collaborations.

Digital networks facilitate the emergence of social production, where informational works are increasingly generated through collaboration and exchange outside of the organizational structures of firms and states. Large scale collaboration – the ability of individuals to act together without the formal structures of governments and corporations – is one of the most significant phenomena of the information age. New technologies enable individuals to act together, organizing a political demonstration, initiating and implementing a political campaign or commercial boycott, without the organizational structure of political parties. Individuals can also collaborate in generating information works, as in Wikipedia and free software, without the managerial structure of corporate hierarchies.

The proprietary model aims at internalizing the negative externalities associated with the use of resources. Therefore, it does not address the needs of parties who are collaboratively generating new resources. The individualistic focus on the sovereignty of the owner regarding the use of the work and the legal power to exclude others, which is the essence of the proprietary approach, may conflict with the fundamentals of social production. The proprietary emphasis on the sovereignty of owners further weakens social cohesion by emphasizing difference and disparities of interests rather than shared values and goals. This emphasis on the right of each owner in her respective contribution creates impediments to large-scale collaboration, as it gives each and every contributor the power to decide how his or her contribution will be exploited.

The property framework defines rights against strangers – rights of owners against non-owners. It entitles the owner to stop the unlicenced use of the work by potential exploiters. It lacks a framework for addressing the rights and duties of collaborators towards one another regarding their respective contributions and the exploitation of their joint effort. Furthermore, the proprietary model, which concentrates control over an asset at the hands of a single owner, does not provide sufficient answers on how to govern the output of social production and resolve conflicts and disagreements related to it. This deficiency is particularly crucial in the case of large-scale collaboration among a massive number of users who are not organized by any formal legal structure.

Many questions may arise regarding the ongoing processes of generating and exploiting content through large-scale collaboration. For instance, who has the right to edit and transform a work created by many? What rights should each participant have over their individual contributions? What rights should each of the users have to the outcome as a whole? If each participant is entitled to control her own individual contribution how should the output of collaborative production be governed? Should users be free to use their contributions to a collaborative endeavor as they please? Is each user entitled freely to change, edit, transfer or otherwise distribute such works? What if editing the content or implementing a particular business model affects the endeavor as a whole, or at least the micro-contributions made by others? Are participants free to exploit the outcome commercially? Are they entitled to prevent others from using it?

The proprietary model, which focuses on the sovereignty of owners, does not provide a functional way of addressing these questions in large-scale collaborations. Consider, for instance, new ways of exploiting Wikipedia. This free, web-based encyclopedia, which is the output of large-scale collaboration, is now facilitating printed versions through print-on-demand offered by printing services such as PediaPress or publishers, such as the German publisher Bertelsmann,which published a special edition of selected items from German Wikipedia. Can any user publish a printed edition of selected entries from Wikipedia for commercial purposes? Some users may view this as an abuse of their team effort. A printed version, edited by a single publisher and sold at a price, may contradict some of the values Wikipedia stands for: a free online encyclopedia that reflects the input of thousands of users/editors, where knowledge is constantly subject to challenge; a collaborative endeavor that promotes a non-authoritarian and a pluralistic view of knowledge; and the widest possible dissemination of that knowledge. At the same time, however, a printed version may promote access to knowledge and may widen the potential readership of Wikipedia, making it useful outside the online environment. Commercial exploitation, one may argue, would not compromise free access. Free access to the online version will still be provided, but the printed version will provide some added value. How should we decide between these conflicting views? Regardless of our position on this particular matter, it is evident that it does not offer any useful framework for addressing questions regarding this new use of Wikipedia, either on the normative level or on the functional one.

The legal toolkit, offered by a proprietary rule, is rather limited. Take copyright for instance. Structurally, copyright law creates a governance structure that assigns the power to authorize use in the hands of a single owner: the individual author, employer, exploiting firm, or even partners who share ownership. The law rests on the notion of a singular author, with only two exceptions to this rule: the doctrine of work made for hire and the notion of joint authorship. A work made for hire covers any work prepared by employees in the scope of their employment or commissioned works of certain categories listed by law, which the parties have defined as a work for hire in a signed written agreement. Within the framework of work made for hire, the employer is considered a single author who orchestrates the production process implemented by many employees who are basically acting as the employer's long arm. The collaborative nature of online production does not fit neatly under this exception. That is especially true in the case of massive collaboration by thousands of contributors over time. Users who work together cannot simply be considered employees of a social media platform, or of the NGO, or indeed the corporate entity that operates it. They are often not officially hired by platforms to do any particular work, and they are not paid. There are rarely any formal employment relations between the social media platform and the collaborating users. The actions of users generating content are often spontaneous and independent and are not orchestrated by the social media platform or any other single entity. In fact, even when users have engaged in tasks that were seen as an integral part of the platform's operation, they have been considered by the courts to be volunteers.

Several scholars conceptualized the relationship between a platform and users as labor relations, emphasizing the economic value that users contribute to the platforms and the way the relations are shaped by ownership and control over the means of production. Indeed, any interpretation of the work relations between social media platforms and participating users needs to consider the economic role of users, regardless of the existence of any formal employment agreement. The crowd of creative volunteers lowers production costs by allowing businesses to take advantage of amateur users without having to compensate them or guarantee their employment environment. Yet it is hard to accept the view that users/authors are employees. What characterizes social production is that users voluntarily engage in it. When users generate reviews of books and movies and share them online, they do so as a matter of social practice. Therefore, users participating in social production cannot be conceived of as workers. Social media platforms such as Amazon can extract an economic value from user-generated reviews, but this does not turn the practice of offering comments into work that establishes labor relations between Amazon and the users.

Another exception to the notion of a singular author is joint authorship, which results in joint ownership. Under the 1976 US Copyright Act, for example, '[a] joint work is a work prepared by two or more authors with the intention that their contributions be merged into inseparable or interdependent parts of a unitary whole'. In some cases, online collaboration lacks any such intention to contribute to a unitary whole as contributions are separate and independent. In other cases, however, such as that of Wikipedia, it is arguable that users intend to contribute to a unitary whole. These cases might be treated under copyright law as jointly authored, and therefore would be considered joint ownership.

Yet joint ownership under copyright does not offer a useful framework for governing the output of large-scale collaboration. Joint owners share equally the ownership of copyright, unless a contrary agreement is made. The rules related to co-ownership in copyright derive from co-ownership in tangible property. Each owner can act unilaterally and independently of the other co-owners. This does not mean that each contribution should be copyrighted to the individual user. The collaborative nature of such creative projects may weaken the claim of each individual user for exclusivity over the bits and pieces she contributed to a collaborative endeavor.

Large scale collaboration demonstrates the limits of the proprietary model in an organizational framework for the production and use of intangible assets. It is rather superficial to apply the legal constructs of joint authorship and work made for hire to large-scale collaboration of the type that is taking place in the social web. These legal doctrines do not provide sufficient protection for the interests of collaborators in their joint work. Social production reflects a joint effort, but here value is created by the accumulated effort of a massive number of participants. Viewing the output of online collaboration as a single coherent work often fails to address the special nature of such collaboration: that it is a dynamic and interactive process. Social production creates new space for collectivity. The contributions of users that are facilitated online often reflect spontaneous expression and engagement with each other's works by rating, tagging and commenting. The output of such collaboration is actually more a reflection of an ongoing social process than of a commodity that can be owned and transferred.

Social production generated institutions of self-governances: licenses, contracts and term of use (ToU) enable online communities to opt out of the standardized rights and duties applied by copyright and to establish a legal regime that fits their needs. A classic example is the general public license

(GPL) of the Free Software Foundation (FSF), which secures the freedom to run, edit and share software. As further discussed in Chapter 5, these private ordering arrangements rely on property rights.

From the perspective of social production, such private ordering arrangements have an important advantage, as they allow communities to tailor the governance of content to fit the nature of collaboration, the group identity and the values shared by its members. At the same time, however, private ordering provides only a limited remedy to some of the deficiencies of the proprietary model.

It seems that in a similar way to Ostrom's analysis of common natural resources, social norm and institutions play a major role in informational commons, a fact that points towards the inefficiency of the contemporary proprietary regime and calls for an exploration of an alternative regulatory structure outside the proprietary model.

### *4.4.5 Deconstructing traditional property and the proprietary paradigm of IP*

We elaborated above the main points of criticism against the proprietary paradigm to IP which implicitly assumes informational products to be an object of property right. In this section we would like to approach the issue from a different direction and raise some preliminary and tentative thoughts about property right in general in view of its expansion into intellectual creations. In other words, the proprietary model of IP requires a fresh look at the meaning of property right in general and whether the justifications for the legal definition of this right when tangibles or land are involved remain intact when applied to informational and intellectual creations.

Property right, or ownership, is an established and veteran legal concept but, in fact, this right is understood in a different way by economists (Smith 2011) and even in the legal world it is an abstract concept, which includes a bundle of particular rights related to its object. The five main components of private ownership are the rights to access, withdrawal, management, exclusion and alienation (Ostrom 2000). When the law recognizes the right of property it implicitly acknowledges different exclusive rights of the owner to access the property, to use it, to manage it, to transfer it to others, to exclude others from using it, and to destroy the property. All the economic benefits that result from these activities belong to the owner. There is no obvious reason to consider automatically the whole bundle of rights as a single legal concept.

Indeed, the rulings of American courts regarding natural resources, such as oil, gas and waters on private land have developed a more complex allocation of rights. For example, courts have ruled that while individuals have the right to drill on their private property and that the retrieved oil is owned by them in the sense of usage, transfer and exclusion, they are not allowed to alienate the oil and will be liable in damages for doing so (Epstein 1985: 221). This ruling, in fact, creates a right that includes exclusive access and withdrawal, common management and no right of alienation. This is an exception to the general perception of full private property as a 'thick' and integral concept.

It is possible that transaction costs were the main reason in the past not to break up the concept of property into its different components, or rather to group those rights under a common legal title in the first place. In the information environment transaction costs are significantly lower (Elkin-Koren and Salzberger 1999). More sophisticated and fine tuned enforcement measures are available through innovative technologies (see Chapter 6). New technologies may require new rights to protect new types of interests and may enable the design of new types of rights that could be enforced (ie exclusive access for a limited time). It might be an interesting exercise to examine the justification of each of these components separately and their optimal degree of propertization. For example, the optimal duration of each of these rights might be different. While restrictions on access are the most heavy-handed measure vis-à-vis the implications on the flow of ideas and the sources for new creations, management, exclusion and alienation are less harmful. On the other hand, from the point of view of the individual incentives to create, allowing greater access (for example by a wide definition of fair use and its extension beyond copyright) might pose a minor disincentive to create in comparison with allowing exclusivity in management or alienation.

The breakage of the full property right into different components is not only a normative analysis of the desirable extent of IPR; it can be analysed on the positive level. Projects such as creative commons (further discussed in Chapter 5), in fact, break the full private property right into sub-components, using contractual tools. Again, the decrease of transaction costs in the new information environment enables these developments. From a law and economics perspective these developments point to inefficiency of the current legal arrangements, but the good news is that reduced transaction costs brings us closer to Coasian efficiency, in the shadow of the positive legal rules.

The broadening of the objects of traditional property to intellectual products has also significant effects on the old property. For example, let us assume that the government changes the designation of particular common land into private property. This piece of land is subsequently purchased by an individual who builds an architectural masterpiece on it. This new building is privately owned in the sense that no one can enter the building, use it, sell it or eliminate it, save its private owner or under her permission. But the pleasure of viewing the building for the rest of the community, the inspiration it creates, its contribution to future architectural plans, which are not part of the owner's property according to positive law, should be regarded according to the new paradigm as also part of the owner's property. Why should we distinguish between the economic benefits an owner is entitled to when a physical object is their source, and the equivalent benefits when their source is an idea or non-physical creation? The new architecture masterpiece can be the source for new ideas in architecture, the source of inspiration of poets and writers and, in general, a source for utility enhancement for members of the community and even the cause for an increase in the monetary values of the private properties of the neighbors. All these benefits cannot be claimed, under present legal doctrine, by the private owner of the new building; thus they are things, which belong to the public domain. This example demonstrates that property (in its traditional definition) is not necessarily the antonym of the public domain, because it is very possible that had this piece of land been kept in common ownership or declared res nullius, everyone could have made any physical use of it, but the total welfare or utility of the community would have been lower.

From a law and economics perspective (defined broadly on the bases of utility maximization or narrowly on the bases of wealth maximization), property rights are a mechanism to increase the total utility/wealth of the population and on this path we can resort to Demsetz and his externalities analysis of the emergence of property rights or to the public goods analysis of the incentives model, and portray the public domain as also comprising positive externalities from private property (a different version of the same idea can be found in Wagner 2003). However, if we expand the traditional objects of property to include all economic benefits that can be extracted from information, ideas and other intellectual creations, the result would be a decrease of total utility or wealth not only in the traditional realm of IP but also as a consequence of indirect modifications of the extent of property rights in tangibles and land. As our example above shows, under this framework, propertization or commodification can in fact enlarge the public domain. Under the proprietary paradigm, which assumes that everything of value is an object of property, this is not the case, and the essential goal of economic analysis might be altogether frustrated.

## 4.5 The 'tragedy of the commons' and positive analysis of intellectual property

So far we have discussed the application of the 'tragedy of the commons' to the normative analysis of intellectual property and the emergence of the proprietary model. As we mentioned at the beginning of this chapter, Demsetz's original theory of property was a positive analysis in which he explained when and how property rights emerge. The theory offered by Demsetz to explain propertization can be extended also to explain depropertization, and in the context of IP it might be even more relevant in explaining the latter. As we emphasized above, Demsetz's theory focuses on the positive analysis of the creation (or lack of creation) of property rights. Thus, according to his rationale, if governments (or in this case any other central decision-making bodies, including courts) intervene in the market of property rights in an inefficient way, as can be argued is the case of recent changes in IP rights, market activities can lead to depropertization. The phenomena of free software, creative commons and other activities of enhancing the public domain can be understood as market responses to the inefficient expansion of property rights by central agencies. It is noteworthy that these current depropertization movements use the existing legal framework of both contracts and property law to perform the shift towards depropertization. The same positive and dynamic analysis offered by Demsetz for describing the creation of property rights can serve to analyse the expansion of the commons or of the public domain in the shadow of a too robust property rights regime. Demsetz himself (Demsetz 1967: 357) hinted at this direction by asserting that:

> . . . [t]he greater are diseconomies of scale to land ownership the more will contractual arrangement be used by the interacting neighbors to settle these differences. Negotiating and policing costs will be compared to costs that depend on the scale of ownership, and parcels of land will tend to be owned in sizes which minimize the sum of these costs.

Demsetz's theoretical framework does not only allow for a dynamic of depropertization but it also specifies the variables that can predict such a process, some of them can fit the description of the new mode of production of informational goods (e.g. Benkler 2002). Demsetz referred to the analysis of corporations as an alternative structure of property rights (Demsetz 1967: 357), stating that:

> . . . the interplay of scale economies, negotiating cost, externalities, and the modification of property rights can be seen in the most notable 'exception' to the assertion that ownership tends to be an individual affair: the publicly-held corporation. We assume that significant economies of scale in the operation of large corporations is a fact and, also, that large requirements for equity capital can be satisfied more cheaply by acquiring the capital from many purchasers of equity shares. While economies of scale in operating these enterprises exist, economies of scale in the provision of capital do not. Hence, it becomes desirable for many 'owners' to form a joint-stock company.

Benkler (2002) emphasizes the peer production mode as an alternative to production within a firm. However, if we focus on the property rights aspects of this new production mode, the analogy between corporations and the market-driven enlargement of the public domain can be of great interest. In other words, Demsetz's 1967 statement regarding the nature of the corporation can actually, with small modifications, describe the property rights aspect of the peer production process emerging today (Elkin-Koren and Salzberger 2004: 62, 130–36). The decreasing transaction costs and contract forming costs are leading to greater production outside firms and back into the markets. However, the atomization of joint work efforts enabled by the new technologies creates a new type of market activity not seen in the pre-Internet era.

In our times, de facto depropertization can also be the result of a rational corporate business model, as we have been witnessing recently. Some major players in the IT world today, such as Facebook and Google, are opting to give up some IPR protection as a result of a rational calculation that other sources of funding, primarily advertising, might be maximized when IPR are actually voluntarily given up. This phenomenon is different from the much discussed peer production outside the corporative framework and extends the Demsetz framework even further. However, in both cases, depropertization is the result of spontaneous individual action rather than a spontaneous collective action described in the original work of Demsetz. It signals the inefficiency of the current positive IP regimes, which are in a course of significant expansion endorsed by the proprietary model.

## 4.6 Conclusion

The incentives paradigm, which has been the main law and economics framework for the analysis of intellectual property, generated frustration in its inability to direct policy-makers in the crucial issues of the optimal duration of IPR, the optimal exceptions and other important details which have immense consequences for information policy decisions. This was perhaps one of the prime reasons for the paradigmatic shift within law and economics to the proprietary model, the adoption of which bypasses the crucial questions of tailoring IPR. This paradigmatic shift was facilitated by resorting to traditional economic analysis of physical property, where Demsetz's 1967 theory was a major anchor.

The shift, alas, overlooked various differences between physical property and information, as well as the positive nature of the 'tragedy of the commons' analysis, which was transformed into normative analysis by the new paradigm. The incentives framework is a pure normative analysis, while the 'tragedy of the commons' emerged originally from a positive analysis. In this sense, the 'tragedy of the commons' framework for property rights can be presented as creating an inner equilibrium between positive and normative analyses. Once central intervention is required in the information markets, such equilibrium cannot be guaranteed. Intellectual property rights have to be created by law-makers and their distributional effects exposes them to manipulations by interests groups, social choice problems and other public choice obstacles. Economic analysis, therefore, cannot predict that the desirable (optimal) solutions will indeed be implemented on the bases of the same fundamental assumptions of the law and economics framework, especially the assumption of rational, self-maximizing, behavior.

# Part III

# Central intervention and private ordering

# 5 Intellectual property and the rise of private ordering

In recent years we have witnessed a dramatic increase in the use of contracts for determining the terms of access to creative works and inventions, thus affecting the de facto status and scope of intellectual property rights. Digital networks offer new opportunities for content providers and innovators to contract directly with the end users of their respective works at low cost. At the same time, however, private ordering is employed by rightholders for expanding the rights awarded to them by intellectual property laws, such as limiting the right to sell a used copy of the work, or lend it to others. On the other hand, license agreements are employed by individual creators, businesses and NGOs to promote open access and open content agenda, shrinking the rights awarded by IP. Even in areas traditionally governed by patents alone, contracts are becoming more pervasive. Patentees, for instance, are increasingly using license agreements containing 'no challenge' clauses that either bar or otherwise deter a licensee from challenging a licensor of intellectual property rights. By contrast, some public institutions in biomedical research are conditioning the license on assurances that grantees and licensees will not assert patents to impede further scientific inquiry.

The proliferation of private ordering reflects a shift from property to contracts as a major mechanism for implementing intellectual property policy. Consequently, a growing number of issues related to the exploitation of informational works, is now regulated by contracts (*private ordering*) alongside patent law, copyright law and other legislation of IPR (*public ordering*). Contracts and licensing schemes, therefore, should become a focus of theoretical and empirical analyses and policy-making in this area. This is the purpose of this chapter.

The dominance of private ordering destabilizes intellectual property laws on two levels: institutional and normative. On the institutional level the shift to private ordering blurs the distinction between property and contracts. As further explained below, this is a result of the pervasive nature of licensing in digital format, and to the legal policies that hold such contracts enforceable against third parties. Once terms of access, established by a contract and applied to third parties govern each and every access to a work, they have the same impact as proprietary protection. This self-help mechanism for governing information challenges the norms designed through collective action (intellectual property laws) and require reconsideration as to the type of desirable government intervention. On the normative level, questions arise as to whether the state should enforce privately created norms when they are inconsistent with copyright, patents and other IPR, and what should be the considerations for such enforcement.

On the positive level of analysis, digital networks introduce new modes of production and distribution of creative works (Benkler 2006). The Web 2.0 enables individual users to actively engage in creative processes, where users independently generate and mass-distribute their creations, using different licensing strategies. Governing access to user-generated content (UGC) by private ordering raises a whole set of issues related to licensing through platforms, the interdependency of users and platforms, and the licensing by many to many.

The coexistence of a public ordering (legislated IPR) regime and a private ordering, (contractual) regime for regulating ownership (access, management, exclusion etc) in information raises a whole set of challenges to the economic analysis of IPR. It calls into question the justification for intellectual property, which is often assumed as non-excludable by technical and other legal means. We will return to this question in Chapter 6, which focuses on regulation by technology. The proliferation of private ordering in areas governed by IPR requires further consideration of the interface between intellectual property laws and contracts, which are governing the use of informational works. What legal status should be accorded to norms established by 'private ordering'? Should the state defer to such norms? What should be the legal validity of norms that are inconsistent with the policies that intellectual property laws seek to promote? Should the state enforce such norms? Under what circumstances should the state provide remedies for a breach of such contracts? The blurring of distinction between property and contracts, and new types of licensing schemes of many-to-many, are challenging the assumptions of the standard economic analysis of contracts, property, and intellectual property, and may require adjustments of its analytic framework.

This chapter takes a closer look at the interface between intellectual property and contracts. It is meant to examine whether the changing nature of knowledge production gives rise to different considerations related to private ordering for governing access to creative works. We begin by describing the rise of private ordering as a dominant strategy for governing creative works and inventions in the information environment (section 5.1). We introduce the general approach of law and economics in favor of private ordering and their broad enforcement (section 5.2) and raise the main points of critique against this approach (section 5.3). Subsequently, we address the effects of these developments on the dichotomy between contract and property (section 5.4). Finally, we describe the use of private ordering by social media platforms and the implications of the changing nature of content production (section 5.5).

## 5.1 The rise of private ordering for governing informational goods

Licensing agreements and contracts are playing an ever greater role in governing the terms of access to creative works and inventions. Digital networks offer new opportunities for content providers and creators to contract directly with the end users of their respective works. The proliferation of private ordering reflects a shift from property (*public ordering*) to contracts (*private ordering*) as a major mechanism for implementing intellectual property policy.

*Public ordering* and *private ordering* are two fundamentally different ways of governance. *Public ordering* refers to rule-making processes, which are designed by the state and its apparatus. Its norms reflect the outcome of collective action mechanisms, which are formulated and applied from the top down by public institutions. *Private ordering*, by contrast, concerns bottom-up processes, where each party voluntarily chooses to undertake the norms that will govern its behavior. This definition captures the fundamental justifications for the enforcement of norms created by *private ordering*: their self-imposition by the parties is considered not simply morally justifiable but also economically efficient. One of the questions addressed by this chapter is whether this description holds for private ordering when applied to licenses governing access to inventions and creative works, which aim at altering the intellectual property regime set by public ordering.

The rise of *private ordering*, as discussed in this chapter, refers to practices that are applied within a legal system and enforced by law enforcement mechanisms. The term *private ordering*, however, is much broader. It sometimes refers to self-adopted rules – social norms – followed by a community in the absence of any formal legal rules and sanctions. A classic example is the seminal work of Robert Ellickson on cattlemen in Shasta County, California (Ellickson 1991). In recent years we have witnessed a growing body of literature which documents the existence of different creative communities, where private ordering mechanisms are supplementing formal intellectual property laws in regulating the use of creative output. Two recent examples are the recipes of French chefs (Fauchart and von Hippel 2008) and the jokes of comedians (Oliar and Springman 2008). Here, however, we focus on a more narrow sense of *private ordering* referring to decentralized processes by which norms are formulated, where enforcement is achieved through the legal system.

Contracts are one of the main mechanisms for creating new norms of IP. Contract law defines when a mutual undertaking by parties constitutes a legally enforceable right, offering remedies against those who breach the contractual obligations. Similarly, technological measures, which often govern the use of digital works, define the scope of permissible use authorized by the vendor. Anti-circumvention regimes in the USA (the Digital Millennium Copyright Act 1998) and in Europe (Article 6 of Directive 2001/29/EC of the

European Parliament and of the Council of 22 May 2001 on the harmonization of certain aspects of copyright and related rights in the information society) provide immunity against circumvention of some technological protection measures employed by copyright owners. This latter type of private ordering will be further discussed in Chapter 6.

For the past two decades, licenses and contracts have become more pervasive in governing the use of works and inventions. End user license agreements (EULAs) define the scope of permissible uses of the work or invention and the terms under which it is authorized for use. Rightholders often use EULAs to expand the scope of protection provided under copyright law, by limiting the rights of users under legal doctrines such as 'fair use' and 'first sale'. Licenses may impose duties on the licensee related to the unprotected aspects of a work or an invention for which the licensor has no copyright or patent. Private ordering has also been employed in recent years by open access initiatives, to promote access to creative works and facilitate interaction, exchange and sharing of creative materials.

Contracts and intellectual property rights have always coexisted. Intellectual property regimes constitute basic entitlements, granting owners a set of exclusive rights against the world and requiring all potential users to acquire a license to use the protected information. Contracts are therefore the legal instrument for exercising property rights, enabling owners to exploit their property by licensing and assigning particular rights. Moreover, contractual arrangements between inventors and users offered an alternative to intellectual property protection. If one seeks to avoid the high transaction costs, or the disclosure, involved in registering a patent, an inventor may keep her invention a secret and rely on 'trade secrets' law to secure her interests. To keep the invention a secret, and at the same time enable its implementation by users, inventors must subject any user to a non-disclosure agreement (NDA). The threat that inventors would use NDAs to deny the public of their scientific and technological knowledge is often raised as a justification for expanding the scope of patent protection and strengthening the incentives to inventors to patent their inventions.

Digital technology gave rise to new mechanisms to govern the use of creative works. Content providers can contract directly with the masses of end users connected via digital network. Creative works, once a non-excludable public good, for which exclusivity was established only by intellectual property rights, are increasingly subject to terms of access drafted by content providers, at times enforced by technological means. Prior to the digital era contractual arrangements were prohibitively expensive for governing informational materials. Most of the content produced by the content industry during the 20th century was distributed in physical copies (books, newspapers, records, and later CDs and DVDs). Millions of copies produced by book publishers and the recording industry were distributed to anonymous buyers through intermediaries and retail stores. It was simply unfeasible for publishers to identify each and every purchaser of their copies and to make a bargain with each. Having no direct contractual relationship with potential consumers of their works, publishers had to rely on copyright laws to secure their rights in copyrighted materials.

Digital networks made it much easier to contract. Direct communication between owners and users allows creators and copyright holders to identify potential users and to conclude a bargain. Rightholders may further establish a long-term relationship with users, offering renewable licenses and monitoring the performance of contractual obligations. Contract formation is also easier. Rightholders can make access to informational products contingent upon acceptance of the terms of a license. Downloaders of content made available online are required to agree to the terms of use before gaining access. Digital copies may also be distributed with a license attached, which is prompted during installation of the digital copy, requiring consent by clicking 'I agree' (clickwrap license), or simply pops up on the screen before the music plays or the video clip runs (browsewrap license).

EULAs were used early on by software providers to define the scope of protection for software, at a time when it was still unclear whether software was entitled to any intellectual property protection. When copyright laws worldwide were expanded to cover computer programs, and in some jurisdictions software was even granted patent protection, licenses were used for acquiring additional legal protection. Restrictions on the use of software include provisions limiting the right of consumers to resell or give away the purchased copies of a computer program (often secured under the 'first sale' doctrine) or the right to reverse-engineer the program (often secured under 'fair use'). In some cases, EULAs were employed to limit the use of informational goods, which were not otherwise protected under copyright law, such as a database of phone numbers (*ProCD Inc.*, 86 F.3d 1447).

Digital networks further facilitate self-help measures that were not effectively available for governing information in the analog environment. TPMs enable information vendors to distribute creative works subject to terms codified by the code itself. Content providers can set the terms of access in the digital package that wraps the content, so the terms literally become part of the product – that is, the copy of the work purchased by the consumer. TPMs could be designed not only to enforce copyright as defined by legislation but also to expand the scope of protection by disabling uses that are explicitly exempted under copyright law.

The use of EULAs and TPMs not only changes the transaction between owners and users but may also transform the nature of the commodity which is the subject of the transaction. Computer programs are classic examples. Software is a functional product, comprised of sequences of instructions intended to operate particular tasks in a computer. Software vendors are claiming, however, that software is licensed rather than sold. The legal framing of the transaction as a license may limit, for instance, the right of software users to sell their used copy. Another example is eBooks. Printed books are usually widely distributed as commercial products and typically consumers are not required to undergo any approval process or to undertake any additional commitments before they can use the book. eBooks, by contrast, are not sold but rather licensed. The eBook is subject to a license agreement, setting limits on the freedom to use the book in a certain way, such as prohibiting the lending of the eBook or the selling of the copy to others. Publishers may further restrict the number of readings or, in the case of libraries, restrict the number of eBook checkouts a library can perform before it is required to pay again for the eBook. Only recently HarperCollins, a major publishing company, announced that it is revising the lending terms of eBooks so that libraries will be licensed to circulate an eBook only 26 times before the license expires. Such restrictions are likely to compromise the ability of libraries to perform their fundamental role of preserving and lending content. This may not only lead to the elimination of public libraries but may also abolish altogether the rights of users to access content they have not purchased.

Private ordering has also been employed in recent years by open access initiatives to facilitate access to creative materials. There is no strict definition of open access, or open content, and the term is often used to describe a wide range of activities with different strategies, goals and ideological commitments. Some initiatives focus on availability, promoting free and unrestricted access to all kinds of content, such as open access journals (e.g. BioMed, Public Library of Science (PLoS)) and courseware (e.g. MIT Open Courseware project). Other initiatives emphasize freedom to use copyrighted materials, and especially to modify, remix and tinker with pre-existing materials. The conviction shared by many open content initiatives is that the online environment facilitates new ways of sharing and collaborating in the production of creative works, and that copyright law in its current form creates an obstacle to exercising these new opportunities (Lessig 2001; Litman 2004; Benkler 2006).

The pioneering attempt to secure freedom in software through a matrix of licenses was the innovative general public license (GPL) designed by the Free Software Foundation (FSF) in the late 1980s. FSF licenses endorse four freedoms related to computer programs: to run the program, to study it, to modify it, and to share or redistribute the original program and any modified versions thereof. The Free Software Foundation, founded by Richard Stallman, manages the GPL, which aims at securing these free software principles. The GPL is a 'copyleft' license, which has a viral effect: it applies automatically to any new copy of the software and any derivative program based on the original one. Subsequent creators and users therefore are bound by the terms of access defined by the license, and must strictly apply them to any subsequent work they create using the original free software. The open source initiative, launched in 1998, adopted a more liberal strategy, defining minimal key elements that must be met for a license to qualify as an open source license. Consequently, over 100 different open source licenses are estimated to be available today.

The colossal success of the free software movement was followed by successful licensing initiatives for other creative works such as creative commons, as well as licenses for scientific building blocks such as BiOS. Creative commons offers a user-friendly licensing scheme which applies to copyrighted materials of all sorts. The licensing platform allows authors to generate licenses of their choice. This licensing scheme is modular, and licensors can therefore mix and match predefined provisions requiring attribution (Attribution), banning commercial use (Noncommercial), prohibiting the preparation of any derivative work (NoDerivs), or stipulating that any subsequent derivative work will be subject to the same terms as the original (ShareAlike). While creative commons' Attribution license is the least restrictive on access, permitting any use as long as credit has been given, the Attribution–NonCommercial–NoDerivs license is probably the most restrictive creative commons license. The license permits the copying of the work 'as is', bans any alteration or transformation which builds upon the work, and excludes any commercial use. Creative commons' automatic licensing platform simplifies the licensing process and is also intended to help end users easily to identify works authorized for use. The license is accessible in a legally enforceable format, but also in comprehensible language, intended for potential users, and in machine code, so that works subject to more permissible terms could be automatically located by search tools.

The different goals of private ordering, and the different ways in which these strategies are employed, should not conceal the fact that it has become a dominant source of the norms governing access to creative works. Consequently, two competing models for governing the use of informational works are emerging. One is the traditional intellectual property rule created by centralized institutions of the territorial state; the other is the emerging regime of standard contracts generating rules via private ordering. Whereas in the past the use of informational products was governed almost exclusively by intellectual property laws, it is currently governed also by contracts.

Should we welcome these developments? Can private ordering better tailor access to accommodate different needs and preferences of different industries and communities? Is it likely to generate optimal terms of access to creative works and inventions? Should licenses and TPMs take priority over norms defined through public ordering, or should private ordering be subject to intellectual property law and take force within its boundaries only? The following discussion will address some of these questions.

## 5.2 The canonic position of law and economics towards private ordering

### *5.2.1 From social norms to private ordering*

Private ordering outside the IP context has been the focus of several law and economics studies examining how systems of norms, which were not generated by the state, but instead voluntarily adopted by communities, regulate the behavior of their members (e.g. Ellickson 2005; Bernstein 1992; Cooter

1991). The notion of 'private ordering' has several meanings. It refers to the way in which norms are being created and enforced outside a legal regime, namely to extralegal systems in which rules are followed in the absence of any legal obligation to do so. 'Private ordering' may also refer to the origin of norms, namely to decentralized processes by which norms are formulated, and thereafter enforced by the legal system. This chapter focuses on the latter. It examines attempts to regulate relations among people regarding the use of information by voluntarily committing to sets of norms.

For many scholars of law and economics 'private ordering' regimes are appealing. The economic approach generally presumes that private ordering regimes would be more efficient and therefore hold them superior to regulation by government. This reflects a general suspicion towards central governments, which presumably lack sufficient information regarding the most efficient arrangement and the sufficient flexibility for tailoring it to changing circumstances. Governments are also presumably exposed to public choice distortions.

This view resonates in the law and economics scholarship pertaining to the rise of private ordering in informational works. The idea that we may no longer need to rely on centralized regulatory institutions, and may individually make our own choices on the terms and conditions for using information, seems to be liberating. 'Private ordering' is seen as a manifestation of fundamental values such as autonomy and freedom. If intellectual property laws were perceived by some as a 'necessary evil' of the pre-digitized age, the prospects of replacing such property rules with a free and diverse 'market for norms' is welcomed most favorably. One can point to two main arguments of law and economics scholars in favor of private ordering: the limits of public ordering by government, and the efficiency of contracts. These arguments are further discussed in the following sections.

### *5.2.2 Private ordering and the limits of central intervention*

Advocates of private ordering believe that using it for governing access to creative works is superior to public ordering. In essence they argue that private ordering is more efficient than intellectual property laws since the bargaining parties are often better informed. Therefore, private ordering, rather than rules designed by central governments, will better serve the parties' interests and better promote overall social welfare. Essentially they make the following claims: first, governments cannot determine the optimal terms of access to creative works; and, second, that information markets are capable of generating the most efficient terms (Bell 1998; Dam 1999; Easterbrook 1996; Hardy 1996; Merges 1997; O'Rourke 1997).

Underlying this approach is a deep distrust of governmental rule-making processes. According to private ordering advocates, governments are unable to determine the requirements of different owners and users of creative works, and lack reliable means to ascertain the appropriate level of protection that should be assigned to each work (Easterbrook 1996; Merges 1997). Therefore, regulators are likely to define restrictions on access to information either too narrowly, thus diminishing incentives to authors and inventors, or too broadly, thus restricting efficient access to creative works and inventions. The risk of error escalates when rapidly changing technologies require flexibility and constant adjustment to ever changing needs. Legislators, it is argued, simply lack the necessary flexibility to respond promptly and efficiently to the changing circumstances created by technological developments. Furthermore, the legislative process itself is inefficient. The processes of defining rights in informational works, or amending and refining such rights, involve high transaction costs (Hardy 1996). Such processes involve costs of conducting hearings, preparing reports, processing comments and revisions, drafting, and lobbying. These high costs deter the parties involved – legislature, industry, and interest groups – from engaging in frequent attempts to revise and amend existing provisions. At the same time, however, rapid technological change requires adapting the legal rules to the changing needs of the online environment (Hardy 1994: 995–96). The legislative process is therefore perceived as inefficient for regulating rights of use in informational works.

### *5.2.3 The contract-as-product approach*

Advocates of private ordering further assume that market processes are better suited for governing the terms of access to creative works. Owners and consumers of informational works, it is argued, have several advantages over governments in this regard. In the absence of a market failure, such as the presence of a monopoly, the market will generate efficient arrangements for the use of informational works as reflected in the end user license agreements (EULAs).

From an economic perspective, EULAs are perceived as a commodity, an integral part of the product. Terms and conditions that govern the use of information are determined in the same way that the quality and price of goods are determined, namely through competition. Individuals are expressing their preferences for various license terms directly through market transactions. Just as a computer program can be priced by its features, it could also be priced based on the scope of permissible uses provided by the license. A licensee's consent to purchase a restricting license at a lower price is no different from her consent to purchase a computer subject to a one-year (rather than a three-year) warranty at a lower price. This approach was expressed in the opinion of the US Court of Appeals of the 7th Circuit in *ProCD, Inc. v. Zeidenberg* (86 F.3d 1447). Terms of the contract, the court held, should be determined by competition: 'Terms of use are no less a part of "the product" than are the size of the database and the speed with which the software compiles listings. Competition among vendors, not judicial revision of a package's contents, is how consumers are protected in a market economy' (*ProCD, Inc.*, 86 F.3d 1447, 1449). The contract-as-product view becomes even more powerful when TPMs are employed, and both the terms of the use and the creative work are represented in the same digital format (Radin 2006: 1230).

Essentially, private ordering advocates believe that terms governing the use of creative works are shaped by market forces, in the same way as the quality and price of goods are determined through free competition. Individual users express their preferences for particular terms of use through their purchasing choices, and content providers satisfy the demand by adjusting the license restrictions and price. The market reflects the preferences of the relevant parties more accurately. This lowers the chances of error in setting the optimal level of use for informational works and reduces inefficiencies (Easterbrook 1996: 211). Efficiency in transactions regarding the use of informational works will lower the price of accessing information and, thus, make access more available to the public.

One important advantage offered by private ordering, in this regard, is enhancing efficiency by facilitating price discrimination (Fisher 2004; Meurer 1997). Rather than distributing information at a fixed price, subject to copyright restrictions alone, providers of content can tailor different packages for particular consumers, selling limited rights at a lower price. Users will pay for precisely the type of use they wish to acquire. Users who want to make a special use of the copyrighted materials will pay a higher price for expanded authorizations. Users who place high value on receiving timely information could pay a premium (e.g. news service, hardcover books) and, similarly, users who seek to make specific exploitations will be willing to pay a higher price for expanded rights. Users who make basic use (such as making a single copy, or displaying the work for personal use) will be charged a lower fee for a limited license. If the licensee is willing to pay a higher price for less restrictive licenses, the market will provide for it (Easterbrook 1996: 211). This theoretical approach was echoed by Judge Easterbrook in the *ProCD* case (86 F.3d 1447). In *ProCD*, the court examined restrictions on the use of a database (that is non-copyrightable under US law) in a shrinkwrap license. Judge Easterbrook interpreted the restrictions in ProCD's license as an attempt to engage in price discrimination, namely selling its database for personal use to the general public at a low price while selling to commercial businesses at a higher price. If ProCD could not have charged commercial users a higher price, it would have been forced to raise the price to private end users. This would have harmed end users and limited public access to the work. The court concluded that it is therefore necessary to give force to the contract in such cases, to enable a control arbitrage that would make price discrimination work (*ProCD, Inc.*, 86 F.3d 1447: 1449).

### 5.2.4 *Implications of the law and economics position*

The claim that private ordering is superior to rules defined by intellectual property laws carry some important policy implications. As we discuss further below, if contracts are superior to IPR there is stronger justification for substituting IPR with private ordering, Moreover, there is no ground for government interference in such contracts under freedom-of-contract principles. The 'private ordering' discourse thus might be invoked to limit the scope of legitimate government intervention in such transactions. Advocates of private ordering rely on a conventional, although controversial, distinction between public and private. The public/private distinction is central to liberal political theory, which perceives the private sphere as immune from any governmental interference. Viewing the private sphere of contracts as a manifestation of individual autonomy renders it free from state intrusion. Furthermore, contracts are considered private in the sense that they affect only the contracting parties. Such private arrangements in the marketplace raise no public interest and, therefore, any government intervention in such arrangements will be considered unjustified.

The economic approach assumes that market forces of supply and demand may guarantee the optimal level of use of information. Use restrictions will reflect the preferences of users to pay less for limited usage rights or pay more for expanded privileges. Consequently, in the case of conflict between the terms of contracts and intellectual property law, the contract should prevail, unless certain market imperfections exist (O'Rourke 1995: 527–28). Robert Merges concludes that 'unless serious third-party harm or constitutional rights are implicated, intellectual property holders should be free to craft contracts as they see fit' (Merges 1997: 126).

On a practical level, if private ordering regimes are more efficient than copyright it follows that contracts (private ordering) should be given priority over copyright laws (public ordering), and terms of a contract that conflict with copyright policies should nevertheless be effective. From this perspective, the role of law is, therefore, limited to providing the two legal fundamentals of the market: assigning property rights to owners and facilitating an efficient exchange system by contract law (Easterbrook 1996: 210–212).

## 5.3 Private ordering: a critical view

The governance of creative works in the digital environment through private ordering was highly controversial from the start, and has remained so for over a decade (Elkin-Koren 1997, 1998; Cohen 1998; Lemley 1999; Guibault 2002; Easterbrook 2005; Epstein 2010). The proposition that private ordering is superior to a copyright regime since it would lead to more efficiency rests on several key assumptions. One set of assumptions relates to contract formation. Contracts are expected to generate optimal outcomes since the process of contract formation is presumably voluntary, reflects the bilateral assent of informed parties and occurs in a competitive market. Another set of assumptions relates to the ability of market mechanisms to produce efficient outcomes. Opponents of private ordering disagree with this description of the market for licenses (Elkin-Koren 1998; Cohen 1998; Lemley 2006; Radin 2006). They challenge the proposition that private ordering will lead to greater efficiency in governing access to creative works. Below is a brief summary of some of these arguments.

### *5.3.1 The contract-as-product re-examined*

For contracts to be efficient they must reflect the voluntary consent of all parties involved. Key aspects of transactions in information, however, render this assumption unsound (Elkin-Koren 1998). The main critique raised by opponents of private ordering is that unilateral licenses and TPMs are not really contracts, and therefore should not be perceived as reflecting the consent of end users of creative works (Cohen 1998).

Indeed, EULAs, which are unilateral documents drafted by rightholders, are often enforced even in the absence of assent by end users. Courts have held online contracts enforceable based on very minimal evidence of assent. For instance, shrinkwrap licenses were enforced even when the licensee became aware of the terms only after the computer program was purchased (*ProCD, Inc.*, 86 F.3d 1447). Similarly, browsewrap licenses were held enforceable even where the license provisions were simply posted online stating that the mere use of the product or website constituted acceptance of the terms of the license (*Register.com, Inc.*, 356 F.3d 393; but see *Specht*, 306 F.3d 17).

This outcome reflects a general approach by courts to electronic contracting, thinning the requirement of consent. Courts expect a fairly minimal demonstration of assent in treating a unilaterally drafted license as a binding contract (Lemley 2006). As eloquently described by Margaret Jane Radin (2006: 1231):

> The idea of voluntary willingness first decayed into consent, then into assent, then into a mere possibility or opportunity for assent, then merely fictional assent, then to mere efficient rearrangement of entitlements without any consent or assent.

Moreover, with respect to licensing works protected by copyright, the enforceability of licenses might become even stronger. It is often suggested that these online contracts are in fact a *property license*, which is not a contract (see for instance, *Jacobsen v. Katzer*, 535 F.3d 1373 (Fed. Cir. 2008)). It is a unilateral legal action, through which a property owner can exercise her rights and define the scope of the authorized use. The binding force of a property license does not derive from exercising autonomous will and therefore it does not require consent by the user. The binding force of the license stems from the property rules, in this case copyright law. Copyright law empowers owners to exclude others from making certain uses of the work, and a license is necessary to permit what the law otherwise prohibits. Such permission to use the work could be conditional and might be subject to various restrictions. Under this view of EULAs as property licenses, the burden of proof rests on the user, who must show that the use was properly authorized by the rightholder.

The choice of interpreting the transaction as a *property license* rather than a *contract* has significant legal implications. If it is a conditional license (such as a requirement that credit would be given to the original author) and the condition is not satisfied, the use of the work would be a violation of IPR. If the required attribution is simply a covenant, then failing to give credit would amount to a breach of contract. While a remedy for a breach of contract would be damages, the remedy for an IPR infringement would often be an injunction. Thus, for instance, the US Court of Appeals in *Jacobsen v. Katzer* held that an open source software was subject to a conditional property license. Consequently, incorporating the open source software into commercial software without meeting the conditions (proper attribution, reference to the license and the tracking of changes in the program) was an unlicensed modification and distribution of copyrighted materials and therefore constituted a copyright infringement. The Court of Appeals in that case recognized the significance of the license in enabling collaboration among a large number of collaborators and providing assurance to downstream users against liability.

The pervasiveness of standard form contracts, and their economic advantage in reducing transaction costs, may support their enforceability in many circumstances, even in the absence of meaningful assent. It does not follow, however, that simply because standard form contracts are enforceable one may assume that the parties in fact have agreed to their terms (Cohen 1998). For contracts to be efficient, however, they must reflect the voluntary consent of all parties involved. But this is often absent in mass-license transactions related to informational works. Users cannot be considered as agreeing to terms of use if they are not adequately informed of the contract terms and do not properly understand them.

One cannot seriously talk about a *license-as-product* when the terms of use are often non-transparent, and are hardly ever read by anyone. The lack of knowledge of the contracting party regarding the provisions of a contract is a problem suffered by all standard form contracts. It is widely acknowledged that the vast majority of consumers do not read standard form contracts. Consequently, if buyers are unaware of the contract terms and do not factor the contract provisions into their purchasing choices, the terms are likely to remain biased towards the seller who drafted them and will not reflect an efficient bargain. This argument has recently received some empirical support. A study of EULAs' provisions in the software industry found that terms are biased toward the seller, even though there was still a great variety in terms offered by different sellers (Marotta-Wurgler 2007).

One response to this issue in the law and economics literature claims that such market imperfection could be fixed by a few purchasers who have the greatest interest in reading the terms of the license agreement and could cause the seller to modify the terms. Thus, it is argued, an 'informed minority' of buyers, who have a greater interest in the standard terms and will read the terms, are sufficient to address this problem. A seller who cannot distinguish between reading and non-reading buyers, will offer the better terms to all buyers (Schwartz and Wilde 1983). As numerous scholars have argued, however, an 'informed minority' is insufficient for assuring optimal terms and when consumers do not read the terms or do not understand them, sellers have no incentive to modify their standard terms (Goldberg 1974; Katz 1990; Cruz and Hinck 1995; Gazal-Ayal 2007).

The terms of use for informational works raise even greater difficulties, as some information failures are inherent in the market for informational works (Elkin-Koren and Salzberger 2004). Shopping for legal terms is of course different from shopping for price or quality of a product, as terms and conditions are less transparent. This is especially true for TPMs, where restrictions on the use of content are embodied in the computer program and therefore are often non-transparent at the time of the bargain. This point is further elaborated in Chapter 6.

As a general matter, terms of use for creative works and inventions are not as transparent as price or other salient attributes of a product such as speed or power. License restrictions, defining the scope of use of intangibles, are often highly abstract and very difficult to comprehend. Even people who are capable and willing to read the terms of use are hard pressed to determine accurately the impact of these terms on their utility. Apart from incomprehensible legal drafting, this is also a result of the abstract nature of copyright restrictions and legal definitions of intangible uses. Since information lacks physical boundaries, we may often be unaware of the type of usage that we are employing. The legal description of acts covered by the license is often unintuitive and controversial. For instance, simply browsing would not commonly be conceived as reproduction, and saving a file in the shared documents library would not be commonly understood as public distribution or as 'making available', which may trigger copyright liability. The idea that the license is the product and the terms of use are simply part of the creative work is therefore unsound.

Furthermore, informational works may be used in many unpredictable ways. It is usually difficult to determine ex ante what type of usage one would wish to make. It is even more difficult to attach a value to all uses of information in advance. Creative uses are likely to be more spontaneous and to emerge through engagement in reading, listening or otherwise experiencing a work. Consumers' purchase decisions are therefore less likely to be motivated by specific terms of use. Consumers are more likely to treat the license as a general name for an authorization to use the work.

Another informational failure arises from the fact that the market for creative works is likely to suffer from information asymmetries. Mass producers of content are repeat players who enjoy a systematic information advantage over end users. The former can better assess the risks and benefits associated with any provision and can better understand the impact of any given term on the potential exploitation of the work. Since they execute a large number of similar transactions over time, they have sufficient incentive to collect information about the legal implications of each provision and the validity of different terms included in the license. Such information asymmetries should make us more skeptical about the outcome of free bargaining for formulating terms of access to creative works.

Efficient bargaining requires not only informed consent but also free choice. Consent and choice are related concepts. We are unlikely to hold a party as agreeing to the terms of a contract unless she had a choice not to do so voluntarily. But 'consent' requires not merely the ability freely to exercise one's will, but also the necessary knowledge required to act deliberately and not arbitrarily. From an economic perspective, an efficient bargain requires that parties enter the transaction voluntarily. This would guarantee that the bargain indeed reflects their preferences. Absent the voluntary consent of all parties, the private ordering regime merely reflects an exercise of power by information providers and enjoys no supremacy over other types of governance.

Contracts and licenses supplement protection by intellectual property, and therefore are likely to be performed in a monopolistic environment. Intellectual property provides owners with a monopoly power over the exploitation of their particular work or innovation, which, in light of the lack of substitutes, enables owners to monopolize the market. As we further discussed in Chapter 3, the extent to which inventions and creative works actually have substitutes is a controversial issue, and the answer may vary depending on the type of work and the type of user involved (Landes and Posner 1989: 328). Although some informational works may have perfect substitutes (such as telephone listings), many works, from critical medications to unique pieces of art, may not. To the extent that an informational work is indispensable, information suppliers will have the power to dictate the terms of use (Cohen 1998: 526). Thus, uniformity of terms may reflect disparities in bargaining power. In many cases, individual users will simply lack the necessary bargaining power to change industry standard contractual provisions. Although recent empirical studies of EULAs in the software industry found little correlation between pro-seller terms and the level of competitive conditions (Marotta-Wurgler 2008), this is only one finding within an under-researched field. At any event, a low level of competition over the terms of use renders the assumptions regarding choice and mobility problematic, to say the least.

### *5.3.2 Markets cannot be trusted to secure optimal access to creative works*

Skeptics of private ordering argue that it is unlikely that market mechanisms will secure efficient access to creative works, due to market failures. A major problem with private ordering for governing access to creative works is externalities. From an economic perspective, contracts are generating efficient outcomes, since all those who are affected by them are part of the bargain. Yet, in the case of contracts pertaining to informational works, not everyone affected by the rights and duties created by the license are represented in the transactions pertaining to their interests. Assuming that terms of use are agreed upon by the licensor and licensee, the most they can reflect is the preferences of users to pay less for limited rights or to pay more for expanded privileges. The terms may reflect the immediate value users place on any given transaction, but will fail to reflect the public utility and the benefits to society as a whole. For instance, an EULA restriction on reverse engineering may not only affect the purchaser of the computer program, but also the public at large, which would be denied compatible programs that may foster innovation and lower the price. A schoolteacher may be reluctant to purchase a license to perform a certain documentary film even though it might be socially beneficial if she made the work available to her elementary-school students whose welfare is not taken into account in the transaction.

Terms of access often carry positive or negative externalities for others. Access to creative works is necessary to foster further innovation, creativity and progress. That is because creative works are ingredients used in generating subsequent works. Access to cultural goods cultivates the workforce for further creation: it educates; it stimulates our minds; it expands our understanding of the world around us; it provides inspiration and facilitates creativity and innovation. Therefore, wide and indiscriminate access to creative works is necessary to make it possible for subsequent authors and inventors to create further (Elkin-Koren 2007). Indiscriminate access to creative works is also essential for widespread participation in the creation of culture. Such participation does not necessarily involve actively generating new works. It may also take the form of engaging with creative works, and constructing meaning which arises from the way it is represented through our reading of novels, listening to music and making actual use of technological artifacts in our everyday lives (du Gay et al. 1997).

The social utility encompassed in the use of creative works may not be accurately reflected through individuals' purchase choices in market exchanges, also because of the positive network effects of information, on which we elaborated in the previous chapter (as more people are using the same technology the greater the utility each user is likely to benefit from such usage). These considerations make us generally more skeptical of the ability of market mechanisms and private ordering efficiently to regulate the use of information.

### *5.3.3 The inconsistency of the law and economics approach*

On top of the two points raised above, one can point to an inconsistency of the pro-private ordering arguments with the canonic law and economic approach regarding the justification of IPR and especially the proprietary model and its endorsement of intellectual property rights expansion by public ordering (see Chapter 4). First, under the law and economics assumption that private ordering reflects real consent and thus efficient outcomes, the mere fact that we witness significant departures from the legislated arrangements point to inefficiency of the legislated arrangements endorsed by the same group of scholars. Second, the support for private ordering, which partly relies on the analysis of the deficiencies and inefficiencies of IPR legislated by governments, does not correspond to the support advocated by law and economics scholars to legislated amendments of IPR and to IPR laws in general.

Third, the analysis of private ordering as yielding desirable results is in contrast to the main premises of the normative analysis of IPR, which is founded on the bases of the public goods and externalities market failures of the free market. In other words, if contracting in the free market is sufficient to enable an efficient production of informational goods, why do we need IPR in the first place? As we elaborate below, the endorsement of private ordering encompasses implicit new meaning of contracts and property and the distinctions between them, as well as new meaning for private and public and the borders between them,

## 5.4 Viral contracts and the new property

Viral license is a term first coined by Margaret Jane Radin (2000) to describe the widespread effect of such contracts that limit the rights of subsequent owners or users of the property. Viral provisions were first included in the 1989 GPL which authorized anyone to copy, modify and distribute its code as long as any copies or derivatives based on the original code were distributed subject to the same license. By asserting copyright in the code, the GPL enabled developers of free software to secure compliance with the license terms and prevent others from capturing the code and making it proprietary. The licensing scheme, often called copyleft, intends to ensure that the original license conditions would apply to all downstream versions of the software.

The viral effect of the license is achieved by requiring that every copy of the program and every derivative will be subject to the same license. The viral provision of the GPL (Section 2(b) of GPL v2) states as follows:

> You must cause any work that you distribute or publish, that in whole or in part contains or is derived from the Program or any part thereof, to be licensed as a whole at no charge to all third parties under the terms of this license.

The license further provides that each time a GPL licensee redistributes 'the Program (or any work based on the Program), the recipient automatically receives a license from the original licensor to copy, distribute or modify the Program' (Section 6 of GPL v2). Similarly, the creative commons ShareAlike provision provides: 'If you alter, transform, or build upon this work, you may distribute the resulting work only under the same or similar license to this one'. The power to set restrictions on subsequent users of the work is particularly important for open content initiatives, such as free software and creative commons that seek to offer an alternative to the current IPR regime. But viral licensing is also employed by proprietary licenses.

The legal strategy of using viral contracts may cause some inefficiencies by increasing the cost of coordination and even preventing coordination altogether. One issue is incompatible viral licenses that may prevent the mix and match of pre-existing materials. New informational works often incorporate pre-existing materials. When a new work is derived from a couple of sources that are subject to incompatible viral licenses it may not be generated at all.

This would reduce interoperability and the freedom of subsequent users to remix existing materials. If we want to promote use and reuse of works, and allow creators to incorporate previous works into their art, we must ensure compatibility with other licenses. But diversity of licenses inevitably leads to conflicts. Some of the creative commons licenses are incompatible in themselves. For instance, if a computer game developer wants to use some images that are subject to a creative commons non-commercial ShareAlike license and another picture that is subject to a creative commons attribution ShareAlike license she will not be able to mix the two images. Attribution–SA would require that subsequent works would be distributed without any further restrictions and non-commercial ShareAlike would require that subsequent works be licensed for non-commercial uses only.

### 5.4.1 *Is it a contract?*

As discussed in the previous sections, standard law and economic analysis of contracts justifies the enforcement of contracts as they presumably reflect a voluntary transaction between two or more consenting parties. Such consent implies that the contracting parties benefit from it and hence it contributes to society's total welfare. This is not the meaning of 'contract' within the emerging private ordering in the digital environment. To secure the interests of the rightholders effectively contracts should apply to third parties. The fact that licenses are enforceable against their immediate contracting parties is simply insufficient. Creative works tend to be used and reused over and over again, changing formats while being molded into new forms of expressions. If subsequent users of the original work were not subject to the terms of the original license, the licensing scheme would shortly become meaningless; third parties who gained access to the work without directly contracting with the rightholders would be able to use the work against the will of the original owner (Elkin-Koren 2005).

What types of legal claims does a rightholder have against third parties who fail to comply with the terms of the license? The simplest case concerns a third party who appropriates the work in a way that is covered by copyright. In such a case, copyright owners would have a copyright (property) claim against infringing third parties. For instance, if the license of a computer program prohibits unauthorized copying, a user who accepts the license agreement and is bound by the contract may not copy the program for purposes other than those listed by the license. If a third party who did not agree to the contract, copies the software, such unauthorized copying would constitute copyright infringement.

The situation is different, however, when the licensor seeks to establish new rights, not enumerated under copyright law; for instance, a license agreement of software prohibiting any subsequent sale of copies which is in conflict with the right of purchasers under the first sale doctrine. If a third party acquires copies and redistributes it, the rights of the copyright holder against her are less clear.

One way to view these contracts is as a property license. To the extent that copyright empowers owners to exclude others from certain uses, a license to use the work permits what the law otherwise prohibits. Permission to use the work could be subject to various restrictions. Under this view, the burden of proof rests on the user, who must show that the use was properly authorized by the rightholder. A property license is not a contract. It is a unilateral legal action, through which a property owner can exercise her rights, and it defines the boundaries of legitimate use. Its binding force does not derive from exercising autonomous will. The restrictions imposed by the license are enforceable due to property rights, and they do not require voluntary consent. It is arguable that copyright owners have the legal power to restrict the use of their works indefinitely. Yet, enforcing legal obligations outside the scope of the property right against third parties could subsequently lead to new forms of property. Owners could precondition the license upon behaviors that are related neither to the use of the work nor to the use of copyright. Owners may wish to condition a license upon the purchase of another product, or license the work for non-competing uses only, or license a work provided that users would refrain from criticizing the work or exploring its innovative secrets. Should such restrictions hold against third parties? We may of course distinguish between different types of license provisions, based on their constitutionality or the antitrust issues they provoke. Yet, if such restrictions are treated as a property license, the grounds for legal intervention in the sovereignty of the property owner are likely to be limited.

Typically, rights and duties created by contracts are rights in personam, namely, they bind only the parties to any given contract. Contracts create rights against parties to the contract who undertook an obligation by consenting to the terms of the agreement. Holding parties legally obliged to keep their promises is not only considered morally justifiable (Fried 2006) but also efficient. The parties are thought to be in the best position to ascertain the cost and benefits associated with the rights and obligations designed by the contract. Therefore, from an economic standpoint, a contract is considered efficient only if it reflects the free will of consenting parties. That is why contracts typically do not impose duties on third parties who do not accept their terms.

There is a slippery slope from concluding consent or acceptance on the bases of very minimal evidence, as exemplified by Easterbrook J's ruling in the *ProCD* case on shrinkwrap licenses or by the *Register.com, Inc.* case regarding browsewrap licenses, and the extension of this conclusion to third parties' obligations. What makes someone a party to a binding agreement? Would simply using a copyrighted work constitute acceptance? When access to the work constitutes a legally binding consent, all access to the work is in fact governed by the contract. The terms of use thus become effective against all. Minimizing the legal requirements for online contract formation and enforcing licenses even without an explicit indication of consent on the part of the licensee may give rise to contracts that run with the asset.

Both the property license analysis and contractual analysis require further consideration. The property license analysis assumes a rather expansive interpretation of the legal powers vested with copyright and patent owners. If owners are able to create indefinite restrictions on the use of their works, beyond the bundle of rights defined by the intellectual property rule, they could unilaterally constitute new types of property forms. This analysis entails an understanding of intellectual property rights as absolute property rights, which undermines the delicately balanced regulatory regime set by the law. Is this broad interpretation of copyright and patents justifiable? Lowering the requirements necessary for establishing consent by contracting parties further allows content providers to enforce contractual restrictions against third parties. Such standard licenses that 'come with' each work would define its terms of use, changing de facto the legislative arrangement.

### *5.4.2 Blurring distinctions: private/public, contracts/property*

Treating EULAs as contracts, even in the absence of any meaningful consent, or viewing EULAs as property licenses, which allow enforcement against every conceivable user, might carry serious consequences on access to copyrighted materials. First, when the mere use of copyrighted materials is seen as constituting consent to a legally binding contract, access to works is automatically governed by unilaterally defined terms of access. These provisions, drafted by private parties, acquire general applicability and become effective against all, not just the parties who have undertaken them voluntarily. The distinction between private and public ordering collapses.

Second, enforcing standard licenses against parties who did not undertake the terms of use, blurs the distinction between property and contracts. IPR differ from contractual obligations, in that the right and the corresponding duties they impose on third parties 'run with the asset' (Hansmann and Kraakman 2002). Copyright and patent law allocate the initial entitlements, while contract law governs their transfer; intellectual property law creates rights against the world (in rem), whereas contracts apply only to the parties (in personam). A legal policy that treats contractual restrictions as enforceable against third parties gives rise to contracts that run with the asset. Enforcing standard licenses against parties who did not assent to the contract blurs the distinction between property and contracts. It allows distributors, rightholders and possibly others to establish rights in rem through contracts (Elkin-Koren 1997: 102–104).

Third, when rightholders can enforce use restrictions against third parties, beyond the bundle of rights defined by the property rule, they can unilaterally constitute new types of property. Property rules reflect an exclusion strategy for regulating the use of resources: they restrict access rather than specify the permissible or prohibited uses of any particular resource. They automatically inflict a standard bundle of duties on all persons in society to avoid a use, unless authorized by the owner. When the legal duties defined by the license become enforceable against all subsequent users, all users must bear the burden of learning the content of each and every license term in order to avoid violation. That is why typically the law does not enforce contracts that run with the asset, and claims against third parties are normally denied. Merrill and Smith (2001) explain that the objection to new forms of rights in rem aims at reducing information costs. Property rights, they argue, communicate a standard bundle of rights related to an asset, thereby reducing transaction costs involved in determining the type of rights and obligations that are associated with that asset. When we allow content providers to create property-like rights (rights of exclusion, which are automatically imposed against everyone who uses the resource) we substantially increase the information cost of potential users. These are the costs incurred by third parties, ie non-owners, who seek to avoid an infringement of IPR (Long 2004). End users of creative works, who simply seek to avoid inadvertent interference with copyright or patents, will be required to investigate which restriction of the many applicable licenses applies to their respective use. These costs of avoidance may undesirably increase barriers on access to creative works and inventions (Elkin-Koren 2005).

## 5.5 Private ordering and the social web

The digital environment not only fosters greater reliance on private ordering for governing access to creative materials but it also transforms the structure of the content market. The lower cost of coordinating creative efforts and distributing materials to a large audience enables individuals to play a bigger role in generating and distributing new content. Individual users can *mass self-communicate* original content (Castells 2009) and collaborate with others in the production and distribution of creative works. Bloggers may post news and analysis, professional and amateur photographers may upload their photos to Flickr or Picasa, independent musicians may share their music clips on YouTube and programmers may collaborate in creating new software. The mass content industry of the 20th century, which was dominated by media conglomerates and large publishing houses, is being at least partly replaced by the social web. Likewise, the share of innovations and new technologies, which is a product of individuals or small companies, has increased significantly, as opposed to the past in which big corporations were their main source.

Does the ascendancy of UGC, the social web and collaborative innovations outside the firm hierarchy give rise to different considerations related to private ordering for governing access and usage? Put differently, does the current usage of private ordering and its endorsement by courts pose an obstacle to the new mode of production of information and the development of the social web? Some of the arguments raised against private ordering for governing access to creative works have presumed an environment where standard licenses were designed by the content industry to govern mass-produced content in a unified and often restrictive manner. Would the same concerns apply equally to the emerging creative landscape of UGC?

The social web introduces new challenges to the standard economic analysis of private ordering: one issue arises from the fact that users are both consumers of services and producers of content. Another issue has to do with the social dimension of the new mode of production that is not fully captured by market transactions. A third issue relates to the high transaction costs involved in governing social production by private ordering.

### 5.5.1 *The dual nature of users and platforms*

In the social web, terms of access to content are often defined by platforms. The key players in the new social web environment are users/authors and social media platforms, which enable users to share their content with one another and to collaborate in producing new works. These players have distinct stakes and interests, which are different from those involved in the mass production of content. Consequently, the economic analysis of these contractual arrangements is different from the standard analysis of market transactions.

Users/authors, or 'prosumers', a term coined by Alvin Toffler in 1980 to describe the dual role of a producer-consumer, are generating content and at the same time using content originated by others. Users in the UGC environment actively engage in creating cultural flows. In sharp contrast to the consuming audience of the old media, prosumers have greater capabilities to act upon creative materials, and therefore they have a special interest in appropriating and sharing creative works. At the same time, however, new modes of production enhance the commercial pressures on individual users, as these users become independent units of production. Conflicting desires to share and control content may come into play. Users of social media platforms are playing a dual role: they generate original content, which is made available by the platform, and at the same time they use content originated by the platform and by other users.

Social media platforms are commercial and non-profit online platforms that are making UGC available. Platforms perform a wide range of functions, from technical enabling to social facilitation. Platforms coordinate and facilitate access to UGC via search engines (for example, Google and Yahoo!), hosting facilities (such as YouTube and Flickr), social networks (including MySpace, Friendster, Facebook, Orkut and Bebo) and virtual worlds (such as World of Warcraft). Social media platforms facilitate exchange and collaboration, enabling users to communicate with friends and colleagues and also to connect with new people and establish online communities.

The market for social media platforms is highly concentrated and dominated by a relatively small number of players resulting from economies of scale and network effect. Since much of the cost of producing a platform (design, technological innovation) is unrelated to the number of users of the service, the average cost of providing a service to each additional user may fall as the number of users increases. But economies of scale reduce the level of competition. The cost of entry is rapidly rising as the Internet continues to grow and as competition becomes more sophisticated. A strong network effect gives advantages to large-scale intermediaries such as Google's search engine, and to global social networks such as Facebook and Twitter, which attract the most traffic by users on a global scale.

Competition is further weakened as platforms converge and crosslink to one another, giving users added value by enabling them to make their output in one social media an input in partnering social media. Such convergence creates new barriers to entry and makes it even harder for new applicants to penetrate the market. Another issue affecting the level of competition among platforms is stickiness, which is a function of users' switching costs. If users are able to transfer valuable assets, such as personal contacts, social graphs, personal histories and original content to another facility, they can more easily switch their social media platform. If these assets cannot be transferred to another platform, users might find themselves locked into a particular platform.

As we further discussed in previous chapters, social media platforms, unlike the content industry, do not engage in mass production and distribution of content. Platforms make use of a wide range of business models that affect information flows and shape the relationships between users and platforms. Advertising is the most common source of income for many social media platforms. Revenues from advertising depend on the ability of social media platforms to attract users. This should sound familiar. Advertising-supported radio and television broadcasters are also generating revenues by attracting viewers and selling their captive audiences to advertisers. New platforms, like old intermediaries, monetize on users' attention. One critical difference between old media and social media, however, is that content in the latter is generated by the users themselves. Users generate original content or simply perform editorial functions; they provide eyeballs for advertisers and produce data for marketers. The platform's economic value arises from a network of connected users and it generates revenue by maintaining an engaged community of creative participants. In fact, social media are attracting users not simply by offering access to the content created by their peers, but also by producing a social context. There is no value in the platform other than the users who actively engage in it. From the platforms' perspective, the community of users constitutes its main generative asset; the stronger this community becomes, the higher the value for the enterprise.

Consequently, social media platforms often do not depend upon exclusive control over creative works. Quite the contrary: social media platforms often seek to promote open access and free exchange of information in order to attract more users to their social networks. Content is both generated and made available by users. The content produced by users constitutes the building blocks of these virtual communities. Consequently, the business models of social media platforms are very different from those typical of the content industry; they are based on social motivation and preservation of a sense of community, loyalty and social commitment. They do not require exclusivity because what attracts users to the platform is their fellow users and not necessarily some particular content; what keeps users attached to a platform is the robust information flows and the ability to connect their online presence with content and peers across platforms. Social media platforms need to maintain a vibrant community. They must keep their users/authors engaged and encourage them to share content with other users. This may require wide distribution of content and better mechanisms for sharing it.

### *5.5.2 Governance*

The multi-level relationship, platform-user/social network, has bearing on the analysis of private ordering in the social web. Governance of UGC in the social web is multi-layered; access to any particular work might be subject to a variety of licencing strategies. Some terms of access are drafted by platforms. Such terms of use (ToU) would often reflect the dual nature of social media platforms as commodities of their owners and communities of their users. Other rules are selected by users/authors and are attached to the content that is made available online, often by using licencing schemes such as creative commons licenses or free software standard contracts.

The user/author dual role may affect the economic pressures that shape the terms of access to content. Terms of access of mass-produced content were drafted unilaterally by multinational corporations and enforced against uninformed bodies of consumers. Terms of access in EULAs were therefore relatively restrictive, limiting the freedom of consumers to make full use of their purchased copies. The contract-as-product perception, discussed in the previous sections, expects content producers to respond to consumers' preferences by either reducing the price and introducing harsher terms or increasing the price for better license terms. Yet, often these were not reflected in the EULA provisions since markets rarely developed any special demand for particular terms of access due to several market failures.

The situation is different for the social web. In their capacity as producers of content and generators of economic value, users are more likely to care about how their intellectual property rights are being used. Users are more likely to be informed and motivated to negotiate the terms of access to creative works in social media platforms. They will generally seek more say in determining the terms of access to their own works and the works of others. At the same time, users might be more vulnerable, and suffer various disadvantages vis-à-vis the platform. Many online services are provided free of charge. Users do not pay with their money, but invest other types of resources: their free labor, their social connections, their engagement in online discussions, their personal data and their privacy.

In recent years we have seen an increase in diversity of licensing terms. Open licensing, described in section 5.1 above, is offering a wide range of alternatives to EULAs of commercial vendors. The creative commons license is one example where creative content is offered under more liberal terms. Open source programs such as Open Office provide an alternative to MS Office, authorizing free copying, modification and distribution of the software. Sometimes the same computer program will be subject to different licencing strategies, open and close, thereby serving the different preferences of potential users.

When terms of access are designed by users/authors, should we expect them to opt for fewer restrictions on the use of their works? Presumably, yes. Since end users act concurrently as producers and consumers of creative works they are more likely to take into account, on the whole, all the significant interests involved. It can be claimed that this dual role may enable owners to reach the terms of access reflected through public ordering. This may constitute a social contract intended to reflect our shared understanding of the optimal access to creative works, regardless of our immediate vested interest in any particular moment. General rules adopted by society through collective action mechanisms are arguably more distant from temporary interests of particular parties. Public rule-making processes allow a choice to be made behind a Rawlsian 'veil of ignorance'. That is true, of course, if we momentarily put aside the deficiencies of collective decision-making processes, especially those identified by public choice theory.

Are users in a UGC environment more likely to exercise their rights in ways that facilitate more access to creative works? Are they more likely to act in a socially informed manner when selecting the terms of access that would apply to their works? Several anecdotes suggest that this may not always be the case. The story of Danica Radovanovic's blog highlights the commercial pressures and the confusion among creative commons' licensors over the purpose of the license. Radovanovic runs a blog called Belgrade and Beyond, hosted by WordPress.com. Her blog was subject to a CC–BY–ND license. She changed it to a CC–BY–ND–NC license. She was upset to discover that her blog was mirrored by a Chinese user, who used Google AdSense to generate profits from advertisements. Radovanovic notified the blog hosting service, and also sent a notice to Google AdSense service regarding the alleged infringement. Within a few days she managed to block the Chinese mirroring site (which apparently also made Wikipedia available in China).

Danica Radovanovic's story reflects the evolving interests and commercial pressures in the UGC environment. She did not want to lose income generated through Google AdSense, and also wanted to stop what she saw as unjust, preventing the mirroring site from benefiting from her own efforts. In the absence of any commitment to values of access in the licensing scheme, Danica enforced her license to block access. The story further shows how commercial interests of users can take priority and are likely to push for further restrictions.

Another example is the lawsuit brought by the celebrity Adam Curry against a Dutch magazine. It demonstrates how creative commons' license could be used to gain control over the use of a picture, and restrict its dissemination and use. The *Weekend* magazine published photos of Curry's daughter without his permission. The photos were posted by Curry himself on Flickr and were marked: for public use. A sidebar titled 'Additional Information' was linked to creative commons' logo. Another click linked the photo to the creative commons attribution–non-commercial–ShareAlike license. The license allowed free use of the photos for non-commercial purposes as long as credit was granted. Curry argued that the use of his photograph violates his privacy, a claim that the court dismissed. He further argued that the publication by the magazine violates the license and infringes his copyright. The court held that the republication of photos by the magazine was commercial and therefore violated the terms of the creative commons license. The license, the court held, was enforceable, and automatically applied to the use, even when the user had not explicitly agreed to its terms and was not even aware of it (*Curry v. Audax, Rechtbank Amsterdam*, Docket No. 334492 / KG 06-176 SR, 3/9/06).

The court held that the defendant should have diligently investigated the applicable terms, and conducted a thorough and precise examination before publishing photos from the Internet. In case of doubt, the court ruled, the defendant should have requested authorization from the copyright holder. Curry used his copyright to protect the privacy of his daughter (even though he himself posted her pictures on the web). Others may wish to use copyright for other purposes, not necessarily consistent with free and open access. Such a wish was that of the Canadian photographer David Wise who threatened to sue Betty Hinton, a Canadian politician, for using his photograph in her campaign. The picture was downloaded from Flickr and was subject to the creative commons Attribution–ShareAlike license. The photographer said that he would not have allowed the use of the photograph for the campaign since he disagrees with the campaign's political views.

These anecdotes reflect the power that comes with copyright, that is, control over creative works and the way they are used. The stories further reflect the wide range of interests that this type of control over the use of works may serve. Commercial interests, as in the case of Radovanovic, are probably the most pressing. Commercial pressures are actually likely to increase as the UGC environment matures and new business models evolve, allowing users to benefit from their labor. But even for Radovanovic it was probably not just about money. It was also about justice, the wish to prevent others from making profit from the fruits of her creation. Protecting privacy, political convictions, moral beliefs and reputation can also impel rightholders to limit access to their creative works. They may do so even if they themselves wish to access and freely use other people's works, and generally support a rule that provides more liberal access and use of creative materials.

Recent examples suggest that end users actually care about terms of use, and in some cases have been successful in exerting pressure on providers to modify what they believed were unreasonable terms. For instance, the website Fark.com revised its copyright terms after public outrage following a story on BoingBoing. The original terms provided that every submission by users 'carry with it an implied assignment of the entire copyright interest in the submission'. Terms of service by other hosting services such as Yahoo! (early in 1999) and MySpace were revised in response to complaints by end users. These examples are consistent with eBay's sellers' boycott following eBay's announcement of a new fee structure. Another story relates to Digg, a social aggregator using the editorial functions performed by its users. Digg faced a community revolt following its decision to remove an HD-DVD decryption post after receiving a cease and desist letter from the owner of the IP. The community of users protested against Digg's editorial intervention, and its front page was rife with HD-DVD decryption posts. Finally, Kevin Rose, Digg's founder, posted a public apology promising in future to avoid such interventions as taking materials down.

These stories demonstrate that even though terms of access might be drafted by the platforms, they are not determined unilaterally in the same way as EULAs are. They reflect the complexity of uses/social media dependency. Users of platforms are more engaged in setting the terms, and platform owners must be more attentive to users' preferences since they are more dependent on the community's vitality.

There are several reasons to believe that social media platforms might be good fora for negotiating such a social contract among participants on the social web regarding the terms of access to creative works. Let us examine this hypothesis by the following example. Facebook used to have a provision in its ToU, authorizing Facebook, and its users, to use any content uploaded by other users of the social media network. The license was set so that it would expire when a user successfully quitted Facebook. The provision provided as follows:

> You may remove your User Content from the Site at any time. If you choose to remove your User Content, the license granted above will automatically expire, however you acknowledge that the Company may retain archived copies of your User Content.[22]

Accordingly, any contributor to Facebook who uploaded any content including clips or pictures retained the copyright in the contribution and granted the platform and its users a license to use it as long as they remained on Facebook. Once the user/author left Facebook, however, the license would expire. In the spring of 2009 Facebook made an attempt to change this legal situation by deleting that provision from its ToU, so that Facebook, and its users, could continue to use any content even after a user had decided to terminate membership. On 15 February 2009, The Consumerist, a consumer rights advocacy blog, reported that Facebook had revised its ToU. The news traveled swiftly and provoked an online flame, which quickly ran out of control. Users were outraged, describing Facebook's actions as a 'rip off' and accusing it of sneakily gaining a perpetual ownership in UGC. Many have joined the 'People Against the New Terms of Service' group to protest against the alleged change in the ToU. Following a three-day vocally public campaign, Facebook decided to

22 www.facebook.com/terms.

abandon the initiative to amend its ToU. Instead it initiated a vote for a new Bill of Rights and Responsibilities among its hundreds of millions of users.

This incident demonstrates the special character of social media platforms and their relationship with their users. One way to understand this story is of course to think of Facebook as trying to exploit the free labor of users and deprive them of their rights. From this perspective the ToU proposed by Facebook should be treated as a type of unconscionable contract or, in the European framework, as a standard form contract that is subject to some scrutiny by the courts. Another way to understand the actions taken by Facebook is as representing the interests of its users as a whole. Users of social networks often make use of content provided by others and incorporate it into their own content: pictures, songs or clips. A photo distributed on Facebook may become part of someone else's collage. Some friends on Facebook may also create together – drafting a text, editing a clip or creating a shared album of pictures. Users who incorporated a photo, which was uploaded to Facebook, into their online albums, or those who incorporated some music clips into their own works, have relied on the license that was originally granted by the contributing user. If this license were to expire every time someone quits Facebook, the ability to use any content on a social network would be seriously compromised.

The deletion of the said provision from the ToU was actually serving the mutual interests of all users. Facebook protected the users who relied on the content provided by their peers. From this perspective, Facebook's reformed ToU might be viewed as a social contract frustrated by distorted collective action.

### *5.5.3 The social web – between a market and a community*

Social media platforms facilitate a community, not merely a market for users. For end users a platform is not simply a means for distributing information and facilitating the sale of goods. It also functions as a social community. End users may have a vested interest in social media platforms. They are invested in their profiles, creative efforts, social connections and the social status and reputation they have earned. Quitting the social media platform might be costly. When data and content created on a platform can neither be easily transferred nor the community of users easily reproduced, users might not have an exit option so they might not be in a position to demand particular terms.

From the platforms' perspective users are perceived as one of the company's assets. The community of users is a commodity that increases the market value of the enterprise. Social media platforms generate profits by maintaining an engaged community of creative participants. The platform's economic value derives from the network of users, who create value. Users generate original content or editorial functions; they provide eyeball to advertisers and produce data for marketers. In fact, there is no value in the platform other than that of the users who actively engage in it. To a large extent platforms may find themselves at the mercy of their users, especially if users have decided collectively to play by different rules.

The reason that social media platforms, such as Facebook, could facilitate a social contract, is that their sustainability depends on the ongoing engagement of all of its users. Their dependency on users' active engagement requires social media platforms to be very attentive to the needs and interests of the unorganized crowd interacting and collaborating via the platform.

However, a social contract for a community of users, which is defined by ToU of a social media platform, may suffer several limits. One set of issues arises from users' vulnerabilities in social media platforms and the type of activities they engage in. The nature of the bargain between users and social media platforms is that platforms provide access for free and users are 'paying' with a special type of 'currency' – a social currency: social graphs, personal interactions, social engagements and creative works. This type of 'currency' is related to some sensitive aspects of the human condition, such as labor, identity, personal interactions, intimacy and social engagements. Consequently, this bargain between users and platforms raises new interests, which require special legal protection.

Another reason for concern regarding ToU facilitated by platforms relates to the dual nature of social media platforms. On the one hand, a social media platform forms a community of users and cultivates social production. At the same time, however, for the platform the community is simply a corporate asset, which is intended to maximize profits. Platforms are increasingly torn between those two roles. These new vulnerabilities of users and communities may overlook issues that may not be sufficiently addressed by the crowd or by the social media platform.

A third set of issues relates to the tyranny of the crowd. In recent years many writers have been praising the 'wisdom of the crowd', especially in the online environment. The story of Facebook's bylaws demonstrates, however, that the crowd may sometimes act in a non-efficient manner, and in fact may not necessarily represent all the constituencies and may not lead to a rational choice for the benefit of all participants. This suggests that the pressure on platforms created by the crowd of users may act as a mitigating force to the power of platforms, but cannot entirely safeguard the interests of the community of users itself.

These concerns suggest that some intervention of regulators might be necessary in these private ordering arrangements and ToU. Regulation should set limits on private ordering by platforms to safeguard the civil liberties of participants against abuse by the social media platform and also against the crowd that may put pressure on the platform to disregard the interests of individual users and serve the needs of the community as a whole.

How can we secure the rights of individual users and, at the same time, protect the interests of the community of users? Such checks and balances should be based on the principles of public law. One mechanism for securing the rights of individual participants is voice. Rules adapted by social media platforms should explicitly enable participants to select the norms, which apply to their works and shape them as circumstances change. Voice would require the transparency of the terms of use that apply to content, so that each user could clearly understand the type of rules that apply to the content she generates and shares. It further requires that participants be given notice prior of any legal change in the ToU intended by the platform. Voice also requires an opportunity for an ongoing deliberation and negotiation of the terms by the community of users, where users are given an opportunity to express their opinion over the proposed changes.

Another mechanism is exit – the ability to leave a platform and transfer content and data. Participants should be able to opt out, to make sure that their choice to stay in a particular social media and to participate is sufficiently voluntary. To secure the right to exit it is necessary to identify the necessary conditions that would make exit a viable option. Enabling this option might require external regulations.

### *5.5.4 Private ordering and social production*

Large scale collaborative initiatives are using licenses and contracts to opt out of the standardized rights and duties applied by IP laws (copyrights and patents) and to establish a legal regime that fits their needs. A classic example is the general public license (GPL) of the Free Software Foundation (FSF), which secures the freedom to run, edit and share software. Another example is the Creative Commons Attribution ShareAlike license that is used by Wikipedia.

From the perspective of social production, such private ordering arrangements have an important advantage, as they allow communities to tailor the governance of content to fit the nature of collaboration, the group identity and the values shared by its members. At the same time, however, private ordering suffers from several disadvantages. A major shortcoming of private ordering is that obtaining the consent of thousands of collaborators to a contract, and to any revision thereof, might be a very difficult (and costly) task. This process of collective action is much more difficult to achieve than simply coordinating the work of collaborators in creating new content. Collective action requires a procedure that would enable the group to reach decisions that are binding on the entire group of collaborators regarding the exploitation of the work. It is difficult to reach such agreement in large-scale collaboration where the parties are not bound together by any formal legal structure.

Moreover, once a consensus is reached, it is very difficult to move away from it. Since private ordering of social production relies on the proprietary rights (copyrights or patents) of each contributor, relicencing requires obtaining permission from all the contributors to the endeavor. For large-scale collaborations, any process of identifying the rightholders and getting their permission to relicense their content under different terms would be prohibitively costly and most likely unfeasible. This becomes a critical issue as there is a constant need to revise the terms of such licenses. That is because the online environment is dynamic and changes rapidly with new technological developments, new business models and changes in circumstances and power relations.

Processes of license migration in social production are not only cumbersome and time-consuming but also difficult to achieve. Legally, every owner has to agree to license her content under new license terms. But every new license must also gain the legitimacy of the entire community of right holders. Practically, if contributors do not opt in the new license becomes useless. In this respect, social production is fundamentally different from corporate production of content. Social production depends on the enduring contribution of users. If they cease to collaborate, the endeavor will dry out and the content will vanish.

One example of these difficulties is the migration to the GPL v3 administered by the FSF. The draft of version 3 of the GNU GPL was distributed in January 2006, and the version was finally released in June 2009, after a public consultation and a long and intensive consensus-building process within the free software and open source communities.

Another example is Wikipedia license migration. The Wikimedia Foundation, the non-profit organization that supports Wikipedia, was recently faced with the need to modify its license. Wikipedia entries used to be subject to the GFDL license, a GNU free documentation license that permits copying and distribution in any medium for either commercial or non-commercial purposes. The license imposed significant burdens on print distribution (such as attaching the printed version of the license) and was incompatible with other free content licenses such as the creative commons license.

The migration to creative commons CC–BY–SA was legally complicated and somewhat controversial within the community. Legally, each Wikipedia contributor retains copyright in the content that they submit, and Wikimedia was therefore unable unilaterally to relicense the content under a different license. What enabled the migration to CC–BY–SA was the release of a revised version of the GFDL, which was jointly announced by the FSF and the Wikimedia Foundation and which explicitly authorized the relicensing of content posted on massive multi-author collaboration (MMC) sites for a limited time. Even though the amended version of the GFDL authorized Wikimedia to relicence under CC–BY–SA, it nevertheless brought this issue to a general vote and subsequently created a dual-license for Wikipedia content so that it is available under both the GFDL and CC–BY–SA licenses.

To sum up, private ordering within the social web takes a different shape than in the more traditional EULAs. One cannot draw conclusions from the developments in the social web to justify and enforce private ordering in general as based on markets, free will contractual relationship. Even the more balanced (vis-à-vis conflicting interests and general social welfare considerations) private ordering in the social web is not lacking deficiencies, which might call for a different approach to private ordering from that expressed by the canonic law and economics approach.

## 5.6 Conclusions

Private ordering is becoming increasingly significant in defining and shaping rights in information. Its substantive arrangements depart from the scope and duration of IPR set by legislation. The law and economics approach supports this development, because it assumes that private ordering reflects contractual relations between benefiting parties and thus is geared to promote overall efficiency.

The position of law and economics regarding private ordering is inconsistent with the same scholars' position justifying strong intellectual property rights regime and indeed endorsing the expansion of IPR. If the endorsed de facto intellectual property regime is so different from the legislative one, the public ordering of IP is inefficient. Another point of critique is the characterization of private ordering as reflecting real consent, which is the basis for assuming its efficiency. Such real consent is doubtful when we analyse the conduct of the direct parties to these licenses, and is lacking when we talk about third parties who are bound by the terms of license, despite not being a side to the contract.

Critics of *private ordering* as the dominant mechanism for governing access to creative works are also skeptical about the idea that market mechanisms can adequately secure access to creative works. This skepticism derives from a fundamental disbelief in the existence of a market for different access terms, and the view that what rightholders call 'contracts' are simply unilateral provisions which are held enforceable against third parties. Skepticism regarding a market mechanism for governing access to creative works also assumes that access to informational goods involves externalities and therefore may call for central intervention. Overall, skeptics of *private ordering* to govern access reject the view of 'contract-as-product'. Consumers' choice to acquire content, they argue, should not be viewed as acceptance of the terms and conditions that define the scope of permissible use.

The law and economics analysis of private ordering is further challenged by the social web. The contract-as-product approach presumes that mass copies of creative works are produced and distributed by the content industry, just like any other commodity. Content in the UGC environment, by contrast, is produced by individual users who interact and collaborate via social media platforms. These differences between mass-produced content and UGC may entail different considerations in governing access to creative works.

First, as the analysis shows, access to UGC is often governed by the facilitating platform. Users control the means for producing and distributing content, but coordination is facilitated by platforms. Users who produce the content do not have the legal power to determine the terms of access. In some cases users may not even own the content they produce. Individual creators might have interests and stakes different from those of the platform. This is not to suggest that regulation by platforms would necessarily produce more restrictive terms. For instance, platforms that use UGC to draw attention and increase traffic to their facilities may have an incentive to minimize the control exercised by each user/producer over the content they have produced. But in other cases individual users may have greater incentives than those of a platform to share content freely on a non-commercial basis.

Second, users in the UGC environment have multiple roles. Vis-à-vis the platforms, users consume some services, and in return produce some content. At the same time, they are consuming content produced by others. The dual role of users as both consumers and producers challenges the view that consuming UGC is simply a bargain between platforms and users/consumers for the purchase of products or services. We cannot seriously argue that consumers of UGC express their preferences for particular terms of use through their purchasing choices. The fact that users 'pay' for access with free labor, social connections and personal data makes users in the UGC environment far more vulnerable than consumers of commodities. The notion of a 'bargain' that is central to the law and economics view may not fully capture the complexity of processes taking place in online communities of UGC.

Third, the UGC environment blurs more traditional distinctions between commercial and non-commercial. Platforms facilitate communities of users, but at the same time this virtual community is also a commodity for platform owners. Platforms are often commercial entities, which turn the content and social interactions produced by end users into a market commodity. A similar duality characterizes participating users. Conflicting desires to share and control content may come into play. The interdependency of platforms and users make both individual users and platform vulnerable in novel ways that require further study.

Fourth, social media platforms facilitate new forms of collective action. For instance, individuals in the UGC environment act collectively by posting their homemade videos on YouTube and are rating the videos posted by others. Action by individual users in the UGC environment is not 'collective' in the classical sense. It is not an act of collective governance, which generates norms of general applicability. Individuals' actions are coordinated rather than bound by a single set of formal rules expressing their choices at any given moment. It is not exactly a group action either, since it does not entail the long-term commitment of community affiliation. People may go in and out of social networks, and may engage in ad hoc collaboration with others. Yet the content they produce endures. Therefore, governing the rights and duties regarding access to such content is long-term. Collective action in this context is also not a market transaction. Participating users are not paid for their actions, and they make no purchasing choices. The nature of such coordination and self-management is yet to be explored.

On a conceptual level, the emerging environment may require us to be more cautious in applying our traditional notions of consumers and to examine our presumptions about legal doctrines such as contracts of adhesion. The discourse of disparities of power may have to make way for a more egalitarian view of partnership, where platform owners and users may have to collaborate to attain the optimal terms of use that will maximize the interests of all.

We need to develop a framework that will help us conceptualize a social activity that is a commercial asset, a market commodity and, at the same time, a community. That social media platforms also constitute communities of users loosens somewhat the strict economic view of this phenomenon. For the platform the terms of access must serve a commercial interest, maximizing the economic value of the online activities. For users, however, the terms of access may have to guarantee more than just economic viability. Their vested interests are more profound. Content produced in social media platforms may reflect a user's personality and identity. It may reflect a joint effort, a community asset, which goes beyond the sum of the different parcels of ownership of each contributor. The relationship of each user to such content may reflect a sense of belonging and a long-term commitment to a community of peers. Issues related to sovereignty, autonomy and liberty may come into play.

# 6 Intellectual property in the digital era

## Economic analysis and governance by technology

The introduction of digital technology in the second half of the 20th century dramatically changed the economic setting of information markets. On the one hand, it became extremely easy to copy copyrighted materials in a digital format and to make it available through digital networks. At the same time, however, digital technology enables powerful mechanisms of self-help to control the use of information works, from limiting access to authorized users only, to long-term ongoing control over the use of copyrighted or patented materials long after they were purchased by authorized users. These developments call for a re-examination of economic analysis of IP laws, particularly, but not exclusively, in the field of copyright law. This chapter explores the implications of the rise of digital locks vis-à-vis the justifications for central intervention in the market for informational goods. It focuses on the economic analysis of technological protection measures (TPM) or as often called digital rights management (DRM) systems and on the major tool of central intervention that has been employed in this context so far – anti-circumvention legislation.

DRMs are particularly interesting from an economic perspective. They turn information – once a non-excludable resource – into a more excludable asset, and they extend the time span of excludability and control, long after the informational product was purchased by a consumer. This fundamental change transforms not only the nature of informational works but also the relationship between rightholders and recipients of IP protected materials. DRMs facilitate a long-term relationship between suppliers and recipients of informational works and it also affects subsequent users who were not engaged directly with the original rightholder. DRMs can be designed to enforce IP rights as defined by legislation – rights whose initial rationale often becomes obsolete upon the disappearance of the very market failure that justified their introduction in the first place. However, DRMs may also change the relevant legislative arrangements by extending the duration of the rights, abolishing legal exceptions or providing protection to works or inventions otherwise not protected by IP laws. These developments call for a more general examination of theories of law and the economic analysis of law, to which we turn in this chapter.

Section 6.1 will elaborate on the rise of regulation by technology and its implications on the definition and theory of law. Section 6.2 will offer some insights related to the economic analysis of information in the age of regulation by the code and will question the premises of the traditional economic justification for IPR. Section 6.3 will elaborate on the main legislative reaction to the DRMs phenomena – the anti-circumvention legislation which was introduced in the US and the EU to prohibit the bypassing of regulation by technology. Section 6.4 will focus on one of the important unique features of DRMs – their ability to control uses long after purchase was made and the ramifications of this option on the economic analysis of information and consumers' rights. Section 6.5 deals more specifically with competition in light of regulation by technology. Section 6.6 will offer several insights into the economic analysis of anti-circumvention legislation and its effects on the general economic model of informational markets. Section 6.7 will conclude and offer tentative alternative courses for central intervention in the shadow of regulation by technology.

## 6.1 The rise of digital locks

### *6.1.1 What are DRMs?*

Digital rights management systems (DRMs), often also referred to as technological protection measures (TPMs) enable control over the access and use of digital content. These measures enable owners to monitor and manage the use of their respective works and to license specific uses, while restricting others. Consider, for instance, the Adobe Digital Publishing Solution for eBook. This system enables authors to distribute text in digital form but at the same time restrict certain functions related to the files, such as editing, copying, printing or annotating. The encrypted version enable publishers to manage the rights on the eBook files and the types of authorizations will differ from book to book or from one reader to another. As opposed to private ordering on which we elaborated in the previous chapter, the terms and enforcement mechanism do not use contract, licenses or the law altogether, but rather rely on technology to achieve similar goals. However, works protected by DRMs are often distributed subject to a license as well.

DRMs come in various forms and types. DRMs may facilitate control by creating a gatekeeper, thereby controlling access. Just as concert halls are allowed to sell tickets, but they and their audience are prohibited from recording public performances of musical works, some platforms enable the exclusion of digital content by forcing people to pay for access to songs and videos (Bomsel and Geffroy 2005a). A common way to secure content is by encrypting it, namely by scrambling the digital information through an algorithm. As long as the content is scrambled it is inaccessible. For instance, if you have tried to copy a DVD video to your computer and you received a warning announcing that the CD is copy protected, it means that a DRM system is in effect.

DRMs are often divided into two categories: hard DRMs and soft DRMs. Hard DRMs place control over access, copying and distribution in the hands of the copyright owner by providing her the tools to actually prevent 'unauthorized' actions. Sometimes the content is accompanied by physical support (Bomsel and Geffroy 2005b: 13). CDs and DVDs that disable copying are one example of such support. The second category of DRMs is known as soft DRMs. Such systems do not prevent unauthorized actions but simply monitor the user's interaction with the content. The system then submits the information to the content owner (M.E.L.O.N. 2007). A common example is a digital watermark, which embeds additional information into the content and enables verifying the authenticity of the content or signaling the identity of the owner. The signal could be a text, an image, a video or an audio, adding a distinctive mark to any unauthorized reproduction. The watermark could be visible to viewers (ie the logo of the content displayed on the video clip) or invisible to users and detectable only by tracking systems, media players or copying devices.

DRMs may be installed on copies of works distributed to the public (such as MP3 files or DVDs), or may be implemented through the platforms that provide access. For instance, Microsoft Windows Media Digital Rights Management system offers a platform that allows owners electronically to define the terms of access and disable the playing of content on the media player. The Microsoft system packages the digital media files in an encrypted format. To play a file the user must acquire a license and a 'key' that will permit access. Once a license has been retrieved by the system, the user can play the file according to the rules defined by the owner of the file. These rules may define the duration of the license, the region for which it is granted, the number of times a file may be played, the devices it may be played on, or times it may be copied. For instance, a movie that is licensed to be viewed only in the United States will not be playable on a media player encoded for any other region. Thus, the terms of the license are not merely drafted in a license agreement but are technically embedded in the code attached to the work.

### *6.1.2 Regulation by code and the theory of law*

Digital technology – the code – increasingly substitutes the law – the main tool of governance traditionally held by the state. Take for example the wish to protect minors from exposure to sexually explicit materials on the Internet. This goal brought the American Congress to legislate the Child Online Protection Act (47 U.S.C. §231), which criminalized the act of knowingly posting online, for commercial purposes, materials 'harmful to minors'. The law was struck down by the US Supreme Court as being not sufficiently narrow and thus in conflict with freedom of speech and violating the First Amendment (*Ashcroft v. ACLU*, 542 U.S. 656 (2004)). However, achieving the same result is simply done by using blocking and filtering software that would prevent minors from seeing harmful content, a technological self-help mechanism that de facto changed the law and is outside the radar of the courts.

The power of digital technology to enable governance and control was recognized early on in the information law literature by scholars such as Joel Reidenberg (1998), describing the *lex informatica* and Lawrence Lessig (1999), who coined the popular term 'code is law'. Rather than prohibiting by law a certain behavior, the design itself can simply block it.

DRMs are one of the most profound examples of regulation by code. Encryption and digital management systems are often employed to block technically what the law prohibits with rules. Copyright law prohibits the creation of copies without authorization from the copyright owner. The owner may cease unauthorized use of her work by seeking an injunction in court and subjecting the infringing copier to damages. Using encrypted platforms, owners may prevent through technological means the creation of digital copies, while permitting printed copies, or choose to restrict any copying whatsoever. In theory, owners may also inflict some damage on copiers by, for instance, disabling any device on which an unauthorized copying attempt was made. Where copyright law fails to deter millions of music file-sharing program users around the world from infringing copyright, DRMs hold the potential to replace the law and simply prevent copying completely. Not every user of P2P networks might be aware of the particulars of copyright law, but if copying is disabled physically, the user is barred from copying and distributing music files.

Self-regulation by technology raises some interesting theoretical questions regarding the essence of regulation and the theory of law: For instance, what is law? What counts as regulation by rules and how can one distinguish between physical constraints, social norms and legal norms?

The prevailing positivist theories of law attribute the creation of law to man-made institutions: legislatures, courts and delegated bodies, such as the executive or administrative agencies. Since the rise of legal positivism (see especially Austin [1832] 1995; Kelsen 1949; Hart 1961), we perceive law as hierarchical, territorial and backed by the physical ability to enforce it through sanctions. Legal norms are created based on the authority of strong ruling powers (Austin), higher legal norms (Kelsen) or social conventions (Hart). As such, regulations are valid because statutes authorize their construction; statutes are valid to the extent that they do not conflict with constitutional norms. Furthermore, legal norms claim a monopoly on power and superiority over other types of societal norms and, in fact, the power of the state to enforce legal norms physically affirms this superiority (Bentham [1789] 1948; Austin [1832] 1995). Hence the perception of law as territorial and correspondent to political regimes employing physical or conventional enforcement powers.

Legal and economic theory may treat technology simply as a design that restricts behavior. Technology has always shaped people's behavior, determining what is possible and what is not, what is allowed and what is forbidden. For example, a fence would prevent one from entering another's property, and an electric fence would make it even more difficult to trespass. It can be argued that preventing access to a website without a proper password is the technological equivalent of a fence. However, contemporary regulation by code is arguably substantially different from the physical and technological constraints of the past. Two major differences are worth mentioning. First, in the past technological frontiers were very similar for all members of community and within the realm of common knowledge, whereas today technological know-how varies significantly among individuals and in most cases is beyond the knowledge of the ordinary user. Second, in the past man-made law was still dominant over technology, while today the opposite might be true. An illegally erected fence preventing people from entering a space to which they have the right to enter by virtue of law, will likely be removed by enforcement authorities, whereas, in contrast, today's technological tools can surpass legal rights. In other words, while technology in the past existed in the shadow of human institution-made law, and merely as one mechanism for enforcing those laws, technology today overpowers democratic man-made laws, no longer serving solely as an enforcement tool, but also as creator of norms and rights.

From a law and economics perspective, one of the key questions in this new environment is whether it is justified to discuss enforcement by code as law. The law limits people in a straightforward manner; it encourages them to do the right thing by sanctioning them if they contravene the rules. Even when formal law is absent, social norms usually fill the void (Grimmelmann 2005). The notion of regulation under the economic analysis of law presumes *choice*. The underlying assumption is that rational agents are able to control their behavior and direct it towards what they perceive as a desirable, utility maximizing, outcome, thus choosing also whether to comply with or violate the law. Rules are sometimes necessary to correct an otherwise distorted set of incentives, and provide individuals instead with appropriate incentives so they would choose to behave in accordance with the public welfare, but they may choose otherwise and bear the legal consequences. Unlike legal norms, however, enforcement (and indeed rule-making) by code provides neither a definition of undesirable behaviors, nor a matrix of incentives. Regulation by code makes it possible to eradicate certain behaviors while enabling others. If a design simply prevents a particular act, we can no longer talk about regulations and incentives, since choice may no longer be exercised.

More importantly, DRMs do not simply offer an efficient enforcement mechanism for rights defined by intellectual property laws. These systems enable content providers to limit the use of content in ways which the law alone does not facilitate. For instance, book owners currently enjoy the right to lend and even resell their books to others under copyright 'first sale' doctrine. Some eBook vendors, however, such as Barnes & Noble, set limits on lending options so that eBooks can only be lent to owners of a similar eReader (ie Nook) and can only be lent once, for a non-extendable period of two weeks (Barnes and Noble, Nook: User Guide Version 1.5 at 131 (2009–2010)).

In this sense, DRMs offer substantive rules, providing copyright protection over areas in which democratically elected human-made law chose not to grant property or other substantive rights. The new mode of norms originating from technological self-help action, does not meet basic conditions of democratic theory and the rule of law principle. They are not adopted by democratically elected representatives or by their explicit authority, after deliberation in public; they are not brought to the public knowledge ex ante, and they do not necessarily apply equally to all those who are affected by them.

## 6.2 The economic analysis of information in the digital environment

### *6.2.1 Is information still a public good?*

The predominant economic justification for intervening in information markets is the public good market failure associated with informational products and services. It is presumed that information, once created, cannot be efficiently excluded. Therefore, market players lack sufficient incentives to invest in exploring new inventions, developing new creative works, and improving existing materials. Thus informational goods may not be created in the first place, or may be insufficiently produced. This market failure was thought to be corrected through the creation of intellectual property rights. The idea is that a set of legal rights to exclude would remedy the inability to physically exclude the use, and would thus provide incentives to create. At the same time, however, in contrast to physical exclusion, legal rights leave room for flexibility, thereby ensuring optimal grounds for the widest possible availability of informational goods by limiting rights in time and allowing exceptions.

Does the introduction of digital technology have any impact on the analysis of public goods failure of informational products? On the one hand, digital networks intensify the market failure of public good by sharply reducing the cost of copying and distributing informational materials. When copying was performed by hand it involved substantial costs; the invention of photocopying and recording devices significantly lowered these costs. In digital format, it becomes almost costless to create a large number of identical copies. The same devices we are using for creating original text, music and pictures, such as personal computers, tablets and smart phones, are also capable of mass production of identical copies at no cost. These same devices connected to the Internet also enable mass distribution by individual users, and no additional equipment is necessary for the distribution of copies. This decentralized distribution structure also renders standard intellectual property enforcement far less effective. IPR are legal rights that must be enforced by law enforcement agencies applying national laws. Enforcement through state apparatuses must cope with the global nature of digital networks, which enables any offender to cross territorial borders without exposing her physical identity. The public good market failure is thus intensified.

On the other hand, the digital environment enhances the ability of content providers to exercise unprecedented control over the use of works, as we demonstrated in the previous section, thus making them more excludable.

One reason has to do with the availability of encryption measures that makes it easier for owners of informational materials to exclude technologically non-payers at minimal cost. If music distributors are capable of effectively encrypting their music files, it is possible to enable access to paying consumers only, and deny it to free-riders.

Another reason relates to processing devices, which are the gatekeepers for access to digital content. The use of digital content is recorded in files. Digital bits, saved as files, must be processed by computers in order to become a melody or a text. Thus, reading a book, listening to music, or sending and downloading files all involve data processing. Every process is recorded by various files on the servers involved in the transmission and therefore leaves 'digital tracks'. These digital footprints make it easier to trace and block 'unauthorized' uses of works. Consider, for instance, books. Printed books could be read directly, but reading an eBook is always mediated by a device that converts the binary code into readable text. eReaders, such as Kindle, Nook or a multipurpose device such as the iPad, may limit the use of the eBook to a particular device. eReaders may enable a whole range of limits on content, such as the conversion of content from one format to another, the ability to cut and paste text, print the eBook, or transfer the eBook to another location. The control over the use of informational works, in contrast to the old world, is also available long after the purchase of the works by consumers.

DRMs challenge the characteristics of informational products and services as non-excludable public goods and, therefore, the justification for protecting these goods by intellectual property. DRMs are capable of facilitating efficient enforcement to a degree that has not existed in the print environment. Unlike standard copyright enforcement, which is ex post, DRMs create ex ante excludability. In other words, they can prevent violation of copyright from occurring in the first place. DRMs involve relatively lower costs, as they eliminate the costs of identifying, seizing and prosecuting copyright infringers, as well as maintaining the legal enforcement apparatus, such as police and courts. The level of enforcement and its success do not depend on the extent to which the public comprehends and internalizes the rules; rather, they depend on technological effectiveness.

The availability of cost-effective, self-help, technical measures that govern the use of informational works weakens the public good nature of those resources. The classic assumption that informational goods are non-excludable, presumed that exclusion of non-payers cannot be achieved in a cost effective way. If informational works no longer suffer from the public good deficiencies, however, then government intervention is neither required nor desirable. Likewise, if DRMs offer an efficient means of excluding non-payers, then it may no longer be necessary or justifiable to exclude non-payers through copyright regulation; that is, at least under the public goods approach to intellectual property.

This analysis, however, overlooks a key factor – technological stability. For every protection measure created, there is always a counter-technology to crack it. The effectiveness of DRMs requires resistance to hacking. Once a DRM has been hacked, the information is vulnerable to unlimited copying. The primary response by governments to this new development is anti-circumvention legislation, to which we dedicate a significant share of this chapter.

It seems that, vis-à-vis the economic rationale of the incentives public goods analysis, the ability to exclude technologically trumps the decreasing costs of copying, so if one considers seriously the economic analysis for intellectual property laws, then the digital revolution of the past several decades ought at least to have changed the balance struck by existing IP rights in terms of their scope and the length of time for which they are granted, if not to abolish IPR altogether. Such a change has not yet taken place; instead we witness new regulatory components added to the field, primarily anti-circumvention laws. Although these laws might be viewed as additional enforcement tools, they may also be perceived as de facto broadening the scope of substantive IP rights. We discuss anti-circumvention legislation in section 6.3, but beforehand we will elaborate on other variables related to the effects of the new digital world on the economics of information.

### *6.2.2 Digital networks and the economic analysis of information*

Excludability is a matter of cost. It has always been possible to exclude creative works but it was often the case that the cost of exclusion was greater than the marginal costs of provision, such that it was inefficient to expand resources excluding non-payers. When the costs of preventing copying by a printing house or excluding unauthorized recording of music on the air were high, copyright law was tailored to create the legal exclusivity, deterring potential copiers. Nevertheless, despite copyright protection, tracking the private copying of protected works, such as photocopying a poem from a book, involved relatively high transaction costs, rendering it unpractical. Consequently, copyright law and enforcement policies focused on public exploitation of works, prohibiting unauthorized public performance and public distribution (even though, technically, every unauthorized reproduction constitutes a copyright infringement). Copyright enforcement efforts often aimed at intermediaries, such as competing publishers and unauthorized printers. Such intermediaries, who were responsible for mass reproduction and distribution of infringing copies, were relatively easy to detect, and successful legal actions against them were likely to secure the market for the original work. The cost structure of exclusion also had an effect on the distribution strategies of creators. Films, for example, were displayed initially in theaters, rather than being released as copies for purchase, to ensure that viewers will buy a ticket for watching them and will not be able to forward copies to friends.

The cost of exclusion is decreasing dramatically. It is much easier to control the use of text in a PDF format than to prevent photocopying of a printed version. The Adobe Acrobat application, for instance, enables a generator of a document to limit the preparation of copies, or the annotation of the file, at a click of a mouse. Digital networks, which facilitate colossal distribution of copies, also enable electronic monitoring, by automated crawlers, file trackers and central monitoring systems located at different junctions of the communication infrastructure. Informational works in digital format could often be monitored in a cost effective way. Automated self-policing options offer cost efficient solutions to the enforcement challenge. YouTube, for instance, is offering rightholders a service called 'Content ID', that automatically detects unauthorized use of their copyrighted materials on YouTube servers. Rightholders provide the proprietary content – TV shows, video clips, music tracks, for which the system generates a fingerprint – the content ID. Next, the system automatically matches content uploaded to YouTube (or content that is already posted on YouTube) with the content ID provided by the copyright owner. The service offers rightholders to choose whether automatically to detect and remove the files – in which case YouTube will notify the user that a notice of infringement was served, or, instead, to allow the rightholder to benefit from the content, receiving statistics on their use and collecting the royalties for advertisements.

Efficient and cheaper enforcement in the new digital environment would arguably decrease the price of informational works and thus increase access to information. The price of informational works reflects not only the large investment in creating and marketing the work, but also the cost of enforcement, as well as the expected loss from failure fully to enforce the rights of the IPR holder. If the expected market for a music publisher is substantially encumbered owing to piracy, music publishers are likely to raise the price per copy in order to cover their expenses and risk. Conversely, if DRMs reduce the level of piracy, the price of copyrighted works should decrease.

Yet, enforcement by code is not costless – it involves the costs of developing a technology and preserving its technological superiority, such that it will not be bypassed by counter-technology. One should bear in mind that DRMs are not immune from hacking and cracking (Hanbidge 2001; Rosenblatt 2007). The vulnerability of DRMs raises the issue of government intervention and the extent to which the law should encourage and strengthen the use of DRMs as a matter of policy. This issue will be discussed further in the following sections.

Another issue that arises is the efficiency of DRMs as a private ordering regime. DRMs are private goods, which, unlike public law (and even contracts), do not rely upon any law enforcement institutions, such as courts or other administration of justice apparatuses. Enforcement is self-executed and self-implemented. Whereas significant share of the burden of the administrative costs of traditional IP enforcement is typically distributed among all taxpayers, the costs of self-enforcement by DRMs are usually borne by content owners and subsequently reflected in the price of the copies (Samuelson 1999, 2001; Cohen 2000). Park and Scotchmer (2005) argue that the effect on prices depends on whether the content providers use independent protection standards or a shared one and, if shared, on the monitoring of the system.

It has been suggested that utilizing DRMs may foster efficiency by facilitating price discrimination, or rather the fragmentation of the product into different packages. DRMs enable rightholders to provide multiple pricing schemes for different types of uses and formats for the same product (Petrick 2004; Picker 2005). Implementing DRMs may allow producers to charge different prices depending upon how many times the user wishes to listen to a song or to an entire album, the number of personal copies she wishes to make, how often she wishes to export the music from one device to another and whether she wishes simply to sample the music. For instance, Amazon Instant Video is using DRMs to offer videos for rentals or for purchase. When a video is rented from Amazon Instant Video, DRM is used to enable one viewing only. Movies downloaded to be watched at a later time are automatically erased after the duration of the rental expired. Amazon is also offering videos for sale, enabling online and offline viewing options at any time. Similarly, book publishers may tailor new products to libraries. Libraries were purchasing books for an indefinite and unlimited lending to its patrons. eBooks publishers offer libraries a set of more limited rights, disabling the copy of an eBook after a fixed number of checkouts.

Picker (2005) argues that employing DRMs for product differentiation, enable content producers to tailor the product and price to different consumers' preferences and may expand the range of ways the rightholder is able to recover her fixed costs, as well as achieving wider distribution. Some of these economic benefits of DRMs may come, however, at a cost to competition, to consumers' interests and to innovation. In a sense, DRMs enable information producers to become complete discriminating monopolies, which generate efficient equilibrium at the cost of stripping consumers from all added value from market transactions, which is added to the producers' profits. We further explore some of these factors in section 6.4. We can conclude, however, that DRMs shift the cost-benefit analysis of information, which should have had significant ramifications on the normative analysis of IPR. Policy-makers, it seems, were not interested to address the substance of intellectual property rights and instead introduced legislation preventing the bypassing of regulation by technology, as elaborated in the next section.

## 6.3 The anti-circumvention legal regime

The efficacy of technological protection depends on their resilience to hacking attempts and the absence of cost-effective circumvention means. The development of exclusion measures often encourages users to develop countertechnologies for code-breaking and hacking tools. For instance, once the Adobe Acrobat eBook was released back in 2001, a decrypting program (AEBPR) was developed. Dmitry Sklyarov, an assistant professor at Moscow Technical University, originally wrote this decrypting program as a practical application of his dissertation. The program was later released by his employer,

Elcomsoft Co. Ltd, on the latter's website. Files decrypted with the AEBPR program were no longer protected by encryption and could therefore be copied and annotated like any other digital file.

The effectiveness of DRMs requires full resilience to hacking. Once a DRM has been hacked, the information it protects becomes vulnerable to unlimited copying (EFF Report 2005). The primary response by governments has been anti-circumvention legislation. Anti-circumvention legislation outlaws the circumvention of protective measures.

### *6.3.1 Legal background*

Anti-circumvention legislation was officially aimed to provide extra protection to copyright owners threatened by the dramatic increase of piracy in the digital age. The pressure mounted by lobbyists of copyright owners on their national governments to strengthen their rights led to the adoption in 1996 of the WIPO Copyright Treaty. The treaty entered into force in 2002, after more than 33 countries agreed to ratify it (as of today the treaty was ratified by 89 countries). Article 11 of the WIPO Copyright Treaty and Article 18 of the WIPO Performances and Phonograms Treaty, require the contracting parties to 'provide adequate legal protection and effective legal remedies against the circumvention of effective technological measures' used by *authors, performers or producers of phonograms* in connection with the exercise of their rights, and which restrict acts that are not authorized by the owners or permitted by law. The respective provisions of the treaties lack a definition of key terms and, consequently, caused much strife during the implementation process as different interest groups sought to shift the balance in their direction (Gasser 2006: 11).

The United States was the first country to implement the WIPO Treaties in 1998 by enacting the Digital Millennium Copyright Act (DMCA). The Act was followed by the European Union's Directive on the harmonization of certain aspects of copyright and related rights in the information society (2001). The legislative histories of anti-circumvention laws in Europe and the United States share some similarities. In both Europe and the United States, a preliminary committee advocated the need to provide legal protection for technological measures from circumvention. In the United States, these efforts were initiated through the White Paper on Intellectual Property and the National Information Infrastructure (NII White Paper), prepared by the Working Group on Intellectual Property Rights established by the Clinton Administration in 1995. Owing to strong domestic opposition the recommendations of the NII White Paper regarding circumvention were not implemented in legislation until after they were adopted into the WIPO Treaties.

Similarly, in Europe, a Green Paper on Copyright and Related Rights in the Information Society was published in 1995 (COM(95) 382 final 27 July 1995), but was incorporated into the EU Copyright Directive only in 2001 (Articles 6 and 8). While in 2004 only eight Member States were in a pending implementation status vis-à-vis the Copyright Directive, currently all Member

States have incorporated the directive into their national law (Study on the implementation and effect in Member States' laws of Directive 2001/29/EC on the harmonization of certain aspects of copyright and related rights in the information society 2007).

### *6.3.1.1 Scope of protection*

Anti-circumvention regulations restrict two categories of legally cognizable behaviors: *breaking and entering* and *trafficking* (Nimmer 2000). The ban on the first behavior, as enacted in the US, prohibits the circumvention of any DRM in order to gain unauthorized access to copyrighted materials, and it covers any type of tampering with control mechanisms that are protected by law (DMCA §1201(a)(1)(A)). Circumvention is prohibited, regardless of whether it infringes any copyright. The European approach is slightly different, as under Article 6(1) of the EU Copyright Directive users must know, or have reasonable grounds to know, that their actions are causing the circumvention of a protective measure without authority. The scope of the provision is very broad: it applies to any act of circumventing technical measures to gain access to a work. Such acts may include circumventing technical measures that block initial access to copyrighted works, or even subsequent access after expiration of the time period or volume initially licensed to the user. The ban on circumventing *access control* measures applies, regardless of whether the work has actually been copied. It is also important to note that since informational works are composed of both protected expression and non-protected ideas, which are intermingled and inseparable, a digital lock would necessarily block access to the unprotected aspects of a copyrighted work and anti-circumvention rules will also apply to it.

The second type of behavior banned by anti-circumvention regimes is trafficking, namely any act of facilitating circumvention by manufacturing, importing, offering to the public or otherwise providing devices that make circumvention possible (DMCA §1201(a)(2), §1201(b); EU Copyright Directive Article 6(2)). Under the EU Copyright Directive, not only are manufacturing and trafficking prohibited, but also the possession of the aforementioned devices for commercial purposes. The trafficking ban covers any device or service that is marketed as a circumvention tool; that is primarily designed or produced for circumventing technical measures; or that has only limited commercially significant purposes or uses, other than to circumvent protective measures (DMCA §1201(a)(2); EU Copyright Directive Article 6(2)(b)). The trafficking ban is much broader than the former regime, which held enablers of copyright infringement liable under the contributory liability doctrine. In the US these principles were set forth in *Sony v. Universal City Studios*, 464 U.S. 417 (1984). In *Sony*, the US Supreme Court addressed the potential liability of a manufacturer of a device, the Sony Betamax Videocassettes Recorder that enabled unlicensed copying of copyrighted movies. Under the *Sony* rule, a manufacturer will not be held liable for contributory infringement for the distribution of copying devices with 'substantial non-infringing use'. But, as US courts have held, the Sony defense does not apply to the trafficking liability under the DMCA. Therefore, when a defendant designed products primarily for the purpose of circumventing an access control measure, which effectively control access to a copyrighted work, the defendant was violating the DMCA (*RealNetworks v. DVD-CCA* (2009)).[23]

Similarly, in Europe, the circulation of devices intended to circumvent technical protective measures was regulated prior to the new regime by the Computer Programs Directive 1991. It covers only technological measures whose 'sole intended purpose' is to facilitate circumvention (Council Directive 91/250/EEC of 14 May 1991 on the legal protection of computer programs, Article 7(1)(C)). The definition of circumventing devices under the EU Copyright Directive is broader.

The scope of protection afforded by the anti-circumvention regime remains controversial. Some believe that the ban should be interpreted broadly. For instance, it has been suggested that because circumvention devices that allow the decryption of non-copyrighted materials may also enable decryption of copyrighted materials, it is necessary to outlaw all dual-use devices (Koelman 2004: 625–26). Nevertheless, from an economic perspective, outlawing dual-use devices involves high social cost, namely the loss of benefits yielded by legal uses of the same devices. Assuming that sufficient social benefit is derived from additional anti-circumvention legislation protections, in the form of additional incentives, it is necessary to determine whether this social benefit outweighs the losses associated with outlawing legitimate uses.

In any case, as we will elaborate below, the draconian scope of outlawed anti-circumvention measures enable DRMs to broaden the scope of intellectual property protection and immunise their actions relying on anti-circumvention laws. Hence these laws de facto extend IPR.

### *6.3.1.2 Exceptions and limitations*

The anti-circumvention regime established a rather narrow list of exemptions alongside the broad ban on circumvention. The DMCA, for instance, deems

23 See also *Universal City Studios, Inc. v. Corley*, 273 F.3d 429 (2d Cir. 2001), in which the lawsuit of producers and distributors of films, television programs and home videos against distributors of a decrypting algorithm (DeCSS) was allowed. When the motion picture industry launched its digital distribution in DVDs, it encrypted the copies using an encryption-based security system, called CSS (Content Scrambling System), which was designed to prevent copying of the DVD. The CSS was based on an algorithm installed (subject to a license) on standard DVD players or personal computer operating systems. The decrypting program, DeCSS, emulated the 'key' to CSS and, thus, enabled users to play a DVD even in the absence of an authorized key. The court held that CSS is a technological measure limiting the user's ability to make unauthorized copies of DVDs and, therefore, distributors of DeCSS are liable for distributing circumventing devices.

circumvention permissible when necessary for the protection of privacy; for parental control, law enforcement and national security purposes by government agents; and in public libraries, for the sole purpose of determining whether to acquire a particular work. Several limitations in the anti-circumvention regime are designed to allow legitimate encryption research (DMCA §1201(g)), computer security testing (DMCA §1201(j)) and reverse engineering (DMCA §1201(f)). Additionally, the DMCA established an ongoing administrative rulemaking procedure, monitored by the Library of Congress, authorizing the latter to exempt certain classes of works where anti-circumvention legislation is likely adversely to affect the ability of users to make non-infringing uses (17 U.S.C. §1201(a)(1)(B)–(E)). This authority was exercised three times: in 2000, 2003 and 2006 (Federal Register/Vol 64, No 226 (2000), Federal Register/Vol 68, No 211 (2003) and Federal Register/Vol 71, No 227 (2006), respectively).

The rule-making procedure established under the DMCA added only a few narrow exemptions to access control (Library of Congress (October 2003)). Those exemptions include: accessing filtering software (other than antivirus and anti-spam software); circumventing computer programs protected by hardware locks that are outdated and prevent access merely due to malfunction; circumventing computer programs and video games distributed in formats that have become obsolete and require the original hardware to allow access; and circumvention necessary to enable the reading-aloud function in literary works distributed in an eBook format that does not allow this function. In November 2006 the US Library of Congress, upon the recommendation of the Registrar of Copyrights, announced six classes of works that would not be subject to the prohibition against circumventing access controls for a period of three years (17 U.S.C. §1201(a)(1); Federal Register/Vol 71, No 227 (2006)). The exemptions announced include, among other things, audiovisual works used by the educational library of a college or university's film or media studies department for the purpose of creating compilations for educational use in class, computer programs and video games distributed in formats that have become obsolete, and circumvention of cell phone programs that control wireless network connection.

Thus far, in interpreting the anti-circumvention rules of the DMCA US courts have held that the Act is not subject to the fair use exemption. This holding, in effect, strengthens the legal safeguards afforded to informational materials protected by technical measures, allowing content providers to utilize such measures to prevent uses traditionally permitted under fair use.

The European approach to the question of the relationship between anti-circumvention prohibition and traditional copyright limitations was an issue of intense debate during the drafting of the EU Copyright Directive of 2001 (Bechtold 2004: 374–81). The Copyright Directive eventually adopted a narrow view: it allows Member States to take 'appropriate measures' to ensure that beneficiaries of copyright limitation are able to take advantage of the exceptions or limitations afforded by their respective national copyright legislation. Nonetheless, unlike the DMCA, which stipulates a list of (narrowly defined) exemptions, the Copyright Directive does not explicitly allow circumvention by beneficiaries of copyright limitations (Bechtold 2006: 391). Instead, the Copyright Directive calls for rightholders to undertake voluntary measures to allow users to benefit from some copyright limitations (Article 6(4) of the EU Copyright Directive; recital 51 of the EU Copyright Directive). Article 6(4) provides that 'voluntary measures taken by rightholders, including agreements between rightholders and other parties concerned' take precedence over any legislative action. Only if rightholders fail to provide such 'voluntary measures' may beneficiaries of limitations resort to other means. In giving priority to contractual arrangements, the Copyright Directive rendered the protection of user privileges meaningless (Bechtold 2004: 374–76). Rightholders are unlikely to have any incentive to undertake such measures. Thus, copyright limitations could be overridden by technological protection and contractual agreements (Guibault 2002; Bechtold 2004: 378).

Furthermore, Member States are only authorized to facilitate limitations under very limited circumstances. Article 5 of the Copyright Directive provides a list of 22 limitations to copyright law which Member States may incorporate in their national copyright laws. Yet, Article 6(4) severely restricts the authority of Member States to safeguard the rights of beneficiaries under those exceptions. It mandates state intervention with respect to only a number of copyright limitations, such as copying privileges for libraries, researchers, museums, hospitals and disabled persons. Pursuant to Article 6(4) Member States are not obliged, but are entitled, to take steps to secure the privilege to make copies for private purposes. Thus, Article 6(4) weakens the limitation on copyright permitting copying for private purposes. Finally, Member States are not required by the directive to provide exemptions to the anti-circumvention ban with respect to other categories, such as quoting for the purpose of criticism or review, parody, or temporary copying under Article 5(1) (Bechtold 2006: 391–92).

### *6.3.2 The economic rationale of anti-circumvention legislation*

Two economic rationales have been offered in support of the anti-circumvention regime: one is the need to provide disincentives against circumvention, and the other is the need to minimize what some believe is a wasteful technological race.

The first rationale is fairly simple: the ability to exclude non-payers is essential to maintaining incentives to create; exclusion is made possible by technological means, while the act of circumvention reduces the effectiveness of such means. DRMs are basically useless without effective sanctions against those who disable them. In case of a market failure, the role of law is to alter the pay-off functions of market players (Basu 2000). Outlawing circumvention measures creates disincentives for developing those technologies; and even if the law cannot entirely prevent such technologies from emerging, banning circumvention renders their development riskier to hackers and, therefore, more expensive. As a result, anti-circumvention legislation may have the effect of chilling investments in circumvention technology. Furthermore, if circumvention measures are not widely available, it becomes more difficult and expensive for end users to circumvent copyright protection measures. Consequently, so the arguments go, government intervention is necessary to curtail circumvention. Thus, the law should ban the manufacturing of any technology that is primarily designed for the purpose of circumventing technological measures that protect copyright.

This rationale was reflected in recital 47 of the European Union Copyright Directive:

> Technological development will allow rightholders to make use of technological measures designed to prevent or restrict acts not authorized by the rightholders of any copyright, rights related to copyright or the sui generic right in databases. The danger, however, exists that illegal activities might be carried out in order to enable or facilitate the circumvention of the technical protection provided by these measures. In order to avoid fragmented legal approaches that could potentially hinder the functioning of the internal market, there is a need to provide for harmonised legal protection against circumvention of effective technological measures and against provision of devices and products or services to this effect.

A second rationale for banning the manufacture and distribution of circumventing measures is the desire to put a stop to the technological race between exclusion tools and their counter-technologies. It has been suggested by several economists that the development of circumvention measures represents an economic waste. Such a race, they argue, may divert funds that could otherwise be invested in more productive directions (Dam 1998).

Both rationales reflect the limits of the current economic framework for encompassing the complexity of the dynamic information environment. First, this approach presumes that the mere availability of technological measures necessarily renders their use socially desirable. Dam, for instance, argues that '[a]llowing people to protect by their own means what they create is usually socially optimal where the law does not provide a cheaper, more effective, remedy' (Dam 1999: 397). Therefore, he argues, there should be no limit on the use of self-help methods. If one has labored to prepare a telephone directory, she should be entitled to protect it using her own means. If someone invades, or circumvents, those means, according to Dam she has committed 'theft' and the state should outlaw the act. This argument, however, fails to distinguish between private ordering, the reliance on self-help means and public ordering, that is, protection by the state. The case of DRMs resembles private ordering, but in fact relies on public ordering. The DRMs themselves are not necessarily efficient means of exclusion as their effectiveness involves continuous investment in preventing hacking attempts. To determine whether these means are cost-effective one must take into account the costs of developing a technology and preserving its technological superiority, such that it will not be bypassed by counter-technology. What turns self-help means into effective measures of exclusion is government intervention through anti-circumvention legislation.

Second, the current economic framework fails to acknowledge the dynamic nature of such a technological race. The dynamics of developing technology and counter-technology may fuel the technological race and may ultimately contribute to further innovation and further sophistication of exclusion tools, but also other technologies. In other words, the contribution of the race between technological exclusion tools to circumvention tools may result with technological progress in other areas, benefiting in total innovation, progress and collective welfare. We will further elaborate on this in section 6.5 below.

Third, in view of this dynamic nature of developing technological measures and counter-technology, regulating circumvention measures could be viewed as cost allocation. As legal risks become involved, prohibiting the development of circumvention measures increases the costs of their production. Moreover, a ban on circumvention technologies shifts the cost of keeping up with new technologies from copyright owners to other parties. Given the dialectic nature of protective and subversive technologies, this cost could prove substantial. The anti-circumvention regime, thus, cuts costs for copyright owners, no longer required constantly to update and improve their protective measures in order to maintain their effectiveness against hacking. Instead, copyright owners may rely on the legal system to enforce their technological standards and secure their immunity against any circumvention. In this sense, anti-circumvention legislation provides a sort of subsidy to copyright owners, enabling them to maintain the excludability of their copyrighted materials through the use of DRMs. It is therefore arguable that without this subsidy, the use of supposed 'self-help' means would be inadequate. Although subsidies could be used to create incentives for enterprises to act in a way that would lead to social benefits (Truett and Truett 1982), in some cases, as the following section will demonstrate, this arrangement may lead to market distortions. Stated more generally, the traditional economic analysis of law assumed technology to be exogenous to the market. Once technology is viewed as an integral aspect of the market, the implications of any intervention for technological development and the type of technology that would become available should be taken into account (Elkin-Koren and Salzberger 2004: 998–1101).

Fourth, the offered economic analysis endorsing anti-circumvention legislation assumes that the current substantive IP rights are efficient, whereas, as we explained above, the new technological abilities should have an effect on the IPR balance (unless one adopts the proprietary model which pre-assumes intellectual creation to be a natural object of property). In other words, the current IP balance cannot be considered as an exogenous variable in the analysis of the desirable anti-circumvention legislation.

Finally, if DRMs enable restrictions on materials not protected by IPR and anti-circumvention legislation outlaws devices enabling their use, directly by broad interpretation, or indirectly because of the inability of the technological device to distinguish between legal and non-legal use, then anti-circumvention legislation changes the substance of IPR which are assumed to be efficient.

These points of criticism can be simplified by arguing that the combination of strong IP regime (which cannot be justified if technology can enable effective exclusion) with anti-circumvention legislation (meant to enable this efficacy), both endorsed by the law and economics analysis, cannot be justified simultaneously.

### *6.3.3 The nature of regulation by technology*

Are DRMs facilitated by an anti-circumvention legislation to form a new type of IPR? Are they supplanting traditional IPR or simply supplementing rights defined by public ordering, strengthening the self-help enforcement capabilities of right holders? One way to examine the issue is to consider the legal effect of the ban on circumvention for the purpose of gaining access to a work. Under such a view anti-circumvention laws may prohibit access to non-copyrighted materials and thus expand rights, adding a new property right, *a right of access*, to the bundle of rights already granted to copyright owners (Ginsburg 1999: 140–44). If so, technological measures could provide unlimited protection – and control – to rightholders. It would be sufficient for a copyright owner simply to employ technological protective measures to outlaw any circumvention, thereby gaining unlimited control over the use of copyrighted materials, as well as any intermingled non-copyrighted informational materials.

Alternatively, one could argue that anti-circumvention rules should not be interpreted as defining a new property right, but rather as simply providing additional means for enforcement of existing rights. Under this view, these rules are intended to strengthen enforcement of copyright but not to alter the property regime (Hollaar 2002). This approach was expressed by several US courts in cases such as *Corley* and *Chamberlain Group, Inc. v. Skylink Techs., Inc.*, 381 F.3d 1178 (Fed. Cir. 2004). From their perspective, entitlements are defined by copyright law (public law), and the ban on circumvention (public law enforcing private regulation) is limited in scope to the extent necessary for enforcing copyright.

From an economic perspective, the anti-circumvention legislation marks a different approach to the role of government in addressing the public good failure. Often government intervention take the form of either providing the good directly (ie national security, space and human genome research) or securing incentives to invest in the production of public goods by assigning intellectual property rights enforced by the state. Banning the manufacture of circumvention technologies takes government intervention a step further. Here, the government is neither called upon to provide the public good nor to establish the legal means to enable its production by profit-maximizing firms. Central intervention grants a privileged status to information access restrictions unilaterally defined by information providers. Indeed, what enables restrictions on the use of informational works is not the legal rule, but the availability of encryption and other protective technologies. Had it been legal to develop and distribute circumventing technologies, the market effect could have mitigated the power of content owners. Instead, a rule that prevents the development of circumventing measures assigns a privileged status to self-created regulation measures. On the one hand, it strengthens the ability of rightholders to exercise self-help by essentially immunizing such measures against circumvention. On the other hand, it limits the power of end users to implement their respective self-help measures, an act that could be crucial to securing their rights and interests. In order to regulate the implementation of self-help measures, anti-circumvention legislation directly addresses the development and use of new technologies. This type of central intervention regulates technological development and, consequently, directly interferes with competition and innovation. These ramifications of anti-circumvention legislation are the focus of the following sections.

## 6.4 Post-purchase control and consumer protection

DRMs have an extensive impact on the essence of transactions involving informational works. These technical measures, that were originally designed to prevent infringing copying, not only bolster excludability but also limit the functionality of content to a set of permitted uses predefined by vendors (Bomsel and Geffroy 2005b: 16). The uses of DRMs allow content providers to control the use of works long after they have been distributed to the public. For instance, a computer program may simply disable the creation of unauthorized copies or, alternatively, require a code each time a new copy is made. Every time a user logs onto the Internet, a program may transmit a special file notifying the software vendor on which hardware the materials are being used, and how.

Post purchase control may be exercised in several ways. One way of implementing control is through the copies themselves. Adobe PDF, for instance, allows the distributor of a file to prevent certain uses of it, such as saving and printing. The Adobe eBooks platform facilitates control over access restrictions, allowing access to stored information for a limited time, after which the file will 'expire'. Region coding prevents the use of a CD purchased outside the region. Another way of implementing control is through the platform or device which enables access to the content.

DRMs redefine the relationship between rightholders and users of informational works in several ways. First, they create an ongoing relationship between copyright owner and consumers, allowing vendors of content to control rights of access over time and intermittently change content authorization requirements. Rightholders may also occasionally change the terms of access to the content embodied in the platform. Apple, for instance, reserves the right to change at any time how consumers are able to use music purchased at the iTunes Music Store. Currently songs purchased on iTunes can be downloaded to a computer and may be transferred to an iPod, or burned on CD. However, in April 2004, for example, Apple decided to modify the DRM such that consumers could no longer copy their playlist 10 times, but were limited to only seven times. Consumers who had already invested in creating a collection of music prior to April 2004 could have done very little about this retroactive change.

DRMs enable online retailers remotely to control the use of content which was already purchased. A striking example of the lack of consumers' control over their eBooks is the Orwellian 1984 saga, in which Amazon.com remotely removed purchased copies of George Orwell's book, *1984*, from Kindle owing to some copyright concerns. Following a public outcry, Amazon.com apologized and later settled a class action brought against it for violating its terms of service by remotely deleting purchased copies of the book.

Second, DRMs facilitate direct relationship between content distributors and an individual user. While the purchasing of books or CDs was typically anonymous and did not require consumers to identify themselves, online purchasing often involves identification. That is the case when music or apps are downloaded to a smartphone or an eBook is downloaded to a Kindle. Content providers may further collect and retain detailed information about consumers and their habits. Information on purchasing habits was used by Amazon.com, for instance, to enhance its innovative recommendation system, which tailors promotion strategies to particular consumers' preferences. eBooks easily track data, so as to monitor habits and details about the reader's preferences: what she likes to read, how often, for how long and at what times. eBook providers can also track information related to the paragraphs that were highlighted and the annotations that were added by the reader. This may turn the reading experience, which used to be intimate and private, into public knowledge. This transition is not only a threat to privacy but also to free speech, as awareness of such monitoring may create a chilling effect.

Many DRMs allow rightholders to monitor and track the use of their digital content, thus generating new information about intellectual preferences and consuming habits (Cohen 2003). In order to secure content, copyright holders employ technological measures to restrict rights of access to their works to authorized consumers, using different methods for identifying users and authenticating their identity. This process often exposes personal information about the consumer, or at least provides tools that could lead to disclosure of personal information when matched with other databases. Moreover, in order to enjoy the privileges afforded to her under the 'first sale' doctrine, a user must furnish the buyer with her username and password.

The law provides very little tools to curtail DRMs violation of basic rights such as free speech and privacy. US law offers very limited protection to consumers' data privacy. Under the DMCA, consumers are permitted to circumvent a technological measure that collects or disseminates personally identifying information (DMCA §1201(i)). In the absence of available devices and without a similar exception applying to the manufacturers of such circumventing devices, this exemption only benefits consumers who are technologically savvy and thus cannot be considered a meaningful remedy to privacy infringement.

In Europe, the protection of personal information is governed by the EU Directive on Personal Data (1995). Recital 57 of the EU Copyright Directive requires that technical measures incorporate privacy safeguards in accordance with the Directive on Personal Data, which limits the collection and processing of personal data to the extent necessary for a specific lawful purpose and based on legitimate grounds (EU Data Protection Directive, Article 6(1)(b)), and provided that the data subject has unambiguously given consent (EU Personal Data Directive, Article 7(a)). Consequently, under the European regime, rightholders may collect and process personal data only when necessary to the operation of a DRM, and after having explained the purpose of processing such data to consumers and acquiring their consent. However, even if protection exists in principle, without technological anti-circumvention tools, consumers cannot even detect the violation of their rights.

A third aspect relates to consumer rights and especially to the fact that ongoing control by rightholders through DRMs can regulate areas far beyond the rights and protections granted by traditional IP law. As elaborated above, DRMs often set limits on the use of the eBook to a particular device, or disable the option to convert content into a different format, activities that are only available because of post-purchase control.

It had been suggested that post-purchase control interferes with consumer rights and, therefore, warrants government intervention in the form of privacy laws and consumer protection laws. Such laws will guarantee the right of a consumer purchasing a copy to use it with every player she owns, as well as to copy it for personal use, such that she may view the movie on her computer, or listen to the music track on her portable player (Helberger 2004). This perspective was reflected, for instance, in the *Chamberlain* decision of the US Court of Appeals for the Federal Circuit, in which the court rejected a garage door opener (GDO) manufacturer's claim that a universal remote opener infringed his rights under the DMCA (*Chamberlain Group Inc.*, 381 F.3d 1178). Consumers, the court noted, having purchased the plaintiff's GDO system, hold the right to use the copyrighted software embedded therein. Similarly, the French Court of Appeals treated the issue of private copying of a DVD as an aspect of consumer protection law, holding that consumers bear a reasonable expectation to make copies of a DVD that they have purchased for their private use (Helberger 2005). From a strictly legal perspective, the question is to what extent DRMs (and for that matter other types of private regulation, such as end user license agreements) should be allowed to interfere with the statutory rights of consumers who purchased copies.

While the consumer protection doctrine is often useful in resolving these kinds of problems, it also suffers from several shortcomings. At the outset, the nature of the claims invoked under consumer protection laws is restrictive because the laws themselves provide a limited framework both for conceptualizing the harm created by DRMs to information consumers and for defining the scope of the latter's rights vis-à-vis copyright owners. Currently, consumer protection laws offer a relatively limited set of remedies to consumers of information goods, primarily attempting to remedy deficiencies through informed consent, thereby often relegating consumers' interests to questions of notice (Elkin-Koren 2007).

The economic analysis of consumer protection law covers a variety of theories that assume information failure, asymmetry and disparities of power arising from the use of monopolies (van den Bergh 2003; Haupt 2003). Under the current framework, government intervention is limited to securing full information, while the remedy prescribed for lack of information is often the imposition of disclosure duties. On the other hand, if the market produces the necessary information, intervention in the form of compulsory disclosure becomes unnecessary. Furthermore, if consumers are informed by appropriate notice, there is little need for government intervention on the basis of consumer protection.

Consumers in the information environment suffer, however, from information overflow. The proliferation of information makes it expensive to extract and focus on the information necessary for a particular decision-making process. 'Data smog', a term coined by David Shenk (1997), describes the human experience under information overload. For many users, the sheer volume of information is overwhelming. Rather than optimizing their performance, it impairs their ability to make decisions and take actions (Simon 1971: 40–41). Under such circumstances, there is no reason to expect that full disclosure regarding the invasion of privacy in DRM systems will be sufficient for establishing a functioning market. If consumers are not aware of privacy invasion in DRM systems, they will not develop a demand for systems that are privacy friendly.

Some of the ramifications of weakening competition are the narrowing of consumer choice and the weakening of consumer power. Consequently, there is growing concern regarding consumers' rights and the need for consumer protection in the market for informational goods (Schaub 2005). From an economic perspective, consumer bargaining power and the signaling power of their cumulative acts of consumption, must be secured through shifts in demand. Consumers' choice, however, depends on the level of competition. The implications of DRMs for competition are further discussed in the next section.

## 6.5 DRMs and competition

Anti-circumvention legislation was originally intended to grant copyright owners extra protections against the growing threats of digital piracy. In order to reduce piracy, if not entirely prevent it, the new regime sought to deter the creation of endless free copies that would substitute the market for authorized copies. When anti-circumvention legislation was first adopted, it raised serious concerns that the legal regime might expand the market power of copyright owners and that DRMs could be used to reduce competition and increase concentration (Samuelson 1999; Koelman 2004: 626). Indeed, DRMs are increasingly employed for strategic advantages. DRMs enable rightholders to control downstream distribution by making it technically impossible to resell used copies. For instance, a system can be designed to prohibit reinstalling a program once it has been uninstalled, or requiring a match between the hardware and software serial numbers.

DRMs are also employed to prevent the development of complementary products that require interoperability, and thus consumers find themselves tied to a specific hardware device owing to the inability to transfer content from one device to another. The consequences of the anti-circumvention regime have already exceeded the proclaimed legislative intent. Moreover, a growing number of commodities incorporate software that control their functions and interfaces with other systems (from cameras and media players to watches, cars and microwaves). As a result, the anti-circumvention regime is increasingly viewed as troublesome by a wide range of industries and it is receiving growing attention from policy-makers.

### *6.5.1 The virtues of interoperability*

A major concern regarding the anti-circumvention regime is that it will be used for anti-competitive purposes. Indeed, DRMs have been used to create platforms, content and products that are incompatible with others. Interoperability between systems refers to their ability to work together and exchange information directly. It is the ability to transfer content from one platform to another, and interact with information acquired on another platform or merge several types of content from different sources together. Interoperability could directly affect creativity and innovation. It enables experimenting and interacting with different systems and creating new content by using different sources.

The ability to transfer data and content acquired or generated on one platform onto another platform is required to guarantee competition. In the absence of such transferability content users are likely to be locked in one platform, thereby weakening the competition among providers. Interoperability may therefore affect the level of competition and consequently the price of accessing copyrighted materials. Interoperability among competing platforms may allow end users to switch between different brand technologies and encourage vendors to compete for quality and price. Sony, for instance, can achieve exclusivity in the market for games developed for its Sony PlayStation video games console, by preventing competitors from developing games compatible with its game console. Thus Sony can eliminate competition in this specific market and gain the power to dictate the price of PlayStation games. This would allow Sony to sell its consoles at low prices, while further increasing its market share in the video games market.

In the absence of competition, content might end up being too expensive and therefore available only to a limited segment of consumers. But competition in the market for content may have other important implications that go beyond the price of informational works. The shift to digital content affects access to knowledge and may have far-reaching implications for privacy, free speech, political freedom, research and development. Competition is not only the best way to promote progress in this context by increasing the volume of content and its availability at a reasonable price, it is also the best way to secure human rights and free speech in the digital environment.

The power to limit interoperability may further enable rightholders to leverage their monopoly, established by law, in the market for copyrighted content into a monopoly in the market for platforms, products and services. If a DRM is only compatible with systems produced by a single vendor and is incompatible with other systems, rightholders can expand their control from the market for the work, to the market for accessories and other products, thereby increasing their overall market holding. One example is Apple's Music Store, iTunes, and Apple's music player, the iPod. By using FairPlay, Apple prevented users from playing music purchased from the iTunes Store on other companies' music players, and also prevented purchasers of iPod from playing music acquired from other music stores. Consequently, Apple was accused of leveraging its market power from one market into the other.

Furthermore, controlling interoperability by DRMs may even allow vendors to interfere with independent markets for accessories and spare parts. Such interference could become a widespread phenomenon, not only in the market for informational materials, but also in other markets for consumer goods. After all, the computer programs embedded in many consumer products, from cars to watches, are copyrightable materials. Compatibility could be governed by a computer program set to allow interface with authorized products and prevent it with others. For instance, Lexmark, a printer manufacturer, installed an 'authentication' mechanism between its printers and toner cartridges. Static Control reverse engineered the authentication procedure and developed a chip that emulated the 'handshake' between the printer and the toner cartridge, thus enabling the company to refill and remanufacture cartridges that would be compatible with Lexmark printers. The court denied a lawsuit brought by Lexmark against Static Control, finding no copyright infringement or violation of the anti-circumvention ban. Adopting a narrow interpretation of the law, the court held that the authentication sequence employed by Lexmark did not 'effectively control access' to copyrighted materials (*Lexmark Int'l Inc. v. Static Control Components*, 387 F.3d 522 (6th Cir. 2004)). Another case in which the court decided to dismiss a similar lawsuit was the garage door openers, the *Chamberlain* case, on which we elaborated in section 6.4. In fact, the US Federal Circuit Court of Appeals in *Chamberlain* warned against applying a broad interpretation to the DRM/DMCA ban, that:

> . . . would allow any manufacturer of any product to add a single copyrighted sentence or software fragment to its product, wrap the copyrighted material in a trivial 'encryption' scheme, and thereby gain the right to restrict consumers' rights to use its products in conjunction with competing products. In other words, Chamberlain's construction of the DMCA would allow virtually any company to attempt to leverage its sales into aftermarket monopolies – a practice that both the antitrust laws . . . and the doctrine of copyright misuse . . . normally prohibit.
>
> (*Chamberlain*, 381 F.3d, 1178 at 1201)

While the courts were willing to apply the DMCA narrowly when technical measures controlled the compatibility of mundane consumer devices, in other somewhat similar circumstances involving online games, DVDs and music players, they actually applied a more expansive interpretation of the ban on anti-circumvention, as will be discussed further below.

### *6.5.2 Legal impediments to interoperability: the new IPR regime*

When DRMs are invoked to prevent interoperability they serve two goals: one is to ensure that copyrighted materials are used only as authorized by the copyright owner and the second is to verify that protected content may be used solely with selected platforms. It is this latter goal that could threaten competition. When DRMs are used to tie together platforms, content and products, they function as technical standards, which enjoy a special immunity against circumvention under the anti-circumvention regime. DRMs may impede the adoption of shared standards of interoperability that could otherwise facilitate competition. Ensuring interoperability with competing products and services could help restrain the market power of owners of intellectual property who enjoy exclusivity in the market for content. Interoperability of content, platforms and products could bring newcomers to the market, thereby safeguarding against attempts to drive a monopoly in the market for content into a monopoly in the market for platforms and products. In the past, competitors could bypass compatibility impediments by engaging in reverse engineering. Anti-circumvention legislation, however, makes such attempts illegal.

Generally speaking, reverse engineering entails the process of analysing the workings of a computer program, or any other device, by taking it apart. This process can reveal the components of a product, as well as how they function. Computer programs present prime subjects for reverse engineering, as they are released in 'object code', while the 'source code' is protected as a trade secret. Reverse engineering of software reverses the program's object code, namely the machine code composed of strings of the numbers 0 and 1 that are sent to the logic processors, back into the source code, which is the human readable language in which software is written and from which the internal design of a program can be deduced. While reverse engineering a computer program could be essential for facilitating compatibility, it often requires copying significant portions of the original work. Unless exempted by the law, the creation of such unauthorized copies might constitute copyright infringement.

As a matter of policy, exempting reverse engineering from liability has important advantages. As has been suggested by Samuelson and Scotchmer (2002), allowing reverse engineering in traditional manufactured goods is economically sound policy, given that reverse engineering only captures some of the know-how embodied in the goods. To illustrate, reverse engineering could reveal what a spare part looks like, or what its component substances are; it would not reveal, however, how to manufacture the good, allowing that fact to remain a trade secret. Furthermore, since reverse engineering is costly and time-consuming, it creates a delay that enables a lead time advantage of the first-comer and allows her to recoup her initial R&D investment. In information-based products, by contrast, the lack of concealed information means that if one knows how a product operates, one knows how to make it. However, reverse engineering is still adequately time-consuming and cost-prohibitive to render it an inefficient means of developing competing products, particularly in the case of computer programs.

Reverse engineering may further encourage innovative activity by allowing developers to learn from what their competitors have already achieved and build upon it. It also facilitates new entrance to the market by enabling the development of complementary products. Understanding the functionality of a computer program is critical to the process of establishing compatibility with other products and services on the market. Additionally, reverse engineering encourages developers to introduce products and services of competitive quality.

These rationales were reflected by law. In the US reverse engineering used to achieve interoperability is considered fair use that does not require permission by copyright owners (*Sega Enters. Ltd. v. Accolade, Inc.*, 977 F.2d 1510 (9th Cir. 1992); *Sony Computer Entertainment v. Connectix Corp.*, 203 F.3d 596 (9th Cir. 2000)). Similar laws exist in Europe. However, the anti-circumvention regime prohibits the type of exploration once permitted under the reverse engineering regime. Once a computer program is encrypted, for instance, any attempt to decrypt it constitutes circumvention. Some limitations in the anti-circumvention regime are designed to allow reverse engineering, including legitimate encryption research (DMCA §1201(g)), computer security testing (DMCA §1201(j)) and other limited reverse engineering (DMCA §1201(f)). But these exemptions were narrowly drafted and do not cover the range of potentially efficient explorations. Reverse engineering, for instance, is only permissible when necessary to achieve interoperability and used solely for that purpose (DMCA §1201(f)(1)).

Under the DMCA, information acquired through reverse engineering can only be revealed to others for the same purpose for which it was acquired, namely, to achieve interoperability among computer programs (DMCA §1201(f)(3)). The reverse engineering exception under the DMCA was also narrowly interpreted by the US courts. In *Universal City Studios, Inc. v. Reimerdes*, for instance, the defendant claimed that DeCSS circumvention of the CSS DVD encryption was necessary to achieve interoperability between the DVDs and the Linux operating system, and thus constituted lawful use of lawfully purchased DVDs on another platform (111 F.Supp.2d 294 (S.D.N.Y. 2000)). The court denied the reverse engineering defense, holding that the right to circumvent and acquire the information through reverse engineering extends only to dissemination 'solely for the purpose of achieving interoperability' and does not apply to the public dissemination of circumvention means.

In 2005, the US Eighth Circuit Court of Appeals narrowed even further the scope of the reverse engineering exception in the *Davidson & Associates v. Jung* case (422 F.3d 630 (8th Cir. 2005)). In that case, the plaintiff had developed a computer game, 'Blizzard', with an optional online multi-player platform, 'Battle.net Mode', which required a password (a CD-key that was printed on a sticker and attached to the product packaging). The defendant was held liable for offering a non-commercial online gaming website that allowed users to play the game without a password. The court found that the reverse engineering of the original copyrighted 'Blizzard' games, in order to emulate Battle.net, was a violation of the EULA, which explicitly prohibited reverse engineering. Furthermore, the court held that the defendant's alternative server (bnetd.org) circumvented Blizzard's technological measures controlling access to the original multi-player's online website (Battle.net) under §1201(a)(2) of the DMCA. This interpretation of the term 'circumvention' was criticized for being overly broad (Zimmerman 2006), particularly given that the reverse engineering defense under §1201(f) did not exempt the use in this case.

As was previously mentioned, in 2006, the US Library of Congress established six new exemptions from the ban on circumvention of DRM systems. One of those exemptions applies to the circumvention of a computer program used to enable wireless telephone handsets to connect to a wireless telephone communication network. Prior to this ruling, the circumvention of such programs by owners of cell phones for the purpose of switching to another wireless carrier was considered illegal. The new exemption permits 'unlocking' a phone in order to achieve compatibility with any wireless network.

The situation under European law is slightly more complex. Article 6 of the EU Copyright Directive does not apply to computer programs, since software is already covered by Article 7(1)(c) of the EU Software Directive (EU Copyright Directive, recital 50). Under the Software Directive, the right to reverse engineer is secured. For instance, Article 5(3) of the Software Directive allows reverse engineering for the purpose of studying the essential ideas and principles behind a program. A lawful owner of a copy of the program may 'observe, study or test the functioning of the program in order to determine the ideas and principles which underlie any element of the program' (Software Directive, Article 5(3)). Under Article 6, decompilation is permitted for the purpose of achieving interoperability, but the use of information gained in the course of reverse engineering is prohibited for purposes other than to achieve the interoperability of the independently created computer program (Software Directive, Article 6(2)). Article 6(2)(c) permits reverse engineering for the development of a new program, provided that it is not substantially similar in its expression to the original program and does not involve copyright infringements.

### *6.5.3 Interoperability and competition in information markets*

Understanding the role of DRMs in shaping competition in the market for informational goods requires paying attention to the distinct characteristics of markets governed by intellectual property and the interface between intellectual property policies and competition. Apparently, when DRMs are used to protect the market for copyrighted content, there is a stronger economic justification for the interference with competition. When the motion picture industry sought to protect DVDs from unauthorized copying, it was presumably desirable to legitimize the anti-circumvention ban, which is directly related to the rationale of securing incentives to invest in future creation. The monopoly and the resulting decline in competition are considered part of the package designed by intellectual property laws and are therefore justifiable under its premises. In contrast, when Lexmark sought to use DRMs to control the market for toner cartridges, there was no justification for legal intervention to facilitate Lexmark's attempt at achieving dominance. Competition policy would render such an outcome undesirable.

At the same time, however, since markets for content are not free markets, but are based on intellectual property monopolies, the risk to competition is even greater in the case of IP markets. Whereas many of the markets for consumer devices are presumably competitive, copyright owners enjoy exclusivity and, in some cases, in the absence of perfect substitutes for the work, the copyright owner might hold a monopoly. Therefore, the risks to competition associated with legally-immune DRMs are even greater.

Consider, for instance, the emerging market for eBooks. Access to eBooks is technically controlled either by DRMs or by the reading device, which enables control of a variety of issues related to the digital copy: who can use it, what users can do with it and what data is collected on the users. eBooks and eReaders should therefore compete not only for price, but also for the level of connectivity, functionality, privacy and use restrictions. In the absence of competition, eBooks might become too expensive, limiting use to a particular device or format, and might limit the types of use available to consumers. Competition in the market for eBooks should facilitate diversity in books and applications for eBooks by enabling developers and self-published authors to distribute their content under fair terms. Competition should further enable online intermediaries – such as online retailers, search engines and social networks – to provide added value to books and develop supplementary services (Elkin-Koren 2011).

The eBooks market consists of four layers: hardware, software, distribution and content. Contrary to paper books, eBooks require a reading device and therefore involve a layer of hardware and software. The hardware – either multipurpose devices such as tablet computers and smartphones, or eBook readers such as Kindle – must be compatible with an eBook format. The combination of hardware and software will affect the functionality of an eBook and what users will be able to do with it: whether they can transfer it, whether they can read in private free of monitoring and whether they can copy, print, or listen to it. The need to use compatible hardware and software makes eBooks vulnerable to becoming locked in by technical standards.

The level of competition in the eBooks market will depend on the ability of vendors to use content, application and hardware together. At the distribution level, access to eBooks is facilitated by a variety of online intermediaries: online retailers such as Amazon.com and Apple, search engines such as Google, and ISPs and social networks. These new gateways to eBooks combine some control over the content with powerful capabilities of collecting personal data on users. A strong network effect gives advantages to large-scale intermediaries that attract the most traffic by users on a global scale. Economies of scale, the rising cost of large-scale exposure, and the need to operate globally across international borders further reduce competition and lead to domination by a small number of mega-platforms (OECD Report 2007). Consequently, online intermediaries may raise serious concerns regarding the competitiveness and openness of future information markets.

At the content level, digital books, with new search and hyperlink capabilities, become more valuable as they are linked to other books. Some business models which are based on providing added value, such as search capabilities or the ability to share comments, may also take advantage of access to a large number of books. Providers of eBooks may gain a strong competitive advantage by offering a comprehensive collection of digital books. The increased dependency on reading devices, the rise of new intermediaries, and the increased value of comprehensive book collections may affect competition in the market for eBooks. Taken together, these features of eBooks may concentrate economic and cultural control in the hands of a few dominant players.

Copyright in books may enable publishers to shape the eBook market at all layers. For example, Amazon.com first released the Kindle in 2007. In order to create demand for its eReaders, Amazon.com had to offer books in a digital format. To stimulate further demand, Amazon.com sought to sell eBooks at a discount. Therefore, it bought eBooks for Kindle from publishers at $12.00 to $13.00 and offered them for sale to consumers at $9.99, taking a loss in order to gain a market share for its Kindle. When Apple introduced the iPad in January 2010, it was anticipated that, with more competition, there would also be a reduction in the price. Indeed, the release of the iPad and competition from Barnes & Noble, Borders and Sony pushed down the price of eReaders. But the introduction of the iPad only increased the price of eBooks.

Apple sold eBooks at $14.99. The reason was copyright. The publishers, who hold the copyright in the vast majority of books, refused to licence eBooks to Amazon.com unless it complied with the higher retail price Apple was charging. The publishers argued that a lower price for eBooks might diminish sales of paper books, and might also devalue the prestige of books. In response, Amazon.com posted an announcement calling on consumers to boycott eBooks with the publishers' fixed price.

In this eBooks price war, copyright was used to tie together content and hardware, to the detriment of consumer welfare. Such lock-in is precisely what enabled iTunes to become dominant in the market for music distribution. As long as copyright holders can prevent the publication of their books in eBook format, competition in the market will be limited. Copyright holders may further affect the design of eReaders and its functionalities. For instance, the Authors Guild objected to the introduction of a text-to-speech feature by Amazon.com in the Kindle 2, which enabled users to listen to the text as it was read aloud. It argued that this feature constituted copyright infringement. Ultimately, Amazon.com was forced to give authors and publishers the option to decide whether to enable the feature.

Another example that demonstrates how the combination of IPR and DRM may stifle competition and lead to inefficient outcome is the use of DRMs in the market for video games. The case of Sony PlayStation is particularly illustrative. Sony, like many other vendors of DVDs and videogames, such as Nintendo and Microsoft, uses a region code indicating the area of the world in which distribution and playback are authorized. DVD video players are often designed to comply with such region codes, and consumers in one region can only play discs that contain its region code. In the case of PCs, definitions are incorporated into the operating system. This distribution model allows the motion picture industry and game manufacturers to control distribution of their movies and games, respectively, on a region-by-region basis. Movies and games may be released in different regions and at different times. More importantly, this distribution model enables differential pricing among regional markets. For consumers, however, the model may pose a burden. It has been argued that the region coding system interferes with consumers' expectations. A tourist who rents a movie at Blockbuster at full price expects to be able to play it on her portable computer, even if the computer is coded for a different region. Similarly, tourists who purchase games and DVDs abroad would like to be able to play them at home. Thus, regional coding interrupts the free movement of goods and services, preventing parallel importation.

The stability of this business model depends on the ability to prevent the manufacturing and distribution of software and devices that allow users to bypass the region code and play a DVD or a video game outside their region. As long as consumers cannot play an imported DVD or game bought outside their region, a distributor can prevent genuine competition in international markets and fix the price for each region. Yet, many DVD players are equipped as multi-systems – they automatically identify region codes and enable users to play DVDs from all regions. There are also codes and computer programs that allow users to override regional coding in personal computers and video games consoles.

Copyright therefore becomes essential for securing this business strategy. On several occasions Sony successfully sued distributors of devices allowing users to bypass region codes. For instance, in *Sony v. GameMasters*, 87 F.Supp.2d 976 (N.D.Cal. 1999), the court found that a game enhancer that permitted users to play imported games, intended for Japanese or European PlayStation consoles, violated the DMCA. The court held that the device 'circumvents the mechanism on the PlayStation console that ensures the console operates only when encrypted data is read from an authorized CD-ROM' (ibid: 987).

Recently, Sony brought suit in Australia against the manufacturers of 'mod chips', which allow users of Sony PlayStation to play games purchased in different regions. The High Court of Australia distinguished between pirating a game and playing legitimate copies using a mod chip: while making a pirated copy of a game was found illegal, playing a game using a mod chip was not. The High Court held that regional coding intentionally reduces global market competition and limits consumers' rights (*Stevens v. Kabushiki Kaisha Sony Computer Entertainment*, 79 ALJR 1850 (2005)). Mod chip devices, however, are considered illegal in other countries. For example, the High Court in England ruled that mod chip devices were used to make infringing copies of copyrighted material and were, therefore, illegal (*Ball*, E.C.D.R. 33).

### 6.5.4 *Can the market take care of the problems on its own?*

The previous sections described how DRMs could be used in anti-competitive ways. The question for policy-makers is whether these uses pose a threat to competition, which the market cannot resolve? In other words, economists may predict that consumers will adjust their expectations regarding the available uses of platforms and content and that the current state of affairs would eventually affect the demand for platform and content and would lead to more efficient purchasing of media content (Grimmelmann 2005).

In answering this question several considerations may come into play. One factor is lock-in. Consumers of iTunes music who are using the iPod become dependent on the Apple-supported DRM. For a consumer who invests in equipment and selection of music, the costs of switching could turn out to be prohibitively expensive. These costs, in turn, create a barrier to re-entry in a market for songs and media players and may reduce competition in these markets. However, the costs could also prove damaging to Apple. If iPod only supports the FairPlay DRM, the attraction to iPod for new consumers may decline, as consumers interested in purchasing a portable digital player increasingly take these extra costs into account. The lock-in factor could lead to competition among companies over the dominant standards of DRMs. The question is whether this fight is beneficial for consumers.

Another factor that must be considered is the tension between inter-technology and intra-technology competition within the market. When companies are restricted to one common standard of DRM, intra-technology competition may result. Likewise, competition in the market no longer surrounds the model of the DRM, but rather the price, quality and service (Bomsel and Geffroy 2005b: 35). Intra-technology competition could benefit consumers both by facilitating interoperability, thereby increasing the functionality of goods for consumers and by improving competition over price and quality.

Competition among technologies leads to increased efficiency, as long as the technologies are interoperable. Interoperability is socially desirable since it allows using content without being limited to one type of standard. From an economic perspective the question is whether government intervention is necessary in order to achieve and maintain interoperability and, if so, in what form. Naturally, content providers are motivated by self-interest – if they are able to control the use of works after their distribution to the public, one can reasonably expect that those controls will be tailored to maximize content provider profits.

However, it is also within the content provider's self-interest to take the consumer's interests into account. If DRMs are viewed simply as technology that inhibits copying (Dam 1998) then one could expect markets to react to unreasonable restrictions on use. In other words, if Lexmark prevents the purchase of toner cartridges produced by competitors, or the refill of the original toners, and requires users to purchase new cartridges made only by Lexmark and at relatively high prices, consumers will eventually prefer competitors that allow choice in refill and replacement. Moreover, the price of maintaining these restrictions will be absorbed by the consumer and reflected in the price listed when the consumer makes her choice of purchase. It follows logically that this arrangement would subsequently place Lexmark at a disadvantage and would force the company to change its policies. For similar reasons copy protection technology, which prevented users from producing additional copies of computer programs, failed in the market. Thus, one could claim that providers who use DRMs will respond to consumer preferences and will be market-regulated by these types of shifts in demand.

This argument nevertheless suffers from several weaknesses. First, the claim fails adequately to identify the stakeholders and their interests. The market for content is affected by content providers, DRM and consumers. Content providers enjoy a dominant position due to their exclusivity over content based on intellectual property rights. Many of them are organized in associations such as MPAA or RIAA, which coordinate standard terms of access determined through a particular DRM. Consequently, users who wish to acquire content that is distributed by members of such associations will be governed by the terms of access determined through collective action. The extent to which competition occurs in the market for content depends on the availability of substitutes. In the case of online distribution, content providers are increasingly using standardization of platforms, in the interest of reducing the costs of both distribution and copyright enforcement.

Another dynamic that affects the availability of platforms is the relationship between hardware and software providers and the content industry (Besek 2004: 487). This relationship involves a complex web of interrelations. Content providers no longer produce DRMs, but rather purchase ready-made systems from specialized DRM suppliers. At the same time, DRM suppliers refuse interoperability, seeking a dominant position in the market. Security considerations play in this dynamic too: if standards are compatible, content may easily migrate from secure to insecure format (Farchy and Ranaivoson 2005).

While the hardware and software industries seek to produce market platforms and applications that will meet consumer preferences, content drives the sales of applications. After all, no one has an interest in an MP3 player on which there is no music to play. The content industry wishes to maximize profits generated from content by distributing in secure format to the greatest extent possible. The buyers of DRM systems are not individual consumers but members of the content industry. Therefore, the DRM standards that emerge are likely to respond to demand in the content industry, which is interested in encouraging tight restrictions on access. The hardware and software industries, which depend on content, typically follow these standards. As the example of Apple demonstrates, the incorporation of DRMs in the distribution model (here, a music store and portable music player) may also serve the strategic interests of hardware manufacturers. Thus, the potential is quite high that a single standard will dominate.

Digital technologies create a dependency by content providers on technology designers, the power of which is reinforced by the legal rules that aim to protect DRMs (Farchy and Ranaivoson 2005: 65). This reality may also bear ramifications for barriers on entry and the level of competition that is to be expected in the online world. While the costs of producing content are decreasing and the means of production (computers, home studios) are broadening, the increasing dependency on new online intermediaries for distributing content, such as search engines and DRM providers, renders it more difficult to penetrate the market. Therefore, the use of DRMs should be analysed within the broad economic and technological context that facilitates control (Cohen 2003), in which the market is governed by a small number of content and access providers. As Cohen contends, describing DRMs in terms of private regulation does not capture the system of control on which it relies.

Second, the belief that markets for content protected by DRMs will reach equilibrium through market forces of supply and demand overlooks the lack of information that is associated with DRMs. The efficiency of DRMs, as in the case of any other type of private regulation, depends on their ability to reflect the will of consenting parties. Permissions defined by DRMs are often unknown to consumers. This problem arises from the fact that DRMs are not transparent. The rules, as well as the code, are not directly accessible to lay people. In many instances, users are not adequately informed about the rights and obligations embodied in any particular system and thus it is difficult for them to know what to anticipate. A consumer who purchases a DVD may expect to be able to play it on the DVD players installed on her computer, or on the DVD player connected to her home movie theater system. However, regional coding systems might prevent the consumer from doing so. If users inaccurately perceive the impact of the bargain on their utility, we can no longer be confident that the exchange will, in fact, leave both parties in a better position (Cohen 1998).

Indeed, initial studies show that many online music services do not respect consumers' legitimate and legal expectations of personal use (Mulligan, Han and Burstein 2003). A recent survey shows that consumers are not pleased with the status of DRM systems in the online music industry. The study, which was aimed squarely at the music-buying public, shows that 68 percent of the respondents believed that the only music worth paying for is DRM-free music (Entertainment Media Research 2007).

The analysis above as well as the empirical findings may point to the need of central intervention in order to protect consumers' expectations. The lack of information regarding the terms of the bargain, as they are encoded electronically, and the ability to continuously alter access to copyrighted materials, weaken the power of consumers to shape the terms of access by creating a strong demand for alternative conditions. Consequently, whereas normally it would be foreseeable that market competition over prices would thrive, it is unlikely that competition over terms of access designed by DRMs will develop. In this sense DRMs might be viewed as infrastructure, like roads, which require central provision (Frischmann 2012).

## 6.6 Anti-circumvention legislation and the economics of innovation

From an economic perspective the prime goal of the IPR system as a whole is to maximize innovation, which is the basis for wealth maximization and growth. Does anti-circumvention legislation contribute or rather frustrate innovation?

Anti-circumvention legislation regulates innovative activity. It explicitly prohibits the development of certain technologies. Thus, anti-circumvention legislation may directly affect encryption research, which focuses on identifying the vulnerability of systems and is therefore critical for the safety of information systems and network infrastructure. Programmers and computer scientists, as a result of anti-circumvention legislation, may fear publishing research that analyses the vulnerability of security systems. The chilling effect of anti-circumvention legislation on research and development is best demonstrated by the case of Princeton professor Edward W. Felten. When Felten identified deficiencies in the DRM system announced by the music industry, he was threatened with litigation by the Recording Industry

Association of America (RIAA) if he presented his research results at a workshop. His request for a declaratory judgment that the threat violated his constitutional right to free speech was rejected by the court. Similarly, a Dutch computer scientist, Niels Ferguson, was reported to have withdrawn publication of a paper explaining security flaws in Intel's video encryption system for fear of legal consequences (Ferguson 2001).

The chilling effect on computer science and encryption is more severe under the US regime than in Europe. The reason for this difference is that in Europe technological measures that protect computer programs (in contrast to other copyrighted materials) are subject to the EU Software Directive, which does not prohibit the act of circumvention as such. In the US, the exemptions for encryption research are provided under the DMCA (DMCA §1201(g)). Both regimes, however, prohibit publishing the results of analysing technological measures and exploring their operations (DMCA §1201(g)(3)(a); EU Copyright Directive Article 6(2)).

Commentators have expressed concerns that strong anti-circumvention rules will threaten high-technology research, particularly in the area of security (Brown 2003; Samuelson 2001). When protective technology is tested in the open market and challenged by counter-technologies, there is less concern. Competition will fuel technological progress and the best technology will survive.

As elaborated in section 6.3 above, DRMs may diminish the ability of consumers to rely on copyright exceptions and limitations in gaining access to informational works (Petrick 2004). Currently, there are no sufficient incentives for DRM developers to enable distinctions between unauthorized copying and privileged uses under copyright law. Restrictions imposed by DRMs often strip users of some of the privileges awarded to them under standard copyright law. Changing the balance maintained by copyright laws means deviating from efficient arrangements that take into account the fact the informational products ought to be widely distributed once produced in order to enable future creation and innovation. Likewise, limiting the technical ability to explore works and adapt them to one's own needs could severely hamper innovation. Thus, the ability of a DRM to prevent (rather than prohibit) the use of works may negatively impact the 'freedom to tinker' and alter the state of innovation (Lockton 2005).

The issue at stake, therefore, is whether DRMs can override exceptions and limitations provided by copyright law. Some would contend that from an economic perspective, DRMs are a means of self-help and as such they constitute a form of private regulation that is arguably more efficient than public regulation (Bell 1998). The main advantages of private regulation are that it reflects the specific circumstances pertaining to the parties and that it lowers administrative costs. Yet, in some cases public regulation should prevail. The advantage of public regulation is that it innately takes into account how decisions made by the particular parties affect the welfare of others not represented in the transaction. The strong presence of externalities in the area of copyright regulation may warrant government intervention in setting limits on the outcomes of private regulation.

Just as innovation policy is affected by direct restrictions on the freedom to explore computer programs, it is also influenced by competition in informational markets. Several points on this topic are worth mentioning. First, the cost of innovation depends on the price of access to copyrighted materials. This is because research and development are incremental. New developments are established on the basis of previous developments. Copyrighted materials are often used as resources for producing new works. Therefore, an increase in the price of copyrighted materials and thus access to the wealth of innovative achievements, renders research and development either stagnated, or simply more expensive. In many cases, higher prices increase production costs and may slow innovative or creative activity; simultaneously, the cost of access affects the depth and quality of human resources that may engage in producing more works. For instance, if a new game is built upon a previous game, as is the case in derivative works, a price increase of the original game would lead to higher production costs of the subsequent game and might prevent it from being produced altogether.

Second, DRMs bring about a decentralization of control over copyrighted materials. When an interface between a platform and a game or music track is entirely controlled by rightholders, they may unilaterally determine what type of content will be produced and by whom. For instance, if Sony can use DRMs to prevent the use of a game enhancer that allows games to be played in a different manner, or the development of applications that would allow playing PlayStation compatible games on PCs, then Sony can exercise full control over the subsequent development of its copyrighted program.

This advantage may not only affect the competition for price of accessories and compatible applications, but it may also influence the likelihood of inventing improvements. This particular point questions the extent to which it is economically efficient to concentrate control over decisions of improvement at the hands of the intellectual property owner. The original creator is not necessarily in the best position to develop potential applications, or even to identify them (Lemley 1997a). There is no apparent advantage in forcing potential developers to negotiate with the rightholder of the original work prior to developing a new application, given that the information is non-rival and there is no significant need to coordinate the development of further applications. Many developers could be encouraged to compete and the effort made by one would not detract from the ability of others to develop their own applications based on the original work. In fact, the open source experience suggests that further development of computer programs could be achieved more efficiently if improvements are enabled by many participants, working in an open platform.

Finally, as evidenced by Sony's legal strategy, there is no reason to believe that rightholders would refrain from using their absolute control over the platform strategically, for the purpose of leaving any potential competitor out of the market, or at least creating very high barriers to entry. From the perspective of innovation policy, control by DRMs could affect the freedom to innovate and the diversity of products and applications introduced in the market.

## 6.7 Conclusions: designing regulations for regulation by design

In this chapter we have examined the effects of digital technologies on the economic analysis of IP law, focusing on DRMs as technological tools to enforce IP rights and on anti-circumvention legislation, the new method of central intervention to protect the superiority of DRMs.

The substantive arrangements of intellectual property rights have been justified by law and economics on the basis of the public good market failure of information products and services. Consequently, IP rights are limited in time and include various exceptions intended to balance the conflicting desire to maximize the welfare of society or to achieve efficiency. This balance is contingent upon the extent and nature of the public good market failure in informational goods. The production and distribution of copyrighted materials in digital format enhances the ability of content creators and providers to exercise unparalleled control over the use of works, thus causing them to be more excludable. The availability of encryption measures allows creators of informational materials to technically exclude non-payers at low costs. If one takes the economic rationale for intellectual property laws seriously, the digital revolution of the last couple of decades ought to have changed the balance struck by existing IP rights in terms of the length of time for which they are given and their scope. Such a change has not taken place so far, and instead we witness new regulatory components added to the field, primarily anti-circumvention laws, which may be viewed as additional enforcement tools, but also broaden the scope of substantive IP rights. In other words, new regulatory tools respond to the balance struck by traditional IP rights, instead of re-examining this balance prior to the deployment of new legal avenues to enforce these traditional rights.

Our elaborate description and analysis of DRMs from an economic perspective reveal that they possess the ability to turn information, once a non-excludable resource, into a more excludable asset and exceed the time span of excludability long after purchase by consumers and, indeed long after the expiration of IPR granted by legislation. This fundamental change transforms not only the nature of informational works but also the relationship between rightholders and consumers of copyrighted materials. It enables a long-term relationship between suppliers and recipients/users of informational works, as well as affecting subsequent users who were not engaged directly with the original content producers. Although DRMs can be designed to enforce IP rights as defined by legislation (rights which themselves may lose their initial rationale upon the disappearance of the very market failure that justified them in the first place), they can also change legislative arrangements by extending the duration of rights, abolishing legal exceptions and more. If substantive IP laws are efficient, the self-regulation and self-help provided by DRMs might justify central intervention in the opposite form of IP laws – ie through restricting the ability of private parties to extend IP rights and to control their creations beyond what substantive IP laws grant.

The primary response of governments to the new digitalized information environment failed to adapt to the first two points summarized above. Instead, they resorted to an opposite strategy by enacting anti-circumvention legislation, which prohibits the development of technological tools aiming to circumvent the digital protection of information products and services. Not only did law-makers fail to re-examine the IP rights balance in light of the technological changes, but the anti-circumvention legislation in fact expands IP rights. Anti-circumvention is not restricted to violation of traditionally protected IP rights; rather, it extends to new substantive rights created by individual DRM designs. The two main rationales mounted in support for anti-circumvention legislation – establishing disincentives to circumvention and creating obstacles to the technological race between exclusion tools and their counter-technologies – are not persuasive in light of the first two points. Moreover, these rationales are even less convincing in the absence of a consensual framework to incorporate technology and technological change as an endogenous variable in the traditional economic models of markets, market failures and the justification for central intervention in the market.

The rise of this new type of regulation in the information environment raises a whole new set of concerns. DRMs and their protection by anti-circumvention laws enhance the likelihood of intensifying market failures caused by monopolies and externalities. The anti-competitive environment created by DRMs and their legal protection relates to their ability to bind content with platforms and other related products, as well as their ability to create separate technological standards that are incompatible with others. In such an environment, access to content is limited for users of particular products or platforms. The new IPR environment enhances externalities by the legally protected abilities to control the informational products long after they are sold to users, to change the terms of usage unilaterally and to control their usage beyond the contracting parties, affecting various types of third parties.

Anti-circumvention legislation is only one model for regulation in the area of technology. There are other regulatory options, which governments can employ in technological markets to secure excludability, but also competition and innovation. These regulatory options reflect the consequences of expanding intellectual property protections in recent years and the implications they have had on other areas normally governed by different bodies of laws.

Governments could intervene to prevent the misuse of DRM and anti-circumvention rules and to regain control of standards. Competition law could offer a framework for monitoring market abuse. Governments can also facilitate interoperability by imposing standards for DRMs. One could argue that standardizing DRMs may cause social loss. If DRMs are interoperable, meaning that there is a common standard DRM system, an ex post intervention will decrease incentives to create new DRM systems and society will lose the benefits of 'standards races' (Valimaki and Oksanen 2006). Notwithstanding this risk, it should be noted that even with the standard HTML code for websites, intense competition has flourished between web browsers when Microsoft's Internet Explorer was challenged by others, such as Mozilla's Firefox and Opera Web Browser.

Alternatively, a hands-off policy could allow a bottom-up development of standards. This type of policy, however, warrants the abandonment of an anti-circumvention ban in cases that involve compatibility.

A third way of addressing the issues of technological standard abuse through regulation is by requiring manufacturers of consumer electronics devices to design their products to satisfy certain common standards of technological protection. The DMCA does not require such implementation of technical standards, as long as the main purpose of the device is not to circumvent a technological measure (DMCA §1201(c)(3)). It includes, however, mandatory requirements regarding certain analog devices. For instance, analog recording devices must contain automatic gain control copy control technology (DMCA §1201(k)).

Additionally, governments may intervene by setting technological standards, thereby preventing misuse of technological standards to create barriers for competition. This method has been used in areas unrelated to IP. One sort of government interference in the market is imposing technological requirements on device manufacturers or providers of infrastructure. The most detailed example of a technological capability requirement is the US Communications Assistance for Law Enforcement Act of 1994 (CALEA). This legislation mandates that telecommunications services design their technology so that it may be wiretapped by the government, pursuant to lawful authorization or a court order. CALEA does not require a specific technological design or prohibit any particular technology, but it requires the design to enable certain functions, such as government access to call-identifying information and the transmission of the intercepted information to the government.

In the context of copyrighted materials, government standard setting is demonstrated by the US Federal Communication Commission proposed Broadcast Flag regime. Broadcast Flag is a DRM system for controlling consumer treatment of high definition TV broadcast content. The flag consists of machine readable data that is inserted into digital television (DTV) signals and contains instructions for the treatment of DTV content. The flag requires a reader on the receiver equipment, allowing broadcasted content to be played only on devices that comply with the flag. In 2011, several years after the US Court of Appeals invalidated the order on jurisdictional grounds (*American Library Association v. FCC*, 406 F.3d 689 (D.C. Cir. 2005)) the FFC finally abandoned this attempt to require a code embedded in HDTV content to prevent copyright violations.

The dangers in implementing such legal strategies, which impose technical standards designed by governments, are reflected in the experience of the US Audio Home Recording Act (AHRA) of 1992, one of the most comprehensive pieces of legislation demonstrating the difficulties associated with regulating equipment. Aside from prohibiting the tampering of copy control mechanisms of digital recording devices (AHRA §1002(C)), the AHRA requires all digital audio recording devices to implement the SCMS (serial copy management system), or similar technological measures that allow an unlimited number of first generation copies, but no second generation copies (AHRA §1002(A)). The AHRA incorporates a tax levy regime, whereby consumers are exempted from copyright infringement suits based on certain noncommercial uses of digital or analog musical recordings (AHRA §1003–1007) and rightholders are compensated for such digital recordings through a tax imposed on the sale of digital audio recording devices and media. The taxes collected from distributors, importers and manufacturers of digital audio recording devices are distributed to copyright owners of sound recordings and musical compositions. In return for the tax levy, the Act prohibits suits against consumers for non-commercial copying of music using digital or analog equipment designed for that purpose (AHRA §1008).

Since the enactment of the AHRA, both digital recording media and devices have changed. Digital distribution of music files is conducted primarily through MP3 files and CDs, which are not covered by the AHRA regime. The broad scope of copyright, which covers a wide variety of works and the rapid changes in information technology, may render the standardization of technological measures through legislation inefficient.

To summarize, regulation by technology introduces a whole set of new challenges to the economic analysis of law. It requires consideration of the technological race and consequently to the dynamic nature of technological protection which involves constant breaking and updating. It must also consider the interconnection between law and technological development and the ways in which regulation directly shape technological progress. Finally, the economic analysis should consider the distinctive ways in which technology regulates, enabling ex ante, long-term control over the behavior of users. These distinctive aspects of regulation by technology may bear implications for the circumstances warranting government intervention, the scope of intervention and optimal measures for such intervention. These characteristics of regulation by technology, which is different from private ordering or public ordering, may further require adjustment of the conceptual framework of the economic analysis of law as applied to informational goods.

# Part IV

# Positive analysis

# 7 A positive analysis of intellectual property law

In Chapters 3 and 4 we focused on normative economic analysis of intellectual property. We elaborated on the incentives/public goods paradigm and examined its theoretical and practical shortcomings. Subsequently, we dealt with the 'tragedy of the commons' framework and criticized the shift of canon law and economics literature towards the proprietary model of intellectual property. This chapter will bring on board some insights of positive analysis. We will examine through three theoretical perspectives of law-making what are likely to be the rules generated by legislatures regarding the protection of IP, explain more closely arrangements within specific legal systems and the possible sources for differences between various countries and evaluate to what extent the existing legal arrangements correspond to the desirable legal regime discussed in previous chapters. The last point highlights why some treatment of IPR from a positive analysis perspective is essential for a complete picture of normative theories.

Positive economic analysis is not a mere description of existing legal rules using economic language.[24] Like normative analysis, positive analysis is exercised in the framework of models constructed on the bases of various assumptions exogenous to the models. In our case we examine three models of how policy-makers make their decisions vis-à-vis the preferences of the political community in large and the structure and procedures of law-making institutions. Normative analysis tries to ascertain the desirable legal or constitutional arrangement. To perform such an analysis one has to define a normative objective (e.g. utility maximization, wealth maximization), the source of which is outside the scope of the science of economics. The normative objective is one of the simplifying assumptions of the methodology of the science of economics. Positive economic analysis tries to predict what kind of legal rules will be adopted as the result of different decision-making procedures, structure of institutions and set of individual preferences. As in normative

24 For the differences between positive economic analysis and descriptive economic analysis see Veljanovski (2007).

analysis, the conduct of positive analysis is based on simplifying assumptions as to the way preferences of voters, representatives and judges are formed and being expressed in the course of collective decision-making. Different sets of assumptions yield different positive models. We distinguish between three such basic frameworks and apply them to collective decision-making in the realm of intellectual property.

As elaborated in Chapter 1, one of the soft points of the law and economics project in general is the inner equilibrium between normative and positive analyses. The distinction between normative and positive analyses is not exclusive to the economic approach. However, this distinction is crucial in law and economics, because both positive and normative analyses are founded upon specific assumptions as to human behavior, such as rationality or self-maximizing behavior. What is the use of constructing a normative theory if the same assumptions, which are in its bases, direct us to predict that the recommended solution does not stand a chance of being selected. In this sense there is a major difference between free and fully competitive economic market and the political market. Within the former, the individual conduct of the players, each of which is led by self-interest goals to maximize his or her preferences, is expected to lead to efficient equilibrium, hence also creating an equilibrium between positive and normative analyses (in terms of both utility maximization and wealth maximization). In the latter, self-interested conduct by politicians, bureaucrats or judges does not necessarily lead to equilibrium of positive analysis with normative analysis or to the prediction that central intervention will result with efficient outcome of utility or wealth maximizing collective choices.

In other words, while in a perfect competitive world we can expect an equilibrium that reflects the desirable end-state of efficiency (in terms of both wealth maximization and Pareto optimality) and utility maximization, once a market failure is identified and central intervention is required, it cannot be predicted that such central intervention will lead to efficiency or utility maximization.

This problem of lack of equilibrium between normative and positive analysis might be less acute in some areas of private law. Thus, if normative analysis points to the desirable rule regarding the leading remedy for breach of contract, or to the desirable rule regarding contingency fees or other types of substantive or procedural rules, there is a fair chance that legislators, who do not have direct stakes in the selected solution, or who are not under specific pressure to enact a certain arrangement by powerful interest groups, will vote for such an arrangement. Partly, this is the result of the high degree of generality of legislation, which cannot be perceived as acting for the benefit of certain and constant individuals or groups. Likewise, a whole body of literature has shown why the common law – norms derived from individual precedents of courts – is geared towards efficiency. Given efficiency as the leading normative goal, this literature points to equilibrium between normative and positive analyses.

Lack of equilibrium between normative and positive analysis is a much more acute problem in the realm of public law and especially in economic analysis of constitutional law. When politicians are voting on rules that bind their future discretion, either through the establishment of other institutions which check and balance their output (structural rules of government – either constitutional or post-constitutional) or through constitutional or administrative substantive limitations on political power (such as a bill of rights), it will be difficult to present their choices as falling in line with normative arguments regarding separation of powers, bill of rights or basic rules of administrative law. If one assumes self-interested politicians, then it is not straightforward to present the positive analysis of separation of powers, for example, as falling in the same line as the normative argument which is usually used by legal theorists to describe the concept, unless one can point at an equilibrium in which the normative goal of consensus building fits a politician's self-interested goals (see in this context Salzberger 1993; Salzberger and Voigt 2002).

The realm of IP is characterized by central intervention – the creation of carefully designed and limited property rights – and thus this is a field in which lack of equilibrium between normative and positive analysis might materialize.

Our prime task in this chapter is to apply the tools of law and economics to analyse the political markets regarding norms in the field of intellectual property and, more specifically, to examine what are the different outcomes that will result from different institutional structures of different regimes and whether they are likely to conform to the desirable arrangements *à la* normative analysis. We will examine whether the regulation of IP is closer to the issues in which equilibrium between normative and positive analyses is likely to emerge (notably many fields of private law), or to the fields in which such equilibrium is much more difficult to achieve (notably issues within the realm of constitutional and administrative law). We will see why in the area of IP such equilibrium is difficult to obtain.

Positive analysis of IP laws is contingent upon a general framework theory of legislation. We present here three basic positive theories of legislation – the pluralist model (section 7.1), the republican model (section 7.2) and the public choice model (section 7.3) – and examine the consequences of each model on IP laws, which are likely to be enacted, and on their connection to the desirable IP laws as derived from normative analysis. We also dedicate a section (7.4) to rule-making on the intra-national and international levels, which are becoming more significant in regulation of IPR, and a short discussion on positive analysis of court rulings (section 7.5).

## 7.1 The pluralist view of legislation

In a democracy laws are enacted by a parliament on the basis of majority rule. Members of parliament are elected periodically by the general public and are accountable to their voters who can choose to oust them in subsequent elections if they do not represent their interests faithfully. Thus, one could have expected that the legislative outcome will represent the opinion of the majority of the population. This view of the political process is dubbed 'pluralism' (Farber and Frickey 1991: 13). One can attach to this description a positive or negative value, which, in turn, will set a basis for a normative theory of constitutional limitations on the majority, a form of separation of powers and definitions of the roles of the judiciary vis-à-vis the task of correcting majoritarian decision-making. This normative theory might be different from a positive analysis of constitutional restraints, separation of powers etc.

An important point to emphasize in this context is that even if the pluralist description of legislation as representing the will of the population's majority is correct, the legislative outcome under this framework will neither be efficient nor utility maximizing, and it will not represent any natural law or protect natural rights. It is quite straightforward to see why popular vote will not result with the materialization of any external natural truth of right and wrong. The main reason why popular vote will not result in efficiency is that unlike the operation of economic markets in which the willingness to pay reflects not only a decision whether to buy or not to buy a product or a service, but also the price for which this decision (or rather decisions) is made, the decision-making in the political market is based on dichotomous – yes or no – voting, which does not take into account the intensity of the preferences, neither in utility terms nor in wealth terms.

In other words, if the majority of law-makers (who are assumed by the pluralist approach to represent the view of the majority of the general public) have to choose between two alternative legal arrangements regarding, for example, copyright law, the option that will be legislated is the one that reflects the choice of the majority, ignoring the intensity of preferences. The option that will be legislated, therefore, will not reflect maximization of utility or maximization of wealth. It is very possible that the intensity of preferences of the minority is much higher than that of the majority and therefore the voted arrangement will bring about a decrease in total utility or wealth. The pluralist view of politics, therefore, cannot predict an actual arrangement of IPR based on the normative justification of natural law, or such an arrangement based on the incentives paradigm or other variant of normative law and economics.

An interesting example in which natural law arguments played alongside utilitarian and wealth maximizing interests was the debate about the EU directive supporting the legal protection of biotechnological inventions – the Biotech Directive (1998). The pro-legislation lobby, which consisted mainly of self-interested industrial entities and trade associations, asserted that IP protection was crucial for innovation and for advanced scientific research. In opposition were various activists' groups that, based on natural law type of reasoning (rather than natural rights of innovators) claimed that modifications of either animal or human genomes is immoral and that patenting organisms is unethical. The final result, the Biotech Directive, reflects a compromise but is biased towards the ideology or interests of the industry (Thaker 2003). The end result reflects neither natural law nor efficiency.

What is the expected IP regime under the pluralist model of legislation and how is it different from the desirable IP regime under the incentives model? It seems that IP legislation under pluralism will provide under-protection in comparison to the efficient or utility maximizing IP regime. There are two main reasons for that prediction. First, the incentive-based normative framework for IP is wealth maximizing but not necessarily Pareto optimal. On the contrary, those who gain from IP protection, at least directly and in the short term – the rightholders – are few, while most people are only consumers of informational products or users/authors who are not motivated by monetary incentives. Therefore, for the majority IP rights increase the costs of the protected goods and services and the cost of future individual creation. Even if the total cost-benefit analysis of IPR is on the benefit side, such welfare maximizing arrangements are not likely to be supported by popular vote (or by its representatives *à la* the pluralist model) because of this distributional factor. In this sense there is a significant difference between the protection of regular property, which can be enjoyed by almost everyone, and thus is likely to be supported by popular vote, and the protection of IP, which works for the benefit of some and against the short-term welfare of most. This argument might be particularly valid in the last few decades when potential IP rights are mostly held not by individual creators and inventors but by mega corporations whose owners and managements are listed on the richest people lists of the world.

A second reason for lack of equilibrium between normative – efficiency enhancing – analysis and pluralist positive analysis in the specific context of IP is that the normative theories of IPR geared towards efficiency are based on a long-term or medium-term maximization of welfare. The essence of the incentives model is that the protection of IP rights today provides incentives to create, some fruits of which we will be able to enjoy only in the medium or long term, indeed even beyond the ordinary human life cycle. While in various areas of the law efficiency is calculated (also) for short term (e.g. strict liability and obligatory insurance for car accidents or damages as the prime remedy for breach of contract) the IP calculation is distinctly a longer term one. For the majority of the population no protection or low protection of IP means lower costs of informational services and products, and thus if the level of protection of IP is left to popular decision-making and if most people set their preferences taking into account their own personal welfare without considering the welfare of the next generations, no protection or very low protection will be chosen. The positive analysis will in this case predict under-protection of IP laws in relation to the normative analysis.

Consider, for example, the proposal to extend copyright for an extra 20 years of protection – so copyright would last for life plus 70 years rather than life plus 50 years. The immediate effect would be that a range of informational products that would have become free or priced only according to the marginal copying cost, will now be protected and subject to the price determined by the IP owner. The longer terms effect might be (emphasizing 'might' as we critically discussed this initiative in Chapter 4) the production of more informational goods. Many people will feel the immediate effect and not the future one and thus will vote to defeat the motion. Likewise, a motion to strip patent protection from essential drugs (e.g. life saving drugs) will have the immediate effect of cutting the prices of such drugs to their marginal cost (at times this decrease of price can be of thousands of percentages). The longer effect might be a decrease in incentives to invest in the development of life saving drugs and a lower chance that other drugs will be developed. Many people will vote for the motion, thinking about the immediate drug price, overlooking the longer effects of the decision, which requires an understanding of the processes of knowledge production in society.

The facts on the grounds in the real world of national legislatures are different. Copyright was extended by legislation (e.g. the 1998 Sonny Bono Act in the USA, which was affirmed in *Eldred* 123 S. Ct. 769) and patent protection was not stripped to enable wide distribution of essential drugs. The public outcry regarding the high death rate from AIDS in Africa ended up with no legislative amendments limiting the scope of IP protection to AIDS drugs. The expansion of intellectual property rights that we have witnessed in the past two decades around the world stand in sharp contrast to the predictions of the pluralist model. This can negate the pluralist model of legislation altogether or alternatively indicate that the majority has a more complex view on the issue than the one we described above. Maybe the majority believes that the effect of IP rights are quite immediate – if you give protection to genetic sequences – this industry and research will attract more investments in the stock markets and there will be more R&D that is beneficial to all. One example that comes to mind is that of Cellera and the Human Genome project – the introduction of IP and private sector investments shortened the period necessary for mapping the human genome significantly. Similarly, perhaps the majority's perception is that granting patents to computer programs means more incentives to high-tech industry and granting copyright to music means more incentives to music composers, resulting with the present benefits to local industry, securing jobs and national prosperity. At the same time, however, the effects in terms of higher prices for products are negligible because of their wide distribution. These views are often echoed in political debates regarding expanding IP protection.

If this is the case, the majority decision might deviate from the desirable balance in the opposite direction – towards over-protection of IP, as it might ignore or have more difficulties to digest the long-term effect of stronger IP rights on the public domain and on the availability to use free information for new creations. The public domain is an abstract concept, whereas copyright and property rights are more concrete. The notion of the public domain and the thoughts about IPR as impediments for creation and innovation requires an understanding of the processes of knowledge production in society, which the majority might lack.

The actual conduct of the majority with regard to the level of obedience to IP laws might support the negation of the pluralist model. The level of disobedience in this realm is high. Downloading and copying music or P2P file sharing might indicate that current IP laws are not supported by the majority of the general public, and thus pose a serious challenge to the pluralist model. However, different individual considerations may apply in the individual decision whether to obey a law, different from the ones that lead to his or her support or objection to the law itself. Moreover, studies have shown that in some areas of IPR, such as copyright, there is a growing gap between social norms, about what is considered right and wrong, and legal rules as defined by copyright law. In some places this sentiment was also translated into a political power. Sweden is an example in hand: after the Pirate Bay verdict, which sent the operators of the illegal file-sharing website in Sweden to prison, the Swedish Pirate Bay Party won two seats in the 2009 elections to the European Parliament.

An interesting example of disobedience, which affected also rule-making and thus might lend support to the pluralist model in this context, relates to the EU piracy legislation. In April 2007, the EU Parliament passed piracy legislation, which aimed to protect consumers from imitation products such as fake Viagra pills or imitation designer handbags. This legislation, which endorses a set of common criminal penalties across the EU, was considered necessary by many owing to the 125,000 workers who lost their jobs because of unfair competition from counterfeiters around the world. However, exemption from the measures adopted in the directive was granted to piracy committed by individuals for non-profit purposes, such as downloading music files from the Internet. A possible explanation is that while Internet piracy benefits many and harms only a few, other imitations harm many and therefore were criminally outlawed, unlike Internet piracy. In section 7.4 of this chapter we address the rule-making of IPR on the international level which might conform more to the pluralist model in comparison to national legislatures.

Be that as it may, while a pluralist view of legislation can predict equilibrium between normative economic analysis and positive analysis in various areas, including the basic arrangements regarding contracts, torts and real property, it cannot predict such equilibrium in the area of intellectual property. Let us examine two other positive models of legislation.

## 7.2 The republican view of legislation

The pluralist view of legislation was attacked from two major directions: the republican theory and the public choice theory. Despite their very different roots and normative backgrounds both approaches have an important common insight – that, unlike the pluralist theory's analysis, legislators can act to certain degree independently from the immediate preferences of their voters. While public choice asserts that legislators will act in the benefit of powerful interest groups, a positive republican analysis of legislation asserts that legislators work towards the 'public interest', that legislative (and, indeed, popular) deliberations are likely to result in the rejection of 'bad' private preferences towards other-regarding preferences and common goals; towards the 'common good'. The republican perception of legislators (in this sense on both levels of positive and normative analyses) is of trustees rather than representatives (Edmund Burke 1896) whose goal and actual conduct is not merely to reflect their voters' popular opinions, but to shape these opinions and convince the voters to support the common good.

In economic language, the republican approach differs from the pluralist and the public choice approaches in its assumption as to the voters' preferences. While the latter approaches assume that preferences of voters are exogenous to the political process and are pre-given in the context of the positive analysis of political decision-making, the republican approach can be viewed as endogenizing the preferences of the public. It thus assumes that the political markets do not only aggregate a set of pre-given preferences, but alternate preferences, portraying a picture of mutual influence of voters on representatives and other public figures, and vice versa, rather than a one-way influence of voters on their representatives portrayed by the pluralists (and by the public choice theory).

Within a republican view of politics, the normative goal of IP – either in the framework of natural law and rights or in the framework of normative economic analysis of law – can be materialized. However, from a positive law and economics perspective, the problem of the republican approach is that legislators are not portrayed as *Homo economicus*. In other words, the basic assumption of the republican approach is that legislators work towards what they perceive as the common interests of their society rather than promoting their own interests, or promoting their political powers or chances of re-election. Some would present, therefore, the republican view of legislation as altogether outside the scope of the law and economics movement. This is not necessarily the case. Although very few law and economics works have gone in this direction, the economic analysis of law can, in fact, incorporate republican thinking on both normative and positive levels (for such an attempt see for example Salzberger and Voigt 2002; Elkin-Koren and Salzberger 2004: 142–74).

If one relaxes the assumption that individual preferences are fixed and exogenous to the political market, and replaces it with the assumption that individuals' preferences are endogenous to the political process, ie that the structure of state institutions, civil society and decision-making processes will affect individual preferences, and by derivation the collective decision-making outcome, an interesting difference will emerge between the pluralist analysis and the republican one, within law and economics methodology. Likewise, one can relax the rigid assumption that politicians are aiming only to maximize their powers and chances of being re-elected, and replace it with the assumption that politicians do have utility functions which have a major component of their perception of the public good or public interest, alongside the wish to maintain power and be re-elected, partly in order to realize their vision of the public good (Brennan and Hamlin 2000: ch 2).

One of the major implications of the republican model on the analysis of legislative outcome is that the state's formal and informal institutional structure, decision-making processes, information sources and the nature of the forums of deliberation and debates on various policy issues, do matter a great deal and that politicians will strive to construct institutions and decision-making processes that will enable them to optimize the desirable outcome and still remain in power. Such new assumptions can explain, for example, why politicians delegate powers to other decision-making bodies which are not accountable to the majority, such as courts, central banks, anti-trust authorities, international organizations etc (for such a model see Brennan and Hamlin 2000; Salzberger and Voigt 2002). Such delegation will be made when politicians are interested that decisions, which they view as good for society but are unpopular decisions, will be adopted, and the mechanism to achieve this is through delegated bodies.

In the IP context, the republican model may explain, for example, the delegation of IP related decisions to special agencies and courts and likewise the process of internationalization and globalization of IPR as a type of delegation of the decision-making powers in this field. Such delegation can be explained in light of the unpopularity of broadening IPR, which politicians might view as desirable, taking into account the long-term welfare of their societies, despite the short-term negative consequences for consumers. Like tailoring and expanding IP rights by court decisions, decisions by international bodies or transnational bodies have a 'democratic' deficit. The public is less involved in the decision-making process and thus a greater segment of the field is left to experts and decision-makers who are not bound to be influenced by the election cycle and thus can (but not necessarily will) take the decisions which are the most 'desirable' for the medium and long term. Public choice theory will explain the same phenomenon of delegation to domestic as well as international and transnational bodies as beneficial to politicians exactly because such forums have a democratic deficit and therefore are much more prone to manipulation by interest groups, predicting that the outcome of an increase in IP rights is not the 'desirable' one, in contrast to the republican prediction and evaluation.

An example that comes to mind in this context is the European Union's directive on the legal protection of databases (Directive 96/9/EC). The directive does not have an equivalent across the Atlantic, or in fact in most states. It provides for IP protection of those who compile a database (a collection of information stored and accessed by electronic means) on top of the copyright of those who produced the pieces of information themselves and regardless of whether there is a copyright on the information itself. The EU Commission in the green paper leading to the directive (COM(88) 172 final) stated that there is a need to provide protection against copying of the mode of compilation, even if the compilation itself is not entitled to copyright protection. Such protection would give the database operator a right similar to the right of the phonogram producer, who normally has a specific statutory right to protect his interest in the recording itself, regardless of whether or not he is recording a protected work.

The argument with regard to phonogram producers was that in order to combat piracy, the general introduction of producers' rights in sound recordings would appear to be a desirable development. Thus, according to the Commission, introducing corresponding right for databases operators to pursue unauthorized reproduction in their own right is a logical next step. Such a right may prove to be an important tool in the combat against data piracy. The unauthorized reproduction of data will more often than not involve works of several authors. The individual author may not be in a position to establish that an infringement has taken place and even in case of having such knowledge may consider the infringement of marginal importance in respect of the economic exploitation of his work. To the database operator, the infringement may nevertheless be of considerable importance. He is often better placed than the author to detect infringements and has more pressing incentives to react.

From a normative law and economics point of view there are no first order justifications for granting IP rights in databases. If the information in the database is protected, contractual relations can transfer the rights to the database compiler. A second order justification might be that the transaction costs of contracting the copyright of very small segments of information and the transaction costs of enforcing copyright infringement related to databases are so high that such contracts would not be signed and enforcement would not take place, increasing illegal copying – what is termed by the Commission as 'piracy'. However, no empirical data was provided to prove this argument and the statistics that are mentioned in the green paper do not support it. These statistics show a growth in the number of databases since the beginning of the 1980s (from 400 in 1980 to 2,901 in 1986) and indicate that lack of IP protection has not been a hurdle in the growth of these informational goods.

The green paper stated that database protection prior to the directive, given under international conventions, covers the characteristics of the works stored therein, rather than the database itself as a collection of information. Therefore, potential difficulties might arise where the extracts from protected works are themselves not covered by copyright, in particular, those in the public domain. In such cases a considerable degree of skill and investment in the compilation might be required, in order to gain copyright protection. In particular, the compilation will have to be designed to ensure ready access to the information and to create features attractive to particular groups of users; otherwise the work will be part of the public domain. It is not clear, however, why this pre-directive legal arrangement is not desirable and why it is justified to commodify information that already exists in the public domain, because it was justifiably not protected by copyright. The real motivation of the Commission is revealed in the green paper, when it mentions the background facts according to which US companies control 80 percent of the market share in the total worldwide turnover of electronic publishing (true for 1985). In other words, the directive was probably meant to advance European businesses and grant them economic advantages over their American counterparts.

Be that as it may, the fact that such a directive was adopted in the EU and not in the USA or other countries may be explained against the background of the republican model of legislation. The directive increases the cost of various types of information for many, while benefiting the few producers of these databases. Thus, on popular vote (or legislative vote according to the pluralist model) it would have been rejected. By delegating the issue to Brussels, this popular view could have been bypassed and a 'desirable decision that is in the public interest' could have been adopted. A counter argument, which also corresponds to the public choice view of legislation, is that lack of wide debate among the citizens of the EU who feel remote from its Brussels decision-making institutions, may have brought to decisions of the EU central organs, which are different than in other jurisdictions, in which such public debates do take place effectively. The question remains whether this delegation brought to a better decision or rather exposed the decision-making process to excessive influence of narrow interest groups. We will return to the database example when discussing the public choice view of legislation below.

The argument regarding database protection in the EU can be generalized. The migration of critical decision-making in the area of IP to the international level is said to be the result of the rise of digital information markets that cut across states and political boundaries. But the consequence of this shift is that it is much more difficult to mobilize against broad copyright and other IPR reforms on the international level than on the municipal level. While many of the largest companies are active in international markets and therefore have close relationships with trade authorities, consumer organizations and new entrants generally do not have such relationships, since the trade authorities do not view them as an important constituency. Thus, the decision-making will reflect over-protection of IP.[25] This is an insight of positive analysis of IP laws, which is common to the republican approach and the public choice approach discussed next.

In any case, the key question of the republican model applied to the IP field is what is the best IP regime to create a just and attractive society and, in a similar way to the pluralist approach, equilibrium between positive analysis and normative analysis of IPR cannot be assumed or proved.

25 On other examples concerning WIPO see Bach (2004).

## 7.3 The public choice view of legislation

The public choice approach to the positive analysis of legislation, in contrast to the republican one, is constructed upon the basic assumptions of the pluralist approach regarding the fixed nature of individual preferences (or their exogenous nature vis-à-vis the political markets). Elected legislators are viewed by the public choice approach as any other rational players who are interested in maximizing their own utility or preferences. One can distinguish between two main schools within public choice, which can be dubbed as a rigid school and a moderate one. The rigid school assumes that politicians are driven by immediate self-interest goals of enhancing their power and maximizing their chances of re-election (Stigler 1971; Peltzman 1976). The moderate school assumes that politicians seek *also* to promote their ideological beliefs as to the good society and as to the policies that will promote that good (Frey and Lau 1968; Brennan and Hamlin 2000); but in order to implement their ideological beliefs, legislators will also have an interest to remain in power as long as possible. The tricky business of politics is to trade off long-term ideological goals with short-term interests of re-election (Voigt and Salzberger 2002). This moderate school, therefore, has common grounds with the republican model.

Two of the most important ingredients of the public choice approach (common to the two schools) are social choice, on the one hand, and interest groups theory, on the other. Social choice theory is engaged in normative and positive analysis of the interaction of three factors: decision-maker groups, optional decisions group and decision-making rules. In our context it is used to analyse the legislative process, as being a product of a collective process rather than a decision of one person. Interest group theory analyses the fact that legislation is a product of representatives' vote rather than principals' direct vote. It is therefore focused on the way in which preferences in society as a whole are reflected by the individual preferences of legislators.

Interest group theory, departing from the pluralist view of legislation, asserts that in a perfect political market the distribution of votes among legislators would indeed have been a mirror picture of the distribution of opinions among the general public. However, the political market is not fully competitive, for three main reasons. First, lack of sufficient information for ordinary voters as to the record of their representatives enables legislators to depart from full representation of their immediate voters' interests. Second, in order to be elected or re-elected legislators have to rely on expensive election campaigns, which are mostly financed by powerful and wealthy individuals and institutions, rather than by ordinary people. Those wealthy individuals and groups can also better monitor the record of the representatives, creating information asymmetry with ordinary people, and thus the legislators will over-represent these interest groups at the expense of the majority of their voters. Third, there is asymmetry between the ability of narrow interest groups to influence the legislative outcome and the equivalent ability of wide interest groups or the public in large, owing to organization costs. Much of the public choice literature is focused on this third factor and on the analysis of interest groups and rent-seeking activities in the framework of a market in which legislation is sold by legislators to interest groups.

In fact, it was James Madison who argued (*The Federalist Papers* nos 9, 10, 51, 62, 78) that the pluralist model does not work because of factions (interest groups), which are likely to distort the pluralist legislative outcome. Madison used this analysis to argue in favor of federalism with a strong central government, in which he thought that the relative power and thus impact of interest groups would be lower than in collective decision-making on the level of smaller political units such as the pre-federation American colonies. This analysis was also the basis for his advocacy for a checks and balances style of separation of powers in which the power of interest groups vis-à-vis the legislature would be muted by a strong executive and an independent judiciary. While Madison's analysis might have been accurate in his era, the prescriptions he offered are probably not sufficient in our days. In other words, while the shift from a state to federal decision-making in the 18th century might have posed serious obstacles to the success of then powerful groups, even the larger entity of the US federal administration is not sufficient nowadays against mega conglomerates and corporations. We will return to this theme in the IP context below.

An important contribution to modern public choice analysis was made by Mancur Olson's theory of collective action (Olson 1965). When a specific legal rule is favored by a few, because it is likely to bring them significant profits, collective organization of these few is likely to occur. The collective organization will materialize because the organization costs of a small number of individuals or firms is likely to be lower than the rents that this organization can seek through its collective action, ie the benefits from organizing are higher than the costs. The majority that opposes the rule is not likely to be organized collectively because the costs of organization will be higher than the benefits. Politics, therefore, is likely to be dominated by rent-seeking special interest groups and the legislative outcome would be biased towards the preferences of these groups.

Intellectual property is a classical area for interest group analysis. The benefits from protection of IPR are not distributed equally. While the creators are granted monopoly powers, which enable them to make potentially immediate high profits from selling their creations, the benefits for each member of the general public are lower. In fact, in the short term the general public suffers losses because of the increased prices of the protected creations, and the longer-term benefits of IP protection, which are in the form of more creations, are more difficult to identify, quantify and individualize, and they are distributed among the vast membership of the general public.

Copyright holders, for example, have benefited from an extremely favorable asymmetry of interest concentration. Whereas copyright holders, ie the publishers, are a small, homogenous, well organized and well financed group, the other camp of the copyright debate – consumers and potential new entrants – is a heterogeneous crowd with very slim collective organization abilities. Most consumers have not ever been aware of the implications of copyright reforms (Bach 2004). Furthermore, all major copyright industries have developed effective lobbying arms over the last two decades. Good examples of actual interest group activity in the realm of copyright in the US are MPAA and RIAA. These organizations collectively create lobbying groups in order to push for stronger copyright laws. We already discussed extensively in Chapter 4 how this collective organization brought the American Congress in 1998 to extend retroactively copyright protection from 50 to 70 years, what was dubbed the Mickey Mouse Law (extending copyright protection on Disney's famous cartoon which was about to expire). This success only encouraged the copyright lobbying to enhance its activities. In May 2007, for example, these two organizations teamed up with mega-corporations such as Disney, Viacom and Microsoft, to create 'The Copyright Alliance' (Masnick 2007). A month later (June 2007) they joined forces with the US Chamber of Commerce and a diverse collection of other industry groups in order to press the US Congress and the White House for new anti-piracy and anti-counterfeiting laws (Sweeting 2007). The pro-copyright lobby approached the legislators as a well defined, highly motivated and apparently effective lobby. Those who advocated for common law rights and for the public domain had relatively little impact on the legislative process. This basic asymmetry influenced the legislature to depart from an efficient or desirable level of IP protection towards over-protection. Against this background it is not surprising that copyright duration was extended by the US Congress several times in the past century from 28 years to life plus 70 years.

This lobbying activity has not focused only on the extension of copyright duration, but also of the scope of extension. In Chapter 6 we discussed in length the anti-circumvention legislation. A more recent example is the development in the legislative process of the Design Piracy Prohibition Act in the US. After aggressive lobbying from the industry group, consisting also of retailers such as Zara and H&M, the bill that has been under consideration in the House of Representatives was joined by a Senate version in August 2007. The bill expands copyright protection for fashion designs and the garment itself (Sanchez 2007). The latest example for such intensive lobbing activity is the SOPA (Stop On Line Piracy Act) on which we elaborate below.

Similar accounts hold for patent expansion. Although patent duration was extended only moderately from 17 to 20 years, the range of objects protected by patent was considerably broadened. For example, until the 1940s new seeds that were developed were not patented because seeds coming from natural reproduction could not be distinguished from those coming from plant breeders. During the 1940s, the hybridization technique became available. The hybrid seeds cannot be reproduced because they are sterile, and so the distinction between these two types of seeds was enabled. From this point, companies producing hybrid seeds started lobbying for new and special legislation for plant patents and in 1960 the Plant Varieties Protection Act was enacted (Boldrin and Levine 2004) and seeds gained patent protection. Likewise, in the first half of 2007 a group of over 60 high-tech companies and trade associations (including Microsoft Corp. and Apple Inc.) paid over $300,000 to lobby the federal government to promote a patent reform which would shift the US law from a 'first-to-invent' to a 'first-to-sale' system. In September 2007 the bill was passed in the House of Representatives and on September 2011 President Obama signed it into a law, which is the first major change in patent doctrine in legislation in more than half a century. The main reason that patent duration was not significantly extended, in contrast to copyright, is that among the main industries of patent holders there are two very strong camps with opposing stances as to patent duration, which reflects the average life spans of their products and reliance of new creations on existing ones. The high tech industry belongs to one camp, with short life span of products constructed upon existing patented ones. It thus opposes extended patent duration. The pharmaceutical industry with longer product life span is in favor of extended patent duration.

The dynamics of IP expansion in recent years all over the world can be explained in the framework of the public choice model. The technological developments of the Internet and accompanied technologies made copying less expensive. When copying is expensive relative to the cost of expression, the added value of intellectual property rights is limited; authors do not need IP rights in order to be protected from copying, or need only limited protection. But as the cost of copying falls and its speed increases as a consequence of technological developments, the potential benefits of IPR for creators rise. With no significant change in the cost of collective organization (or diminishing such cost) the potential net benefits from collective organization of creators increase and we can expect to witness more rent-seeking activities that will eventually result in the expansion of IP rights.

An interesting example for collective organization in the digital era is the American entertainment industry, whose lobbying activity resulted in the 1998 Sonny Bono Act in the USA (CTEA), extending copyright protection for an additional 20 years, including on existing creations. This extension, and particularly its retroactive application to existing creations for which the production cost were already covered, meant granting net benefits to the powerful industries who held copyrights that were about to expire. Landes and Posner (2004: 16) provide interesting figures about the financial contributions of the most powerful copyright holders to Congress members who promoted the 1998 Sonny Bono Act, demonstrating how the theory can be substantiated on this particular case. The content industry, which was the biggest engine behind this Act, was also the biggest donator in the year of 1996 to six of the Act's eight sponsors and co-sponsors in the American Congress (donating more than US$1,419,717).

Likewise, the Patent Reform Law, which was debated during 2007, involved tremendous amounts of money poured by various interest groups. The numbers are amazing. The Coalition for Patent Fairness has spent

US$860,000 in one year on lobbying, while the total resources of lobbying by the computer industry were estimated at US$47.7 million! These groups have given Democrats 60 percent of its US$9.2 million in campaign contributions. Other parties, such as TechNet and the Business Software Alliance, supported these measures and spent nearly US$1 million (Argyres and Mayer 2007).

It ought to be emphasized that the regular asymmetry between groups who wish more IP protection and the general public who lose from such a move, is even more significant when an extension of the copyright protection is applicable to existing works. Since the costs of creating existing works have already been borne, the additional revenue generated by the extension of their copyrights is almost entirely profit, that is, economic rent. As a result of this asymmetry, it is easier to organize a collective effort of IP owners to expand intellectual property rights than it would be to organize a copiers' interest group to oppose such an expansion. The most obvious evidence for this is the music performing-rights organizations (mainly ASCAP and BMI), which act collectively in order to obtain the IP owners' rights and had a great influence on the content and wording of the 1976 Copyright Act and the 1998 Sonny Bono Act in the USA. This analysis can be substantiated by Jessica Litman's findings according to which the wording of the 1976 amendments to the Copyright Act in the USA are not those of members of Congress but those of the main rightholders themselves who were lobbying Congress intensively (Litman 1987: 860–61).

Another example is the database protection discussed earlier. Granting IP protection for databases has the immediate effect of monopolistic gains, which firms involved in gathering and compiling data can make, by selling their products, or charging fees for usage of their data. The general public is likely to suffer immediate losses as data that was freely available before is now costly. However, while the potential gains of database 'creators' from IP protection are likely to be high, indeed much higher than the costs of collective organization in order to lobby the legislature for such protection, the expected losses for every member of the public who wants to make use of databases is relatively low, loss that will not economically justify massive collective organization for lobbying against laws that grant IP protection to databases. It is possible that normative analysis within the incentives paradigm will conclude that some protection of databases is desirable as it provides an incentive to create databases which enhance our available information and, in turn, our ability to make more sensible decisions. However, the interest group effect on the legislature distorted it from efficient equilibrium towards over-protection. With regard to the database example the insights of the public choice model of legislation coincide and complement the insights of the republican model. The combination of interest group analysis in different institutional settings and the institutional structure of the decision-making and policy-making bodies, the channels for wide public debate and individual participation, may explain the different results in different jurisdictions. The European Union in this respect is a very interesting and unique entity. On the one hand, its institutions and decision-making processes resemble a national unit more than an international one. On the other hand, its institutions lack a democratic environment in which wide public debate can take place, in which representatives can be singled out by their voters, held accountable to their voting record etc. This combination brings into greater importance the power of interest groups.

As Greenwood (2003) puts it, organized interests are the 'natural constituencies' of the European Commission and of the European Parliament. As allies in the drive for European integration, they reduce the dependence of these institutions upon national administrations and form a demand constituency upon Member States. Organized interest groups are a source of support for the Commission in drafting legislation. They are a means of 'testing' proposals among stakeholders, and they are a source for valuable information about the implementation of measures. Moreover, the small size of the Commission sometimes makes it dependent upon expertise that external interest groups bring for drafting policy proposals. One can expect, therefore, that the legislative result will reflect the agenda of these interest groups more than in the national context. In the borderless world of IP this general description has to be supplemented by an additional crucial factor – that the Commission also assumes an important role in representing Member States in world trade negotiations.

Performers' rights provide another example for the public choice model. From a normative law and economics perspective it is difficult to justify distinct IP protections for performers. As the creation is already protected by copyright, all the derivative usages and expressions are also protected by the same initial copyright and, therefore, questions regarding income from public performance of the creation are only distributional questions. A song, for example, enjoys the initial copyright protection for both its lyrics and music. When such a song is performed by a singer, there is no justification to grant the singer any property rights for the performance or for the recording. Even if the singer is popular and only her performance brings the creation to the attention and popularity of the masses, contractual arrangements between the initial copyright holders and the derivative users of the creation is enough to achieve efficiency. However, in many legal systems we witness the existence of separate and independent IP protection for performers. This phenomenon can be explained in the framework of interest group analysis. On the one hand, the gains that performers can obtain by collective organization are huge, while such an organization is rather cheap because of the relatively small number of performers. On the other hand, the losses that the general public suffers for paying more for records, and indirectly for the operation of broadcasting platforms, are too small economically to justify collective organization to oppose the extension of IP to performers. Thus, the legislative outcome is likely to be distorted towards over-protection.

The most recent example for interest group activity in the field of intellectual property is the SOPA (Stop Online Piracy Act) bill, which, while this book is being concluded, is still under a heated debate in the US. The SOPA initiative demonsrates also the blurring boundaries between national and international law discussed in the next section. Currently, US federal laws empower the enforcement authorities to act against Internet websites that offer infringing material, only if they are US based. They cannot overpower foreign websites (such as Pirate-Bay). The SOPA, alongside the PIPA (Protect IP Act), is designed to alter this status, by prohibiting American companies to grant any funding whatsoever to foreign websites that offer infringing materials. Those bills will enable the American enforcement authorities to order Internet service providers (ISP's) to block access to these websites and, de-facto, to shut them down entirely and permanently (The Wall Street Journal 18.1.2012). Furthermore, it allows the content companies to sue directly the ISP's for hosting infringing content. This feature broadens the liability of the ISP's in comparison to the DMCA, which grants immunity to the ISP's, assuming that they act in good faith to remove the infringing content when asked to do so ('Notice and Takedown' safe harbor).

The foreseen problematic character of this bill is that the authorities will be able to shut down websites that, generally, do not store infringing content, or websites that happen to host infringing content that they are not aware of, such as Facebook. The state of thing, as described above, might harm severely freedom of speech of both the websites and the users. This move is being promoted vigorously by the leading media companies in the US. The Motion Picture Association, one of the leading proponents, claims that piracy costs the US dozens of billions of dollars a year, and threatens dozens of millions of jobs (The New-York Times 1.1.2012). The opponents argue that the bill, if made to a law, would not eliminate piracy and that the collateral damage would be enormous, that the cure – the laws – would be worse than the disease. The bills are being held as dangerous and destructive to the open web and will affect adversely the free transfer of information (The New-York Times 1.1 2012).

As part of the protest wave against the SOPA, many popular websites, such as Google, have put black banners on their logo. Others, such as Wikipedia, have darkened themselves completely. Currently, both houses of Congress are obstructing the legislation process, so it is too early to say whether the powerful IP interest groups will have their way in this case.

It should be emphasized that, in contrast to intuitive wisdom, the interest groups representing the beneficiaries from IP protection will not be always interested in unlimited property rights. Most creators of intellectual property, or performers, use intellectual property created by others as inputs into the creation of their own intellectual property. Hence, they would not favor a law that would strengthen the IP rights beyond the level necessary to assure maximum profits from their creations, taking into account also the input costs, which rise with the broadening of IP rights. This factor can explain the various limitations on IP rights in the flow of new rights-expanding legislation. It can also explain the asymmetric development of different sub-fields of IP. For example, while in the area of copyright we witnessed a significant extension of IP in the last century (in the US from 14 years to life plus 70 or 120 years for corporation produced content) in the field of patent the duration was extended only from 17 to 20 years. One explanation for this disparity is that while in the copyright terrain the preferences of the industry used to be homogenous, in the area of patent law the preferences are much more diverse: the pharmaceutical industry is much more interested in patent extension than the high-tech industry, which relies much more on previous inventions. In any case this diversity of interest, which is reflected by the legal dynamic, can be presented in line with the public choice model of legislation.

An important angle of interest group analysis, which has not been dealt with extensively in the literature so far, is the possible inverse connection between economic market power and the power to motivate political collective action. Producers or suppliers who can create a cartel in the market by, for example, coordinating prices or levels of production, will be less in need of seeking rents in the political markets. Cartelization in industries in which there are high costs of entry, for example, is likely to be more effective than cartelization in industries with low costs of entry. Cartels in markets of a handful of producers (e.g. the car industry) are likely to be more effective than in markets of hundreds or thousands of producers (e.g. farming). One can expect, therefore, to find more rent-seeking activities in the latter, as political organization is easier and cheaper than collective organization in the market. In addition, it can be expected that a more effective antitrust authority will channel producers or suppliers to the political market and vice versa – in countries where such authority is less effective firms will be using relatively more their market power than their potential political powers.

How can this angle shed light on the positive analysis of IP protection? Here is a potential (and indeed initial) insight. There might be interesting differences between the various types of IP vis-à-vis this line of argument. Some segments of patents markets, notably the bio-medic and pharmaceutical ones, can be characterized as markets with higher entry barriers than markets of copyrighted products. If our line of argument is correct, one would expect a more intense use of the political markets with regard to copyright than with regard to patents, because in the area of patents the high barriers to entry create significant market power. Thus, as we explained before, the firms in such markets will coordinate with each other and would put less effort into generating political collective action. The markets of copyright, on the other hand, are not characterized with high barriers to entry. Hence, the firms in these markets will find it more difficult to form market coordination among themselves and political collective action will be the prime route to extract rents.

If the number of laws, amendments and their volume can serve as a good indicator for rent-seeking activity, then our argument may be supported by the comparison between legislative developments in the area of copyright as compared to the field of patents. Landes and Posner (2003a: 403–419) found that there was an expansion in intellectual property protection over the last fifty years. The greatest changes were in copyright laws, where the number of words in legislative instruments in the US increased from 11,500 words in 1946 to 124,320 words in 2000; in trademarks law from 10,640 in 1946 to 24,750 words in 2000. The size of the US Commercial Code increased at an annual rate of 3.6 percent compared to 4.4 percent for copyright, 3.0 percent for patents, and 1.1 percent for trademarks. The conclusion is that copyright law was the only intellectual property area in which the expansion was more rapid than the overall growth in federal statutes in the years 1946–1994 (see also Landes and Posner 2004).

The fact that there was more legislative activity in the field of copyrights than in patents might be considered as a puzzling one, since patents offer potential of greater economic rents than copyrights. Landes and Posner offer possible explanations for these findings, which relate to different levels of delegation of decision-making powers to other governmental bodies (such as the Federal Circuit), the requirement of registration that exists with regard to patent and does not exist in copyright, enabling the changing of the filtering process with no legislative change, and differences in the structure of the IP laws in the two areas. While copyright law tends to specify the nature of the protected work, patent and trademark law protect respectively inventions and brand names more broadly. Hence, when new types of expressive works arise, there is a need for new legislation in order to bring them under the copyright umbrella, a factor that does not exist with regards to patents. These explanations might be correct, but we think that these findings may also support our hypothesis as to the inverse relations between the potential economic market power and the need for collective action and also the diversity or lack of diversity in the industries who benefit from copyright as opposed to patents. This may explain why patent owners or potential patent owners have not lobbied more for amending the patent laws in order to gain equivalent protection to copyright.

## 7.4 The intra-national and international dimensions in the positive analysis of IP

As we have already indicated in other places throughout this book, an important feature of intellectual property or informational goods is their borderless nature. This characteristic is significant not only for the normative analysis of the desirable IP laws, but also for the positive economic analysis of IP laws. In addition to collective organization and rent-seeking in national arenas, IP is a tool for national gains and, therefore, for rent-seeking activities in the international arena by both governments and corporations. Countries in which relatively more intellectual creations are produced will be interested to expand international IP rights because this expansion can increase the rents that they can obtain from countries, which are primarily consumers of intellectual creations and in which relatively less creation is produced. A nation that has a comparative advantage in producing IP is more likely to favor stronger international IP rights than a nation that does not.

The United States, for example, in fact the prime example, has a very large positive balance of trade in informational products. This means that the access costs imposed, whenever IP rights are enforced and indeed extended, are shifted in part to foreigners, who neither vote nor are permitted to make campaign contributions in US elections. Moreover, a dynamic of decline in the competitiveness of the relevant industries, attributed to a loss of technological momentum to competing nations (notably Japan), as happened in the US during the 1970s, is likely to lead to an increase in the scope of IP rights, as indeed happened then. The expansion of IP rights, originating again in the US, was also propelled by a desire to alleviate chronic trade deficits by increasing the income of owners of copyrights, patents and other IP rights, most of those owners being American.

In 1994 the US suffered from a significant trade deficit. TRIPs was a way to promote the competitiveness of US industry by making products from the 'Asian Tigers' more expensive through IP protection and as a mechanism for generating higher levels of protection abroad to sustain balance of payments by royalty fees to be paid to IP holders in the US. More recently (11 March 2010) President Barack Obama endorsed the Anti-Counterfeiting Trade Agreement (ACTA) as discussed below, by these words:

> We are going to aggressively protect our intellectual property. Our single greatest asset is the innovation and the ingenuity and creativity of the American people. It is essential to our prosperity and it will only become more so in this century.

Intra-national rent-seeking will express itself with an attempt to create a supra-national and international regime regarding IP rights. Indeed, European harmonization in this field, as well as international treaties and enforcement agencies characterize the more significant development in intellectual property law in the last decades.

In the EU, the 1988 green paper on 'Copyright and the Challenges of Technology' was the starting point for copyright harmonization. The process resulted with the Directives for 'Legal Protection of Computer Programs', 'Rental Rights, Lending Rights and the Main Neighboring Rights', 'Satellite Broadcasting and Cable Retransmission', 'the Duration of Protection of Authors' Rights and Neighboring Rights', 'the Legal Protection of Databases' and on 'Artists' Resale Right'. A more ambitious Directive on 'Copyright and Related Rights in the Information Society' was enacted in 2001 (Directive 2001/29/EC of the European Parliament and of the Council of 22 May 2001, on the harmonization of certain aspects of copyright and related rights in the information society). Unlike the earlier directives, which focused on relatively narrow areas, the 2001 directive covered a wide range of issues.

The major share of this harmonization process was completed before the biggest enlargement of the EU in 2004, despite the knowledge that this enlargement was due to take place and that the new Member States were relatively more on the consumer side rather than the producer side of IP related products. In other words, the harmonization entrenched the status quo, which did not benefit the new mostly eastern and central European Member States; it merely protected the interests of incumbents, before offering equal opportunities for new entrants (Oksanen and Valimaki 2003).

With respect to each of the above directives, several parties had conflicting interests and the parties were trying to use lobbying to get the most favorable outcome from their perspective. The fight was very ugly at times, where the adversaries were the content industry, on the one side, and the telecommunication industry and library associations, on the other. Consumer organizations and wider interest groups have not played any major role and there were no EU-level cyber-rights organizations in effect. The outcomes reflect this set up. For example, although the 2001 directive does not grant full copyright on computer programs, its 'legal protection of technical protection measures' part (TPMs) applies also to software, as long as it is used as a tool for creating TPMs. This dual nature of software, being a work itself and a gatekeeper to other works, gives content owners more choices between different protection alternatives. This outcome reflects the fact that there were no real counterbalancing forces, which could prevent the rent-seeking of the content industry and the fact that some American content corporations participated actively in the lobbying process. The telecommunication companies were active, but their goals were limited. Practically, no one was defending the general public, who were the biggest losers from the outcome.

During the debates on the Software Copyright Directive a number of dominant American companies (Microsoft, IBM, Apple, Lotus) established the Software Action Group for Europe (SAGE), which was aiming to achieve as stringent a law as possible to curtail the European competition. They were lobbying to add user interfaces under the scope of copyright and, perhaps more importantly, trying to ban reverse engineering altogether. The economically weaker European software industry (Amstrad, Bull, Olivetti and Fujitsu from Japan) formed the European Committee for Interoperable Systems (ECIS) in order to counter this threat and to secure an open competitive environment, and they were partly victorious, as the final version of the directive is silent on the subject of user interfaces. But again, the Software Copyright Directive is a classical example of a case in which two powerful parties with opposite interests were engaged in a lobbying competition. The interests of the public at large were not properly represented (Oksanen and Valimaki 2003).

At the same time that the EU was beginning to work towards its harmonizing directives, it was also pushing for the same agenda in international forums. So did the Americans. The history of international law relating to IP is very interesting vis-à-vis positive theories of legislation and especially the public choice insights. The World Intellectual Property Organization (WIPO) was established by the United Nations as one of its organs in 1967. It began operating when only minimal standards of IP protection, agreed upon in the Paris and Berne conventions, were guiding international IP law. However, since the ground rule of WIPO is that each of its 184 member states have equal votes in the decision-making process, and with the majority of countries consuming IP rather than producing it, WIPO's operation has not resulted in an expansion of IP protection on the international level. In fact the operation of WIPO has been instrumental in blocking significant expansion of IPR. This led the US and Europe to push for forum shifting of IP related issue to the General Agreement on Tariffs and Trade (GATT), which later evolved into the World Trade Organization (WTO).

The tactics of the powerful players – the US and the EU – was to tie free trade, which can also benefit the developing world, into the expansion of the minimal standards for IP protection. TRIPs resulted in 1994 with substantive strengthening of both the copyright and patent protection (a bold example is software). Many countries were required to make major internal legislative changes in order to comply. TRIPs is used as the main tool to harmonize the enforcement of IPRs on a global level. Unlike the other IPR-treaties, it has an effective sanctions regime against countries that do not fulfill their obligations. In the field of software, for example, the most relevant TRIPs articles require that software should be treated as literally work under copyright law and that software should be patentable as well. There are essentially no requirements for exemptions to less developed countries. This suggests that the acquisition costs of software in less developed countries as well as barriers to entry to international markets have risen significantly (Oksanen and Valimaki 2003). The carrots and sticks to bring on board the developing world was in terms of increase in the Foreign Direct Investment (FDI) and significant increase in imports (Lesser 2002), as opposed to potential trade sanctions.

The next phase of development in the international IP arena was the emergence of bilateral trade policies that are designed to promote US IP standards as IP standards to be respected abroad (as reflected by the Bipartisan Trade Promotion Authority Act 2002). Countries that want to have preferential market access to the US were required to accept TRIPs-plus US standards (e.g. data exclusivity). The EU, Japan and EFTA followed suit, and subsequently a condition for those countries aspiring to join the WTO (e.g. China, Cambodia, Russia) was made – to accept TRIPs-plus standards in order to join.

Recently, a new initiative of several developed like-minded countries was launched, aspiring to rise above the TRIPS and to crowd out the norms that the TRIPS had established. This is the Anti-Counterfeiting Trade Agreement (ACTA) which gained the infamous title 'The Country Club Agreement'. ACTA generates a new approach of negotiation, and de facto seeks to form an additional copyright enforcement framework to the existing ones. It aims to establish an international legal framework for targeting counterfeit goods, generic medicines and copyright infringement on the Internet, creating a new governing body outside existing forums, such as the World Trade Organization, the World Intellectual Property Organization, or the United Nations.

The agreement was signed in October 2011 by Australia, Canada, Japan, Morocco, New Zealand, Singapore, South Korea, and the United States. In January 2012 it was joined by the European Union and its 22 Member States. It can be seen that ACTA fails in tailoring its characteristics to the non-developed countries, and that it excludes important players like Brazil, China and Russia. Among the private actors pushing for this agreement were the big American lobby groups such as the MPAA and the Pharmaceutical Research and Manufacturers of America. According to ACTA, its members will be the ones who will determine the standards and principles they wish to apply, attempting to force them on the non-members as well (Gervais 2011). So far ACTA has not come into force, as it has not been ratified by 6 countries as required by the agreement.

The negotiation and formation of ACTA attracted severe criticism from numerous civil and digital rights organizations and from the public in general, reflected by street demonstrations which took place on February 2012 throughout Europe. As the agreement is not at all transparent, it has the potential to harm the future of the Internet as we all know it, to endanger free speech and privacy rights and to undermine the foundations of democracy. The opponents argue that ACTA shatters the delicate balance that has been achieved between authors and users, and may even be considered as a 'tipping point' (Gervais 2011).

These developments can point to a lack of equilibrium between normative analysis of global IP regime with positive analysis of the actual laws. While normative analysis, which takes into account wealth or utility maximization in all world nations, would have resulted in less protection, the actual global IP regime reflects the desirable level of protection of only the strong nations.

## 7.5 Positive analysis of the role of courts

We have examined in this chapter so far the positive analysis of IP laws on both the domestic level and the intra-national and international levels. Our focus was mainly on rule-making by legislatures and other rule-making bodies. We cannot conclude without short and tentative words about the function of courts. Courts are also important players in shaping legal policy toward intellectual property. It was the American Supreme Court, for example, that shaped the American patent regime during the period from 1865 to 1885, when patent experts threatened farmers and railroads. Even today, it is argued, the US courts have been tailoring the patent system and are more instrumental than legislatures in generating norms in this field (Bessen (2007) provides examples in the context of the Microsoft related lawsuits). The courts are usually thought to be less prone to interest group pressure and influence, and are portrayed even as a mechanism to counterbalance majority decision-making, self-interests of politicians and rent-seeking activities. Indeed, this is one of the major rationales for the existence of an independent judiciary as a separate branch of government in the first place (Salzberger 1993). However, even on this level we can find successful indirect efforts by interested parties, such as the calls to establish special courts to deal with IPR related disputes. In Taiwan, for example, a bill presented by the Judicial Yuan (the judicial branch) had led to a legislative process in which an IP court was established. The court, which is authorized to settle all civil and criminal litigation regarding IP rights (Kuo and Wang 2007), began its work in 2008. Such a court has also existed in Thailand since December 1997. The central IP & IT court has the power to adjudicate both civil and criminal cases regarding intellectual property and civil cases regarding international trade (Nagavajara 2003). An exclusive IP court might be much more exposed to pressure by special interest groups than the general courts system and the effects of this move are yet to be empirically examined.

However, even in the framework of general courts' litigation, their effect on the norms governing IP rights is immense. It can be argued that since in the field of information the path of development and change is so intense, legislation is always lacking behind reality and thus the judicial role is much more significant than in other areas of the law. Legal issues arising in the field of IP rights, more than in any other legal area, often reach the courts for primary resolution and the decision can affect both economic and technologic advancement. An example of such a case is *Diamond v. Chakrabarty* (447 U.S. 303), where the American Supreme Court enabled commercialization of patents on life forms. In the last two decades, the US Court of Appeals for the Federal Circuit methodically undertook to restore the patent law to the legal mainstream. In decisions applying across all areas of technology, the court implemented the patent statute and revived dormant legal principles (Newman 2007).

One of the most interesting recent examples of judicial policy-making in the field is the recent development in the threshold of patentability. In the last couple of years, the US Supreme Court has arguably raised the threshold for patenting by, inter alia, changing the non-obviousness standard and ruling that injunctive relief is not mandatory upon a finding of patent infringement. In 2006, the Supreme Court limited the use of permanent injunction, deciding that because a patent holding company did not use its patent and therefore was not harmed – Ebay's use in the discussed patent will not lead to a permanent injunction (Holzer 2006). Only recently, the American Supreme Court also addressed and indeed set the norm regarding patentability of business methods (*Bilski v. Kappos*, 130 S. Ct. 3218, 561 US, 177 L. Ed. 2d 792 (2010)).

The influence of judicial ideology has been the subject of many articles and been demonstrated across a number of issue areas. Some argue that according to the 'attitudinal model', which asserts that judges vote their political preferences, the judges' ideology is the most important factor in the court's process of shaping legal policy (Epstein and Jeffrey 2006). A recent study had shown that judges' ideology is a significant determinant of IP cases (Sag, Jacobi and Sytch 2007). In other words, attitudes about IP are part of the liberal-conservative ideological continuum and not an exception to it. In contrast, some IP scholars claim that IP law is a function of its own peculiar jurisprudential complexities and is not amenable to conventional ideological analysis (Beebe 2006; Moore 2001). However, this research is considered to be narrow in scope and to have negative results from which no conclusive inferences can be drawn.

Be that as it may, there is no institutional mechanism that directs courts to correct inefficient IP laws and thus courts' influence on IP policies cannot be regarded as mitigating positive analysis of rule-making with the normative analysis of the desirable IP regime. Hence one of the core problems of the law and economic analysis of intellectual property is yet to be sorted.

# References

## Books and articles


Abramowicz M. (2004), 'Perfecting Patent Prizes', *George Mason Law & Economics Research Paper No 01–29*. Retrieved 29 August 2007, from http://law.gmu.edu/faculty/papers/docs/01-29.pdf.

Ackerman B. A. 'The Storrs Lectures: Discovering the Constitution', *Yale L.J.*, 93, 1013, 1983–1984.

Acs J. Z. and Audretsch B. D. (1988), 'Innovation in Large and Small Firms: An Empirical Analysis', *American Econ. Rev.*, **78(4)**, 678.

Adobe Acrobat eBook, 'Can I Print and Copy my eBook?', retrieved 29 August 2007, from http://www.adobe.com/support/ebookrdrfaq.html′intcopy.

AIDS Legal Network, 'Victory in South Africa, But the Struggle Continues', retrieved 29 August 2007, from http://www.aidslaw.ca/Maincontent/issues/cts/updateSA.htm.

Alchian A. A. and Demstez H. (1972), 'Production, Information Costs, and Economic Organization', *American Econ. Rev.*, **62(5)**, 777.

Andersen B. (2004), 'If "Intellectual Property Rights" is the Answer, What is the Question? Revisiting the Patent Controversies', *Econ. Innov. New Techn.*, **13**(5), 417.

Andersen B. (2006), 'How Technology Changes the Scope, Strength and Usefulness of Copyright: Revisiting the "Economic Rationales" Underpinning Copyright Law in the Light of the New Economy', prepared for the conference 'Copyright and New Technologies' in Case Western Reserve Univ., Cleveland, Ohio. Retrieved 29 August 2007, from www.copyright.bbk.ac.uk/contents/workshops/andersencase.pdf.

Anding M. and Hess T. (2002), *Online Content Syndication – A Critical Analysis from the Perspective of Transaction Cost Theory*, in Proceeding of the Tenth European Conference on Information Systems (Wrycza S. ed), 551–63.

Andjelkovic M. (2006), 'Intellectual Property Rights and Access to Knowledge Models: Managing Innovation, Public Goods and Private Interest', *BSIS Journal of International Studies*, **3**, 1.

Android Open Source Project (http://source.android.com/index.html).

Antelman K. (2004), 'Do Open Access Articles Have a Greater Research Impact?', *College & Research Libraries News*, **65(5)**, 372.

Apple Press Release (2004), 'iTunes Music Store Catalog Tops One Million Songs', retrieved 29 August 2007, from http://www.apple.com/pr/library/2004/aug/10itms.html.

Argyres N. and Mayer K. J. (2007), 'Contract Design as a Firm Capability: An Integration of Learning and Transaction Cost Perspectives', *Academy of Management Rev.*, 32(4), 1060.

Arno K. (2005), 'Dual Licensing – A Business Model from the Second Generation of Open Source Companies', in *How Open is the Future? Economic, Social and Cultural Scenarios Inspired by Free and Open-Source Software* 479 (Marleen Wynants and Jan Cornelis eds).

Arora A., Ceccagnoli M. and Cohen W. M. (2004), 'R&D and the Patent Premium', *National Bureau of Economic Research, Inc, Working Paper Number 9431*. Retrieved 29 August 2007, from www.nber.org/papers/w9431.

Association of American Publishers (2000), 'Digital Rights Management for Ebooks: Publisher Requirements', retrieved 29 August 2007, from www.publishers.org/digital/drm.pdf.

Austin J. (1832), *The Province of Jurisprudence Determined*, reprinted in Rumble W. E. (ed.) (1995), UK: Cambridge University Press.

Aviram A. (2003), 'A Network Effects Analysis of Private Ordering', *Berkeley Program in Law & Economics Working Paper Series No 80*, retrieved 29 August 2007, from http://repositories.cdlib.org/blewp/art80.

Bach D. (2004), 'The Double Punch of Law and Technology: Fighting Music Piracy or Remaking Copyright in a Digital Age?', *Business and Politics*, 6, 1089.

Bailey C. W. (2006), 'Strong Copyright + DRM + Weak Net Neutrality = Digital Dystopia?', *Information Technology and Libraries*, 25(3), 116.

Baldwin J. R., Hanl P. and Sabourin, D. (2000), 'Determinants of Innovative Activity in Canadian Manufacturing Firms: The Role of Intellectual Property Rights', *Statistics Canada Working Paper No 122*. Retrieved 29 August 2007, from http://ssrn.com/abstract=229792.

Band J. (2009), 'The Long and Winding Road to the Google Books Settlement', The John Marshall Review of Intellectual Property Law, 9, 227.

Basu K. (2000), *Prelude to Political Economy: A Study of the Social and Political Foundations of Economics*, UK: Oxford University Press.

Beccaria C. (1764), *On Crimes and Punishments*, republished in 1986, US: Hackett Pub.

Bechtold S. (2004), 'Digital Rights Management in the United States and Europe', *Am. J. Comp. L.*, 52, 323.

Bechtold S. (2006), 'The Present and Future of Digital Rights Management – Musings on Emerging Legal Problems', in *Digital Rights Management – Technological, Economic, Legal and Political Aspects* (Becker, Buhse, Günnewig and Rump eds). Germany: Springer.

Beebe B. (2006), 'An Empirical Study of the Multifactor Tests for Trademark Infringement', *Cal. L. Rev.*, 94, 1581.

Bell W. T. (1998), 'Fair Use vs. Fared Use: The Impact of Automated Rights Management on Copyright's Fair Use Doctrine', *North Carolina L. Rev.*, 76, 557.

Bellis M., 'Viagra, the patenting of an aphrodisiac', retrieved 29 August 2007, from http://inventors.about.com/library/weekly/aa013099.htm.

Benjamin W. (1968), 'The Work of Art in the Age of Mechanical Reproduction', in *Illuminations*, US: Schocken.

Benkler Y. (2000), 'An Unhurried View of Private Ordering in Information Transactions', *Vanderbilt L. Rev.*, 53(6), 2063.

Benkler Y. (2001), 'A Political Economy of the Public Domain: Markets in Information Goods vs. The Marketplace of Ideas', in *Expanding the Boundaries of Intellectual Property: Innovation Policy for the Knowledge Society* (Dreyfuss R., Zimmerman D. and First H., eds).

Benkler Y. (2002), 'Coase's Penguin, or, Linux and the Nature of the Firm', *Yale L.J.*, 112, 369.

Benkler Y. (2006), *The Wealth of Networks: How Social Production Transforms Markets and Freedom*, US: Yale University Press.

Bentham J. (1789), *An introduction to the principles of morals and legislation*, reprinted in Wilfrid Harrison (ed) (1948), UK: B. Blackwell.

Bergh R. van den (1996), 'The Growth of Law and Economics in Europe', *European Economic Rev.*, 40, 969.

Bergh R. van den (2003), 'Competition Law and Consumer Protection Legislation', in *Economic Analysis of Law: A European Perspective* (Hatzis ed).

Bernstein L. (1992), 'Opting Out of the Legal System: Extralegal Contractual Relations in the Diamond Industry', *Journal of Legal Studies*, 21, 115.

Besek M. J. (2004), 'Anti-Circumvention Laws and Copyright: A Report from the Kernochan Center for Law, Media and the Arts', *Columbia Journal of Law & the Arts*, 27, 385.

Bessen J. (2007), 'Estimates of Patent Rents from Firm Market Value', *Boston University School of Law Working Paper No. 06-14*.

Bessen J. and Hunt R. M. (2004), 'An Empirical Look at Software Patents', *Federal Reserve Bank of Philadelphia, Working Paper 03-17R*. Retrieved 29 August 2007, from http://www.researchoninnovation.org/swpat.pdf.

Bessen J. and Hunt R. M. (2004a), 'A Reply to Hahn and Wallsten', retrieved 29 August 2007, from http://www.researchoninnovation.org/hahn.pdf.

Birnhack M. D. (2001), 'The Idea of Progress in Copyright Law', *Buffalo Intell. Prop. L.J.*, 1, 3.

Birnhack M. D. (2006), 'More or Better? Shaping the Public Domain', in *The Future of the Public Domain* (P. Bernt Hugenholtz and Lucie Guibault, eds), UK: Kluwer Law International, 59, 65–69.

Birrell A. (1899), *Seven Lectures on the Law and History of Copyright in Books*, US: Harvard University.

Blair D. R. and Cotter F. T. (2005), *Intellectual Property: Economic and Legal Dimensions of Rights and Remedies*, UK: Cambridge University Press.

Boczkowski J. P. (2005), *Digitizing the News: Innovation in Online Newspaper*, US: The MIT Press.

Boldrin M. and Levine K. D. (2002), 'The Case Against Intellectual Property', *American Economic Review Papers and Proceedings*, 92, 209.

Boldrin M. and Levine K. D. (2004), 'The Case Against Intellectual Monopoly', *IER Lawrence Klein Lecture, Federal Reserve Bank of Minneapolis, Research Department Staff Report 339*.

Bomsel O. and Geffroy A. G. (2005a), 'Economic Analysis of DRM's Roll-Out over the Internet', *Center of Industrial Economics* (Paris, France), retrieved 29 August 2007, from www.cerna.ensmp.fr/Documents/AGG-OB-NAEC-2005.pdf.

Bomsel O. and Geffroy A. G. (2005b), 'Economic Analysis of Digital Rights Management Systems (DRMs)', *MediaNet Project Paper*. Retrieved 29 August 2007, from www.cerna.ensmp.fr/Documents/OB-AGG-EtudeDRM.pdf.

Botein M. (1998), *Regulation of the Electronic Mass Media: Law and Policy for Radio, Television, Cable, and the New Video Technologies*, 3rd edition, 401–404, US: West Group Publishing.

Boyle J. (1992), 'A Theory of Law and Information: Copyright, Spleens, Blackmail, and Insider Trading', *California L. Rev.*, **80**, 1413.

Boyle J. (2003), 'Enclosing the Genome: What the Squabbles over Genetic Patents Could Teach Us', in *Perspectives on Properties of the Human Genome Project* (Kieff F. S. ed), US: Academic Press.

Boyle J. (2003a), 'The Second Enclosure Movement and the Construction of the Public Domain', *Law & Contemp. Probs.*, 66, 33.

Braga C. A. P., Fink C. and Sepulveda C. P. (2000), 'Intellectual Property Rights and Economic Development', *World Bank Discussion Papers* **412**.

Branstetter L. G., Fisman R. and Foley C. F. (2004), 'Do Stronger Intellectual Property Rights Increase International Technology Transfer? Empirical Evidence from U.S. Firm-Level Panel Data', *World Bank Policy Research, Working Paper No 3305*. Retrieved 29 August 2007, from http://ssrn.com/abstract=610350.

Brennan G. and Hamlin A. (2000), *Democratic Devices and Desires*, Cambridge: Cambridge University Press.

Breyer S. (1970), 'The Uneasy Case for Copyright: A Study of Copyright in Books, Photocopies, and Computer Programs', *Harvard L. Rev.*, **84**, 281.

Broersma M. (2002), 'Red Hat Defends Controversial Patent Applications', *ZDNet UK*, retrieved 29 August 2007, from http://news.zdnet.co.uk/business/0,39020645, 2111257,00.htm.

Brown I. (2003), 'Implementing the EU Copyright Directive', *The Foundation for Information Policy Research*, retrieved 29 August 2007, from http://www.fipr.org/copyright/guide/eucd-guide.pdf.

Buber M. (1955). 'Education', in *Between Man and Man* **98** (Ronald Gregor-Smith trans).

Burk D. (1996), 'Federalism in Cyberspace', *Conn. L. Rev*, **28**, 1095.

Burk, D. L., Lemley M. A. (2003), *Biotechnology's Uncertainty Principle, in: Perspectives on Properties of the Human Genome Project*, Elsevier Academic Press, San Diego CA, pp. 305–354.

Burk D. and Lemley M. A. (2009), 'Courts and the Patent System', *Regulation*, **32(2)**, 18.

Burke E. (1896), *Speech on Conciliation with America*, New York: Longmans, Green.

Calabresi G. (1961), 'Some Thoughts on Risk Distributions and the Law of Torts', *Yale L. J.*, 70(4), 449.

Calabresi G. (1970), *The Cost of Accidents: A Legal and Economic Analysis*, Yale University Press.

Calabresi G. (1975), 'Concerning cause and the law of torts', *University of Chicago Law Review*, 43, 69–108.

Calabresi G. and Melamed D. (1972), 'Property Rights, Liability Rules and Inalienability: One View of the Cathedral', *Harvard L. Rev.*, **85**, 1089.

Cameron J., Pierce W. D., Banko K. M. and Gear A. (2005), 'Achievement-Based Rewards and Intrinsic Motivation: A Test of Cognitive Mediators', *Journal of Educational Psychology*, **97(4)**, 641.

Campbell-Kelly M. and Valduriez P. (2005), 'A Technical Critique of Fifty Software Patents', *Marquette Intellectual Property L. Rev.*, 9, 249.

Captain S. (2005), 'My Songs, My Format', *The New York Times*, retrieved 29 August 2007, from http://www.nytimes.com/2005/10/06/technology/circuits/06basics.html#.

Carroll M. W. (2006), 'One for All: The Problem of Uniformity Cost in Intellectual Property Law', *American Univ. L. Rev.*, **55(4)**, 845.

Carroll M. W. (2010), 'The Role of Copyright Law in Academic Journal Publishing', in *Working Within the Boundaries of Intellectual Property* (Dreyfuss, First, and Zimmerman eds.), US: Oxford University Press.

Castells M. (2009), *Communication Power*, UK: Oxford University Press.

CNN Money (2006), 'BlackBerry maker, NTP ink $612 million settlement', by Rob Kelly. Retrieved from: http://money.cnn.com/2006/03/03/technology/rimm_ntp/.

Coase R. (1937), 'The Nature of the Firm', *Economica*, New Series, **4(16)**, (Nov., 1937), 386. Retrieved from http://www.sonoma.edu/users/e/eyler/426/coase1.pdf.

Coase R. (1960), 'The Problem of Social Cost', *Journal of L. and Econ.*, **3**, 1.

Cohen J. E. (1998), 'Lochner in Cyberspace: The New Economic Orthodoxy of "Rights Management"', *Michigan L. Rev.*, **97**, 462.

Cohen J. E. (2000), 'Copyright and the Perfect Curve', *Vand. L. Rev.*, **53**, 1799.

Cohen J. E. (2003), 'DRM and Privacy', *Berkeley Technology L. J.*, **18**, 575.

Cohen J. E. (2007), 'Creativity and Culture in Copyright Theory', *U.C. Davis L. Review*, **40**, 1151. Retrieved from http://scholarship.law.georgetown.edu/facpub/58/.

Cohen W. M., Nelson R. R. and Walsh J. P. (2000) 'Protecting Their Intellectual Assets: Appropriability Conditions and Why U.S. Manufacturing Firms Patent (or Not)', *NBER Working Paper, No W7552*. Retrieved 29 August 2007, from http://www.nber.org/papers/w7552.

Coleman S. J. (1988), 'Social Capital in the Creation of Human Capital', *American J. of Sociology*, **94**, 95.

Computer & Communications Industry Association (2003), 'Digital Rights Management', retrieved 29 August 2007, from www.netcaucus.org/events/2003/drm/onepagers/ccia.drm2003.pdf.

Condorcet, Marquis de (1785/1976), Essay on the application of mathematics to the theory of decision-making, in *Baker K. M. Condorcet: selected writings*, Bobbs-Marrill Co Indianapolis, 33–70.

Cooter D. R. (1991), 'Inventing Market Property: The Land Courts of Papua New Guinea', *Law and Society Rev.*, **25**, 759.

Cooter D. R. (1997), 'Symposium: Normative Failure Theory of Law', *Cornell L. Rev.*, **82**, 947.

Cornelli F. and Schankerman M. (1999), 'Patent Renewals and R&D Incentives', *RAND J. Econ.*, **30**, 197.

Crespi S. G. (1997), 'Putting the Chicago School Debate in Proper Perspective: [Reply]', *Law & Social Inquiry*, **22(1)**, 201.

Cruz R. T. & Hinck J. J. (1995), 'Not My Brother's Keeper: The Inability of an Informed Minority to Correct for Imperfect Information', *Hastings L. J.*, 47, 635.

Dagan H. (2009), 'Exclusion and Inclusion in Property', working papers series.

Dalrymple J. (2004), 'Apple Accuses RealNetworks of Hacking', *PCWorld.com*, retrieved 29 August 2007, from http://www.pcworld.com/news/article/0,aid,117183,00.asp.

Dam K. W. (1998), 'Who Says Who Can Access What? The Policy Crisis over Cryptography in the Information Age', in Raymond S. U. (ed), *Science, Technology, and the Law*, US: New York Academy of Sciences.

Dam K. W. (1999), 'Self-help in the Digital Jungle', *J. Legal Stud.*, **28**, 393.

Dau-Schmidt G. K. (1990), 'An Economic Analysis of the Criminal Law as a Preference-Shaping Policy', *Duke L. J.*, 1.

Deci E. L., Koestner R. and Ryan R. M. (1999), 'A Meta-Analytic Review of Experiments Examining the Effects of Extrinsic Rewards on Intrinsic Motivation', *Psychological Bulletin*, **125**, 627.

Demsetz H. (1967), 'Toward a Theory of Property Rights', *Am. Econ. Rev. Papers & Proc.*, **57**, 347.

Demsetz H. (2008), *From Economic Man to Economic System: Essays on Human Behavior and the Institutions of Capitalism*, US: Cambridge University Press.

Depoorter B. and Hiel A. van (2010), 'Copyright Backlash', Working Paper – December, 2010, 35–40. Retrieved from: http://papers.ssrn.com/sol3/papers.cfm?abstract_id=740184.

Dequiedt V. and Versaevel B. (2007), 'Patent Pools and the Dynamic Incentives to R&D', *GATE Working Paper No 07–03, France*. Retrieved 29 August 2007, from www.gate.cnrs.fr/documentation/workingpapers/2007/0703.pdf.

Dhamija R. and Wallenberg F. (2003), 'A Framework for Evaluating Digital Rights Management Proposals', retrieved 29 August 2007, from www.ischool.berkeley.edu/~rachna/papers/EvaluatingDRM.pdf.

Digital Music (2006), 'US Warns of Overzealous DRM Regulation; Reframing the DRM Debate', retrieved 29 August 2007, from http://digitalmusic.weblogsinc.com/2006/09/14/us-warns-of-overzealous-drm-regulation-reframing-the-drm-debate/.

Dinwoodie G. B. (2008), *Achieving Balance in International Intellectual Property Law*, Forthcoming: Oxford University Press.

du Gay P., Hall S., Janes L., Mackay H. and Negus K. (1997), *Doing Cultural Studies: the Story of the Sony Walkman*, UK: Sage.

Duffy F. J. (2005), 'Intellectual Property Isolationism and the Average Cost Thesis', *Texas L. Rev.*, **83**, 1077.

Dutfield G. (2002), 'Literature Survey on Intellectual Property Rights and Sustainable Human Development', retrieved 29 August 2007, from http://www.iprsonline.org/unctadictsd/docs/GDutfield_LiteratureSurveyOnIP_April2003.pdf.

DVD Reviewer, 'Multi-Region Hacks for Domestic DVD Players', retrieved 29 August 2007, from http://www.dvd.reviewer.co.uk/info/multiregion/hackable.asp.

Easterbrook F. H. (1990), 'Intellectual Property Is Still Property', *Harvard Journal of Law & Public Policy*, **13**, 108.

Easterbrook F. H. (1996), 'Cyberspace and the Law of the Horse', *U Chi Legal F.*, **207**.

Easterbrook F. H. (2005), 'Testimony on Civil Remedies before the Antitrust Modernization Commission'. Washington, DC. (July 28, 2005).

EFF and Co-Signers (2005), 'Digital Rights Management: A Failure in the Developed World, a Danger to the Developing World', retrieved 29 August 2007, from www.eff.org/IP/DRM/ITU_DRM_paper.pdf.

EFF Deep Links, 'New DMCA Exemptions Granted', retrieved 29 August 2007, from www.eff.org/deeplinks/archives/005021.php.

EFF Guide to Online Music, 'The Customer Is Always Wrong: A User's Guide to DRM in Online Music', retrieved 29 August 2007, from http://www.eff.org/IP/DRM/guide/.

EFF Unintended Consequences: Five Years under the DMCA, retrieved 29 August 2007, from http://www.eff.org/IP/DMCA/unintended_consequences.pdf.

Elkin-Koren N. (1996), 'Cyberlaw and Social Change: A Democratic Approach to Copyright Law in Cyberspace', *Cardozo Arts & Entertainment L. J.*, 14(2), 215.

Elkin-Koren N. (1997), 'Copyright Policy and the Limit of Freedom of Contract', *Berkeley Tech. L.J.*, 12, 93.

Elkin-Koren N. (1998), 'Copyrights in Cyberspace – Rights without Law', *Chi.-Kent L. Rev.*, 73, 1155.

Elkin-Koren N. (2002), 'It's All About Control: Rethinking Copyright in the New Information Landscape', in *The Commodification of Information* (Elkin-Koren N. and Netanel W. N. eds), US: Aspen Pub.

Elkin-Koren N. (2003), 'The Internet and Copyright Policy Discourse', in *Academy and the Internet* (Nissenbaum and Price eds), US: Peter Lang Publishing Group.

Elkin-Koren N. (2005), 'What Contracts Can't Do: The Limits of Private Ordering in Facilitating a Creative Commons', *Fordham L. Rev.*, 74, 101.

Elkin-Koren N. (2006), 'Exploring Creative Commons: a Skeptical View of a Worthy Pursuit', in *The Future of the Public Domain* (Guibault and Hugenholtz eds), US: Kluwer Law International.

Elkin-Koren N. (2007), 'Making Room for Consumers under the DMCA', *Berkeley Tech L.J.*, 22, 1119 (2007).

Elkin-Koren N. (2010), 'User-Generated Platforms', in *Working Within the Boundaries of Intellectual Property* (Rochelle Dreyfuss, Diane L. Zimmerman and Harry First eds), US: Oxford University Press.

Elkin-Koren N. (2011), 'The Changing Nature of Books and the Uneasy Case for Copyright', *George Washington Law Review*, 79, 101.

Elkin-Koren N. and Netanel W. N. (2002), '*The Commodification of Information*, US: Aspen Pub.

Elkin-Koren N. and Salzberger E. (1999), 'Law and Economics in Cyberspace', *International Review of Law and Economics*, 19, 553.

Elkin Koren N. and Salzberger M. E. (2000), 'Economic Analysis of Unjust Enrichment', *International Rev. of L. & Econ.*, 20(4), 551.

Elkin Koren N. and Salzberger M. E. (2004), *Law, Economics and Cyberspace: The Effects of Cyberspace on the Economic Analysis of Law*, US: Edward Elgar Pub.

Elkin-Koren, N., & Salzberger, E. M. (2005), 'The Effects of Cyberspace on the Economic Theory of the State', in Alain Marciano and Jean (eds) *How to Shape Democratic State*, Edward Elgar.

Ellickson C. R. (1991), *Order Without Law: How Neighbors Settle Disputes*, US: Harvard University Press.

Ellickson C. R. (2005), *Order Without Law: How Neighbors Settle Disputes*, US: Harvard University Press.

Entertainment Media Research (2007), 'The 2007 Digital Music Survey', retrieved 29 August 2007, from www.entertainmentmediaresearch.com/reports/EMR_Digital_Music_Survey2007.pdf.

Epstein A. R. (1985), *Takings: Private Property and the Power of Eminent Domain*, US: Harvard University Press.

Epstein A. R. (2003), 'Trade Secrets as Private Property: Their Constitutional Protection', *U Chicago Law & Economics, Olin Working Paper*, 190. Retrieved 29 August 2007, from http://ssrn.com/abstract=421340.

Epstein A. R. (2010), 'The Disintegration of Intellectual Property? A Classical Liberal Response to a Premature Obituary', *Stan. L. Rev.*, 62(2), 455.

Epstein L. and Jeffrey A. S. (2006), 'Trumping the First Amendment?', *Wash. U. J. L. & Pol'y*, 21, 81.

Fagundes D. (2010), 'Property Rhetoric and the Public Domain', *Minn. L. Rev.*, 94, 652.

Farber D. and Frickey P. (1991), *Law and Public Choice – A Critical Introduction*, US: University of Chicago Press.

Farchy J. and Ranaivoson H. (2005), 'DRMS: A New Strategic Stake for Contents Industries: The Case of the Online Music Market', *Rev. of Economic Research on Copyright Issues*, 2(2), 53.

Fast Company Magazine (1999), 'Inspired by Work', by William Taylor – Interview with Eric S. Raymond.

Fauchart E. and von Hippel E. (2008), 'Norms-Based Intellectual Property Systems: The Case of French Chefs', *Organization Science*, 19(2), 187.

Federal Trade Commission (2003), 'To Promote Innovation: The Proper Balance of Competition and Patent Law and Policy', A report by the Federal Trade Commission. Retrieved from: www.ftc.gov/os/2003/10/innovationrpt.pdf.

Ferguson N. (2001), 'Censorship in action: why I don't publish my HDCP results', retrieved 29 August 2007, from http://www.macfergus.com/niels/dmca/cia.html.

Fink C. and Maskus K. E. (2005), *Intellectual Property and Development: Lessons from Economic Research*, US: The World Bank Publications.

Fisher W. (2001), 'Intellectual Property and Innovation: Theoretical, Empirical, and Historical Perspectives'.

Fisher W. W. (2001), 'Theories of Intellectual Property', in *New Essay in The Legal and Political Theory of Property*, 168 (Munzer, ed 2001), UK: Cambridge University Press.

Fisher W. W. (2004), *Promises to Keep: Technology, Law and the Future of Entertainment*, US: Stanford University Press.

Fisher W. W. and Syed T. (2007), 'Global Justice in Healthcare: Developing Drugs for the Developing World', *University of California, Davis*, 40, 581.

Frey B. S. and Lau L. J. (1968), 'Towards a Mathematical Model of Government Behavior', *Zeitschrift für Nationalökonomie*, 28, 355.

Fried B. (2006), 'Is as Ought: The Case of Contracts', *Vir. L. Rev.*, 92, 1375.

Fried C. (2006), *Contract as Promise*, US: Harvard University Press.

Frischmann M. B. (2007), 'Cultural Environment and the Wealth of Networks', *Univ. of C. L. Rev.*, 74, 1083.

Frischmann M. B. (2007) 'Evaluating the Demsetzian Trend in Copyright Law', *Review of Law and Economics*, 3.

Frischmann M. B. (2012), *Infrastructure: the Social Value of Shared Resources*, UK: Oxford University Press.

Fromer C. J. (forthcoming 2012), 'Expressive Incentives in Intellectual Property', *Virginia Law Review*, 98. Retrieved from: http://www.law.stanford.edu/display/images/dynamic/events_media/Expressive_Incentives_in_Intellectual_Property.pdf.

FTC Report, U.S. Federal Trade Commission (2003), 'Report on Patents and Competition: To promote Innovation: The Proper Balance of Competition and Patent Law and Policy', retrieved 29 August 2007, from http://www.ftc.gov/os/2003/10/innovationrpt.pdf.

Gabel P. (2009), 'Critical Legal Studies as a Spiritual Practice', *Pepp. L. Rev.*, 36, 515. Retrieved from, http://heinonline.org/HOL/LandingPage?collection=journals&handle=hein.journals/pepplr36&div=27&id=&page=.

Gasser U. (2004), 'iTunes: How Copyright, Contract and Technology Shape the Business of Digital Media – A Case Study', *Berkman Publication Series No 2004–07*, retrieved 29 August 2007, from http://cyber.law.harvard.edu/publications.

Gasser U. (2006), 'Legal Framework and Technological Protection of Digital Content: Moving Forward Towards a Best Practice Model', *Berkman Center Research Publication No 2006–04*, retrieved 29 August 2007, from http://cyber.law.harvard.edu/publications.

Gazal-Ayal O. (2007), 'Economic Analysis of "Law & Economics"', *Capital University Law Review*, 35, 801.

Geist M. (2006), '30 Days of DRM – Day 6: Interoperability (Public Protections and Markets)', retrieved 29 August 2007, from www.michaelgeist.ca/content/view/1383/125/.

Geller P. E. (2000), 'Copyright History and the Future: What's Culture Got to Do With It?', *Journal of the Copyright Society of the USA*, 47, 209.

German Guide, 'How to Switch Region Codes on a DVD-Rom Drive', *About Electronics*, retrieved 29 August 2007, from http://german.about.com/library/bldvd2_how1.htm.

Geroski P. A. (2005), 'Intellectual Property Rights, Competition Policy and Innovation: Is There a Problem?', *Script-ed*, 2(4), 423.

Gillen A., Kusnetzky D. and McLarnon S. (2003), 'Five Pros and Five Cons: A Look at Changing User Perceptions on Linux', *IDC study*.

Ginsburg J. (1999), 'Copyright Legislation for the "Digital Millennium"', *Columbia-VLA Journal of Law and the Arts*, 23, 137.

Glave J. (1998), 'Saffo: Leave that middleman alone', *Wired News*, retrieved 29 August 2007, from http://www.wired.com/news/business/0,1367,11756,00.html.

Goldberg P. V. (1974), 'Institutional Change and the Quasi-Invisible Hand', *J. of L. and Econ.*, 17, 461.

Gordon H. S. (1954), 'The Economic Theory of a Common-Property Resource: The Fishery', *J. Pol. Econ.*, 62, 124.

Gordon J. W. (1982), 'Fair Use as Market Failure: A Structural and Economic Approach to the Betamax Case and Its Predecessors', *Colum. L. Rev.*, 82, 1600.

Gordon J. W. (1993), 'A Property Right in Self-Expression: Equality and Individualism in the Natural Law of Intellectual Property', *Yale L. J.*, 102, 1533.

Gordon W. (2002), 'Symposium: Eldred v. Ashcroft: Intellectual Property, Congressional Power, and the Constitution: Authors, Publishers, and Public Goods: Trading Gold for Dross', *Loy. L.A. L. Review*, 36, 159.

Graham S. and Mowery C. D. (2004), 'Submarines in Software? Continuations in U.S. Software Patenting in the 1980s and 1990s', *Economics of Innovation and New Technology*, 14, 443.

Granstrand O. (1999), *The Economics and Management of Intellectual Property: Towards Intellectual Capitalism*, US: Edward Elgar.

Greene W. H. (2001), 'Fixed and Random Effects in Nonlinear Models', *mimeo*, New York University.

Greenwood J. (2003), *Interest Representation in the European Union*, UK: Macmillan.

Greenwood J. (2007), *Interest Representation in the European Union*, US: Palgrave Macmillan.

Griliches Z. (1994), 'The American Economic Review', *ABI/INFORM Global*, 84, 1.

Grimmelmann J. (2005), 'Regulation by Software', *The Yale L. J.*, 114, 1719.

Guibault L. (2002), *Copyright Limitations and Contracts: An Analysis of the Contractual Overridability of Limitations on Copyright*, UK: Kluwer Law International.

Guibault L. (2006), 'Wrapping Information in Contract: How Does it Affect the Public Domain?', in *The Future of the Public Domain* (Guibault and Hugenholtz eds), UK: Kluwer Law International.

Hahn W. R. and Wallsten S. J. (2003), 'A Review of Bessen and Hunt's Analysis of Software Patents', retrieved 29 August 2007, from http://ssrn.com/abstract=467484.

Hall B. H. (2002), 'Testimony to FTC/DOJ (Antitrust) Hearings on Competition and Intellectual Property Law in the Knowledge-Based Economy', retrieved 29 August 2007, from http://www.ftc.gov/opp/intellect/020319cecilquillen.pdf.

Hall H. B. and Ziedonis H. R. (2001), 'The Patent Paradox Revisited: An Empirical Study of Patenting in the U.S. Semiconductor Industry, 1979–95', *RAND J. Econ*, 39, 101.

Hammer M. (2000), 'The Myth of Disintermediation', *InformationWeek*, retrieved 29 August 2007, from http://www.informationweek.com/794/94uwmh.htm.

Hanbidge N. (2001), 'Protecting Rights Holders' Interest in the Information Society: Anti-Circumvention; Threats Post Napster and DRM', *Entertainment L. Rev.*, 12, 223.

Hansmann H. and Kraakman R. (2002), 'Property, Contract, and Verification: The "Numerus Clausus" Problem and the Divisibility of Rights', *J. Legal Stud.*, 31, 373.

Hardin G. (1968), 'The Tragedy of the Commons', *Sci.*, 162, 1243.

Hardy I. T. (1994), 'The Proper Legal Regime for "Cyberspace"', *U. Pitt. L. Rev.*, 55, 993.

Hardy I. T. (1996), 'Property (and Copyright) in Cyberspace', *U. Chi. Legal F.* 261.

Hardy I. T. (1997), 'The Proper Legal Regime for Cyberspace', *University of Pitt. L. Rev.*, 55, 993.

Hardy I. T. (2011), 'Not So Different: Tangible, Intangible, Digital, and Analog Works and Their Comparison for Copyright Purposes', *Univ. of Dayton L. Rev.*, 26(2), 211.

Hargreaves I. (2011), 'Digital Opportunity: A Review of Intellectual Property and Growth', An Independent Report by Professor Ian Hargreaves, 9, 71. Retrieved from http://www.ipo.gov.uk/ipreview-finalreport.pdf.

Hart L. A. (1961), *The Concept of Law*, UK: Clarendon Press.

Haupt S. (2003), 'An Economic Analysis of Consumer Protection Law', *German L. J.*, 4(11).

Hayek F. H. (1960), *The Constitution of Liberty*, US: University of Chicago Press.

Hayek F. H. (1978), *Law, Legislation and Liberty, Volume 2: The Mirage of Social Justice*, US: University of Chicago Press.

Hegel W. F. H. (1821), *Hegel's Philosophy of Right* (Knox T. M. trans, 1967), UK: Oxford University Press.

Helberger N. (2004), 'It's Not a Right, Silly! The Private Copying Exception in Practice', *INDICARE Monitor*, retrieved 29 August 2007, from http://216.239.59.104/search?q=cache:8MXYslxqydQJ:www.ivir.nl/publications/helberger/it%27snotarightsilly. html+%E2%80%98It%27+s+not+a+right,+silly!&hl=en&client=firefox-a.

Helberger N. (2005), 'Not So Silly After All – New Hope for Private Copying', *INDICARE Monitor*, retrieved 29 August 2007, from http://www.indicare.org/tiki-read_article.php?articleId=132.

Helberger N., Dufft N., Groenenboom M., Kerényi K., Orwat C. and Riehm U. (2005), 'Digital Rights Management and Consumer Acceptability: A Multi-Disciplinary Discussion of Consumer Concerns and Expectations', State of the Art Report – First Supplement. Retrieved 29 August 2007, from http://www.ivir.nl/publications/helberger/INDICARESOAReport-Update01.pdf.

Helfer L. R. (2007), 'Toward a Human Rights Framework for Intellectual Property', *U.C. Davis Law Review*, **40**, 971, 981.

Heller M. (1998), 'The Tragedy of the Anticommons: Property in the Transition from Marx to Markets', *Harvard L. Rev.*, **111**, 621.

Heller M. and Eisenberg R. S. (1998), 'Can Patents Deter Innovation? The Anticommons in Biomedical Research', *Science*, 280, 698.

Helsingin Sanomat International (2005), 'Proposed New Copyright Law Would Allow Personal Copies of CDs, but With Restrictions', retrieved 29 August 2007, from http://www.hs.fi/english/article/1101980971029.

Hirshleifer J. (1971), 'The Private and Social Value of Information and the Reward to Inventive Activity', *The American Economic Review*, **61(4)**, 561.

Hobbes T. (1651), *The Leviathan* (Reprinted from the edition of 1651), Oxford: At the Clarendon Press.

Hollaar A. L. (2002), *Legal Protection of Digital Information*, US: BNA Books.

Hollis A. (2005a), 'An Efficient Reward System for Pharmaceutical Innovation', *Draft – Department of Economics, Univ. of Calgary*. Retrieved 29 August 2007, from http://econ.ucalgary.ca/fac-files/ah/drugprizes.pdf.

Hollis A. (2005b), 'An Optional Reward System for Neglected Disease Drugs', *Draft – Department of Economics, Univ. of Calgary*. Retrieved 29 August 2007, from http://econ.ucalgary.ca/fac-files/ah/optionalrewards.pdf.

Hollis A. (2007), 'Incentive Mechanisms for Innovation', *IAPR Technical Paper Series No TP-07005*. Retrieved 29 August 2007, from www.iapr.ca.

Holzer B. (2006), 'Political Consumerism Between Individual Choice and Collective Action: Social Movements, Role Mobilization and Signalling', *International Journal of Consumer Studies*, **30(5)**, 405.

Hovenkamp H. (1990), 'The First Great Law and Economics Movement', *Stan. L. Rev.*, **42**, 993.

Howe J. (2008), *Crowdsourcing: Why the Power of the Crowd Is Driving the Future of Business* 71–130, US: Crown Business.

Hunt A. (1986), 'The Theory of Critical Legal Studies', *Oxford Journal of Legal Studies*, **6**(1) (Spring 1986), 1, 4–8.

Hurt M. R. and Schuchman M. R. (1966), 'The Economic Rationale of Copyright', *American Economic Review*, **56**, 421.

Idris K. (2004), 'Intellectual property, A Power Tool for Economic Growth', *World Intellectual Property Organization*.

International Chamber of Commerce (2005), 'Intellectual Property: Source of Innovation, Creativity, Growth and Progress', http://www.iccwho.org/data/documents/bascap/innovation-creativity-growth-and-progress.

Jaffe B. A. and Lerner J. (2004), *Innovation and Its Discontents: How Our Broken Patent System Is Endangering Innovation and Progress, and What to Do About It*, US: Princeton University Press.

Jardin X. (2004), 'Music is not a loaf of Bread', *Wired News*, retrieved 29 August 2007, from http://www.wired.com/news/culture/0,1284,65688,00.html.

Jaszi P. (1991), 'Toward a Theory of Copyright: the Metamorphosis of Authorship', *Duke L. J.*, 45(5), 455.

Jefferson T. (1813), Letter to Isaac McPherson, August 13, 1813, reprinted in H. A. Washington, ed, *Writings of Thomas Jefferson 1790–1826*, 6 (Washington, DC: Taylor & Maury 1854), 180–81.

Johnson E. E. (2011), 'Intellectual Property and the Incentive Fallacy', *Florida State University Law Review*. Retrieved from http://papers.ssrn.com/sol3/papers.cfm?abstract_id=1746343.

Jullien N. and Zimmermann J. B. (2005), 'New Approaches to Intellectual Property: from Open Source Software to Knowledge-Based Industrial Activities', *GREQAM Working Paper No 2005–39*. Retrieved 29 August 2007, from http://greqam.univ-mrs.fr/pdf/working_papers/2005/2005–39.pdf.

Kahneman D., Knetsch L. J. and Thaler H. R. (1991), 'Anomalies: The Endowment Effect, Loss Aversion, and Status Quo Bias', *The Journal of Economic Perspectives*, 5(1), 193.

Kahneman D. and Tversky A. (1979), 'Prospect Theory: An Analysis of Decision under Risk', *Econometrica*, 47(2), 263.

Kaldor N. (1939), 'Welfare Propositions in Economics and Interpersonal Comparisons of Utility', *The Econ. J.*, 49(195), 549.

Kaplan B. (1967), *An Unhurried View of Copyright*, 72, US: Columbia University Press.

Karjala D. S. (1997), 'The Term of Copyright', in *Growing Pains: Adapting Copyright for Education and Society* (Gasaway L. ed).

Katz A. (1990), 'The Effect of Frivolous Lawsuits on the Settlement of Litigation', *International Review of Law and Economics*, 10, 3.

Katz A. (1996), 'Taking Private Ordering Seriously', *U. Pa. L. Rev.*, 144, 1745.

Kelsen H. (1949), *General theory of law and state*, US: Harvard University Press.

Kennedy D. (2002), 'The Critique of Rights in Critical Legal Studies' in *Left Legalism/Left Critique* (Janet Halley and Wendy Brown eds, Duke University Press, 2002) 179, 224.

Kesan P. J. and Shah C. R. (2005), 'Shaping Code', *Harvard Journal of Law and Technology*, 18, 319.

Kieff F. S. (2001), 'Property Rights and Property Rules for Commercializing Inventions', *Minn. L. Rev.*, 85, 697.

Kieff F. S. (2004), 'The Case for Registering Patents and the Law and Economics of Present Patent-Obtaining Rules', *Stanford Law and Economics Olin Working Paper No 276; Washington U School of Law Working Paper No 04-02-04*. Retrieved 29 August 2007, from http://ssrn.com/abstract=501143.

Kilbey I. (2003), 'Copyright Duration? Too Long!', *European Intellectual Property Rev.*, 25, 105.

Kirkpatrick D. D. (2000), 'Stephen King Sows Dread in Publishers With His Latest E-Tale', *N.Y. Times* (24 July 24 2000, at C1).

Kitch E. W. (1977), 'The Structure and Function of the Patent System', *J.L. & Econ*, 27, 265.

Koelman J. K. (2004), 'Copyright Law and Economics in the EU Copyright Directive: Is the Droit d'Auteur Passé?', *International Review of Intellectual Property and Competition Law*, 35(6), 603.

Kohn A. (1999), *Punished by Rewards: The Trouble with Gold Stars, Incentive Plans, A's, Praise, and other Bribes*, US: Mariner Books.

Kortum S. and Lerner J. (1999), 'What is Behind the Recent Surge in Patenting?', *Research Policy*, **28**, 1.

Krecke E. (2004), 'Economic Analysis and Legal Pragmatism', *International Review of Law and Economics*, **23 (4)**, 421.

Kuhn T. (1962), *The Structure of Scientific Revolution*, US: University of Chicago Press.

Kuo Y. and Wang J. (2007), 'Taiwan: The IP Court is ready to go', *Building and Enforcing Intellectual Property Value* (Taiwan: Formosa Transnational Attorneys at Law), 292.

Lakhani K. R. and Wolf R. G. (2005), 'Why Hackers Do What They Do: Understanding Motivation and Effort in Free/Open Source Software Projects', *Perspectives on Free and Open Source Software* (MIT Press). Retrieved 29 August 2007, from http://freesoftware.mit.edu/papers/lakhaniwolf.pdf.

Landers A. L. (2006), 'Let the Games Begin: Incentives to Innovation in the New Economy of Intellectual Property Law', *Santa Clara L. Rev.*, 46, 307.

Landes M. W. and Posner A. R. (1989), 'An Economic Analysis of Copyright Law', *J. Legal Stud.*, **18**, 325.

Landes M. W. and Posner A. R. (1993), 'The Influence of Economics on Law: A Quantitative Study', *J. of L. and Econ.*, **36(1–2)**, 385.

Landes M. W. and Posner A. R. (2003), 'Indefinitely Renewable Copyright', *University of Chicago L. Rev.*, **70**, 471.

Landes M. W. and Posner A. R. (2003a), *The Economic Structure of Intellectual Property Law*, US: The Belknap Press of Harvard University Press.

Landes M. W. and Posner A. R. (2004), 'The Political Economy of Intellectual Property Law', *American Enterprise Institute-Brookings Joint Center for Regulatory Studies*. Retrieved 29 August 2007, from http://www.aei.org/docLib/20040608_Landes.pdf.

Lawrence K. A. (2004), 'Why Be Creative? Motivation and Copyright Law in the Digital Era', *IP Central Review*, **1(2)**, 1.

Lemley A. M. (1997), 'Book Review – Romantic Authorship and the Rhetoric of Property', *Texas L. Rev.*, **75**, 873.

Lemley A. M. (1997a), 'The Economics of Improvement in Intellectual Property Law', *Tex. L. Rev.*, **75**, 989.

Lemley A. M. (1999), 'The Modern Lanham Act and the Death of Common Sense', *Yale L. J.*, **108**, 1687.

Lemley A. M. (2001), 'Rational Ignorance at the Patent Office', *Northwestern Univ. L. Rev.*, **95**, 1495.

Lemley A. M. (2004), 'Ex Ante Versus Ex Post Justifications for Intellectual Property', *U. Chi. L. Rev.*, **71**, 129.

Lemley A. M. (2005), 'Property, Intellectual Property, and Free Riding', *Tex. L. Rev.*, **83**, 1031.

Lemley A. M. (2006), 'Terms of Use', *Minn L. Rev.*, **91**, 459.

Lemley A. M. and Shapiro C. (2005), 'Probabilistic Patents', *Journal of Economic Perspectives*, **19(2)**, 75.

Leonhardt D. (2007), 'You Want Innovation? Offer a Prize', *The New York Times*, retrieved 29 August 2007, from www.nytimes.com/2007/01/31/business/ 31leonhardt.html?ex=1327899600&en=4aca8bec1f9a18d3&ei=5090&partner=rssuserland&emc=rss.

Lerner J. (2002), '150 Years of Patent Protection', *American Economic Review*, **92(2)**, 221.

Lesser W. (2001), 'The Effects of TRIPS Mandated Intellectual Property Rights on Economic Activities', *WIPO Working Paper, Genève*, retrieved 29 August 2007, from http://www.wipo.int/about-ip/en/studies/pdf/ssa_lesser_trips.pdf.

Lesser W. (2002), 'Intellectual Property Rights in a Changing Political Environment: Perspectives on the Types and Administration of Protection', *AgBioForum*, 8(2&3), 64.

Lessig L. (1999), *Code and other Laws of Cyberspace*, US: Basic Books.

Lessig L. (2001), *The Future of Ideas*, US: Vintage.

Lessig L. (2004), *Free Culture*, US: The Penguin Press.

Levin C. R. (1986), 'A New Look at the Patent System', *American Economic Review*, 76, 199.

Levin C. R., Klevorick A., Nelson R. and Winter S. (1987), 'Appropriating the Returns from Industrial Research and Development', *Brookings Papers on Economic Activity*, 3, 783.

Levine M. (2004), 'RealNetworks Fights Back at Apple', *andPOP*, retrieved 29 August 2007, from http://andpop.com/article/3431.

Lewis N. (2002), 'South African Campaigners Defy HIV Drug Patents', *SciDev.Net*, retrieved 29 August 2007, from http://www.scidev.net/News/index.cfm?fuseaction =readNews&itemid=490&language=1.

Lichtenstein S. and Slovic P. (2006), *The Construction of Preference*, UK: Cambridge University Press.

Light W. D. and Warburton R. (2011), 'Demythologizing the high costs of pharmaceutical research', *BioSocieties*, 6, 34–50.

Lindsay D. (2002), 'The Law and Economics of Copyright, Contract and Mass Market Licences', *Centre for Copyright Studies Ltd.* Retrieved 29 August 2007, from www.copyright.com.au/reports%20&%20papers/IssuesPaper_Lindsay.pdf.

Litman J. (1987), 'Copyright, Compromise and Legislative History', *Cornell L. Rev.*, 72(5), 857.

Litman, J. (1990) *The Public Domain*, *Emory L.J.*, 39, 965, 968.

Litman J. (2004), 'Sharing and Stealing', *Hastings Comm. & Ent. L.J.*, 27, 1.

Litman J. (2006), *Digital Copyright: Protecting Intellectual Property on the Internet*, US: Prometheus Books.

Litman T. (2001), 'Distance-Based Vehicle Insurance Feasibility, Costs and Benefits', *Comprehensive Technical Report*.

Liu P. J. (2004), 'Regulatory Copyright', *North Carolina L. Rev.*, 83, 87.

Lloyd M., Spielthenner D. and Mokdsi G. (2011), 'The Smartphone Patent Wars', Ambercite – Next Generation Patent Mapping. Retrieved from http://www.scribd.com/doc/57285018/The-Smartphone-Patent-Wars-2011.

Locke J. (1690), *Two treatises of government*, reprinted in Laslett P. (ed) (1967), UK: Cambridge University Press.

Lockton D. (2005), 'Architectures of Control in Consumer Product Design', *MPhil Technology Policy*, 10, 1, retrieved 29 August 2007, from http://www.danlockton.co.uk/research/Architectures_of_control_(distilled_eBook_with_links).pdf.

Long C. (2002), 'Patent Signals', *U. Chi. L. Rev.*, 69, 625.

Long J. (2004), 'Understanding the Creation and Adoption of Information Technology Innovations: the Case of Open Source Software Development and the Diffusion of Mobile Commerce', *NDLTD Union Catalog* (United States).

Loshin J. (2008), 'Secrets Revealed: How Magicians Protect Intellectual Property without Law', *Law and Magic: A Collection of Essays*.

Love J. (2003), 'Evidence Regarding Research and Development Investments in Innovative and Non-Innovative Medicines', Consumer Project on Technology. Retrieved from http://www.cptech.org/ip/health/rnd/evidenceregardingrnd.pdf.

Lunney S. G. (1996), 'Reexamining Copyright's Incentives-Access Paradigm', *Vanderbilt L. Rev.*, 49, 483.

M.E.L.O.N. – Multimedia and Entertainment Law Online News (2007), 'DRM: Primer Part 1', retrieved 29 August 2007, from http://beatblog.typepad.com/melon/2007/06/drm_primer_part.html.

Macaulay T. B. (1841), 'The First Speech on Copyright', Macaulay's Speeches on Copyright and Lincoln's Address at Cooper Union, 18, 25 (Charles Robert Gaston ed, 1914).

Madison J. M., Frischmann M. B. and Strandburg J. K. (2010), 'Constructing Commons in the Cultural Environment', *Cornell L. Rev.*, 95, 657.

Managing Intellectual Property – Cost and Duration of Patent Litigation 2009. Retrievedfrom:http://www.managingip.com/Article/2089405/Cost-and-duration-of-patent-litigation.html.

Mann R. (2004), 'The Myth of the Software Patent Thicket: An Empirical Investigation of the Relationship between Intellectual Property and Innovation in Software Firms', retrieved 29 August 2007, from http://papers.ssrn.com/sol3/papers.cfm?abstract_id=510103.

Mann R. J. (2005), 'Do Patents Facilitate Financing In the Software Industry?', *Texas L. Rev.*, 83, 961.

Mansfield E. (1994), *Intellectual Property Protection, Foreign Direct Investment, and Technology Transfer*, US: The World Bank.

Marotta-Wurgler F. (2007), 'What's in a Standard Form Contract? An Empirical Analysis of Software License Agreements', *J. of Empirical Legal Studies*, 4, 677.

Marshall A. (1890), *Principles of Economics (Great Minds Series)*, republished in 1961 (Guillebaud eds.), US: Prometheus Books.

Martin B. (1998), *Information Liberation*, US: Freedom Press (CA).

Maskus K. E. (2000), *Intellectual Property Rights in the Global Economy*, US: Institute for International Economics, Washington, DC.

Maskus K. E. and Penubarti M. (1995), 'How Trade-Related are Intellectual Property Rights?', *Journal of International Economics*, 39, 227.

Masnick M. (2007), 'Lawsuit Over "Theft" Of Digital Items in Second Life Shows Up In First Life Court', *TechDirt*.

Mattei U. (2005), 'The Rise and Fall of Law and Economics: an Essay for Judge Guido Calabresi', *Maryland L. Rev.*, 12, 220.

Maurer S. M. and Scotchmer S. (2006), 'Open Source Software: The New Intellectual Property Paradigm', in *Handbook of Economics and Information Systems*, 1 (Elsevier, Amsterdam).

McCalman P. (2001), 'Reaping What you Sow: An Empirical Analysis of International Patent Harmonization', *Journal of International Economics*, 55, 161.

McCalman P. (2004), 'Foreign Direct Investment and Intellectual Property Rights: Evidence from Hollywood's Global Distribution of Movies and Videos', *Journal of International Economics*, 62(1), 107.

McCarthy A. (2003), 'Report on the Proposal for a Directive of the European Parliament and of the Council on the Patentability of Computer-Implemented Inventions', A5–0238/2003, Committee on Legal Affairs and the Internal Market.

McGowan D. (2004), 'Copyright Nonconsequentialism', *Missouri L. Rev.*, 69, 1.
Menell S. P. (1987), 'Tailoring Legal Protection for Computer Software', *Stanford L. Rev.*, **39**, 1329.
Menell S. P. (1989), 'An Analysis of the Scope of Copyright Protection for Application Programs', *Stanford L. Rev.*, 41, 1045.
Menell S. P. (2000), 'Intellectual Property: General Theories', in *Encyclopedia of Law and Economics, vol 2: Civil Law and Economics* (Bouckaert, Boudewijn and De Geest eds), US: Edward Elgar.
Menell S. P. (2007), 'The Property Rights Movement's Embrace of Intellectual Property: True Love or Doomed Relationship?', *Ecology Law Quarterly*, **34(2)**, 713.
Mercuro, N. and Medema, S. G. (1997), *Economics and the law: From Posner to post-modernism*, Princeton University Press.
Merges P. R. (1997), 'The End of Friction? Property Rights and Contract in the "Newtonian" World of On-Line Commerce', *Berkeley Tech. L. J.*, **12(1)**, 115.
Merrill W. T. (1998) *Property and the Right to Exclude*, *Neb. L. Rev.*, **77**, 730.
Merrill W. T. and Smith E. H. (2001), 'The Property/Contract Interface', *Colum. L. Rev.*, **101**, 773.
Merrill W. T. and Smith E. H. (2007), *The Morality of Property*, *Wm. & Mary L. Rev.*, **48**, 1849.
Meurer J. M. (1997), 'Price Discrimination, Personal Use and Piracy: Copyright Protection of Digital Works', *Buff. L. Rev.*, 45, 845.
Microsoft Windows Media DRM FAQ, retrieved 29 August 2007, from http://www.microsoft.com/windows/windowsmedia/drm/faq.aspx#drmfaq_1_1.
Mill J. S. (1863), *Utilitarianism*, New York: Washington Square Press 1963 (Originally published in 1863).
Millard E. (2004), 'French Courts Give Right Win to Apple', *NewsFactor Network*, retrieved 29 August 2007, from http://www.newsfactor.com/perl/story/28337.html.
Miller D. A. (2005), 'Invention under Uncertainty and the Threat of Ex-Post Entry', provided by *EconWPA* in its series Industrial Organization with number 0510001.
Moglen E. (2002), 'Anarchism Triumphant: Free Software and the Death of Copyright', in Elkin-Koren N. and Netanel W. N. (2002) (eds), *The Commodification of Information*, UK: Kluwer Law International.
Moore D. A. (2001), *Intellectual Property & Information Control*, US: Transaction Publishers.
Moore D. A. (2003), 'Intellectual Property, Innovation, and Social Progress: The Case Against Incentive Based Arguments', *Hamline L. Rev.*, 26, 601.
Moser P. (2003), 'How do Patent Laws Influence Innovation? Evidence from Nineteenth Century World Fairs', *NBER Working Paper, number 9909*. Retrieved 29 August 2007, from https://www.nber.org/papers/w9909.
Mulligan D. K., Han J. and Burstein A. J. (2003), 'How DRM-Based Content Delivery Systems Disrupt Expectations of "Personal Use"', in *Proceedings of the 2003 ACM workshop on Digital Rights Management*, pp 77–89.
Musgrave A. B. and Musgrave B. P. (1989), *Public Finance in Theory and Practice*, US: McGraw-Hill Companies.
Nagavajara S. (2003), 'The Creation of a Specialized Court With Intellectual Property Jurisdiction in Asia', Central IP & IT Count, Bangkok Thailand.

Nelson R. R. and Winter G. S. (1974), 'Neoclassical vs. Evolutionary Theories of Economic Growth: Critique and Prospectus', *The Econ. J.*, **84(336)**, 886.

Nelson R. R. and Winter G. S. (1982), *An Evolutionary Theory of Economic Change*, US: Harvard University Press.

Netanel W. N. (1996), 'Copyright and a Democratic Civil Society', *Yale L. J.*, **106**, 283.

Newman P. (2007), 'Copyright Essentials for Linguists', *Language Documentation and Conservation*, **1(1)**, 28.

Nimmer D. (2000), 'A Riff on Fair Use in the Digital Millennium Copyright Act', *Univ. of Penn. L. Rev.*, **148**, 673.

Nguyen C. (2004), 'Toward and Incentivized but Just Intellectual Property Practice: The Compensated IP Proposal', *Cornell Journal of Law and Public Policy*, 14, 113.

Nozick R. (1974), *Anarchy, State and Utopia*, US: Basic Books Inc.

OECD Report 2007, http://www.oecd-ilibrary.org/economics/oecd-annual-report_19990006

Oestreicher-Singer G. and Zalmanson L. (2010), 'Paying for Content or Paying for Community? The Effect of Consumer Involvement on Willingness to Pay on Media Web Sites', unpublished manuscript. Retrieved from http://papers.ssrn.com/sol3/papers.cfm?abstract_id=1536768.

Oksanen V. and Valimaki M. (2003), 'Some Economic Aspects of the European Harmonization of Intellectual Property Rights in Software and its Impact to Eastern EU', *Helsinki Institute for Information Technology (HIIT).*

Oliar D. and Sprigman J. C. (2008), 'There's No Free Laugh (Anymore): The Emergence of Intellectual Property Norms and the Transformation of Stand-Up Comedy', *Vir. L. Rev.*, **94(8)**, 1787.

Olson M. (1965), *The Logic of Collective Action: Public Goods and the Theory of Groups*, US: Harvard University Press.

Olson M. (1971), *The Logic of Collective Action*, US: Harvard Univ. Press.

O'Rourke A. M. (1995), 'Drawing the Boundary between Copyright and Contract: Copyright Preemption of Software License Terms', *Duke L. J.*, **45**, 479.

O'Rourke A. M. (1997), 'Copyright Preemption after the ProCD Case: A Market-Based Approach', *Berkeley Technology L. J.*, 12, 53.

Ostrom, E. (1990), *Governing the Commons: The Evolution of Institutions for Collective Action*, Cambridge, UK and New York, NY: Cambridge University Press.

Ostrom E. (2000), 'Private and Common Property Rights', *Encyclopedia of Law and Economics*, Vol II.

OUT-LAW-News (2005), 'Antitrust Claim Over iTunes Compatibility Progresses', *OUT-LAW-News*, retrieved 29 August 2007, from http://www.out-law.com/page-6154.

Pakes A. (1986), 'Estimates of the Value of Holding European Patent Stocks', *Econometrica*, 54, 755.

Palmer A. and Vinje C. T. (1992), 'The EC Directive on the Legal Protection of Computer Software: New Law Governing Software Development', *Duke J. Comp and Int'l L.*, 2, 65.

Panagariya A. (1999), 'TRIPS and the WTO: an uneasy marriage', in J. Bhagwati (ed), *The Next Trade Negotiation Round: Examining the Agenda for Seattle, Proceedings of the Conference Held at Columbia University*, 91–102.

Park W. G. and Ginarte J. C. (1997), 'Intellectual Property Rights and Economic Growth', *Contemporary Economic Policy*, **15**, 51.

Park Y. and Scotchmer S. (2005), 'Digital Rights Management and the Pricing of Digital Products', *NBER Working Paper No 11532*, retrieved 29 August 2007, from http://socrates.berkeley.edu/~scotch/w11532.pdf.

Patterson, L. R. and Lindberg, S. W. (1991), *'The Nature of Copyright, A Law of Users' Rights'* The University of Georgia Press.

Peddibhotla B. N. and Subramani R. M. (2007), 'Contributing to Public Document Repositories: A Critical Mass Theory Perspective', *Organization Studies*, **28(3)**, 327.

Peltzman S. (1976), 'Toward a more General Theory of Regulation', *Journal of Law and Economics*, **19**, 211.

Penrose T. E. (1951), *The economics of the international patent system,* Baltimore, US: Johns Hopkins Press.

Petrick P. (2004), 'Why DRM Should be Cause for Concern: An Economic and Legal Analysis of the Effect of Digital Technology on the Music Industry', *Berkman Center for Internet & Society at Harvard Law School Research Publication No 2004–09*. Retrieved 29 August 2007, from http://cyber.law.harvard.edu/home/uploads/408/DRMPetrick.pdf.

Peukert A. (2005), 'A Bipolar Copyright System for the Digital Network Environment', *Hasting Communications and Entertainment L. J.*, **28(1)**, 101.

Picker C. R. (2005), 'Copyright and the DMCA: Market Locks and Technological Contracts', in *Antitrust, Patents and Copyrights: EU and US Perspectives* (Leveque and Shelanski eds.), US: Edward Elgar.

Plant A. (1934a), 'The Economic Theory Concerning Patents for Inventions', *Economica*, **1**, 30.

Plant A. (1934b), 'The Economic Aspects of Copyright in Books', *Economica*, **1**, 167.

Plummer J. (2005), 'Expanding the Market's Role in Advancing Intellectual Property', The Competitive Enterprise Institute, retrieved 29 August 2007, from http://www.cei.org/pdf/4452.pdf.

Posner R. A. (1972), *Economic Analysis of Law*, US: Little Brown.

Posner R. (1979), 'Utilitarianism Economics and the Legal Theory', *Journal of Legal Studies*, **8**, 103.

Posner E. (2000), *Law and Social Norms* (South Asia eds.), US: Harvard University Press.

Post D. (1996), 'Governing Cyberspace', *Wayne L. Rev.*, **43**, 155.

Post D. and Johnson D. (1997), 'And How Shall the Net Be Governed? A Meditation on the Relative Virtues of Decentralized, Emergent Law', in Kahin B. and Keller J. (eds), *Coordinating the Internet*, US: MIT Press.

Priest G. (1986), 'What Economists Can Tell Lawyers About Intellectual Property: Comment on Cheung', *Research in Law and Economics*, **8**, 19.

Radin M. J. (2000), 'Humans, Computers, and Binding Commitments', *Ind. L. J.*, **75**, 1125.

Radin M. J. (2006), 'Copyright Defection', *Industrial and Corporate Change*, **15(6)**, 981.

Rafaeli S. and Ariel Y. (2008), 'Online Motivational Factors: Incentives for Participation and Contribution in Wikipedia' in *Psychological Aspects of Cyberspace: Theory, Research, Applications* 243 (A. Barak ed).

Rafaeli S., Hayat T. and Ariel Y. (2009), 'Knowledge Building and Motivations in Wikipedia: Participation as "Ba"' in *Cyberculture and New Media* 51 (Francisco J. Ricardo ed).

Rafaeli S., Raban D. and Ravid G. (2007), 'How Social Motivation Enhances Economic Activity and Incentives in the Google Answers Knowledge Sharing Market', *International Journal of Knowledge and Learning*, 3(1).

Rai A. K. and Eisenberg R. S. (2003), 'Bayh-Dole Reform and the Progress of Biomedicine', *Law and Contemporary Problems*, 66(1/2), 289.

Rainie L., Horrigan B. J., Wellman B. and Boase J. (2006), 'The Strength of Internet Ties', Pew Internet & American Life Project. Retrieved from http://www.pewinternet.org/~/media//Files/Reports/2006/PIP_Internet_ties.pdf.

Rawls J. (1971), *Theory of Justice*, US: Belknap Pub.

RealPlayer 10.5, RealNetwork, 'More Info On RadioPass Features', retrieved 29 August 2007, from http://uk.real.com/radiopass/.

Regner T. (2004), 'Efficient Contracts for Digital Content', *Leverhulme CMPO Working Paper No 04/108*. Retrieved 29 August 2007, from www.bris.ac.uk/depts/CMPO/workingpapers/wp108.pdf.

Reichman J. H. and Samuelson P. (1997), 'Intellectual Property Rights in Data?', *Vanderbilt L. Rev.*, 50(1), 51.

Reidenberg J. (1998), 'Lex Informatica: the Formulation of Information Policy Rules Through Technology', *Texas L. Rev.*, 76, 553.

Risch M. (Forthcoming 2012), 'Patent Troll Myths', *Seton Hall Law Review*, 42. Retrieved from: http://papers.ssrn.com/sol3/papers.cfm?abstract_id =1792442.

Robbins L. (1932), *Nature and Significance of Economic Science*, UK: Macmillan.

Rocard M. (2005), 'Report on the Council Common Position for Adopting a Directive of the European Parliament and of the Council on the Patentability of Computer-Implemented Inventions', A6–0207/2005 Committee of Legal Affairs.

Rose C. (1986), 'The Comedy of the Commons: Custom, Commerce, an Inherently Public Property', *U Chi L Rev.*, 53, 711.

Rose C. M. (1994), *Property and Persuasion: Essays on the History, Theory, and Rhetoric of Ownership*, US: Westview Press.

Rosenblatt B. (2007), 'Windows Media DRM Hacked Again', *DRM Watch*, retrieved 29 August 2007, from www.drmwatch.com/drmtech/article.php/3689756.

Rousseau J. J. (1762), *The Social Contract*, Translated: by G. D. H. Cole.

Rubin P. (1977), 'Why Is the Common Law Efficient?', *J. of Legal Studies*, 6(1), 51.

Sag M., Jacobi T. and Sytch M. (2007), 'The Effect of Judicial Ideology in Intellectual Property Cases', *2nd Annual Conference on Empirical Legal Studies Paper*.

Sakakibara M. and Branstetter L. (2001), 'Do Stronger Patents Induce More Innovation? Evidence from the 1988 Japanese Patent Law Reforms', *RAND Journal of Economics*, 32(1), 77.

Salzberger E. (1993), 'On the Normative Facet of the Economic Approach Towards Law', *Mishpatim*, 22, 1 (in Hebrew).

Salzberger E. (2008), 'The Economic Analysis of Law: The Dominant Methodology for Legal Research?!' *Haifa Law Review*, 4(1), 207.

Salzberger E. (ed) (2012 forthcoming), *The Law and Economics of Innovation*, London: Edward Elgar.

Salzberger E. and Voigt S. (2002), 'On the Delegation of Powers: With Special Emphasis on Central and Eastern Europe', *Constitutional Political Economy*, 13, 25.

Salzberger E. and Voigt S. (2002a), 'Choosing Not To Choose: When Politicians Choose To Delegate Powers', *KYKLOS*, 55(2), 289.

Samuelson P. (1999), 'Intellectual Property and the Digital Economy: Why the Anti-Circumvention Regulations Need to Be Revised', *Berkeley Tech. L. J.*, 14, 519.

Samuelson P. (2001), 'Anti-circumvention Rules: Threat to Science', *Science*, **293**, 2028.

Samuelson P. (2001a), 'Economic and Constitutional Influences on Copyright Law in the United States', *European Intellectual Property Rev.*, **23(9)**, 409.

Samuelson P. (2002), 'The Law and Economics of Reverse Engineering', *Yale L. J.*, **111**, 1575.

Samuelson P. (2002), 'Toward a "New Deal" for Copyright in the Information Age', *Michigan L. Rev.*, **100(6)**, 1488.

Samuelson P. (2003), 'Should Economics Play a Role in Copyright Law and Policy?', *U. Ottawa L. & Tech. J.*, 1, 3.

Samuelson P. (2003), 'Mapping the Digital Public Domain: Threats and Opportunities', *L. & Contemp. Probs.*, 66, 147.

Samuelson P., Davis R., Kapor M. D. and Reichman J. H. (1994), 'A Manifesto Concerning the Legal Protection of Computer Programs', *Columbia L. Rev.*, 94, 2308.

Samuelson P. and Scotchmer S. (2002), 'The Law and Economics of Reverse Engineering', *Yale L. J.*, **111**, 1575.

Sanchez J. (2007), 'Second Life: An Interactive Qualitative Analysis', in *Proceedings of Society for Information Technology and Teacher Education International Conference* (Crawford et al. eds, US: AACE.

Sauermann H. (2007), 'Turning Knowledge into Action: The Role of Incentives in Innovative Capabilities', *Working Paper*.

Sauermann H. and Cohen M. W. (2008), 'What Makes Them Tick? Employee Motives and Firm Innovation', NBER Working Paper No w14443. Retrieved from: http://papers.ssrn.com/sol3/papers.cfm?abstract_id=1289677.

Schankerman M. (1998), 'How Valuable is Patent Protection? Estimates by Technology Field', *Rand Journal of Economics*, 29, 93.

Schaub M. (2005), 'A breakdown of consumer protection law in the light of digital products', *INDICARE Monitor*, retrieved 29 August 2007, from http://www.indicare.org/tiki-read_article.php?articleId=123.

Scherer F. M. (2001), 'The Innovation Lottery', in *Expanding the Boundaries of Intellectual Property: Innovation Policy for the Knowledge Society* 3, (Dreyfuss, Zimmerman and First eds), UK: Oxford University Press.

Scherrer P. (1999), 'One in Eight South Africans HIV-Positive', *World Socialist Web Site*, retrieved 29 August 2007, from http://www.wsws.org/articles/1999/dec1999/saf-d11.shtml.

Schumpeter J. A. (1912) [1934], *The Theory of Economic Development: An Inquiry into Profits, Capital, Credit, Interest, and the Business Cycle*, US: Harvard University Press.

Schumpeter J. A. (1928), 'The Instability of Capitalism', *The Econ. J.*, **38(151)**, 361.

Schumpeter J. A. (1942), *Capitalism, Socialism and Democracy*, US: Harper and Row.

Schwartz A. and Wilde L. L. (1983), 'Imperfect Information in Markets for Contract Terms: The Examples of Warranties and Security Interests', *Vir. L. Rev.*, 69, 1387.

Scotchmer S. and Menell P. S. (2007), 'Intellectual Property Law', in *Handbook of Law and Economics* (Polinsky and Shavell eds), 2, Amsterdam: Elsevier.

Sen K. A. (1982), *Choice, Welfare and Measurement*, US: Harvard University Press.

Shapiro C. (1999), 'Competition Policy in the Information Economy', University of California at Berkeley, 1–18.

Shapiro J. R. and Hassett A. K. (2005), 'The Economic Value of Intellectual Property, *USA For Innovation.*

Shavell S. (2002), 'Economic Analysis of Property Law', *Harvard Olin Center for Law, Economics and Business Discussion Paper No 399*. Retrieved 29 August 2007, from http://www.law.harvard.edu/programs/olin_center/papers/pdf/399.pdf.

Shenk D. (1997), *Data Smog: Surviving the Information Glut*, US: Harper San Francisco.

Sherwood M. R. (2000), 'Human Creativity for Economic Development: Patents Propel Technology', *Akron L. Rev.*, **33**, 351.

Shiffrin S. V. (2001), 'Lockean Arguments for Private Intellectual Property', in *New Essays in the Legal and Political Theory of Property* (Munzer eds), Cambridge: Cambridge University Press.

Shih Ray Ku R. (2002), 'The Creative Destruction of Copyright: Napster and the New Economics of Digital Technology', *University of Chicago L. Rev.*, **69**, 263.

Shirky C. (2008), *Here Comes Everybody: The Power of Organizing Without Organizations*, US: Penguin Press HC.

Shrestha K. S. (2010), 'Trolls or Market-Makers? An Empirical Analysis of Nonpracticing Entities', *Columbia Law Review*, **110**, 114. Retrieved from: http://papers.ssrn.com/sol3/papers.cfm?abstract_id=1534282.

Siebeck W. E., Evenson E. R., Lesser W. and Braga C. (1990), *Strengthening Protection of Intellectual Property in Developing Countries: A Survey of the Literature*, US: World Bank.

Simon H. (1957), *Models of Man*, US: Wiley.

Simon H. (1971), 'Designing Organizations for an Information-Rich World', in *Computers, Communications, and the Public Interest*, US: Johns Hopkins Univ. Pr.

Skinner B. F. (1985), 'Cognitive Science and Behaviourism', *British J. of Psychology*, **76**, 291.

Smith A. (1776), *An inquiry into the nature and causes of the wealth of nations*, reprinted in Edwin C. (ed) (1961), UK: Methuen.

Smith E. H. (2002), 'Exclusion versus Governance: Two Strategies for Delineating Property Rights', *J. Legal Stud.*, **31**, 453.

Smith S. W. (2011), 'Capital Structure and Entrepreneurial Experience: New Firm Innovation and Survival', in *Oxford Handbook of Entrepreneurial Finance* (Cumming eds.), US: Oxford University Press.

Smith M. A. and Kollock P. (eds) (1999), *Communities in Cyberspace*, UK: Routledge.

Smith T. (2005), 'Microsoft Eyes Disposable, Play-Once DVDs', *The Register*, retrieved 29 August 2007, from http://www.theregister.co.uk/2005/10/05/ms_play-one_dvds/.

Solow M. R. (1957), 'Technical Change and the Aggregate Production Function', *The Rev. of Econ. and Stats.*, **39(3)**, 312.

Sommer R. A. (2005), 'Trouble on the Commons: A Lockean Justification for Patent Law Harmonization', *Journal of the Patent and Trademark Office Society*, **87**, 141.

Stanford News Center – Mobile Computing Giants In Patent Free-For-All (http://www.law.stanford.edu/news/details/4722/Mobile%20Computing%20Giants%20In%20Patent%20Free-For-All/) (2011).

Steinmueller W. E. (2003), 'Information Society Consequences of Expanding the Intellectual Property Domain', *Report Draft No 38, Science and Technology Policy*

*Research*. Retrieved 29 August 2007, from http://ipr.dime-eu.org/files/active/1/steinmueller.pdf.

Sterk E. S. (2004), 'What's In a Name?: The Troublesome Analogies Between Real and Intellectual Property', *Cardozo L. Legal Stud. Research Paper*, **88**.

Stern N., Dethier J. J. and Rogers F. H. (2005), *Growth and Empowerment: Making Development Happen*, Munich lectures in economics, Cambridge, MA: MIT Press.

Stigler J. G. (1952), 'The Ricardian Theory of Value and Distribution', *J. of Political Economy*, **60**, 187.

Stigler J. G. (1971), 'The theory of economic regulation', *Bell J. Econ. Man. Sci.*, **2(1)**, 3.

Stiglitz E. J. (1987), 'Technological Change, Sunk Costs, and Competition', *Brookings Papers on Economic Activity: Special Issue On Microeconomics*, **1987(3)**, 883.

Stiglitz E. J. (2008), 'Economic foundations of intellectual property rights', *Duke Law Journal*, **57**, 1963.

Sunder M. (2006), 'IP$^3$', *Stanford Law Review*, **59(257)**.

Sunstein C. (1995), 'Emerging Media Technology and the First Amendment: The First Amendment in Cyberspace', *Yale L. J.*, **104**, 1757.

Sweeting A. (2007), 'Dynamic Product Repositioning in Differentiated Product Markets: The Case of Format Switching in the Commercial Radio Industry', *NBER Working Paper* 13522.

Sykes A. O. (2002), 'Public Health and International Law: TRIPs, Pharmaceuticals, Developing Countries, and the Doha "Solution"', *Chi. J. Int'l L.* **3** (2002), 47, 59–60.

Tapscott D. and Williams D. A. (2006), *Wikinomics: How Mass Collaboration Changes Everything*, US: Portfolio.

Teece D. J. (1992), 'Competition, cooperation, and innovation: Organizational arrangements for regimes of rapid technological progress', *Journal of Economic Behavior and Organization*, **18**, 2.

Tehranian J. (2005), 'Et Tu, Fair Use? The Triumph of Natural-Law Copyright?', *U.C. Davis L. Rev.*, **38**, 465.

Thaker S. (2003), 'The Criticality of Non-Market Strategies: The European Biotechnology Patents Directive', *Online Research Paper on Biotechnology*.

*The Guardian* – http://www.guardian.co.uk/technology/2011/oct/21/steve-jobs-destroy-android (2011).

*The Guardian* – http://www.guardian.co.uk/technology/2011/aug/04/apple-patents-android-expensive-google (2011).

*The New-York Times* -www.nytimes.com/2007/03/10/world/europe/10europe.html?_r=2&oref=slogin (2007).

*The New York Times* – http://www.nytimes.com/2011/08/17/technology/a-bull-market-in-tech-patents.html?pagewanted=all (2011).

*The Wall Street Journal* – http://online.wsj.com/article/SB10001424053111903639404576518493092643006.html (2011).

*Time Magazine* Person of the Year: You, TIME, Dec. 25, 2006. Retrieved from: http://www.time.com/time/covers/0,16641,20061225,00.html.

Toffler, A. (1980), *The third wave*, New York: Bantam Books.

Towse R. (1999), 'Copyright and Economic Incentives: An Application to Performers' Rights in the Music Industry', *KYKLOS*, **52**, 369.

Towse R. (2003), *A Handbook on Cultural Economics*, US: Edward Elgar.

Towse R. and Hozhauer R. (2002), *Economics of Intellectual Property Rights 4*, US: Edward Elgar International.

Trachtman J. (1998), 'Cyberspace, Sovereignty, Jurisdiction and Modernism', *Ind. J. Global Legal Stud*, **5(2)**, 561.

Truett J. L. and Truett B. D. (1982), *Economics*, U.S: West publishing company.

Tufts Center for the Study of Drug Development Outlook 2011 (CSDD 2011). Retrieved from http://csdd.tufts.edu/news/complete_story/pr_outlook_2011.

Tushnet R. (2009), 'Economies of Desire: Fair Use and Marketplace Assumptions', *William & Mary Law Review*, **51**, 522–27. Retrieved from http://papers.ssrn.com/sol3/papers.cfm?abstract_id=1498542.

UNAIDS Report on the Global AIDS Epidemic – Global Report 2010.

Unicef website – http://www.unicef.org/infobycountry/southafrica_statistics.html.

U.S. Chamber of Commerce, http://www.uschamber.com/ip.

Vaidhyanathan S. (2001), *Copyrights and Copywrongs*, US: New York University Press.

Valimaki M. and Oksanen V. (2006), 'DRM Interoperability and Intellectual Property Policy in Europe', *European Intellectual Property Rev.*, **26(11)**, 562.

Valkonen S. and White L. J. (2006), 'An Economic Model for the Incentive-Access Paradigm of Copyright Propertization: An Argument in Support of the Proposed New §514 to the Copyright Act', *Law & Economics Research Paper Series, Working Paper No 06–15*. Retrieved 29 August 2007, from www.stern.nyu.edu/eco/wkpapers/Valkonen.pdf.

Veljanovski C. (2007), *Economic Principles of Law*, Cambridge University Press.

Wagner J. (2003), 'Are Nascent Entrepreneurs Jacks-of-All-Trades? A Test of Lazear's Theory of Entrepreneurship with German Data', *IZA Discussion Paper No 911*. Retrieved 29 August 2007, from http://ssrn.com/abstract=464641.

Wagner P. (2003), 'Information Wants to Be Free: Intellectual Property and the Mythologies of Control', *Colum. L. Rev.*, **103**, 995.

Wagner, R. P. and Parchomovsky G. (2005), 'Patent Portfolios', *PA. L. Rev.* **154(1)**, 1.

Webster F. (2002) *Theories of the Information Society*, UK: Routledge.

Weimer L. D. and Vining A. R. (2004), *Policy Analysis: Concepts and Practice* (4th ed), US: Prentice Hall.

Wellman B. et al (2003), 'The Social Affordances of the Internet for Networked Individualism', *Journal of Computer-Mediated Communication*, **8(3)**.

West J. and Gallagher S. (2004), 'Key Challenges of Open Innovation: Lessons from Open Source Software', *San Jose State College of Business Mimeo.*

Williamson E. O. (1993), 'Calculativeness, Trust, and Economic Organization', *J. of L. and Econ.*, **36(1)**, 453.

Winter, S. (1989), 'Patents in Complex Contexts: Incentives and Effectiveness', in Weil and Snapper (eds), *Owning Scientific and Technical Information*, US: New Brunswick, NJ: Rutgers Univ. Press.

WIPO Magazine (2010), 'IP Litigation Costs: Special Edition' (2–25). Retrieved from http://www.wipo.int/wipo_magazine/en/pdf/2010/wipo_pub_121_2010_01.pdf.

WIPO Report (2007), 'Patent Report: Statistics on Worldwide Patent Activities'. Retrieved 29 August 2007, from www.wipo.int/ipstats/en/statistics/patents/pdf/patent_report_2007.pdf.

Working Group on Intellectual Property Rights (1995), *White Paper on Intellectual Property and the National Information Infrastructure*. Retrieved 29 August 2007, from http://www.uspto.gov/web/offices/com/doc/ipnii/.

Yen C. A. (1990), 'Restoring the Natural Law: Copyright as Labor and Possession', *O. State L. J.*, **51**, 517.

Zimmerman D. L. (2003), 'Authorship Without Ownership: Reconsidering Incentives in a Digital Age', *DePaul L. Rev.*, 52, 1121.

Zimmerman D. L. (2011), 'Copyrights as Incentives: Did We Just Imagine That?', *Theoretical Inquiries in Law*, 12(1), L. 29.

Zimmerman M. (2006), 'Copyright/DMCA Developments', *IP Litigator*, 12(6), 1. Retrieved 29 August 2007, from www.fenwick.com/docstore/publications/IP/IP_Articles/IP_Lit_1106.pdf.Ackerman B. A. 'The Storrs Lectures: Discovering the Constitution', *Yale L.J.*, 93 1013 1983-1984.

# Index